Media and Conflict

FRAMING ISSUES

MAKING POLICY

SHAPING OPINIONS

Edited by Eytan Gilboa

 Transnational Publishers

CONTENTS

About the Authors .... *v*

World Perspectives on Media and Conflict .... *ix*
        Eytan Gilboa

Part I: Framing

Chapter 1: Media and the New Post-Cold War Movements 3
            Andrew Rojecki

Chapter 2: The Battle in Seattle: How Nongovernmental Organizations
            Used Websites in Their Challenge to the WTO 25
            Melissa A. Wall

Chapter 3: Spiral of Violence? Conflict and Conflict Resolution in
            International News 45
            Christopher Beaudoin and Esther Thorson

Chapter 4: Relational Ripeness in the Oslo I and Oslo II Israeli-
            Palestinian Negotiations 65
            William A. Donohue and Gregory D. Hoobler

Chapter 5: Framing International Conflicts in Asia: A Comparative
            Analysis of News Coverage of Tokdo 89
            Young Chul Yoon and Gwangho E.

Chapter 6: Framing Environmental Conflicts: The Edwards
            Aquifer Dispute 117
            Linda L. Putnam

Part II: Media and Policy

Chapter 7: Sources, the Media and the Reporting of Conflict 135
            Howard Tumber

Chapter 8: An Exploratory Model of Media-Government Relations in
            International Crises: U.S. Involvement in Bosnia 1992–1995 ... 153
            Yaeli Bloch and Sam Lehman-Wilzig

Chapter 9: Global Television and Conflict Resolution: Defining the
            Limits of the CNN Effect 175
            Piers Robinson

Chapter 10: Media Diplomacy in the Arab-Israeli Conflict 193
Eytan Gilboa

Chapter 11: The Russian Media Role in the Conflicts in Afghanistan and
Chechnya: A Case Study of Media Coverage by *Izvestia* 213
Olga V. Malinkina and Douglas M. McLeod

Chapter 12: Effects of Ambiguous Policies on Media Coverage of Foreign
Conflicts: The Cases of Eritrea and Southern Sudan 237
Meseret Chekol Reta

Part III: Media and the Public

Chapter 13: The South African Press: No Strangers to Conflict 263
Arnold S de Beer

Chapter 14: Cultural Conflict in the Middle East: The Media as
Peacemakers 281
Dov Shinar

Chapter 15: The Media and Reconciliation in Central America 295
Sonia Gutiérrez-Villalobos

Chapter 16: The Crisis in Kosovo: Photographic News of the Conflict
and Public Opinion 311
Kimberly L. Bissell

Chapter 17: Internet Public Relations: A Tool for Crisis Management 331
Shannon B. Campbell

Index   345

ABOUT THE AUTHORS

Christopher E. Beaudoin (PhD University of Missouri) is assistant professor in the Department of Telecommunications at Indiana University—Bloomington. He has worked as a journalist in Korea and Japan and as an educator in Lesotho. His research interests include international communication and media effects.

Arnold S De Beer (PhD Potchefstroom University, South Africa) is professor of journalism, School of Communication Studies, Potchefstroom University, and research director of Media Tenor-Institute for Media Analysis in South Africa. He is editor of *Ecquid Novi*, editorial board member of *Journalism Studies*, and co-editor with John C. Merrill of *Global Journalism* (to be published by Longman). He published recently works on news flow, and media and violence.

Kimberly L. Bissell (PhD Syracuse University) is assistant professor in the Department of Journalism at the University of Alabama. She teaches visual journalism, photojournalism and mass communication theory. She is an officer in the Visual Communication Division of the Association for Education in Journalism and Mass Communication and conducts research in the area of visual communication and media effects.

Yaeli Bloch is a doctoral student and an instructor in communication in the Department of Political Studies at Bar-Ilan University in Israel. She received her MA in Political Science and Communication from Bar-Ilan University, and is specializing in mass communication and international relations. She has taught the introductory courses in both these fields.

Shannon B. Campbell (PhD University of Texas at Austin) is assistant professor in the William Allen White School of Journalism and Mass Communications at the University of Kansas. She is a Freedom Forum Fellow who has served as a strategic communications consultant for the Internal Revenue Service (Jacksonville, FL), the federally funded One-Stop Service Centers Conference (Daytona, FL), and the Florida Fund for Minority Teachers.

William A. Donohue (PhD Ohio State University) is Distinguished Professor of Communication at Michigan State University. His main research interests lie in international negotiation, mediation, hostage negotiation, and youth violence prevention. He has published over 50 articles in scholarly journals and five books including *Interpersonal Conflict* (1992), and *Communication, Marital Dispute and Divorce Mediation* (1991).

Eytan Gilboa (PhD Harvard University) is professor of communication and government and Chair of the Department of Social Sciences at Holon Institute of Technology in Israel. He is also affiliated with Bar-Ilan University. He has published extensively on international and political communication. His most recent works were published in *Communication Theory, Gazett, the Harvard International Journal of Press/Politics,* and *International Negotiation*. He is the recipient of the 2001 *Best Article Award* of the International Communication Association, and in 2002 was a Shorenstein Fellow at Harvard's Kennedy School of Government.

Sonia Gutiérrez-Villalobos (PhD University of Massachusetts) is a researcher and professor of Communication at the Instituto de Investigaciones (IDESPO), Universidad Nacional de Costa Rica. She has taught and published on coverage of international conflict and peace, and on intercultural and developmental communications. She is the co-author of *Los Medios y la Cultura de Paz* (2001).

Gwangho E. (PhD Keio University, Japan) is associate professor in the School of Media Science, Tokyo University of Technology, and the co-author *of Changes in Media and News Reporting* (Tokyo: Maruzen, 2000, written in Japanese).

Gregory D. Hoobler is a doctoral student in the Department of Communication at Michigan State University specializing in international conflict. He received his MA from San Diego State University and has taught and published in the areas of international conflict negotiation, intercultural communication, conflict and persuasion, and nonverbal communication.

Sam Lehman-Wilzig (PhD Harvard University) is associate professor and the Head of the Public Communications Program in Bar-Ilan University's Department of Political Studies. He was the chair of the Israel Political Science Association ('97–'99) and is the founder & editor-in-chief of the Hebrew language academic journal *PATUAKH: Politics, Communications & Society*.

Olga V. Malinkina is a native of Moscow, Russia. She received her MA in communication from the University of Delaware. Her research interests include the role of the media in social conflicts in the former Soviet Union, and media coverage of protest groups.

Douglas M. McLeod (PhD University of Minnesota) is professor of journalism and mass communication at the University of Wisconsin—Madison. His research focuses on media coverage of protest groups, the role of the media in social conflicts, and mass-mediated messages as forms of social control. He published numerous articles in leading communication journals including *Journal of Communication, Communication Research, Journalism and Mass Communication Quarterly, Journal of Broadcasting and Electronic Media,* and the *International Journal of Public Opinion Research*.

Linda L. Putnam (PhD University of Minnesota) is professor in the Department of Speech Communication at Texas A & M University and the Director of the Program on Conflict and Dispute Resolution in the Institute for Science, Technology, and Public Policy at the George Bush School of Government and Public Service. She is the co-editor of *The New Handbook of Organizational Communication* (2001) and *Communication and Negotiation* (1992). She has received funding for her research from the National Science Foundation, the Environmental Protection Agency, and the William and Flora Hewlett Foundation.

Meseret Chekol Reta (PhD University of Minnesota) is assistant professor of communication arts at Ashland University in Ohio. He also has extensive experience in international broadcasting from his days as a radio journalist in his native Ethiopia. His earlier publication is entitled "U.S. Media Coverage of the 1994 Elections In South Africa."

Piers Robinson (PhD Bristol University) is lecturer in political communication, School of Politics and Communication Studies, University of Liverpool. His research interests are in post-Cold War intervention and media. He has published articles on the CNN effect in *Political Studies, Review of International Studies, European Journal of Communication* and *Media, Culture and Society*. His forthcoming book on the CNN effect and intervention during humanitarian crisis is to be published by Routledge in 2002.

Andrew Rojecki (PhD Northwestern University) is assistant professor in the Department of Communication at the University of Illinois at Chicago. He is the author of *Silencing the Opposition* (1999) and co-author of *The Black Image in the White Mind: Media and Race in America* (2000). For the last book he received, together with Robert M. Entman, several awards including the 2002 Goldsmith Book Prize of Harvard's Shorenstein Center on the Press, Politics and Public Policy.

Dov Shinar (PhD The Hebrew University) is professor and Chair of the Department of Communication Studies and Head of the Burda Center for Innovative Communications at Ben Gurion University in Israel. His fields of interest include international communications, media in war and peace, and communication technologies. His books include *Internet: Communication, Culture and Society* (2001) and *Palestinian Voices* (1987). His articles were published in periodicals such as the *Journal of Communication, Gazette*, and *Media Development*.

Esther Thorson (PhD University of Minnesota) is the Dean of Graduate Studies and Research at the University of Missouri's School of Journalism. Her research interests include media effects, health communication, and media coverage of ethnic groups. She has published numerous articles in many periodicals including *Political Communication, Communication Research, Journal of Broadcasting and Electronic Media, Journal of Advertising Research,* and *Human Communication Research.*

Howard Tumber (PhD City University, London) is professor of sociology and Dean of the School of Social and Human Sciences, City University, London. He is the editor of *Media Power, Policies and Professionals* (2000); *News: A Reader* (1999); joint author of *Reporting Crime—The Media Politics of Criminal Justice* (1994), and *Journalists at War* (1988); and author of *Television and the Riots* (1982). He is a founder and co-editor of *Journalism*.

Melissa A. Wall (PhD University of Washington) is assistant professor at California State University—Northridge. She studies social movement communications, particularly involving the Internet; Western representations of the Third World; and African journalism. Her research has been published in *Gazette, Journal of Development Communication*, and in *Critical Studies in Media Commercialism*.

Young Chul Yoon (PhD University of Minnesota) is professor in the Department of Mass Communication of Yonsei University, Seoul, Korea. He recently completed a book entitled *Democracy and Media in South Korea*. He teaches media sociology, political communication, and international communication.

WORLD PERSPECTIVES ON MEDIA AND CONFLICT

Eytan Gilboa

The modern media have transformed the management, resolution, and transformation of domestic and international conflicts. They have both helped and hindered the efforts of policymakers to control and end conflicts, and have both functioned as an autonomous independent and influential actor, and as a principal tool in the hands of protagonists, negotiators, and mediators. Yet, despite the significant effects the media have on domestic and international conflicts, only limited attention has been given to this critical topic in the relevant social science disciplines including communication, political science, international relations, management, and sociology. This volume fills the gap by creating awareness, presenting current research methodologies and findings, and charting ways to advance research and analysis.

This book presents, in one volume, the most recent scientific findings and developments in the field. It is truly multidisciplinary, cross-national and cross-cultural. An effort has been made to solicit original research from scholars in many countries on media and conflict in several parts of the world. The 22 contributors are scholars from the United States, Costa Rica, the United Kingdom, Israel, South Africa, Korea, and Japan. Two contributors are presently residing in the United States, but are originally from Russia and Ethiopia. They present research on media and conflict in the United States, Central America, Europe, the Middle East, Africa, Russia, and Asia.

Research on the media roles in different types and levels of conflict are discussed: *domestic* including ethnic and environmental; *international*, where the protagonists are states, including for example the Arab-Israeli conflict and the conflict between Japan and Korea over the Island of Tokdo; and *global*, where states and non-state actors are involved, including the conflict over globalization and the World Trade Organization (WTO). Works both on the traditional print and electronic media and on new media, including the Internet, are included. The media roles in different phases of conflict determined by goal and structure are explored, including *conflict management*, where the goal is to stabilize and prevent deterioration and violence; *conflict resolution*, where the goal is to remove the causes of conflict through agreements, and *conflict transformation*, where the goal is to move rival parties from formal ending to meaningful and widespread reconciliation, friendship, and cooperation.

In order to emphasize the theoretical and methodological contributions of the book, it is organized around analytical areas rather than phases, types or levels of conflict. The media interact with politicians and officials as well as with the public. They are manipulated and used by politicians who wish to advance their political agenda, improve their image, and shape public opinion. At the same time, the media have their own agenda and they also represent and shape public opinion. The public may also have an agenda, that may be different from the preferences of both politicians and the media. This triangular relationship between the government, the media and the public formed the three-part structure of this book. The first part explores framing of issues in the media in the broadest possible meaning, the second deals with media effects on policy and uses of the media to promote policy, while the third part examines the media's complex relationships with the public. The assignment of chapters to each part wasn't easy. Several contributions deal with more than one area, with both framing and public opinion, for example. The final assignment was determined according to the area receiving the greatest weight in those chapters.

Part I presents works on framing in the broadest possible meaning. It refers not only to the traditional media own framing of issues, but also to the ways disputants describe in the media their own role and the other side role in their conflict. Framing has become an important area in research on media coverage, particularly of conflict. The first two chapters deal with coverage of the protests against the 1999 meetings of the World Trade Organization (WTO) in Seattle in the traditional and new media. The policies and activities of this organization, as well as the globalizaton processes that it supports and manages, have become extremely controversial. The battles between supporters and opponents of the WTO have been fought in the streets of the cities hosting the annual WTO meetings, on television screens, and throughout the Internet.

Andrew Rojecki places the media battle over the WTO in a broad theoretical context. He claims that post-Cold War theories of the press and foreign policy and models developed in response to them by political communication scholars, do not seem to map well the press coverage of the anti-globalization movement. He argues for a new theory of the press and oppositional politics in an environment that has altered the equilibrium between media and political elites and interest groups in this new issue domain. His analysis of two streams of media content, news and editorial, on the protests at the 1999 WTO meetings reveals an anomalous reversal for theories of media and elite power in the way the mainstream press covers movement politics.

Melissa Wall focuses on Nongovernmental Organizations' use of websites to challenge the WTO, finding that their power derives in part from their roles as information disseminators. These groups used websites primarily to create new knowledge structures that give voice to the grassroots, and to a lesser extent to encourage political action and to support a two-way dialogue. Wall asserts that this use of websites in Seattle was not an anomaly, but rather the prototype for a global anti-corporate domination movement that will increasingly rely on the Internet.

Christopher Beaudoin and **Esther Thorson** explore coverage of international conflict and conflict resolution in the *Los Angeles Times*, which may represent the U.S. elite press. Through content analysis they found that the newspaper balances coverage in terms of international conflict and conflict resolution, but that there is more conflict in coverage of the developing world. The Middle East for example, is portrayed via conflict and conflict resolution, while coverage of Africa focuses predominantly on conflict. As might have been expected, stories that involve the United States were more positive than other stories. The chapter also theorizes on the potential effects this coverage may have on readers' perceptions of the world, their view of *self* and *other*, and, in a broader sense, the state of conflict and conflict resolution in the world.

William Donohue and **Gregory Hoobler** investigate a very different framing area. They integrate relational communication strategies and theories into the study and practice of conflict negotiation processes. In their chapter, they present a comparative analysis of "relational ripeness" in the Oslo I and Oslo II Israeli-Palestinian negotiations. To examine this issue they use editorials and interviews given by Israeli and Palestinian leaders. The public rhetoric and discourse was analyzed (1) to determine the extent to which the relational context surrounding the negotiations was more affiliation oriented or more focused on power and domination, and (2) to "track" the kinds of relational frames the parties created throughout this broader negotiation process. The findings are significant because they help to better understand how relational messages evolve and are useful to address the social and political context in which conflict negotiations occur.

The chapter **Young Chul Yoon** and **Gwangho E.** wrote represents an interesting joint bi-national research effort to understand how the press in their respective countries, South Korea and Japan, covered a conflict between the two nations over the Tokdo Island. The authors assumed that the news media in each country used frames reflecting their respective national interest—the territorial claim on the Island. They used content analysis and found that indeed the press in each state constructed opposing frames. The authors concluded that the coverage reinforced the negative stereotypes of the opponent nation, and this certainly didn't help to resolve the dispute.

Environmental conflicts are proliferating as more and more people are aware of the need to protect the environment and are ready to battle authorities and companies. Many of these battles are designed to mobilize public support; therefore, for the protagonists, the media become an important arena. **Linda Putnam's** chapter explores the role of media framing in an environmental conflict, and applies it to the dispute over groundwater allocation in the Edwards Aquifer, located in the Texas Hill Country. The chapter draws on identity and characterization frames to demonstrate that the media invokes the language of intractability as it shifts the conflict from interests to institutional struggles and from a plausible agreement to a fight for external control. Overall, Putnam argues, the media tells a tale of intractability that becomes legend among stakeholders in this protracted dispute.

Part II examines the web of contacts and relationships that have developed in recent years between media and policy. One argument is that policymakers use the media as a sophisticated tool to achieve their goals both at home and abroad. They employ a complex spinning system consisting of media and polling experts that controls much of the information the media publish and broadcast. The counterargument is that the media influence policymakers and policymaking simply because of its perceived power to shape public opinion. The CNN effect theory in its extreme formulation even suggests that CNN has taken over policymaking from politicians, at least in humanitarian disaster situations. According to this theory, the CNN televised pictures of genocide, famine, and violence force policymakers to intervene militarily to stop death, even if they don't think it is in the best interest of their country to adopt and implement such policy. The chapters in this part provide fresh insights on this debate and show that the media both influence policymakers and are manipulated by them.

Howard Tumber uses analysis of recent and influential work on the role of sources in the reporting of government policy and primarily applies it to coverage of conflict resolution in Northern Ireland. He critically explores various communication and conflict theories including "primary definition," Bennet's "indexing hypothesis," and Mermin's "critical angel" amendment to this theory. Tumber isn't satisfied with existing theories and thinks that studies of how government sources affect the reporting of conflict and conflict resolution could provide a better picture of the nature, direction and consequences of coverage for policy and public opinion.

The civil war in Bosnia (1992–1995) raised a heated debate in the United States and the West whether to stop the violence through military intervention. Policymakers and the media participated in the exchange of arguments for and against humanitarian intervention. During and after the intervention the question was who brought it about: policymakers who finally decided to intervene or global television that forced them to intervene through horrific pictures of violence and death. Two chapters explore the media's role in this war.

Yaeli Bloch and *Sam Lehman-Wilzig* developed an exploratory model of media-government relations in times of crisis and applied it to the Bosnia war. The model is based on the integration and application of theories from communication and international relations with emphasis on the sundry phases of the crisis, the roles of the media, and the press attitudes toward government policies. Commentary and editorial of the *New York Times* and *The Washington Post* as well as all Presidential and State Department communiqués were examined. The authors found that the elite press actually helped to articulate a rational for humanitarian military intervention, but the government was not sufficiently aware of this, and perhaps if it had been, it might have taken more decisive action and much sooner.

Through critical analysis of the CNN effect theory, **Piers Robinson** examines the role global television played in decisions to intervene militarily in the Bosnian crisis. He distinguishes between two intervention goals: humanitarian relief and conflict resolution. The latter refers to removing the causes of the violence, not only its consequences. He found that the U.S. intervention goal in the 1992–1995 Bosnian war was to enforce narrowly prescribed humanitarian objectives and not to end the conflict. He argues that limitations inherent in current media coverage, coupled with Western reluctance to become involved in "distant" civil wars, means that the CNN effect is limited to influencing forcible humanitarian intervention rather than military intervention to resolve conflicts.

Eytan Gilboa demonstrates how policymakers and journalists employ the media to affect critical elements of negotiation including signaling, mediation, bridging, confidence building, and mobilization of public support for negotiations and agreements. He applied negotiation and communication theories to media utilization in various Arab-Israeli peacemaking processes, and found that uses of the media by politicians and journalists have significantly helped to achieve negotiation goals. However, he also notes that these uses raise practical, professional, and ethical questions.

Olga Malinkina and **Douglas McLeod** explore the effects the Russian media have had on policy toward conflict, and they show how coverage of conflicts has changed from the Cold War years to the Post-Cold War era. They compare the role of the Russian newspaper *Izvestia* in two conflicts: the Soviet conflict with Afghanistan (1979–1989) and the Russian conflict with Chechnya (1994–1996). This comparison enabled them to trace the emergence of *Izvestia* as a source of political pressure on the Russian government. The results reveal content elements for the Chechen conflict that did not previously exist including criticism of Russian institutions and conflict policies, and publicizing evidence of the human casualties and economic devastation attributable to the conflict. Thy also noted however, that since the period under study, the Russian media have ceased to provide diverse coverage, and thus no longer apply pressure on the government to resolve the conflict.

In the last chapter of this part, **Meseret Chekol Reta** attempts to discover how the media perform in foreign conflict situations where U.S. policymakers are uncertain of what position to take. He argues that the propaganda model of Herman and Chomsky cannot address conflicts where the position of U.S. policymakers is ambiguous. Instead, he constructed a "policy uncertainty model" and tested it on the American media coverage of the Eritrean (1962–1991) and Southern Sudan (1983–1996) conflicts. He concludes that the impact of uncertainty on media coverage of these conflicts was minimal but suggest ways to further study this situation.

Part III of the volume explores various diverse relationships, normative and empirical, between the media and the public within a larger societal context. The first chapters deal with the media role in domestic and international reconciliation processes. Several scholars expect the media to make positive substantial contributions to reconciliation, but others think that this isn't what the media should be doing in a democracy, and also that enthusiastic coverage of reconciliation may in fact distort reality by downgrading or ignoring fundamental intractable obstacles. The remaining chapters deal with the traditional and new media effects on public opinion.

The dismantling of the Apartheid regime in South Africa created expectations for a reconciliation process between Blacks and Whites, and the local media was expected to play a significant role in this process. The 1994 democratic elections in South Africa did not only usher in unprecedented hopes for peace, but press freedom was also guaranteed by a Bill of Rights in a new liberal democratic constitution. At the turn of the century the press, though freer than ever, was confronted with a number of crucial issues impacting on a peaceful vis-à-vis a conflict-ridden transition to a fuller democratic society. ***Arnold S de Beer*** examines some of the pertinent issues on a certain group of daily and weekly Southern African newspapers as they affect conflict and peace in the Southern African Society.

Dov Shinar argues that until the eruption of the Palestinian *Intifada* against Israel in 2000, the local and the foreign media adopted the reconciliation/"end-of-conflict" model to guide coverage of Arab-Israeli peacemaking processes. The model well fitted the interest of leaders and the desires of the public. The violence however, forced the media to abandon this model. Shinar claims that the media have ignored the cultural sources and aspects of the Arab-Israeli conflict, and points to the serious consequences of wrongly matching of models and conflicts, such as using the reconciliation model in resolving cultural conflicts. He also discusses the media's building of high expectations for conflict transformation that can't be realized and consequently foment "crises." He concludes that the media must face and resolve the dilemma where on the one hand, they want to contribute to peacemaking, but on the other hand, have to address the negative dimensions of cultural conflict, which may hinder peacemaking.

Like Shinar, ***Sonia Gutiérrez-Villalobos*** discusses the media role in reconciliation processes. She focuses on processes in Central America that ended warfare in El Salvador, Nicaragua, and Guatemala. She found that the media and media professionals were mostly absent from these processes, but were given a role in the political and educational campaign designed to cultivate public support for the implementation of the agreements. She blames the concepts of reconciliation and objectivity as practiced in Central America for this outcome. She thinks the media can contribute much more to reconciliation processes and suggest ways to accomplish this goal.

Kimberly Bissell uses the Kosovo crisis to test traditional agenda-setting hypotheses as well as hypotheses that link agenda-setting with priming theory. Her study tests the news media's ability to prime public attitudes toward specific issues in addition to the traditional agenda-setting measures. The results reported in her chapter indicate that public attitudes toward the Kosovo conflict were correlated with textual and photographic coverage of the conflict. She also found that the media may have primed audiences to think about the Kosovo conflict in terms of "the plight of the refugees" or Serbian atrocities via the photographs published, thereby guiding audiences to favor engagement in the conflict.

In the last chapter, ***Shannon Campbell*** examines the inextricable relationship between crisis management and the Internet. It well illustrates the vital role technology plays in current public relations practices and describes current and future trends for the tech savvy practitioner. Furthermore, Campbell establishes protocol and displays proper procedures for using the Internet to optimize organizational effectiveness. Additionally, her chapter provides the "dos and don'ts" for developing appropriate and mutually beneficial websites.

In addition to following the three parts of the book, readers interested in a particular conflict or issue, can read in a sequence relevant chapters. For example, those interested in the media roles in the Arab-Israeli conflict nay read the chapters by Donohue and Hoobler, Gilboa, and Shinar. Those interested in the Balkan crises may read the chapters by Bloch and Lehman-Wilzig, Robinson, and Bissell. The chapters by Wall and Campbell deal with new media, and those by Robinson, Gilboa, and Bissell with global television.

PART I. FRAMING

CHAPTER 1
MEDIA AND THE NEW POST-COLD WAR MOVEMENTS

Andrew Rojecki

A. INTRODUCTION

The highly publicized 1999 protests against the Seattle meetings of the World Trade Organization (WTO) played a significant part in the failure of these meetings. The protests represented the leading edge of a political movement whose policy aims responded to a global process that had been defended by its proponents as a boon to world prosperity. That a political movement ostensibly opposed to global prosperity could gain any sympathetic traction either in public opinion or in the mass media suggested an altered political dynamic, the most significant since the end of the Cold War. The protests against unregulated economic globalization open a new issue domain and also mark a sea change in the politics of dissent that can be traced to the erosion of state sovereignty on economic policy. As such, they make an ideal case study for examining the validity of post-Cold War theories that account for the press's response to political dissent. Although scholars have offered theories addressing this area, these have been formulated largely for military interventions, which rightfully presume an unchanged monopoly in organized violence held by sovereign states. No such stability remains in the economic sphere, however.

In this chapter a new theory of press and political dissent in a new policy domain that has altered the post-Cold War equilibrium between political elites, interest groups, and mass media is argued, beginning with an analysis of the interacting changes in three domains—the political economy, political discourse, and information technology—and derive a set of propositions about their likely effect on media coverage of dissident movements. These propositions are then developed in an analysis of the mass media's coverage of and editorial response to the Seattle protests.

Beginning with the Vietnam War and continuing through the wars in Central America, the Middle East, Africa, and the Balkans, scholars have grappled with a theory of the press and foreign policy to replace what Hallin (1992) has called the period of "high modernism." In this account the Vietnam War began to fracture a period of extraordinary cooperation between political and media elites based on a consensual view of the Soviet Union as a dangerous implacable foe of the West. The collapse of the Soviet empire eliminated a once reliable template for understanding foreign events and for framing media coverage of foreign policy.

Scholars have developed three general theoretical responses to this new political environment. One sees a continuation of elite hegemonic control, albeit using a number of new strategies (Hallin, 1987; *cf.* Herman & Chomsky, 1988; Parenti, 1993). A second perspective, featuring elite dissensus at the heart of its explanatory framework, has attracted the most empirical study. Bennett's indexing hypothesis (1990) traces the breadth of policy analysis appearing in the mass media to the degree of elite conflict. A number of studies have lent evidentiary weight to the theory (Mermin, 1999), as well as refinement (Entman & Page, 1994; Zaller & Chiu, 2000). A third perspective (Entman, 2000) shifts the balance of power to the media themselves as elites find it more difficult in the absence of the Cold War frame to demonize enemies and thus to invoke the patriotism that once could be counted on to rally public opinion and media support. Though these theories each contribute to our understanding of media response to military interventions and thus to their treatment of dissent to those actions, they do not fully address the economic consequences that followed the collapse of the Soviet bloc and their impact on the pace of globalization.

B. GLOBALIZATION AND RESISTANCE

Anthony Giddens characterizes globalization as the *sine qua non* of modernity, the "intensification of worldwide social relations which link distant localities in such a way that local happenings are shaped by events occurring many miles away and vice versa" (1990, p. 64). Although this process has been at work for well over a century (Tarrow, 1996), an exponential advance in information technologies combined with the absence of a credible alternative to market capitalism has quickened the pace of worldwide economic integration. As Edward Yardeni (2001), chief investment strategist for Deutsche Banc has put it, "the end of the Cold War ended the greatest trade barrier of all times." Modern corporations are indifferent to political boundaries insofar as they do not impede their interests in finding raw materials, cheap labor, and markets for their goods. Ministers appointed by the nation states party to regulatory institutions such as the WTO see their mission as promoting the growth of international markets, which they argue lead to rising national incomes. This growth has led to an erosion of state sovereignty, the extent and significance of which is the subject of some scholarly debate.[1]

---

[1] There are three general views. Scholars such as Zygmunt Bauman (1998) see globalization as inexorably weakening national sovereignty: "Whatever has been left of [post cold war] politics is expected to be dealt with, as in the good old days, by the state—but whatever is concerned with the economic life the state is not allowed to touch; any attempt in this direction would be met with prompt and furious punitive action from the world markets" (p. 66). A sec-

Though the controversy on the extent of the erosion of state sovereignty remains to be settled, there is little doubt that the increased velocity and flows of transnational capital have had profound effects on bond markets, which have, in turn, reduced state discretion on fiscal policy. In the U.S., for example, the Clinton administration implemented the philosophy of the Democratic Leadership Committee, "the third way," in its creation of the North American Free Trade Association and embracing of traditionally conservative calls for reform of the welfare system. Today the policies of laissez-faire in the economic sphere and the gradual withdrawal of the social safety net have put competitive pressures on regional economic alliances such as the European Union to do the same. The rationale is that lean government promotes investment in the private sphere, which encourages international investment and domestic economic growth.

While some tout these developments as the foundation for an increasingly vibrant global economy (Friedman, 2000; Mickelthwait & Wooldridge, 2000), others warn of a transition "toward social and economic stratification, toward walled-in communities and hardening class structures, [and] toward political, business and financial elites that bail each other out . . ." (Phillips, 1994). The gloomy view of globalization sees it as tantamount to a restratification on a worldwide scale owing to the natural tendencies of unfettered capitalism toward inequality, facilitated by institutions such as the IMF and the WTO.

Three kinds of opposition to these governing bodies and their presumed aims have been building over the last decade (Faux, 1999). The first is a reactive nationalism that regards transnational sovereign bodies as eroding American power in general. As a corrective, it would reinstate total national sovereignty over trade—for example, using tariffs to protect U.S. firms from the dumping of cheap foreign steel. Elements of this position made up part of the 2000 Reform Party platform of presidential candidate Patrick Buchanan.

A second source of opposition recognizes the inevitability of global trade but would cushion the excesses of laissez-faire markets. Thus it proposes regulations intended to protect labor and the environment and calls for the introduction of democratic transparency to the WTO that would counterbalance what it considers as to be hegemonic corporate power. Ralph Nader's Global Trade Watch group is one institutional exemplar of this position.

The third view envisions small-scale economic development under the control of local groups. In this world, economic growth would be balanced against

---

ond group, while acknowledging the increasing volume and velocity of finance capital across borders, remain skeptical of its power to erode state power. Mann (1997), for example, argues that capital flows remain based on goods and services tied to specific locations (pp. 481–82). The third is skeptical of the erosion of any state power whatsoever, arguing that strong states have and will continue to bend international law and markets to suit their interests (Mearsheimer, 2001; Barber, 1996).

the need for cultural and biological diversity and politics governed by decentralized civic institutions linked by the internet. Kevin Danaher of Global Exchange, a representative organization, declares the aim is to "replace the money cycle with the natural cycle, to emphasize society rather than the economy, and to remind citizens that nature bats last" (personal communication, October 19, 2000).

To summarize the essentials of the controversy in a metaphor used by both proponents and opponents, laissez-faire global market capitalism represents a tide that for its supporters will, in the long run, raise all boats, but that for its detractors will only float yachts. The difference in political philosophies between these groups parallels the division between Conservatives and Progressives of a century earlier. They also differed sharply on the nature and consequences of a progress that might be attributed to time and nature alone (Hofstader, 1955, p. 5). This division signals one important advantage that contributes to the overall improved gradient of opportunity for this movement.

1. Political Opportunity and Resource Mobilization

Political scholars use the concept of political opportunity structure and resource mobilization theory to account for the expansion and contraction of political movements. While political opportunity structure identifies macro-scale conditions that increase the chances of movement success (McAdam, McCarthy, & Zald, 1996), resource mobilization theory links movement growth and decline to the supply of resources available and the skill with which they are managed (McCarthy & Zald, 1977). These models suggest three major interacting advantages for the coalition making up the anti-globalization movement: elite dissensus on both national and international levels, the end of the Cold War and its dominant ideological presumptions, and the rapid diffusion of new information technologies.

The anti-globalization movement gains its first significant structural advantage by the existence of elite dissensus at both domestic and international levels, driven in part by public worry about the local consequences of globalization. Despite major currents in media discourse that throughout the 1990s highlighted growing affluence, polls indicated public apprehension nonetheless. Thus a survey conducted shortly after the Seattle protests showed that 75 percent of Americans thought that the benefits of the new economy had been unevenly distributed.[2] The same poll (Conlin, 1999) also suggested that over half the public regarded globalization as detrimental to job creation and the environment.

---

[2] Pew surveys reinforce this finding as they point to a positive correlation between income and support for globalization policies. About two-thirds of those with household incomes of $75,000 and higher approve, as compared to only about a third with incomes below $50,000 (Kohut, 1999, A31).

The political consequences of this had been evident in the U.S. for some time before: Bill Clinton's support of NAFTA, for example, created a rift in the Democratic coalition and partly fueled Ross Perot's unusually successful third-party run for the presidency in 1992. Continued labor opposition to NAFTA and other trade pacts (including the admission of China into the WTO) may have also played a role in alienating enough Democratic voters sufficient to ensure a Bush win for the presidency in 2000. In Florida, for example, Ralph Nader received over 97,000 votes, more than enough to have given Gore the presidency, even if the majority of these would not have voted had Nader had not run. Exit polls revealed that only 30 percent of his voters would have skipped the election if Nader was not on the ballot, and that nearly half of Nader voters would have supported Gore had Nader not been in the race. In Florida, this translated into Nader taking about 45,500 votes from Gore (Mishra & Cook, 2000).

Overseas, although the 135 nation states in the WTO share an interest in increasing global trade, they individually enjoy competitive advantages that domestic interest groups seek to preserve. These constraints impose limits on the ability of trade ministers to negotiate agreements, particularly under the pressures imposed by highly visible protests. For example, organizers of the Direct Action Coalition (an umbrella group for some of the organizations involved in the Seattle protests) were aware of rifts between the U.S. and developing nations on enforceable labor rights and of Clinton's need to maintain union support for Gore's presidential run in 2000. The widely publicized turmoil in the streets forced Clinton into a public declaration of support for labor that put the U.S. at odds with India, which depended on its competitive advantage in cheap labor. Similarly, protests regarding the harmful effects of free trade on local farmers and the importation of foodstuffs of unknown origin "delighted" the French delegation:

> "What's happening outside is having an effect on the negotiations," the European Union trade commissioner, Pascal Lamy, said today. The American desire to wipe out government subsidies in Europe that make it difficult for American farmers to export their goods "is even less possible," given the tenor of the protests, he said. (Sanger & Kahn, 1999, p. A14)

The end of the Cold War presents two crucial rhetorical advantages for the movement. First, the elimination of the Soviet Union as a long-standing symbol of repression and the economic system it championed deprives conservative opponents of a dependable ideologically based platform for launching their attacks on dissident movements. During the cold war, the yoking of deeply anti-democratic values to a rival economic system enabled a host of facile rhetorical appeals that conflated the political with the economic and permitted an effortless association of one with the other. The collapse of the Soviet system may have eliminated a powerful real-world exemplar of authoritarian rule associated with a command economy, but a residual association of the two provides a potent advantage for a movement that draws attention to the insulation of the WTO from the influence of public opinion. The organization's secret deliberations draw an ironic parallel to the formerly demonized command economic system, permitting movement participants to impose an implied judgment of authoritarianism on unregulated market capitalism.

A second advantage results from the failure of the socialist economic model as a realistic substitute for market capitalism. As Schiller notes, ". . . the belief is cultivated that there can be no alternative to what exists" (1996, p. xiv). On the one hand, elimination of a real-world economic rival would appear to have shrunken the political spectrum from the left and thus to have rendered movement challenges vulnerable to charges of extremity and preposterous removal from practical reality. Alternatively, however, because no credible rival to U.S. power promotes a rival ideology, elites are deprived of using jeopardy to state security and well-being (e.g., weakened resolve at home) as a conventional reactionary attack on the opposition (see Hirschman, 1991). The tensions between state sovereignty and the border-indifferent dynamics of market capitalism reconfigure the grounds of rhetorical advantage for the anti-globalization dissidents: now it is they who can lay claim to the mantle of loyalty to country and state, its environment and its workers, while corporations and the regulatory bodies that seek to enlarge world markets struggle to find an ethical high ground other than one based on efficiency, profit, and the rhetorical thin gruel of trickle-down economic theory. This widens the field of acceptable discourse and positions movement appeals within a field of resonant, traditional political values.

Freed of the need to protect their flanks from right-wing opponents, movement organizations feel little pressure to impose traditional curbs on their rhetoric and argumentation. As an example, an organizing poster designed by the Direct Action coalition for the Seattle meetings includes this text:

> The WTO is by far the most advanced and far-reaching form of domination that our world has ever known. . . . It is the product of a long history of domination. "Global capitalism" is simply an extension of the colonial experiment. It is not the result of capitalism run awry, but rather of capitalism as it was intended to be. Inherent in capitalism is a propensity for the greater accumulation of wealth in fewer and fewer hands. It's a "grow or die!" economy—and unfortunately it is the oppressed of the earth who are doing all the dying.

The removal of the Cold War ideological presumption also permits a closer alignment of the movement's core message with journalism's historic affinity for the appeals and rhetoric of Progressive reform (Gans,1980; Hofstader, 1955). Take, for example, a collection of essays written by a number of figures associated with the Seattle protests. A representative essay offers a program for reforming global trade policy, including such points as democratizing global institutions, encouraging shareholder activism to drive corporations toward greater accountability, and supporting the development of strong labor unions (James, 2000, pp.

203–208). The underlying appeals to the rule of law and democratic responsiveness are among the foundational elements of Progressive reform (Hofstader, 1955, p. 203) and the substance of a major narrative thread in the tradition of investigative reporting (Ettema & Glasser, 1998). In this light, the recent campaigns against Nike (Bennett, 2001) and other global corporate sweatshops (Klein, 2000) are just the latest examples of a traditional impulse in American reform politics, this time substituting the consequences of globalization for those of urbanization.

Resource mobilization theory (McAdam, McCarthy & Zald, 1977) identifies the third major movement advantage. The Internet offers under-resourced interest groups with tools that provide extraordinary leverage for mobilization and organization (Ayres, 1999; Bimber, 1998). In the case of the Seattle demonstrations, the Direct Action Network coalition used websites, listservs, and e-mail to coordinate activities, to mobilize membership, and to provide expertise on a variety of issues. Participants complained about the slow pace of consensus-building, but organizers argued that majority rule could lead to cleavages that opponents could exploit to divide and fragment what might otherwise be a fragile coalition of reformers and more radically minded participants. Indeed, these cleavages were common in the Cold War movements against nuclear arms. The anti-nuclear movements sought defensive compromises on a single moderate issue for forming a broad-based coalition that could withstand a hostile political environment fraught with elite attacks based on disloyalty (e.g., jeopardizing state security or weakening the U.S. bargaining position vis à vis the Soviet Union). The chief strategist for the movement of the 1980s, for example, decided on a freeze of then current nuclear forces instead of more radical proposals for reduction or elimination of nuclear weapons (Rojecki, 1999). The anti-globalization movements can form a looser coalition of more fragmented but related interests. The result is greater resilience and a decidedly flatter structure. One activist referred to the network of activists and groups in the movement as an "army of equals" (George, 2000, p. 55).

One could see a style of decision-making characteristic of this new kind of movement in the on-the-ground planning in Seattle, which proved to be important during the confusion and violence that would ensue during confrontations with police: "No centralized leader could have coordinated the scene in the midst of the chaos, and none was needed—the organic autonomous organization we had developed proved far more powerful and effective" (Starhawk, 2000, p. 38). These three situational advantages were magnified by the movement's sensitivity to the role of the media in political movements.

2. Media and Political Movements

The political movements of the Cold War had an uneasy relationship with the mass media. Although leaders valued the media's power for mobilizing new members and for influencing public opinion, they were also wary of its tendencies to accept state-favored interpretation of events and to single out conflict and flamboyancy in movement activities. In the anti-nuclear movement of the early 1960s, for example, the Women's Strike for Peace advised its members to wear hats and gloves so as to project a "lady-like" image, to distract the press from the "red diaper baby" origins of some of its participants (Swerdlow, 1993, p. 73). Similarly, in 1963 the editors of *Liberation*, a publication of the Committee for Non-Violent Action, warned its local chapters to avoid ad hoc demonstrations that might attract the beatniks who would distract the media's attention from the mainstream members of the movement or its carefully crafted moderate appeal (Rojecki, 1999). Indeed, Randall Forsberg, chief strategist of the Nuclear Freeze movement, fashioned an image of mainstream respectability just to avoid what she anticipated would be similar press misrepresentations (Meyer, 1990).

Gitlin's ideological analysis of the media's interaction with the Students for a Democratic Society (1980) identified a similar inclination of the media to attend to the actions of the most reckless and thus to exaggerate their significance; this, he argued, drew a similarly minded membership to the New Left movement, thereby radicalizing and weakening it. In his study of the anti-Vietnam War movement, Small (1994) also found a distorting media focus on instability and disruption, part of a larger pattern of what he regarded as hostility to political dissent.

The analysis set out above suggests a much more favorable media environment for the anti-globalization movement. To summarize, the insulation of economic decision making from democratic control and the absence of an institutional means for channeling dissent casts the movement into the role of a sympathetic victim of an indifferent and democratically unaccountable institution. This combined with a loss of the Cold War ideological presumption permits the anti-globalization movement to escape close judgment on the ideological implications of its proposals and thus to benefit by its association with the resonant values of Progressive reform. Finally, because the loose coalition making up this movement is less dependent on a single defensive issue for withstanding an ideologically charged field of resistance, it is more resilient, less likely to falter. All of these conditions suggest a more sympathetic media reception.

C. ANALYSIS OF MEDIA REACTION

To test and further develop these propositions, two streams of mass media content on the WTO meetings held in Seattle in December 1999 are examined: (1) news reports in *USA Today*, the nation's most widely circulated national newspaper, and the evening news broadcasts on CBS, selected randomly from broadcast coverage of all network newscasts after an examination revealed no substantial differences between them;[3] (2) op-ed commentaries in three newspa-

---

[3] National coverage of the issue is selected because this allows a comparison of this coverage to prior studies of national media treatment of Cold War movements and because

pers judged most influential by a panel of editors and other media elites: *The New York Times, Los Angeles Times,* and *Washington Post* ("America's Best Newspaper," 1999).[4] The intent is to monitor the discourse of the most prestigious political and journalistic elites on the assumption that these commentators are read by journalists and other elites attempting to make sense of an issue that, for most audiences, is likely to be obscure. In a sense, these commentators function as master framers who establish the broad contours of public understanding of the uncharted issues of globalization.

Because movements fall outside the perimeter of conventional politics, they need to establish and maintain a sense of legitimacy for their issues and participants. Accordingly, for media framing of issues, assessments of authority and sensibility are explored, whether the ideas presented fall within a range of legitimate controversy or whether they are simply portrayed as outlandish or deviant, and unworthy of further comment (Hallin, 1986).

For media framing of participants, dimensions of comprehension and knowledge are examined, whether movement participants are portrayed as having sufficient grasp of the underlying issues and the knowledge to make reasoned appeals; their position relative to the political mainstream—whether they are portrayed as within its boundaries or as deviants; and their political effectiveness (Rojecki, 1999; Entman & Rojecki, 1993).

Daily press and broadcast news coverage is analyzed first, followed by editorial reaction. The two are separated to get a sense of both the evolving news frames used to depict the swiftly changing events on the ground and the more detached views expressed by columnists and op-ed writers who have a longer time frame to develop their perspectives.

1. The Press and Broadcast News—Evolving Sympathy

Coverage in the popular press followed a trend of evolving understanding of and increasing sympathy to movement positions. Initial focus on surface features—costumes and stunts—quickly deepened to the underlying issues they symbolized.

---

analysis of regional or the local press would add to an already lengthy study. However, in doing so a more definitive connection between sympathetic coverage and local economic dislocations cannot be made and awaits future study.

[4] The papers were selected as the best by the *Columbia Journalism Review* in a two-stage process; in the first by editors of newspapers in all 50 states, and to former American Society of Newspaper Editors' presidents. All papers with circulation over 150,000 on Sunday and several dozen smaller papers were included. "The editors were asked to pick (but not rank) their top ten plus two "wildcards' they thought deserved special notice. A second group, an independent committee, made the final ranking. Judgment was to be based on "writing and reporting quality; editing and graphics; integrity, accuracy, and fairness; vision and innovation; and influence in their community and in the broader journalistic and public world."

In a tone equally frivolous and anxious, *USA Today* began its coverage with an account of an expected "deluge" of protestors. It characterized Mike Dolan, campaign director for Nader's Global Trade Watch, as "an irrepressible cheerleader" for critics of the WTO who guaranteed "a full week of fun," even though threats by the Ruckus Society to shut down the meetings worried city officials (McMahon, 1999, p. 4A). The story also raised an argument that would become one of the frames deployed to explain the failure of the meetings—ineffective PR. Lewis Platt CEO of Hewlett-Packard (also described as a cheerleader) declared, "'We just haven't done a very good job selling it. Industry leaders, the government, the press—we could all be tarred with the same brush.'" The article provided a nuanced account of the advantages to the U.S. economy as well as a less detailed treatment of objections to it by activists who "feel it is exploiting workers, crushing small farmers and businesses, polluting the environment and ravaging natural resources" (Cox, 1999a, p. B1).

Before the protest scene turned violent, coverage favored WTO officials and corporate executives, particularly in *USA Today's* business section where the stories first broke. On the eve of the meeting, for example, the paper reported that 400 CEOs had made themselves available to the press so as to prevent protestors' charges from going unchallenged. (This intervention was perhaps less important for its open admission than for its ultimate ineffectiveness.) In contrast to the thoughtful, reasoned approach of the CEOs, protestors initially suffered under judgments of frivolousness as they were described in terms of their playful dress (some dressed as monarch butterflies, others as sea turtles) and outré actions (rappelling down buildings, hanging from cranes). Even their arguments were trivialized by association with positions that appeared, on the surface at least, untenable: "The thousands of protesters flooding Seattle blame corporations and globalization for everything from child labor in shoe factories to hurricanes sparked by global warming" (Jones, 1999, p. B1). In this early coverage, proponents enjoyed an advantage as they made their case for the wealth created by globalization, the laissez-faire democratic tide theory; no further intervention would be necessary as time alone would resolve the issues of human and labor rights and despoilment of the environment.

Confrontations with police took place on the first day of the meeting when protestors blocked the entrances to the convention center, effectively shutting down the opening ceremonies. Delegates could not gain entry and police began lobbing tear gas at the seated protestors. Significantly, however, Seattle's police chief blamed property destruction on just a small faction of activists: "'we've had an excellent relationship with many of the demonstration's planners'" (McMahon & Cox, 1999, p. A19).

The chief's muted comments coincided with a change in the paper's perspective when the following day's coverage widened to include detailed critiques *offered by movement participants themselves*. With demonstrators being arrested by the hundreds, the protest had "exposed the huge chasm between those who want to harness globalization and those who intend to stop it." Although reporting included the familiar trope of seeking division among elements of the movement ("anti-WTO forces are united by a profound mistrust of globalization—and almost nothing else"), Clinton offered a sympathetic response saying that people in the streets deserved a hearing. The story referred to the "weird jamboree" and to the ignorance of the protestors, but the blame ultimately fell on Clinton who was chided by the head of the U.S. Chamber of Commerce for neglecting to build public support (Cox & Jones, 1999, p. A1).

In contrast to the largely superficial and somewhat negative coverage on the front page, the inner pages of the paper offered considerably more detail on the movement's goals (Cox, 1999b, p. A2) as well as a balanced debate on their desirability. Activists Jerry Mander and John Cavanaugh were offered space on the op-ed pages to make their case against the WTO and its global corporate sponsors: "The central principle of globalization and the WTO is that any obstacles to the expansion of global corporate activity should be suppressed, including laws and standards crafted on behalf of labor, the environment, human rights, consumers, culture, national sovereignty and democracy" (Mander & Cavanagh, 1999, p. A14). An accompanying unsigned rebuttal did not attack the protestors, most of whom it praised as peaceful, nor their concerns about the negative effects of globalization—child labor, dangerous working conditions, and plunder of the environment. Rather, it praised the rise in incomes credited to globalization and argued that the WTO was not the proper forum for dealing with its negative effects: "Far better solutions exist. Thanks to the globalization spotlight, U.S. companies already appoint activists to internal committees and report on labor standards and cleanups at their annual shareholder meetings" ("Smashing Starbucks' Windows," 1999, p. A14).

What was noteworthy in *USA Today's* coverage was not its initial reflexive *ad hominem* attack on the protestors themselves—their ignorance, disorganization, and violence—but its gradual engagement with movement issues and eventual retreat from blanket characterization of movement participants. Over the course of a week, representatives of movement organizations were invited to make reasoned arguments on behalf of their causes, and reporters and officials distinguished the peaceful majority from a small group of window-smashing "anarchists." Increasingly sympathetic coverage permitted the protestors to develop a coherent political critique, untainted by any association with real-world ideological competitors.

Broadcast news followed a similar pattern of evolving sympathy, but with more balanced coverage initially. In its first report, CBS explained the presence of the protestors as a response to the undemocratic nature of the WTO and its lack of recognition of basic labor rights, including the abolition of child labor (*CBS Evening News*, November 29, 1999). As in press coverage, broadcast news was careful to identify and isolate a violent minority from the movement's mainstream. Thus the violence was "carefully orchestrated" by "self-styled anarchists and some moderate demonstrators." In one videotaped sequence, a hooded man kicked in the windows of a Starbucks while an exasperated onlooker shouted, "stop it, you're making fools of our country and our city!" To the hooded figure's response, "it's self-defense," the onlooker cried, "what are you defending yourself against, a window?" Significantly, the reporter said the protest, which to this point had been peaceful, had turned violent not because of the window-kicking anarchists but *because of police overreaction* (*CBS Evening News*, November 30, 1999).

Although the division here of movement participants into categories of responsible and irresponsible protest establishes the potential for future negative framing, the specific coverage here did not by itself discredit the movement because political elites blamed the police for the violence. Prior analyses of political movements would point to elite dissent as the source of positive media framing (e.g., Bennett, 1990), but there is compelling theoretical reason to believe that receptivity to this movement in the present political environment depends less on elite opinion. The absence of a singular ideological field permits this movement to adopt a loose coalitional structure, and this prevents the ready transmission of one group's threat to the whole. Individual groups such as the "anarchists" (whose political program remains unclear from the media reports), may be singled out, but the movement's political integrity remains unaffected and its overall program untainted. Indeed, the following day's coverage reported Clinton's intention to "steer a course between the WTO and protestors" as video footage showed "non-violent" demonstrators helping to clean up graffiti. Michael Dolan of the Nader organization referred to a "few vandals in a crowd of tens and tens of thousands of peaceful protestors," and a demonstrator said, "the protestors aren't hippies on welfare; they are working people trying to keep their jobs and feed their families" (*CBS Evening News*, December 1, 1999).

On the last day of comprehensive coverage the mayor of Seattle declared a state of civil emergency. Despite a blockade by thousands of protestors and the utter collapse of the WTO talks caused by them, Seattle's mayor declared, "there is no battle in Seattle. What there is is a wonderful expression of free speech." Instead of blaming demonstrators, broadcast media highlighted examples of "out of control" police. Accompanying video footage showed police officers chasing demonstrators into neighborhoods beyond the Convention Center, and, in one scene repeated in several network newscasts, a protestor being kicked in the groin and then fired on at point blank range with rubber bullets. The movement was not to blame for the city having lost its pride; rather, broadcast coverage pointed to police overreaction and the implied intransigence of the WTO, described as "undemocratic," "cloaked in secrecy," and "pandering to business interests." After citing some statistics about the WTO's scope of influence on the world stage, the reporter concluded that "protestors have shined a brilliant light on the WTO, and this time the whole world is watching" (*CBS Evening News*, December 2, 1999). This perhaps unintentionally ironic reference to the protests surrounding the 1968 Democratic convention signaled a remarkable reversal of fortune in media treatment of street-level protest. In 1968, initial reports also highlighted police brutality as a principal cause of the disorder, but some of the media backtracked from these characterizations as polls revealed that Americans were split on their assessments of blame (Gitlin, 1980; Small, 1994). Although polls after the Seattle meetings did not specifically address the police brutality issue, a poll conducted for *Business Week* revealed that more than half of Americans were sympathetic with the demonstrators (Conlin, 1999).

In summary, mainstream news took care to distinguish the central message of the protestors from the minority of participants intent on sheer disruption. It did not mount an assault on the credibility or knowledgeability of its participants when their costumes, methods for gaining attention, or civil disobedience and mass arrests could easily have become the focus of coverage. It also offered broad coverage of the essential issues, often offered by its multiple leaders. Though reporters made occasional references to the "weird jamboree," suggesting the absence of a central political organization, this did not undermine the protest's legitimacy (evidenced by scenes of cooperative, thoughtful protestors), or its effectiveness in shutting down the conference and eliciting sympathetic framing nonetheless.

2. Op-Eds: Confounding Convention

Commentators in the prestige press were also at pains to distinguish the legitimate claims of the serious majority in the movement, however diverse, from what they perceived as a few troublemakers. This indicated a serious and a largely sympathetic engagement with the issues raised by the protests right from the start. E. J. Dionne's (1999) comments are characteristic:

> In the short run the attention will go to the violent minority in Seattle who smashed windows, burned trash and tried to shut the city down. Violence begets media attention, and those who rampage usually drown out those who petition peacefully. (p. A41)

Of the three papers, *The Los Angeles Times* tapped the most diverse, and in some cases remarkably radical sources for their op-ed columns. Nearly all, either implicitly or explicitly, used metaphors of impersonal force to characterize globalization—a juggernaut, a steamroller, a force "stalking the earth" (Plate, 1999, p. B9). None were antagonistic to the movement, and only four of 16 could even be characterized as ambivalent. Tom Plate, a contributing editor, wrote several columns in this period charting the benefits of free trade to Asian economies but also noted its negative effects (the end of lifetime jobs in Japan, pornography on the Internet in Singapore): "In a different life or a different fate, at least a few of the ministerial leaders inside Seattle's hotels might have wound up on the other side of the barricades" (Plate, 1999, p. B9). James Pinkerton, columnist for *Newsday*, was also somewhat cautionary as he warned Democrats not to be pulled leftward and thus to allow a Republican victory. "The protestors in Seattle and elsewhere have more leverage inside the party than outside of it" (Pinkerton, 1999, p. B9).

Other commentators were more explicitly positive. Robert Reich (1999) praised the social capital created by "positive nationalism," a sense of generosity extended to fellow citizens and urged that social responsibility replace market efficiency as a cardinal value (p. B9). Jeremy Brecher and Brendan Smith (1999), producers of the documentary "Global Village or Global Pillage," freely used radical rhetoric in their critique of global capitalism: the WTO and its lack of democratic responsiveness symbolized the secrecy of the managers of a global economy who pitted workers against each other and tolerated harm to the environment (p. B9).

Others took positions that mirrored those held by demonstrators themselves. Marc Cooper (1999), contributing editor to *The Nation*, noted an emerging "phantasmagorical" progressive coalition of workers, human rights activists, environmentalists, and family farmers against "corporate-managed" globalization (p. B11); while Michael Lerner (1999), editor of *Tikkun*, compared protestors to the Maccabees' "valiant efforts against a massive Greek empire and its Hellenistic culture." Using rhetoric replete with terms such as "domination," "colonial armies," "imperialist intervention," and "profits uber alles" to characterize the WTO, he concluded that though Americans were opposed to the substance of what the organization sought, they had no effective political leadership to articulate their opposition because politicians remained in the sway of corporate campaign contributions (p. B9).

Robert Scheer (1999), contributing editor, even found good things to say about the violent elements in the movement: "It was not the hundred-odd anarchists who were menacing. They were, like ghetto thugs, only a reminder of the ultimate cost of things going wrong. But we do owe them thanks, for without their militancy, the media would have continued to ignore the WTO and all other elitist and mostly secret arrangements being made for our future"(p. B9).

Most polemical, Edward Luttwak (1999), senior fellow at the Center for Strategic and International Studies, went so far as to call globalizers "the Bolsheviks of their day" who, in the absence of dynamic controlling institutions, destroyed national cultures and societies (p. B9). And illustrating what Giddens refers to as the "double hermeneutic," the process by which the discourse of social science itself becomes an agent of social change, Todd Gitlin (1999) wrote an invited column in which he provided the movement with advice he had gained as an SDS organizer and later as a media scholar: ". . . it is one thing for tiny knots of anarchists to attract front-page pictures, but the real significance of the Seattle turn-out was in the cooperativeness of the disparate groups." Regarding globalization as "unbridled corporate power," he urged activists to build support from the ground up, to talk to people who fear corporate power (p. B11).

Contributors to the op-ed page at *The Washington Post* were more likely to see the failure of the WTO meetings as indicative of the public's misunderstand-ing of the organization's function (Samuelson, 1999, p. A23; Ventura, 1999, p. A43) or recommend that its failures at regulation be dealt with by more capable institutions such as the Department of Justice (Ignatius, 1999, p. B7). Other neg-ative accounts held Clinton accountable: Henry Kissinger (1999) blamed him for inadequate strategic vision and pandering to demonstrators (p. A33); an econo-mist chided Clinton for misleading demonstrators and contributing to their igno-rance (Bhagwati,1999, p. A31); and a former undersecretary of state in the Bush administration accused Clinton of waffling on the issue of labor standards, one of the issues that led to the failure of the meetings (Zoellick, 1999, p. A39).

Even columnists who disagreed with the goals of the protestors tempered their remarks. Contributors, though less effusive than those in *The Los Angeles Times*, were still positive. Sebastian Mallaby (1999), for example, sought to cor-rect the impression that those who opposed the WTO were weak and ineffectual—on the contrary, they represented a "stealth government" whose "reach and clout . . . have since expanded marvelously, courtesy of the Internet." As evidence he cited the movement's blockage of the Multilateral Agreement on Investment (MAI) and the lobbying efforts of Jubilee 2000 for debt relief. Comparing the groups in the movement to business lobbies, Mallaby warned readers not to be distracted by their colorful appearance, evidence for his position that pluralism was alive and well (p. A29).

At *The New York Times*, columnist Thomas Friedman offered the most spirited defense of unfettered globalization. Using an example of a modern Sri Lankan Victoria's Secret factory to support the argument that globalization creates pros-perity, Friedman (1999a) admonished Seattle protesters to go after sweatshops by targeting the specific retailers who use them, not by targeting globalization in gen-eral (Sec. 4, p. 15). Accordingly, on the first day of the protests, he excoriated demonstrators as "Noah's ark flat-earth advocates" (1999b, A23). Despite his com-mitment to free-wheeling globalization and his initial reflexive mockery of the pro-testors, Friedman conceded that the movement may have a legitimate grievance:

> There were some serious groups there raising serious points, particularly the notion that the WTO has no need or right to be so secretive. If it is deciding that a U.S. law banning tuna caught in nets that also catch dolphins is a trade barrier, the WTO should at least allow environmentalists to file a brief or meet with judges. The WTO can't promote open trade by ruling in the dark. It would enhance its own legitimacy if it opened up. (1999c, p. A23)

Here the compelling image of secret proceedings was enough to bring an advocate to the side of reform.

Only two other (implicitly) negative voices appeared in the op-ed pages of the *Times*: Bill Gates (1999), who used Seattle as an example of the prosperity created by free trade (p. A25), and the chief economist for Deutsche Bank, who regarded the protests as an indication of a "civil war" in the U.S. itself: "Quite a few Americans are currently determined to make globalization the catch-all phrase for issues that primarily warrant debate within the United States: American wage inequality and the accessibility of American workers to benefits" (Walter, 1999, p. A33).

With the exception of Thomas Friedman, commentators in *The New York Times* were as sympathetic to the movement as those in *The Los Angeles Times*. Taking issue with Friedman, one contributor argued the protestors were not in fact opposed to globalization but to unregulated corporate power. What had brought this disparate group together was their serendipitous, Internet-enabled discovery of common grievances against multinational corporations (Klein, 1999, p. A35).

Perhaps the most unexpected support came from Robert E. Lighthizer (1999), a deputy trade representative in the Reagan administration. He ridiculed advocates of free trade for arguing that prosperity alone, unfettered by parochial regulation, "will somehow pressure governments into cleaning up the environment, outlawing child labor and enacting workers' rights laws." Regulation would not come without a struggle:

> It rose out of successive waves of industrialization, followed by abuse, followed by reaction and then regulation. The huge monopolies of the last century, for example, gave us the antitrust laws. Only after the fire at the Triangle Shirtwaist Company in New York killed 146 garment workers was legislation enacted that outlawed child labor and protected laborers. The road to enforceable standards will be a long one. But if President Clinton follows through on his words, the Seattle protesters may have had a profound and long-term effect on the international trading system and social conditions throughout the world. (p. A31)

Also approving, though somewhat skeptical of their chances for short-term success, Michael Kazin (1999) compared the WTO protestors to the populists. The movement today would have a harder time because corporate chiefs are much harder to loathe. Nevertheless, quoting C. Vann Woodward, Kazin said ordinary citizens had asserted their ability "to shock the seats of power and privilege and furnish the periodic therapy that seems necessary to the health of our democracy" (Sec. 14, p. 17).

As Hofstader wrote of the "Progressive impulse" of a century earlier, it had the power to transcend traditional political alignments as even high-born political elites responded to what they regarded as a nobler moral purpose (1955, pp. 203–14). Lighthizer's and Kazin's commentaries reveal the resonance of the notion of moral progress to political elites that is a part of the anti-globalization's program of reform, one that this study demonstrates has the power to overcome long-standing political cleavages.

A wide view of these commentaries reveals anything but a monolithic approach to economic globalization or to its antagonists. Those who would have ordinarily been ideological opponents during the cold war—in particular members of the Executive branch in the Reagan and Bush administrations—offer commentaries free of ideological cant. Even more remarkable is the combined breadth and depth of the critiques, the majority of which are in sympathy with the protestors. The evidence from these accounts and commentaries suggests a reversal of the traditional antagonistic relationship between elites and opposition movements. Should this pattern continue beyond this case study (and structurally, there is much reason to expect it), it would call for a modification of models of press coverage and the politics of dissent in this new policy domain.

D. CONCLUSION

Some of the conditions predicting a widened media space for dissent were undoubtedly present in this case study. In particular the indexing hypothesis would have also predicted this kind of treatment. After all, three of the most notable political elites involved in this case—the president and the mayor of Seattle and its police chief—all expressed sympathetic views. What is important to note, however, is that broadcast news was even-handed before the mass arrests and the sympathetic public statements; this despite an unprecedented public relations campaign conducted by corporate CEOs reported by *USA Today*. Further, the range of views in the news and in commentaries was as wide as that expressed by the protestors themselves, creating a critical field that encompassed a heretofore unimaginable combination of conservative elites, traditional reformers, and neo-Marxist protestors. Thus to the extent that globalization will continue to erode national economic sovereignty, one might expect an almost permanent state of elite dissensus on this issue, requiring refinement of the indexing hypothesis on issues of globalization.

One area to consider is the nature of the administration in office. Seeking to build a winning coalition, Democrats are likely to be accommodating to both environmentalists and to labor. Such an ad hoc coalition formed on the ground in Seattle and may have reset Clinton's short-term calculations in favor of the protest and against WTO policy on labor rights. This may not be the case for Republicans, however. In the early months of his administration, for example, George W. Bush said the U.S. would not adhere to the 1997 Kyoto Protocol on reduced carbon dioxide emissions, arguing that he would not sign an agreement that might hurt the U.S. economy and (presumably) the welfare of U.S. workers. Although it may have been the power industry that pressured Bush into this decision, it remains to be seen whether his implicit defense on behalf of labor might work to reduce the structure of political opportunity for the anti-globalization coalition by dividing labor from environmentalists.

Similarly, with the elimination of a real-world socialist exemplar there now exists a greater tension between regarding foreign powers as military competitors or as valued trading partners. China represents a test case where the promise of the world's largest market for goods will be weighed against its superpower aspirations. As the case of the downed American spy plane unfolded in April 2001, the response from what one might have ordinarily expected from a conservative Republican administration was unusually cautious and restrained. Careful study of this case is required for conclusive evidence, but news framing of the incident included as a major theme the mutual Chinese and American desire for a diplomatic solution based on economic interests. This is further evidence of the erosion of elite capacity to demonize foreign enemies and thus to maintain control over news frames. The limiting case, of course, would be an attack of the kind that occurred on September 11, 2001. The swift media condemnation of these acts and the demonization of al-Qaeda terrorists and the Taliban followed as much from a visceral response to the scope and unprecedented nature of the catastrophe as it did from government cues. The effect of that incident on reconfiguring the mental maps of political and media elites and perhaps creating a stable replacement for the cold-war frame remains to be assessed. The suggestion here is of the increasing importance of economic issues that will in the future present greater opportunities for the anti-globalization movement. Under these changed conditions, further study of future protest events would provide a more robust test of the propositions developed in this paper.

The anti-globalization movement's Internet-reinforced tenacity and a widened media sympathy played an important role in creating what John Kenneth Galbraith has called "countervailing power" on unfettered markets. Absent the Cold War and its distorting effects premised on loyalty to the state (Hallin, 1992), the mass media functioned in this case as important intermediaries in linking movement messages to an important segment of the politically engaged public. They helped articulate a critique that is setting an intellectual foundation for a democratic check on transnational economic institutions. The result is a reenergized pluralism in which the mass media may play a constructive effort in building democratically responsive institutions. It remains to be seen whether this new role played by the media will appear in examples beyond extra-institutional politics.

REFERENCES

America's best newspapers. (1999). *Columbia Journalism Review*, 38 (4), 14–16.

Ayres, J. M. (1999). From the streets to the internet: The cyber-diffusion of contention. *Annals of the American Academy of Political & Social Science*, 566, 132–144.

Barber, B. (1996). *Jihad vs. McWorld*. New York: Ballantine.

Bauman, Z. (1998). *Globalization: The human consequences*. New York: Columbia University Press.

Bennett, W. L. (1990). Toward a theory of press-state relations in the United States. *Journal of Communication, 40*, 103–25.

Bennett, W. L. (2001). Consumerism and global citizenship: Lifestyle politics, permanent campaigns, and international regimes of democratic accountability. Paper prepared for the International Seminar on Political Consumerism, Stockholm University, Stockholm, Sweden.

Bhagwati, J. (1999, December 7). Did Clinton take a dive in Seattle? *The Washington Post*, p. A31.

Bimber, B. (1998). The internet and political transformation: Populism, community, and accelerated pluralism. *Polity, 31*, 133–160.

Brecher, J, & Smith, B. (1999, November 26). Score one for little guys in expanding global arena. *The Los Angeles Times*, p. B9.

Conlin, J. (1999, December 27). Hey, what about us? *Business Week, 3661*, 52.

Cooper, M. (1999, December 2). Teamsters and turtles: They're together at last. *The Los Angeles Times*, p. B11.

Cox, J. (1999a, November 26). At what price free trade? Tuesday's clash will highlight impasse of trade's fans and foes. *USA Today*, p. B1.

Cox, J. (1999b, December 2). What protesters want from the WTO. *USA Today*, p. A2.

Cox, J. & Jones, D. (1999, December 2). "This weird jamboree." Teamsters and turtle protectors on same side. *USA Today*, p. A1.

Dionne, E. J., Jr. (1999, December 3). "Something missing." *The Washington Post*, p. A41.

Entman, R. M. (2000). Declarations of independence: The growth of media power after the cold war. In B. L. Nacos, R. Y. Shapiro, & P. Isernia, (Eds.), *Decisionmaking in a glass house: Mass media, public opinion, and American and European foreign policy in the 21st century* (pp.11–26). Lanham, MD: Rowman & Littlefield.

Entman, R. M. & Page, B. I. (1994). The news before the storm: The Iraq war debate and the limits to media independence. In W. L. Bennett & D. L. Paletz (Eds.), *Taken by storm: The media, public opinion, and U.S. foreign policy in the Gulf War* (pp. 82–101). Chicago & London: University of Chicago Press.

Entman, R. M. & Rojecki, A. (1993). Freezing out the public: Elite and media framing of the U.S. anti-nuclear movement. *Political Communication, 10*, 155–173.

Ettema, J. & Glasser, T. (1998). *Custodians of conscience: Investigative journalism and public virtue*. New York: Columbia University Press.

Faux, J. (1999, December 6). Slouching toward Seattle, *American Prospect, 11*, [On-line]. Available: http://www.prospect.org/print/V11/2/faux-j.html

Friedman, T. (1999a, November 21). Y2K plus five. *The New York Times*, Sec. 4, p. 15.

Friedman, T. (1999b, December 1). Senseless in Seattle. *The New York Times*, p. A23.

Friedman, T. (1999c, December 8). Senseless in Seattle II. *The New York Times*, p. A23.

Friedman, T. (2000). *The Lexus and the olive tree*. New York; Anchor.

Gans, H. J. (1980). *Deciding what's news*. New York: Vintage.

Gates, W. (1999, November 29). Shaping the future in Seattle. *The New York Times*, p. A25.

George, S. (2000). Fixing or nixing the WTO. In K. Danaher & R. Burbach (Eds.), *Globalize this!: The battle against the world trade organization and corporate rule* (pp. 53–58). Monroe, ME: Common Courage Press.

Giddens, A. (1990). *The consequences, of modernity*. Stanford: Stanford University Press.

Gitlin, T. (1980). *The whole world is watching*. Berkeley: University of California Press, 1980.

Gitlin, T. (1999, December 16). What was gained at the WTO conference could easily be lost. *The Los Angeles Times*, p. B11.

Hallin, D. (1986). *The uncensored war: The media and Vietnam*. New York: Oxford University Press.

Hallin, D. (1987). Hegemony: The American news media from Vietnam to El Salvador—A study of ideological change and its limits. In D. L. Paletz (Ed.), *Political communication research* (pp. 3–25). Norwood, NJ: Ablex.

Hallin, D. (1992). The passing of the "high modernism" of American journalism. *Journal of Communication, 42*, 14–25.

Herman, E. S. & Chomsky, N. (1988). *Manufacturing dissent: The political economy of the mass media*. New York: Pantheon.

Hirschman, A. O. (1991). *The rhetoric of reaction: Perversity, futility, jeopardy*. Cambridge: Belknap Press of Harvard University Press.

Hofstafder, R. (1955). *The age of reform*. New York: Vintage.

Ignatius, D. (1999, December 5). Global trust busters. *The Washington Post*, p. B7.

James, D. (2000). Ten ways to democratize the global economy. In K. Danaher & R. Burbach (Eds.), *Globalize this!: The battle against the world trade organization and corporate rule* (pp. 203–208). Monroe, ME: Common Courage Press.

Jones, D. (1999, November 30). CEOs go toe-to-toe with pickets. *USA Today*, p. B1.

Kazin, M. (1999, December 3). Saying no to W.T.O. *The New York Times*, Sec. 4, p. 17.

Kissinger, H. (1999, December 20). Making a go of globalization. *The Washington Post*, p. A33.

Klein, N. (1999, December 2). Rebels in search of rules. *New York Times*, p. A35.

Klein, N. (2000). *No logo*. London: Flamingo.

Kohut, A. (1999, December 3). Globalization and the wage gap. *The New York Times*, p. A31.

Lerner, M. (1999, December 3). Modern Maccabees in Seattle. *The Los Angeles Times*, p. B9.

Lighthizer, R. E. (1999, December 3). *The New York Times*, p. A31.

Luttwak, E. N. (1999, December 10). Globalizers are the Bolsheviks of their day. *The Los Angeles Times*, p. B9.

Mallaby, S. (1999, November 30). Big nongovernment. *The Washington Post*, p. A29.

Mander, J. & Cavanagh, J. (1999, December 2). WTO feeds corporate greed. *USA Today*, p. A14.

Mann, M. (1997.) Has globalization ended the rise and rise of the nation-state? *Review of International Political Economy, 4*, 472–496.

McAdam, D., McCarthy, J. D. & Zald, M. N. (1996). *Comparative perspectives on social movements: Political opportunities, mobilizing structures, and cultural framings*. New York: Cambridge University Press.

McAdam, D, McCarthy, J. D. & Zald, M. N. (1977). Resource mobilization and social movements: A partial theory. *American Journal of Sociology, 82*, 1212–1241.

McMahon, P. (1999, November 26). Protesters will deluge Seattle trade meeting. *USA Today*, p. A4.

McMahon, P., & Cox, J. (1999, December 1). "Stop the WTO": Protesters say goal achieved. *USA Today*, p. A19.

Mearsheimer, J. (2001). *The tragedy of great power politics*. New York: W.W. Norton.

Mermin, J. (1999.) *Debating war and peace: Media coverage of U.S. intervention in the post-Vietnam era*. Princeton, NJ: Princeton University Press.

Meyer, D. S. (1990). *A winter of discontent: The nuclear freeze and American politics*. New York: Praeger.

Mickelthwait, J. & Wooldridge, A. (2000). *A future perfect: The essentials of globalization*. New York: Crown.

Mishra, R. & Cook, G. (2000, November 9) Election 2000: Nader, Green Party supporters rebuff criticism. *The Boston Globe*, p. D4.

Parenti, M. (1993). *Inventing reality, the politics of the mass media*. New York: St. Martins.

Phillips, K. (1994). *Arrogant capital: Washington, Wall Street, and the frustration of American politics*. Boston: Little, Brown & Co.

Pinkerton, J. P. (1999, December 7). Anti-trade route is loser for Democrats. *The Los Angeles Times*, p. B9.

Plate, T. (1999, December 1). Globalization isn't a one-size-fits-all answer. *The Los Angeles Times*, p. B9.

Reich, R. (1999, November 24). Nationalism should accent the positive. *The Los Angeles Times*, p. B9.

Rojecki, A. (1999). *Silencing the opposition*. Urbana: University of Illinois Press.

Samuelson, R. J. (1999, November 29). We don't need this trade pact. *The Washington Post*, p. A23.

Sanger, D. & Kahn, J. (1999, December 1). A chaotic intersection of tear gas and trade talks. *The New York Times*, p. A14.

Scheer, R. (1999, December 7). Like it or not, we're all in the same boat. *The Los Angeles Times*, p. B9.

Schiller, H. I. (1996). *Information inequality: The deepening social crisis in America*. New York: Routledge.

Small, M. (1994). *Covering dissent: The media and the anti-Vietnam war movement*. New Brunswick, NJ: Rutgers University Press.

Smashing Starbucks' windows won't free world's oppressed. (1999, December 2). *USA Today*, p. A14.

Starhawk. (2000). How we really shut down the WTO. In K. Danaher & R. Burbach (Eds.), *Globalize this!: The battle against the world trade organization and corporate rule* (pp. 35–40). Monroe, ME: Common Courage Press.

Swerdlow, A. (1993). *Women strike for peace: Traditional motherhood and radical politics in the 1960s*. Chicago: Chicago University Press.

Tarrow, S. (1996). Social movements in contentious politics: A review article. *American Political Science Review, 90*, 874–883.

Tarrow, S. (1998). Fishnets, internets, and catnets: Globalization and transnational collective action. In M. P. Hannigan, L. P. Moch, & W. te Brake (Eds.), *Challenging authority: The historical study of contentious politics* (pp. 228–244). Minneapolis: University of Minnesota Press.

Ventura, J. (1999, December 1). My state and trade. *The Washington Post*, p. A43.

Walter, N. (1999, December 13). Caught in a U.S. civil war. *The New York Times*, p. A33.

Yardeni, E. (2001). Ten big themes for 2001 & beyond. (Available from Deutsche Bank AG, 1 Appold Street, BroadGate, London, EC2A 2HE, U.K.).

Zaller, J. & Chiu, D. (2000). Government's little helper: U.S. press coverage of foreign policy crises, 1946–1999. In B. L. Nacos, R. Y. Shapiro, & P. Isernia, (Eds.), *Decisionmaking in a glass house: Mass media, public opinion, and American and European foreign policy in the 21st century* (pp. 61–84). Lanham, MD.

Zoellick, R. B. (1999, December 14). Clinton's Seattle straddle. *The Washington Post*, p. A39.

CHAPTER 2

THE BATTLE IN SEATTLE: HOW NONGOVERNMENTAL ORGANIZATIONS USED WEBSITES IN THEIR CHALLENGE TO THE WTO

Melissa A. Wall

A. INTRODUCTION

On November 30, 1999, some 50,000 protesters took to the streets of Seattle as part of a growing anti-corporate protest movement that had been slowly building over the last decade. The protesters believed that the World Trade Organization had too much power in setting global trade rules that favored corporations over citizens. Key among the players in Seattle were Nongovernmental Organizations (NGOs), entities that have been identified as part of a global associational revolution (Salamon, 1994). These groups embraced global communications technology, particularly the Internet, in forging the networks that challenged the dominant discourses of the WTO (George, 2000; Morgan, 1999). This chapter specifically examines websites used by NGOs in this challenge, finding that websites were used for providing opportunities for distributing alternative information or knowledge concerning the WTO, and to a lesser extent helping people take concrete action related to the WTO, and enabling participatory dialogue.

B. BACKGROUND TO THE WTO MEETING IN SEATTLE

Located in Geneva, the WTO is run by a secretariat of approximately 500 trade bureaucrats and officials who administer dozens of international trade agreements. It handles trade disputes, sets policies and conducts negotiations. Although officially established in 1995, the idea for the organization originated in 1947 as part of the Bretton Woods Agreement which also established the World Bank and the International Monetary Fund. Today, it is seen as a global institution that actually has teeth because its agreements are accompanied by an enforcement mechanism lacking in many other international arenas. However, the WTO has also gone beyond what was traditionally considered the domain of international trade into areas concerning intellectual property rights, investment measures, services and domestic regulations.

Yet many NGOs do not see the WTO as a helpful institution attuned to the needs of ordinary people; instead they describe it as an undemocratic, secretive organization. Among their main criticisms: The WTO's rules are written primarily for large corporations to benefit their business interests. For example, the U.S. trade representative relies on advisory committees made up of corporate interests for input on trade talks. Citizen groups representing environmental, health, consumer and other areas tend not to be represented. The WTO dispute panels are held in secret and those overseeing them are not screened for conflicts of interest. The WTO forbids regulating a product based on how it is produced, which critics argue, means it supports practices such as child and forced labor. Much of the organization's work goes on in secret meetings where a handful of rich countries make all the key decisions (Beck & Danaher, 2000; Shrybman, 1999). Poor countries are particularly at a disadvantage not only because they are left out of the important decision-making meetings, but because they do not have the resources to adequately analyze the decisions being made (Shrybman, 1999). Prior to the Seattle meeting, the WTO had already attracted attention and criticism from various NGOs. With the announcement of the Seattle meeting, these groups would organize globally—often using the Internet—to an unprecedented degree.

C. THE INTERNET: HOPE FOR DEMOCRACY OR HYPE FOR CORPORATE CONTROL?

No one disputes that the arrival of computer-mediated communications has contributed to fundamental changes in how information is produced, delivered and even used around the world. However, the changes tend to be viewed within two very different frames. One frame views the changes as liberatory and opening new public spaces that can ultimately contribute to a revitalization of democracy (Rheingold, 1993; Gates, 1995; Rash, 1997). This group sees the computer as a tool that government and big business hoped to hoard, but which was freed from their control by an innovative band of young people in the nascent computer industry. They suggest that the Internet will broaden the public sphere, ultimately strengthening or even saving democracy (Katz, 1997; Walch, 1999; Rheingold, 1993). On the other hand, contrarians frame the changes as a mere continuation of ever-greater commercial domination and capital accumulation among large corporate players that has characterized the end of the 20th century (McChesney, 1998; Bettig, 1997). They argue that the Internet is increasingly controlled by corporate interests and that the much hailed liberatory features such as interactivity are either seldom practiced or used to create a mere illusion of participation. They believe the Internet is merely incorporated into pre-existing power structures and used for commercial purposes above all else (Golding, 1998a, 1998b; Bettig, 1997; McChesney, 1998; Schiller, 1995; Hirschkop, 1998; Margolis, Resnick & Tu, 1997).

A step back from the debate reveals some truth to both sides. The Internet does hold incredible potential for turning ordinary people into publishers and disseminators of information. But it is also true that the corporate forces that so dominate much of our lives are seeking to control the Internet as well, and, in some ways, appear now to have the upper hand. However, to dismiss any chance of liberatory action via the Internet seems so dark as to hold no hope for positive social change. While all that the optimists might hope for Internet communication cannot be realistically achieved, some positive actions can be accomplished. Indeed, the next section of this chapter will review some of the ways that computer mediated communication is being used by NGO actors.

D. NONGOVERNMENTAL ORGANIZATIONS, THE INTERNET AND SOCIAL CHANGE

This project is specifically interested in how Nongovernmental Organizations (NGOs) which work toward progressive social change (such as human rights, environmental issues, peace and social justice) have used the Internet. NGOs are defined here as non-profit, voluntary, private organizations that may range from small, grassroots citizens' community-based groups to large, global networks of organizations. This is a particularly compelling moment for examining such groups because they are part of an "associational revolution" sweeping around the world (Salamon, 1994). From Greenpeace to PeaceAction, voluntary, nonprofit organizations are growing in strength and numbers, creating a transformation in the world's political structure (Salamon, 1994; Korten, 1990; Fisher, 1993, 1998). NGOs are devising new channels of action and new channels for discussion of public policies (Clark, 1995; Mathews, 1997; Simmons, 1998). Key among those channels is the Internet. The decentralized nature of the Internet fits well with the decentralized nature of many of those groups (Arquilla & Ronfeldt, 1998; Cleaver, 1998).

The Internet appears to have changed the way Nongovernmental Organizations are communicating in several broad areas:

- *Speed.* The amount of time it takes to get information out and circulating to large number of people has dramatically dropped with the use of the Internet (Ayres, 1999; Kobrin, 1998).
- *Boundaries.* Groups that are physically far apart can now interact with an ease and immediacy unavailable to them previously. Activists from around the world can easily stay in touch with each other and share information despite the fact that they may never meet face to face (Li, 1990; Eng, 1998; Danitz & Strobel, 1999)
- *Efficiency.* Posting information on the Internet can be much less labor intensive than trying to do mass mailings or traveling great distances for face-to-face events (Li, 1990; O'Brien & Clement, 2000).
- *Cost.* The cost of communicating among activists can be significantly lower than with much of the old media (Rheingold, 1993).

Nevertheless, certain caveats remain. Reliance on the Internet may well privilege certain groups, languages, genders, or countries to others' exclusion, thus counteracting claims to give a voice to the marginalized or disenfranchised (Slavin, 1998; Kole, 1998; Kramer & Kramarae, 2000). In addition, it is unclear how NGOs will balance using the Internet with face-to-face organizing and mobilization, as using the Internet may mean diverting precious resources from other areas (Smith & Smythe, 1999; Metzel, 1996). Thus, while the Internet appears to hold great promise, large problems with its widespread use by NGOs remain.

E. COMMUNICATION AND EMANCIPATORY SOCIAL CHANGE

This project draws in particular on the emancipatory communication literature for its analytical framework (Servaes, 1991; Shah, 1996; Escobar, 1995, 2000; Huesca, 2000; Mowlana & Wilson, 1990; Wilkins, 2000). Emancipatory development communication will:

Create new knowledge structures by disseminating original information that critiques the status quo and supports economic, gender, racial, ecological and/or other related forms of social justice and equality.

Encourage self-empowerment or self actualization through providing opportunities to connect knowledge with action. Critique alone is not enough. People must be given encouragement and opportunities to act to change or challenge social, cultural, political and/or cultural injustices.

Provide opportunities for dialogue instead of top-down communication. Ordinary people (those who are not political, social, economic or cultural elites) are given some means of speaking for themselves.

This project asks: In what ways was website use by the NGOs, who challenged the World Trade Organization, emancipatory communication? Where did their communication fail and where did it succeed in being emancipatory?

F. METHODOLOGY

This study analyzed the content of 95 websites that were used by organizations participating in the anti-WTO activities in Seattle in the fall of 1999. A list of every organization participating in that week's events (collected from e-mails, websites, handouts, fliers, reports, etc., as well as via event attendance) was compiled and from this every group with a website containing WTO materials was coded. The unit of analysis was the entire website (not just the first page of the site but all pages). Categories were derived from analyzing the websites' content, although they also were guided by the three elements that have been identified as key characteristics of emancipatory development communication (detailed above). Sites were coded between December 7–29, 1999. Because of the ephemeral nature of Internet content, the findings provide only a "snapshot in time."

Each site was coded for the following: *General categories* includes geographic location of the organization; the type of organization represented by the website (such as environmental or women's); and whether the organization was officially accredited with the WTO. *Encourage self-empowerment* includes encouragement to contact political, social or economic leaders about the WTO specifically; and providing information about the WTO meeting in Seattle that would facilitate attendance. *Participatory dialogue* includes providing directions on joining an e-mail list; providing a guest book, bulletin board or similar space where visitors could contribute ideas or opinions. *Knowledge creation* includes providing NGO's own reports/briefing papers/amicus briefs, etc.; articles, reports or similar information from other NGOs other than the one hosting the website; articles from the mainstream media; articles from the alternative media; external hyperlinks related to the WTO.

G. RESULTS

1. General Information

Area of focus. Environmental/animal groups were the most frequent type of NGO website (29 percent of all websites n = 28). This included groups such as the Sierra Club, the Humane Society of the United States, and West Coast Environmental Law Center. This is not surprising as environmental issues were among the key controversies surrounding the WTO meeting. Those groups with multiple foci such as the Council of Canadians, a broad-based organization whose issues range from culture to trade to the environment, made up the second highest number of NGO websites (19 percent n = 18). This may reflect the fact that the WTO meeting was not perceived as a single-issue event. Economic-issue NGO websites were the third most frequent group (13 percent of all websites n = 12). This included groups such as 50 Years is Enough, and United for a Fair Economy (UFE). Agricultural/food organizations websites were the fourth most frequent group (12 percent n = 11). This included groups such as the Campaign to Label Genetically Engineered Foods or the Institute for Agriculture and Trade Policy. Other results are Women 7 percent n = 7; Peace 6 percent n = 6; Aid/development 4 percent n = 4; Labor 2 percent n = 2; Science/health 2 percent n = 2; Indigenous 2 percent n = 2; Human rights 2 percent n = 2; Consumer 1 percent n = 1.

Indigenous groups made up one of the smaller percentages. Although the low numbers could be because there were simply fewer people of color and their supporting organizations in Seattle, they may also reflect the fact that these groups have less access to computer technology—which should serve as a warning to those hoping to mobilize marginalized voices via the Internet.

Location of organization. The vast majority of the organizations whose websites were analyzed are located in the United States, which made up 68 percent (n = 65) of all websites. The next highest number came from Europe with 16 percent (n = 14), followed by Canada 9 percent n = 9; Asia 4 percent n = 4; Africa 2 percent n = 2; Latin America 1 percent n = 1. As we can see from these results, some 94 percent of all websites were Western. These findings are not surprising. U.S. organizations are more likely to be using the Internet due to its pervasiveness in this country and the overall higher income level. Nonwestern countries are likely to have many more problems—financially and technologically—in sponsoring a website. These findings should remind us that the analysis here with its focus on technology will be biased toward richer countries and richer organizations.

Officially registered NGOs. Of the 95 websites analyzed here, slightly less than half or 47 percent (n = 45) represented officially registered NGOs. Such registration allowed NGOs access to official events arranged by the WTO. This suggests that studies which rely solely on officially registered NGO listings may not fully represent all groups in attendance.

2. Encourages Self-Empowerment

The two primary means of activation directly connected to the WTO meeting were (a) encouraging people to contact political and other leaders (30 percent of all websites n = 29); and (b) encouraging attendance at Seattle events (34 percent of all websites n = 32).

Encourages event attendance. Of the websites, 34 percent encouraged viewers to attend Seattle events. This ranged from including a mention of the event in a calendar of events to large, highly visible calls. The vigor of the calls to participate varied. The national Sierra Club home page[1] featured a "schedule of activities" detailing environment-related events taking place during the Seattle protests, including locations, times, key participants, and contact names and numbers for more information. On its "What you can do" page, the Rainforest Action Network[2] ran a notice reading, "Come to Seattle on November 30 and let the WTO know what You think!" The call included a link to a different organization's home page that contained more detailed information. Aimed at college activists, the Campus Green Vote site[3] headlined its call, "Fuck the Global Economy! Bring the Anti-WTO Message Back to Your Campus!" and went on to describe

> Training @ WTO meeting, Seattle, WA; Dec. 1, 1999. Calling all students and young activists opposed to corporate domination! Join us at the Labor Temple Hall, 2800 First Avenue (at Broad St.) Hall #1, (10 min. walk from Convention Center) from 3–6 p.m. on Dec. 1. For more info: Call Doug at Campus Green Vote . . . [or email] Wanna take your campus by storm after the WTO? Force your University to divest their shares in Shell? Engage stu-

---

[1] http://sierraclub.org/trade/summit/sched.asp.

[2] http://www.ran.org/ran_campaigns/wto/index.html.

[3] http://www.envirocitizen.org/cgv/wto_media_training.html.

dents in actions and debates regarding fair trade? If so, then join students from across the nation for this workshop focusing on WTO follow-up activities to further engage students in environmental and social activism on campus. The workshop will consist of a Media Skills Training and a Divestment/ Socially Responsible Investment campaign training.[4]

Although this study does not argue that websites were sole reason for the large street turnout as it would be difficult if not impossible to attribute the turnout to any one information source, the fact that some 50,000 people showed up in Seattle despite what many organizers called a "news blackout" suggests alternative information sources such as websites must have played an important role. What we can say is that the websites clearly intended to activate their audiences by providing important logistical information and, often, encouragement for visitors to attend the Seattle protests.

Encourages contact with leaders. Nearly a third of the websites (30 percent) encouraged some form of contact with political leaders. For example, the Alliance for Sustainable Jobs and the Environment[5] ran an "Open Letter To All Heads Of State Attending the World Trade Organization Summit in Seattle," which demanded, "the conventions of the International Labor Organization (ILO) must be ratified, implemented and fully enforced in every country!" The letter began:

Dear Heads of State and Government:

We, the undersigned trade union leaders, union activists and supporters of labor rights the world over, address you this Open Letter on the occasion of the World Trade Organization (WTO) Summit in Seattle in November 1999.

It also included a list of initial signatories whom one would join by signing the letter, thus creating a network of allies on this particular issue.

The People for Fair Trade page[6] ran a banner across its homepage reading: "ACT NOW! Contact your elected officials to sign on to the 'WTO must change' letter to President Clinton" with a link to a sample letter containing the email addresses of Washington State's Congressional delegation, King County Council members and Seattle City Council members. The American Lands Alliance[7] website ran an alert advising activists about a "National Call-in Day to Gore." The

---

[4] All citations from websites are taken verbatim and may include typos, misspelled words, etc.

[5] http://www.asje.org/.

[6] http://home.att.net/~sally.pfft/)\.

[7] http://www.americanlands.org.

alert read in part:

> In just a few days, the world's trade ministers will be gathering in Seattle for the Ministerial meeting of the World Trade Organization (WTO). What is the environmental agenda of the U.S. for this meeting? . . . There's not a lot of time, but it's not too late to remedy this injustice . . . please call the Vice President's office at 202/456-2326 to ask for forest protections at the WTO.

This sort of information is not intended merely to educate or inform; indeed such calls clearly intend that their audiences will take action. Information is provided within a context—often accompanied by explanatory material that makes clear what the issues are and why people should be interested in them. The information to act is often presented in an enthusiastic and pressing tone, providing immediate deadlines, thus further urging immediate action.

3. Knowledge Creation

Most websites included some type of knowledge creation materials (93 percent). The presence of information that would support or sustain the creation of an alternative to the status quo view of the WTO is divided here into two sections: (1) original materials which appear to have been created by the NGO itself: press releases as well as reports/briefings and (2) external materials created by other NGOs or by mainstream or alternative media organizations.

Original materials. Of the materials that appeared to be original creations of the NGOs, 45 percent (n = 43) were press releases and a nearly equal amount, 44 percent (n = 42) were reports/briefings, etc.

Press releases. Of the original materials, press releases appeared on 45 percent of all websites. Some releases were written in a traditional inverted pyramid news writing style such as this one which was produced on the Friends of the Earth[8] page on December 7, 1999, just days after the WTO events had ended. Headlined, "Northwest environmentalists claim hard-won victory after tumultuous WTO Seattle meeting," it began with this lead:

> Seattle, Washington—While an exhausted Seattle began its recovery following the traumatic, week-long visit of the World Trade Organization (WTO), Northwest environmental leaders claimed a cautious victory as they turned their attention to evaluating the effects of the failed WTO talks on their efforts to preserve the region's natural heritage.

Likewise, the Sea Turtle Restoration Project[9] ran a post-event press release on December 3, 1999, titled, "Sea Turtle Banner Unfurled Inside WTO Meeting;

---

8   http://www.foe.org/international/wto/nw.html.

9   http://www.seaturtles.org/).

Free Trade = Dead Sea Turtles: Clinton Say No to the WTO." The release began this way:

> Seattle, inside the WTO—Today, a sea turtle activist unfurled a giant banner inside the Seattle Convention Center at the WTO meeting that read, "Free Trade = Dead Sea Turtles: Clinton Say No to the WTO" to protest a ruling last year that declared that the US Turtle-Shrimp amendment to the Endangered Species Act a violation of free trade.

Some releases were notices of a press conference or of an event to which the press was encouraged to come to such as the "Media Advisory" distributed by the Indigenous Environment Network.[10] Titled, "Indigenous Peoples Protest WTO Policies" the advisory notified the press of the time, place and date of an NGO forum during the WTO week that would highlight issues of concern to indigenous people such as treaty rights, biodiversity, intellectual property rights, and border justice.

The appearance of press releases on the websites is important because it suggests that even if a press release is ignored by the media, it can still be distributed to potential audiences—in this case via an organization's own website. Also, a printed press release that might be ignored by one editor or reporter, could, seen online, be noticed and worked into a story by another employee of the same organization or even by a media outlet not targeted by the NGO.

Reports, court or other policy briefings appeared on 44 percent of websites. For example, ActionAid[11] ran a briefing packet focusing on "Government procurement; Working Group on Transparency in Government Procurement Practices" which examined the issue of transparency and the WTO. Development Alternatives with Women for a New Era (DAWN)[12] ran a report titled, "Free Trade or Fair Trade; DAWN discussion paper on the WTO" about the gender impact of the WTO. The Transnational Institute[13] site included studies such as "Towards a World Transnational Organization?" which explains the interaction between Transnational Corporations and the WTO. OXFAM[14] featured its report, "WTO—Loaded Against the Poor" with sections on Free Trade?, Sick People, Healthy Profits, Who's Driving the WTO, and the WTO in Seattle. That so many websites ran these materials indicates a high level of engagement among them with the WTO and related trade issues. Many of these organizations have limited resources and their choosing to devote them to this issue indicates its priority.

---

[10] http://www.alphacdc.com/ien/intellectual_property.html.

[11] http://www.actionaid.org/home.html.

[12] http://www.dawn.org.fj/wtopaperintro.html.

[13] http://www.tni.org/wto/.

[14] http://www.oxfam.org.uk/wto/free.htm.

Imported materials. NGOs also imported materials from other organizations to post on their sites. These consisted of materials from other NGOs, which appeared on 23 percent (n = 22) of websites, as well as articles from the mainstream and alternative media, which appeared on 22 percent (n = 21) and 16 percent (n = 15) of all websites.

Other NGOs. 23 percent of all websites ran material from other NGOs. Such material usually consisted of another organization's reports or press releases. For example, Consumers International[15] ran a WTO-related article from "Bridges Weekly Trade Digest," an online publication by another NGO, the International Centre for Trade and Sustainable Development. Global Exchange[16] ran Amnesty International's press release, "Amnesty International calls for an inquiry into police actions at WTO talks in Seattle." The presence of such shared materials is interesting in light of the belief that NGOs will not cooperate or share information as they must compete for members and donations. This suggests some NGOs see advantages to linking with allies.

Mainstream media. 22 percent of all websites ran information from the mainstream media. For example, The Alliance for Democracy[17] ran an article from Le Monde Diplomatique titled, "State Sovereignty under threat; globalising designs of the WTO." American Lands Alliance ran two articles from Seattle newspapers, one from the Seattle Post-Intelligencer headlined, "Ecologists gain spot on trade panels; Judge rules they can advise on wood talks" and a second one from the Seattle Times, titled, "Environmentalists win seat on trade panel." Global Exchange ran articles about the WTO in Seattle from a range of media including Los Angeles Times, Reuters, MSNBC.com, Business Week, ABCNews.com, and the New York Times among others.

Alternative media. 16 percent of all websites ran articles from the alternative media. The International Society for Ecology and Culture[18] ran an entire edition of the email newsletter, "Rachel's Environment and Health Weekly." The Alliance for Sustainable Jobs and the Environment[19] ran articles from Inter Press Service (IPS), a Third World News agency, ("Environment-Labor: Environmentalists Team Up With Unions") and the Village Voice ("Wobbly Nightmare for the WTO; Hold the Mochaccino"). Consumers International[20] included articles from PANA, the Pan-African News Agency.

---

[15] http://www.consumersinternational.org/trade/updates/update-pana-a.html.

[16] http://www.globalexchange.org/wto/amnesty121099.html.

[17] http://www.afd-online.org/).

[18] http://www.isec.org.uk/ISEC/core.html.

[19] http://www.asje.org/news-village-voice.html.

[20] http://www.consumersinternational.org/trade/updates/update-pana-a.html.

The use of NGO and alternative media articles reflects how NGOs may be able to eliminate traditional hierarchies for the information they use. Articles from leading corporate media such as the New York Times appear side by side by with those by small alternative media organizations or with information collected and distributed by other NGOs. Corporate media do not appear to be seen as superior sources of information or as somehow presenting more important or more valid information. In this way NGOs tend to increase the voice of other NGOs and of alternative media. Certainly, by running mainstream media articles, they increase audiences for that material too, but their subverting of the traditional hierarchy of what or who creates important news may lessen that particular amplification. It should also be noted that by pulling information from various sources for free redistribution, the NGOs appear to be suggesting that they view information as a public good that is meant to be shared and widely distributed rather than as a commodity to be bought and sold.

Hyperlinks. As for hyperlinks, 64 percent (n = 61) of the websites had at least one hyperlink to information specifically related to the WTO and/or trade (total number of links from all websites was 126). Of those links, the majority were NGO/Activist 45 percent (n = 57); followed by Government, 26 percent (n = 33); Media 12 percent (n = 15); Labor, 7 percent (n = 9); Corporations, 6 percent (n = 7); Educational 2 percent (n = 3), Other 1 percent (n = 1); and Faith-based 1 percent (n = 1).

The hyperlinks indicate connections that NGOs are making between their organization and others carrying out similar work. By far, the largest number of links was with other NGOs. Although NGOs are often said to be in competition for funding, this finding suggests that in cases such as the preparations for the WTO challenge, they may have chosen to overlook that competition. For example, the environmental NGO Earthjustice had WTO-specific links to various environmental groups with which it was working—American Lands Alliance, Northwest Ecosystems Alliance and Pacific Environment and Resource Center— as well as to the host of the Seattle Teach-in, International Forum on Globalization. Another environmental group, American Lands Alliance had a broad range of links on its special "trade links" page: AFL-CIO, Center for Concern, Center for International Environmental Law, Institute for Agricultural and Trade Policy, International Brotherhood of Teamsters, National Wildlife Federation, People for Fair Trade, Pacific Environment and Resource Center, Public Citizen's Global Tradewatch, Sierra Club, Third World Network, UNITE, United Autoworkers of America, United Steelworkers, US Congress, US State Department, US Trade Representative, World Wildlife Fund and WTO. Included here are unions, environmental groups, a NGO based in Malaysia, government sites and a Seattle-based citizen's group.

By including links, NGOs are creating a cybernetwork of connections, defining themselves by whose work they also support or believe to be important. This networking reflects what appears to be a tendency to value the distribution of information over the competition that they may have over funding, members or other resources with organizations that have similar agendas. It is also possible that NGOs are linking with other NGOs whose mission does not overlap with their own (i.e., an agricultural issues NGO running links with environmental NGOs). However, it appears many NGOs did link with other NGOs working in the same area—this appears particularly true for the environmental NGOs. Also notable here is the tendency to include the official World Trade Organization website and as well as U.S. government sites. This suggests that NGOs are not afraid to direct those who agree with their point of view to information from the "other side." In contrast, the World Trade Organization did not include links to other points of view.

4. Participatory Dialogue

Of the websites, 44 percent (n = 42) had e-mail lists, and 3 percent (n = 3) bulletin boards.

E-mail. The vast majority of the opportunities for some form of dialogue appear to come through signing up for an e-mail list (44%). The ease of subscription varied. Biowatch South Africa[21] asked visitors to send a blank subscribe e-mail to their list server, the e-mail address of which was listed, but had no direct box or link from the web page. At the Earthjustice[22] site, visitors were encouraged to "Subscribe to our email newsletter. To receive our quarterly email update with news, views and actions you can take to protect our environment, send us your email address here." The last word linked immediately to a pre-addressed e-mail box. Other sites have visitors fill out an on-line form which is e-mailed to the listserv directly from the site. While some sites included links to places where one could sign up for a list specifically set up for the WTO, it was beyond the scope of this project to determine if every e-mail list that was found on the websites examined here contained information about the WTO.

Beyond perhaps stimulating a two-way dialogue, we can say that the e-mail lists also appeared to serve an educational function by providing interested persons with more information about the focal area of the organization. Further, they seem to work as a networking tool, by pulling together a community of individuals interested in the NGO's work.

Bulletin boards, etc. Only 3 percent (n = 3) of the sites featured opportunities to use a guest book, contribute to a bulletin board or participate in other similar forms of dialogue. Of these, the Institute for Agriculture and Trade Policy's special WTO site,[23] allowed organizations to post press releases, reports and other

---

[21] http://www.saep.org/forDB/Biowatch.html.

[22] http://www.earthjustice.org/about/index.html.

[23] http://www.wtowatch.org.

material on-line and those materials would then be automatically added to the site's extensive contents. Global Arcade[24] featured a page of different discussions that could be joined including one specifically about the World Trade Organization which noted, "The WTO meeting in Seattle is also a meeting of the resistance to the vision of the future that the WTO represents. What do you think of the organization and the meeting?" A link jumped to previous postings followed by a box where visitors could post their own comments and were given the option to provide their name and e-mail or to provide neither and remain anonymous.

The lack of bulletin boards and other similar feedback mechanisms suggests that this was not a high priority for NGOs. In part this may be because of the amount of resources necessary to answer postings. Many of the groups analyzed here are simply too small and too poorly funded to do so. That said, it is also possible that some NGOs do not have such a space because they are not seeking to have an Internet dialogue and would rather maintain complete control over the information that appears on their site.

H. SUMMARY OF FINDINGS

The findings presented above suggest that at least some of the NGOs' websites' communication practices such as knowledge creation were emancipatory development communication. In terms of self-empowerment and participatory dialogue, the communication practices, though not as strong, were still emancipatory in a large number of cases.

Self-empowerment. NGO website communication had strong tendencies toward encouraging self-empowerment behaviors among their site visitors. Self-empowerment is important because critique alone is not enough. Once problems have been identified, people must also take action if real social change is to occur. Of course, the indicators (encouragement to attend Seattle events, or to contact leaders about WTO issues) were not found on all sites. This may be because many of the sites examined here were not frequently updated. Such information is time sensitive and some NGOs may not have had time to post it. In addition, some sites may assume that their audience is not located in one region or country (i.e., encouraging visitors to contact President Clinton implies that visitors are Americans). Finally, some organizations included in this study have rejected traditional politics such as contacting legislators, whom they consider to be beholden to special interests and therefore would not answer to voices from ordinary people.

Dialogue. Dialogue consisted almost entirely of opportunities to sign up for e-mail lists—which may or may not be used for two-way conversations—so that the true amount of dialogue may be less than this number suggests. Prior research

---

[24] http://www.globalarcade.org/discus/index.html.

suggests websites in general regardless of their sponsors are not being used for participatory dialogue, so absences here may reflect common uses of the technology. While some might argue it is evidence that the NGOs are simply are not interested in dialogue, numerous observations of their work in face-to-face forums suggests otherwise. Organizations may lack the resources and staff to maintain a participatory site. Indeed, previous research by Smith and Smythe (1999) reveals that many NGOs do not have the personnel to even respond to emails.

Knowledge creation. Most websites included some type of knowledge creation materials. Establishing knowledge was done through providing original and external materials—those created by the NGO and those from other sources—as well as through hyperlinks. Several interesting phenomenon are found here. One is that the NGOs are able to post their own press releases, thus perhaps changing the nature of a press release so that it can be directly distributed to audiences via these websites. Secondly, the websites did not privilege mainstream media articles over information from other NGOs or even the alternative media. All three types might appear in the same space with none receiving higher priority than the others. This suggests that categories such as "alternative" may not apply on these sites. The fact that NGOs would run information from competing NGOs further suggests that they may view information as a public good rather than as something to be hoarded or sold.

Previous research has suggested that for some NGOs the Internet may be serving a media substitution function (Walch, 1999). That is clearly supported by the findings here. Yet unlike mainstream corporate media, these NGOs may be anchored by different values: Their information is non-commercial; it seems to be viewed as a public good (thus NGOs disseminate their own and others' information for free); and, although they sometimes link to the opposition, NGOs are not locked into professional routines such as objectivity, instead urging audiences to take self-actualizing action. More research would need to be done to confirm these trends and to better understand how NGOs themselves are becoming news producers.

In sum, the Internet communication examined here contributed to social change by *organizing* and *mobilizing* ordinary people to take action and participate in events affecting their lives; *networking* local constituencies to work together at the global level; by *amplifying* new information that reframed important policy issues; by *resisting* hegemonic information hierarchies and instead creating new decentralized information structures. The findings further show how grassroots groups were able to re-imagine their own development, creating new ways of seeing and talking about issues in opposition to a dominant discourse that the world's elites had already formulated. Ultimately, any emancipatory challenge to the global expansion of corporate power will also have to be global itself. That is, networks of resistance must also be global. One of the most important ways to ensure that collective emancipatory development communication takes place globally may be through NGO use of the Internet.

I.   CONCLUSION

The findings here suggest that this medium was dominated by rich Northern countries and, to a certain extent, larger organizations with the resources to take advantage of this technology. Many smaller organizations had limited websites that appeared to be fairly static and simplistic in design and content. At later protests following Seattle, participants complained that fliers listed only websites instead of phone numbers or other contact information (Montgomery & Santana, 2000). These findings are not particularly positive. Larger, more mainstream groups could come to dominate the discourse via the Internet and provide much of the research and arguments that will spread throughout the NGO networks. These organizations will be predominantly Western and middle class.

However, some small organizations involved with the WTO protests were able to have large Internet presences which may have helped them attract attention and members. The Internet allowed these organizations to quickly establish themselves with a speed that is simply unimaginable without the web. Groups located in the Global South such as Malaysia's Third World Network, which publishes reports on economic issues such as those covered by the WTO, were able to achieve a higher profile status on-line than some larger Northern-based NGOs. The U.S.-based Direct Action Network, which quickly came into existence in opposition to the WTO's Seattle meeting, was able to post a large, comprehensive site that belied how established the organization itself was. Also not to be overlooked is the accumulated power of multiple sites working on the same issue, articulating similar (sometimes the exact same criticisms) and linking with each other in what has been called the "Lilliput" or "swarming" strategy in which much smaller entities are able to overcome corporate Goliaths with a multi-prong attack (Brecher & Costello, 1994; Arquilla & Ronfeldt, 1998). Further, the Internet facilitates the mutations of sites and organizations that sponsor them so that they can quickly shift attention to the next issue or event. Sites disappear; new sites appear. This mutability and temporality may be a key to understanding these groups and their Internet use in the future.

The Internet in this case appears to have allowed what Appadurai (2000) and others have called "globalization from below" (p. 13). He argues that the only way to counter the overwhelming forces of corporate globalization from above is to work not just at the grassroots level but for those at the grassroots to globalize their struggles. Appadurai specifically calls for researchers to focus on understanding this process of "globalization from below."

This project has made a small attempt to better understand this phenomenon, but it should be remembered that the networking form, which Castells (1996) claims will be the defining organizational form of our society in the future, is at this point impossible to completely delineate and analyze. For example, to locate and examine all the sites that played a role in the Seattle events would be like lassoing a group of butterflies. This is the strength and weakness of the network form that Arquilla and Ronfeldt (1998) argue is the defining characteristic of these NGOs. Just as they can ubiquitously spring to life with impassioned calls to action and reams of supporting data, they can mutate into some other cause in some other place in some other time. Or they can simply disappear.

The post-WTO Internet usage by the same and still other, different groups around the world—from anti-IMF and World Bank protests in Prague on September 26, 2000, to anti-Free Trade Area of the Americas demonstrations in Quebec City on April 20, 2001,—appear to reflect these tendencies. They also show a tremendous learning curve concerning the use of the Internet as a mobilizing tool by NGOs. We are seeing the rise of new political players whose power derives in part from their roles as information disseminators. In the end, we can conclude that Seattle was not an anomaly, but rather the prototype for a global anti-corporate domination social movement that will increasingly rely on the Internet—for its benefit while also at its peril. While other media and even face-to-face organizing will remain vital, this new communication technology has and will continue to affect the face of social change in ways that we have yet to fully comprehend.

REFERENCES

Appadurai, A. (2000). Grassroots globalization in the research imagination. *Public Culture, 12*(1), 1–19.

Arquilla, J. & Ronfeldt, D. (1998). Preparing for information-age conflict; Part 1: Conceptual and organizational dimensions. *Information, Communication and Society, 1(1)*, 1–22.

Ayres, J. M. (1999). From the streets to the Internet: The cyber-diffusion of contention. *The Annals of the American Academy of Political and Social Science*, 566, 132–143.

Beck, J. & Danaher, K. (2000). Top ten reasons to oppose the WTO. In K. Danaher & R. Burbach (Eds.), *Globalize this! The battle against the World Trade Organization and corporate rule* (pp. 98–102). Monroe, Maine: Common Courage Press.

Bettig, R. V. (1997). The enclosure of cyberspace. *Critical Studies in Mass Communication, 14*(2), 138–157.

Brecher, J. & Costello, T. (1994). *Global village or global pillage: economic reconstruction from the bottom up*. Boston: South End Press.

Castells, M. (1996). *The information age: Economy, society and culture. Vol I: The rise of the network society*. Cambridge, Mass: Blackwell Publishers.

Clark, A. (1995). Nongovernmental organizations and their influence on international society. *Journal of International Affairs, 48*(2), 507–525.

Cleaver, H. (1998). The Zapatista effect: The Internet and the rise of an alternative political fabric. *Journal of International Affairs, 51(2)*, 621–682.

Danitz, T. & Strobel, W. P. (1999). The Internet's impact on activism: The case of Burma. *Studies in Conflict & Terrorism, 22*, 257–269.

Eng, P. (1998, April 29). Passing on the word; on-line activists step up fight. *Bangkok Post*. Asia Intelligence Wire. Academic Index. Lexis. Retrieved August 18, 1998.

Escobar, A. (1995). *Encountering development: The making and unmaking of the Third World*. Princeton: Princeton University Press.

Escobar, A. (2000). Place, power and networks in globalization and postdevelopment. In K. G. Wilkins (Ed.), *Redeveloping communication for social change; theory, practice and power* (pp. 163–173). Lanham: Rowman & Littlefield Publishers, Inc.

Fisher, J. (1993). *The road from Rio: Sustainable development and the Nongovernmental movement in the Third World*. Westport, Conn.: Praeger.

Fisher, J. (1998). *Nongovernments: NGOs and the political development of the Third World*. West Hartford, Conn.: Kumarian Press.

Gates, B. (1995). *The Road Ahead*. New York: Viking.

George, S. (2000). Fixing or nixing the WTO. In K. Danaher & R. Burbach (Eds.), *Globalize this! The battle against the World Trade Organization and corporate rule*. (pp. 53–58). Monroe, Maine: Common Courage Press.

Golding, P. (1998a). Worldwide wedge: division and contradiction in the global information infrastructure. In D. K. Thussu (Ed.), *Electronic empires; global media and local resistance* (pp. 135–148). London: Arnold.

Golding, P. (1998b). Global village or cultural pillage: The unequal inheritance of the communications revolution. In R. McChesney, E. M. Wood & J. B. Foster (Eds.), *Capitalism and the information age; the political economy of the global communication revolution* (pp. 69–86). New York: Monthly Review Press.

Hirschkop, K. (1998). Democracy and new technologies. In R. McChesney, E. M. Wood & J. B. Foster (Eds.), *Capitalism and the information age ; the political economy of the global communication revolution* (pp. 207–217). New York: Monthly Review Press.

Huesca, R. (2000). Communication for social change among Mexican factory workers on the Mexico-U.S. border. In K.G. Wilkins (Ed.), *Redeveloping communication for social change; theory, practice and power* (pp. 73–87). Lanham: Rowman & Littlefield Publishers, Inc.

Katz, J. (1997, April 5). Birth of a Digital Nation. Netizen Archive. *Hotwired*. http://www.wired.com/wired/archive/5.04/netizne.html. Retrieved October 10, 1999.

Kobrin, S. J. (1998, Fall). The MAI and the clash of globalizations. *Foreign Policy*, 97–109.

Kole, E. S. (1998). Myths and realities in Internet discourse; using computer networks for data collection and the Beijing conference on women. *Gazette, 60(4)*, 343–360.

Korten, D. C. (1990). *Getting to the 21st century; voluntary action and the global agenda*. West Hartford, Conn.: Kumarian Press.

Kramer, J. & Kramarae, C. (2000). Women's political webs: Global electronic networks. In A. Sreberny & L. van Zoonen (Eds.), *Gender, politics and communication* (pp. 205–222). Cresskill, NJ: Hampton Press.

Li, T. (1990). Computer-mediated communications and the Chinese students in the U.S. *Information Society, 7*, 125–137.

Margolis, M., Resnick, D. & Tu, C. (1997). Campaigning on the Internet; parties and candidates on the World Wide Web in the 1996 Primary Season. *The Harvard International Journal of Press and Politics, 2(1)*, 59–78.

Mathews, J. T. (1997). Power shift. *Foreign Affairs*, 50–66.

McChesney, R. (1998). Media convergence and globalisation. In D. K. Thussu (Ed.), *Electronic Empires; global media and local resistance* (pp. 27–46). London: Arnold.

Metzel, J. F. (1996). Information technology and human rights. *Human Rights Quarterly, 18*(4), 705–747.

Montgomery, D. & Santana, A. (2000, April 2). Rally website also interests the uninvited; *The Washington Post*. Retrieved June 29, 2000, from ProQuest online database.

Morgan, F. (1999). WTO protesters go to the Web. *Salon*. http://www.salon. com/news/feature/1999/12/01/weblog.print.html. Retrieved January 1, 2000.

Mowlana, H. & Wilson, L. J. (1990). *The Passing of modernity; communication and the transformation of society*. New York: Longman.

O'Brien, R. & Clement, A. (2000). The Association for Progressive Communications and the networking of global civil society: APC at the 1992 Earth Summit. In *Proceedings of the Computer Professionals for Social Responsibility Conference* (pp. 177–184). Seattle: Computer Professionals for Social Responsibility.

Rash, W. (1997). *Politics on the nets; writing the political process*. New York: W. H. Freeman.

Rheingold, H. (1993). *The virtual community; homesteading on the electronic frontier*. Reading, Mass.: Addison-Wesley Publishing Co.

Salamon, L. M. (1994, July–August). The rise of the nonprofit sector. *Foreign Affairs, 73*, 109–122.

Schiller, H. (1995). The global information highway: Project for an ungovernable world. In J. B. & I. A. Boal (Eds.), *Resisting the virtual; the culture and politics of information* (pp. 17–33). San Francisco: City Lights.

Servaes, J. (1991). Toward a new perspective for communication and development. In F. Cashmir (Ed.), *Communication in Development* (pp. 51–85). Norwood, NJ: Ablex.

Shah, H. (1996). Modernization, marginalization, and emancipation: Toward a normative model of journalism and national development. *Communication theory, 6(20)*, 143–166.

Shrybman, S. (1999). *The World Trade Organization: A citizen's guide*. Ontario: The Canadian Centre for Policy Alternatives and James Lorimer and Co. Ltd.

Simmons, P. J. (1998, Fall). Learning to live with NGOs. *Foreign policy, 112*, 82–96.

Slavin, B. (1998, May 27). Human rights websites not reaching those in need. *USA Today*. Expanded academic index. Academic Universe. Retrieved August 18, 1998.

Smith, P. J. & Smythe, E. (1999). Globalization, citizenship and technology: The MAI meets the Internet. *Canadian Foreign Policy, 7(2)*, 83–106.

Walch, J. (1999). *In the net; an internet guide for activists*. London: Zed Books.

Wilkins, K. G. (2000). Introduction. In K.G. Wilkins (Ed.), *Redeveloping communication for social change; theory, practice and power* (pp. 1–4). Lanham: Rowman & Littlefield Publishers, Inc.

CHAPTER 3

SPIRAL OF VIOLENCE? CONFLICT AND CONFLICT RESOLUTION IN INTERNATIONAL NEWS

Christopher E. Beaudoin and Esther Thorson

A. INTRODUCTION

When Americans watch CNN or flip through the pages of a metropolitan daily newspaper, they are likely to get the impression that the world is rife with international conflict and violence. This may make sense because, in recent years, there has been civil war in Bosnia, racial war in South Africa, oil war in Iraq, border war in the Koreas, genocidal war in Rwanda, and terrorism war in Afghanistan. The texture and patterns of such news coverage, however, remain somewhat unexplored—perhaps, as illusive as solutions to some of these international problems.

In this light, several questions should be asked. Does it appear that the mass media tell us that conflict is rampant in the world—and that little else happens there? Does such news coverage describe conflict, particularly violent conflict, and ignore the potential for solutions, for resolution, for peace? What patterns exist in news coverage of international peacekeeping efforts and peace accords? And, finally, do patterns in coverage of international conflict and conflict resolution appear to be different when stories involve the United States? We ask these questions not of all news media or even of a sample of daily newspapers, but of one of America's highest quality newspapers, the *Los Angeles Times*.

1. Why International News Content Matters

The mass media play an important role in the process by which people develop a view of the world (e.g., Gitlin, 1980; Hall, 1982; Carey, 1986; Carragee, 1991). Roach (1993) argues that media coverage of international topics, such as war and peace, is especially influential because the public cannot rely on other sources of information, such as personal experience and interpersonal communication.

Zinnes (1968) takes this one step further, contending that perceptions of international conflict are more significant than the actual conflict itself. In this way, whether there is hostility or not is less important than how it is perceived by the nations and peoples of the world. Thus, it could be argued that nations and their citizens may use international news coverage to sculpt predominantly negative impressions of other nations, which can then lead to increased feelings of hostility. Similarly, White (1970) contends that two nations in conflict are prone to develop mirrored negative images of one another. For example, Iraqis and Americans may see each other in a negative light, with this mutual animosity rising from both reporters' selective perception of an opposing nation and a nation's development of a positive view of *self* and a negative view of *other*.

That the U.S. media often fall into the trap of negatively biased international news coverage (Adams, 1964; Aggarwala, 1977; Lent, 1977; Tattarian, 1977; Weaver & Wilhoit, 1981; Wilhoit & Weaver, 1983; Kirat & Weaver, 1984) may, thus, instill in the American public an improper depiction of reality (Galtung & Ruge, 1965). Such news coverage, it appears, may alter international understanding, as well as foment tension (Zinnes, 1968) and prevent resolution (Eldridge, 1979). For these reasons, how the U.S. media present international conflict and conflict resolution to the American public is a matter with great potential ramifications. After all, in being negatively biased, especially in terms of the developing world, media coverage appears to frame the world in a negative, conflict-oriented manner for the public. This, to extrapolate on Zinnes (1968), can result in the creation of a negative worldview, which can then affect voting decisions, political consensus, and, potentially, conflict escalation. Because the mass media play a powerful role in creating public perceptions and portraying conflict and conflict resolution in a light that may give rise to a "spiral of violence," U.S. media coverage of the world—its texture and trends, its characteristics and caveats—is of profound importance for the world today.

The present study attempts to explore the nature of conflict and conflict resolution in U.S. media coverage of international affairs. The medium of analysis is international news coverage in the *Los Angeles Times*. The *Los Angeles Times* is an excellent choice for two main reasons. First, in recent years, the newspaper has undergone a significant effort to upgrade its international news coverage, so it can join the *New York Times* as a national newspaper—or, better, an international one— a newspaper that can properly present the world to the American public (Case, 1998). Second, because of the large proportion of Latino and Asian American immigrants in Los Angeles County (42 percent and 11 percent, respectively) (Los Angeles Times Reader Survey, 1997), there is great pressure on the *Los Angeles Times* to cover Latin American and Asian affairs. With 41 foreign correspondents spanning the globe from Cairo to Johannesburg, London to Beijing, and Moscow to Mexico City, the *Los Angeles Times* aims to bring the world, in accuracy and depth, to its greatly diverse community. Thus, both the emphasis on international reporting and the diversity of the Los Angeles metropolitan area make the newspaper ideal for a study of how international conflict and conflict resolution appear in a highly professional news medium at the millennium.

B. REVIEW OF LITERATURE

To explain international news coverage and its potential effects, this section deals with the following literature: basic definitions; the nature of conflict; U.S. media coverage of the world; and the influences such coverage could have.

1. Definitions and Nature of Conflict

At the heart of the present study are the concepts of conflict and conflict resolution. Bonta (1996) offers useful definitions for these terms. He defines conflict as "the incompatible needs, differing demands, contradictory wishes, opposing beliefs, or diverging interests which produce interpersonal antagonism and, at times, hostile encounters" (Bonta, 1996, p. 405). Furthermore, he defines conflict resolution as "the settlement or avoidance of disputes between individuals or groups of people through solutions that refrain from violence and that attempt to reunify and re-harmonize the people involved in internal conflicts, or that attempt to preserve amicable relations with external societies" (Bonta, 1996, p. 406). Similarly, Bonta explains that peacefulness is "a condition of human society characterized by a relatively high degree of interpersonal harmony"—a definition that includes the resolution of conflict and avoidance of violence (Bonta, 1996, p. 405). Others rely on a dichotomous version of peace: negative peace, as defined by the absence of organized violence; and positive peace, which involves cooperation and integration between groups (Galtung, 1968; Roach, 1993).

Wallensteen and Sollenberg (1997) offer a good overview of peace and conflict happenings over the past decade. Between 1989 and 1996, there were 101 armed conflicts. Conflict prevalence was as follows: Europe (17 percent); the Middle East (11 percent); Asia (29 percent); Africa (29 percent); and the Americas (13 percent). In addition, Wallensteen and Sollenberg pointed out that there were 19 peace agreements during the same period of time. Peace agreements occurred in Europe (16 percent), the Middle East (5 percent), Asia (5 percent), Africa (53 percent), and the Americas (21 percent). According to Wallensteen and Sollenberg (1996), most contemporary international conflict is intranational and takes place in the developing world.

Some scholars believe that conflict and violence are normal aspects of all societies (e.g., Knauft, 1987). Others take this further, stating that not only is conflict inherent to the world, but it is also desirable "because of the close link between conflict and creative, constructive change" (Augsberger, 1992, pp. 5, 21). Yet others say conflict is simply a cultural behavior and should not be valued as "good" or "bad" (Nader, 1991; Ross, 1993). Bonta (1996), however, contends that such viewpoints reflect the Western worldview—and that conflict is not normal or innate to societies in general. He suggests that non-violence is actually the norm in certain non-Western nations.

2. Coverage of the World

U.S. media coverage of the world has long been thought to be flawed. Content analysis studies have dealt with the basic news values of journalists (as defined by domains and frames), global news flow (as defined by region), and the predominantly negative coverage of the developing world (as defined by story tone, frames and domains). Such research has demonstrated that international news coverage is Western-centric and consumed with violence, crisis and disaster.

Content analyses have focused on two measures to explore news coverage: (1) topic domains; and (2) news frames. Domains involve topics like politics and human interest. The concept of frames focuses on the way communications affect individual perceptions by emphasizing particular parts of reality while ignoring or downplaying others (e.g., Entman, 1993; Kosicki, 1993; Pan & Kosicki, 1993).

Via topic domains and news frames, various studies have found that international news is filled with crisis, conflict and disaster (Adams, 1964; Aggarwala, 1977; Lent, 1977; Tattarian, 1977). Wilhoit and Weaver, in their 1981 and 1983 studies of American wire services, showed that this was especially the case in terms of international news coverage of less developed nations. Wilhoit and Weaver (1983) drew the following conclusions about international news coverage: (1) it deals primarily with diplomatic and political relations, internal and armed conflict, political crime, terrorism, and human interest stories; and (2) it is "official" in nature, focusing on news that flows from government and involves "official" sources and actors—with such coverage neglecting social problems, culture, education, health, family planning, international aid and economic matters. The authors found that about 60 percent of international wire stories contained conflict, with 20 percent focusing on violent conflict. In 1983 coverage, Kirat and Weaver (1984) demonstrated an interesting pattern in the proportion of crisis- and conflict-oriented news stories—from 14 percent in 1979 to 27 percent in 1981 to 12 percent in 1983. For developing nations, conflict- and crisis-oriented coverage went from 47 percent in 1979 to 28 percent in 1981 to 10 percent in 1983 (Weaver & Wilhoit, 1981; Wilhoit & Weaver, 1983; Kirat & Weaver, 1984).

Goodman (1999) explored coverage of China in the *Washington Post* and *New York Times*. She found that 24 percent of the stories dealt with severe crisis, 70 percent with conflict, and 32 percent with violence. In terms of Israeli and Palestinian media coverage of the nations' international dispute, Eldridge (1979) found that 60 percent of the coverage dealt with peace, the rest with conflict. In addition, 21 percent of the related news was coded as "good," as compared to 34 percent "bad."

Beaudoin and Thorson (2001) also examined story negativity. In that study, of international news in the *Los Angeles Times*, text was shown to be negative in two ways: (1) headlines were largely negative, 39 percent as compared to 11 percent positive; and (2) presumed story impact on the reader was more negative than positive, 51 percent as compared to 28 percent. Furthermore, the authors found that the developing world was discussed in more negative terms than the developed world.

It should be noted that some scholars hold that the prevalence of conflict and violence in international news coverage should not be surprising. This argument is based on the belief that news coverage is innately determined by conflict (Weaver, 1976; Arno, 1984; Cohen et al., 1990; Jamieson & Campbell, 1992).

Another focus of content analyses of international news has been on how U.S. involvement in a foreign event affects the newsworthiness of related news coverage (e.g., Hicks and Gordon, 1974; Chang, Shoemaker & Brendlinger, 1987). Specifically, Weaver and Wilhoit (1981) determined that international news involves the United States more than half the time.

In the present study, we plan to test patterns found in these studies against those in the *Los Angeles Times*, while expanding this stream of research to examine international news stories in terms of conflict resolution.

3. Potential Effects of Conflict Coverage

The potential effects of international news coverage can be theorized upon in different ways. Some authors contend that international news coverage can actually give rise to conflict or peace. For example, Zinnes (1968) pointed out that there are two components of hostility: (1) a state's expression of hostility toward another state; and (2) the second state's perception that it is the target of the first state's hostility. Importantly, Zinnes argues, hostility can be misperceived or exaggerated, with this disagreement leading to an increase in hostility. Via the same relationship, Frederick (1993) believes it is the responsibility of the media to "play a positive role in education and enlightening the public toward peace" (p. 239). Van Belle (1993) argues that open and free news media can prevent war between democracies while allowing—or possibly even encouraging—war between democracies and non-democracies.

Yet others contend that international news coverage is linked to the stand a government takes on various international happenings. Mermin (1996) found links between U.S. governmental consensus and news coverage of the Panama invasion and the Gulf War, and Gitlin (1980) argued that journalist links to government officials lead to press support for government agendas. In contrast, Hachten (1996) explained that journalists play an adversarial role when it comes to covering governmental affairs.

Other authors have explored how news coverage can elicit divergent perceptions of *self* and *other*. For example, White (1970) explains how nations create similar negative images of one another in two ways. The first way, selective perception, involves how, say, American reporters and editors view global happenings and determine newsworthiness in an ethnocentric manner. The second way involves a positive view of *self*—and a negative view of an opposing nation. White says that we create a vision of *self* that is virile and moral and one of an opposing nation that is diabolical. White suggests that these negative perceptions of two nations lead to selective inattention, lack of empathy, and military over-confidence. Media images, thus, can create a universally negative image, one that links ethnicity to negative characteristics in an oversimplified causal nature. An example of this is how the U.S. media create stereotypes and divergent images of Muslim and non-Muslim nations (Esposito, 1992).

The concepts of *self* and *other* rise from sociopsychological mechanisms innate to all humans—with people naturally "including" and "excluding" (Ross, 1977; Kelly & Michela, 1980). At the global level, these concepts help explain how one nation can begin to define another nation as *other* (Ottosen, 1995), with enemy images resulting from actual tension and conflict and then unifying and legitimizing a nation and its rulers (Luostarinen, 1989). Knightley (1975) says the media play a role in "demonizing" the enemy. Examples of this include how Saddam Hussein was compared to Adolf Hitler (Ottosen, 1995) and how Muslims have frequently been depicted as the enemy since the outbreak of the Gulf War (Ottosen, 1991). In addition, Shah (1993) found that the *Times of India* created an inferior *other* and a superior *self* in its coverage of national politics.

The division between *self* and *other* involves differences between the values and beliefs of two nations. Eldridge (1979) holds that this split can be problematic in terms of foreign policy. He believes that such differential perceptions create a barrier between the leaders of two nations. This makes sense because leaders, like ordinary people, act according to how they perceive a foreign nation—not in terms of the actual reality of that nation. These differential perceptions, Eldridge contends, go a long way in explaining aggression between nations and why resolution is so difficult to achieve.

Other researchers view the gap between how a nation views itself and other nations in terms of conceptualized ideology. Lynch and Effendi (1964) found that the ideologies of a nation pervade its news coverage of other nations. Carragee (1991) explained how neo-Marxist researchers argue that news content supports and extends a dominant ideology. The result of this is that news media may be inattentive to the social and historical roots of problems in the developing world.

C. THE PRESENT STUDY

1. Hypotheses and Research Question

The review of literature suggested dominant patterns that we would expect to find in contemporary international news coverage. First, previous studies indicated that conflict is a common frame in international news coverage (e.g., Adams, 1964; Aggarwala, 1977; Lent, 1977; Tattarian, 1977; Weaver & Wilhoit,

1981; Wilhoit & Weaver, 1983; Goodman, 1999). We wanted to see if this was the case in a prestigious newspaper like the *Los Angeles Times*.

H1: A considerable percentage of international news in the *Los Angeles Times* will deal with conflict.

We also looked for conflict resolution. Because of the negative nature of international news, we expected that less coverage would be devoted to such matters.

H2: A far smaller percentage of international news in the *Los Angeles Times* will deal with conflict resolution than with conflict.

Because previous studies have demonstrated that the developing world receives more than its share of negative and conflict-related coverage (e.g., Weaver & Wilhoit, 1981; Wilhoit & Weaver, 1983), we expected the same pattern to appear in the *Los Angeles Times*, especially when looking at Africa and the Middle East.

H3: The majority of international conflict coverage in the *Los Angeles Times* will focus on the developing world—especially Africa and the Middle East.

A research question was honed to examine whether developed or developing nations would be most common in international conflict resolution coverage. It is possible that such coverage would focus primarily on the developed world because the mass media tend to portray the developed world in a more positive light than the developing world (e.g., Weaver & Wilhoit, 1981; Wilhoit & Weaver, 1983). The opposite is possible, as well, because conflict is more prevalent in the developing world (Wallensteen & Sollenberg, 1996, 1997).

RQ1: Are international conflict resolution stories in the *Los Angeles Times* most common for developed or developing nations?

Because of the innate nature of conflict, we expected to find conflict stories covered via more negative frames than conflict resolution stories. Negative framing of this sort can be found in stories that focus on violence and conflict and emphasize the hopelessness of a foreign nation.

H4: International conflict stories in the *Los Angeles Times* will be handled in a more negative manner than conflict resolution stories.

We expected conflict and conflict resolution stories to be treated differently in other ways, as well. For instance, we expected that conflict resolution stories (in comparison to other stories) would have greater context, whether it be historical, social, economic, political, or environmental. In addition, we expected that conflict stories would be breaking news stories, while conflict resolution stories would be more in-depth and feature-like.

H5: International conflict resolution stories in the *Los Angeles Times* will be presented in a richer historical, social, economic, political or environmental context than international conflict stories.

H6: International conflict stories in the *Los Angeles Times* will be presented as breaking news while international conflict resolution stories will be of greater depth.

Because previous studies have found that U.S. involvement increases the newsworthiness of international coverage (e.g., Hicks & Gordon, 1974; Weaver & Wilhoit, 1981; Chang, Shoemaker & Brendlinger, 1987), we expected to find the same in terms of both conflict and conflict resolution stories.

H7: The United States will be prominent in both international conflict and conflict resolution stories in the *Los Angeles Times*.

Also, per the conceptualization of *self* and *other* (e.g., White, 1970; Shah, 1993), it was expected that international conflict and conflict resolution stories involving the United States would be more positive than other such stories.

H8: *Los Angeles Times* international conflict and conflict resolution stories involving the United States will be more positive in nature than other such stories.

In general, we aimed to explore *Los Angeles Times* coverage of international conflict and conflict resolution in an attempt to expand upon previous international news research and gain a better understanding of the relationship between the mass media and international conflict and conflict resolution.

2. Method

To test these eight hypotheses and one research question, a content analysis was conducted using randomly selected international stories from four constructed-week samples of the *Los Angeles Times* home edition from August 1997 through July 1998. A total of 338 stories composed the data set. Coders, who were graduate students in journalism, analyzed stories that focused on a foreign nation or group of such nations. Stories were considered international in nature if they dealt primarily with a foreign nation—regardless of dateline. Sports stories were excluded because of the difficulty of coding players from various countries on teams from other countries.

Coders examined text and headlines. They also focused on the following factors: story type and context; geographic region where a news happening took place; presumed impact of headlines and stories; domains, frames and metaframes; and the role of the United States. Stories were measured in terms of area (height X width). Story types were categorized by breaking news, feature, editorial, and commentary. The context variable involved what type of context—if any—a reporter offered when explaining a foreign news event. There were five types of context: historical, social, economic, political, and environmental. Presumed headline and story impact, which deals with the influence on the reader, was broken into "positive," "negative," and "neutral." Meta-frames dealt with the hopefulness of a news event and related news coverage. Stories were coded "hopeful," "neutral," or "hopeless"—with concern for whether a foreign country and its people were depicted to have (or not have) hope and potential good fortune. Finally, there were 18 story domains and 11 news frames (see Appendix).

Conflict and conflict resolution were coded in a manner consistent with Bonta's (1996) definitions. News stories were coded as involving conflict resolution if they achieved one of the following criteria: (1) mentioned peacekeeping, peace talks or accord; (2) focused on solutions sought via passivism, diplomacy or non-aggression; or (3) explicitly described a nation as being at peace. Conflict was examined at the international level, as well. It was measured with four news frames: (1) general conflict; (2) nuclear and other arms races; (3) security threats to the United States; and (4) terrorism (see Appendix). If a story met any of these standards, it was coded as a conflict story. If a story also involved conflict resolution (as defined above), it was coded for both conflict resolution and conflict frames.

Regions were defined as follows: the developed world as Canada, Asia and Western Europe—and the developing world as Africa, the Middle East, Eastern Europe, Russia and the former Soviet States, and Mexico and Latin American. Overall coder agreement, via Scott's Pi (1955), was 89 percent—with all variables exceeding 75 percent agreement.

3. Results

a. *General Findings*

The study explored the basic elements of *Los Angeles Times* international coverage. It showed that international news comprised 19 percent of the newspaper's total newshole and that coded stories appeared, by proportion, in the front (73 percent) and business (9 percent) sections. Breaking news comprised 73 percent of the stories, with feature stories making up 13 percent. Coverage in terms of geographic region was as follows: Asia, 29 percent; the Middle East, 15 percent; Western Europe, 10 percent; Russia and former Soviet States, 9 percent; Mexico, 9 percent; Eastern Europe and Africa, both at 7 percent; South America, 5 percent; and Latin America, 2 percent.

The most common story domains were politics and government (48 percent), economics (12 percent), crime (11 percent), military (8 percent), and business (8 percent). Prevalence in terms of news frames was as follows: advancement and conflict/rebellion (both at 24 percent), violence (23 percent), normalcy (16 percent), race/ethnicity (14 percent), corruption (12 percent), terrorism (10 percent), nuclear arms race (7 percent), democracy and security threat to the United States (both at 5 percent), and sensationalism (2 percent). In addition, 17 percent of the stories mentioned peacekeeping, peace talks or accord; 24 percent focused on solutions sought via passivism, diplomacy or non-aggression; and 2 percent explicitly described a nation as being at peace.

4. Tests of Hypotheses

Hypothesis 1 suggested that a considerable percentage of international news would deal with conflict. The study supported this hypothesis. Via the various conflict frames, the study found that 36 percent of the stories dealt with international conflict, which was higher than the rates reported by previous research (e.g., Weaver & Wilhoit, 1981; Wilhoit & Weaver, 1983; Kirat & Weaver, 1984). In fact, our figure is much higher because, in the previous studies, the percentages included not just conflict but also crisis. The story size and placement findings are less conclusive in terms of this hypothesis. Conflict stories were presented in slightly shorter form (35 square inches) than were non-conflict stories (37 square inches)—but the difference here (via an independent-sample t-test) was not significant. Conflict stories received less prominent placement than non-conflict stories in terms of front pages (15 percent for conflict stories, as compared to 19 percent for non-conflict stories) (t = 3.619, p < .058).

Hypothesis 2 suggested that a far smaller percentage of international news would deal with conflict resolution than with conflict. This hypothesis was not supported. Conflict resolution was central to 32 percent of the stories. Therefore, conflict resolution coverage was only slightly less common than conflict coverage. Although contrary to our expectation, this discovery is not a surprise in terms of Eldridge (1979), who found that there was more peace coverage than conflict coverage of the Israeli and Palestinian international dispute.

The story size and placement findings also failed to support this hypothesis. Conflict resolution stories were presented in significantly greater size (42 square inches) than were non-conflict resolution stories (33 square inches) (t = 4.582, p < .033). Conflict resolution stories were also presented with significantly greater prominence than were non-conflict resolution stories (with 23 percent of conflict resolution stories on the front page, as compared to 15 percent of non-conflict resolution stories) (t = 14.172, p < .001).

Hypothesis 3 suggested that the majority of conflict coverage would focus on the developing world—especially Africa and the Middle East. The current study supported this hypothesis. Conflict was more prevalent in the developing world, with 53 percent of developing world stories dealing with conflict, as compared to 31 percent of those dealing with the developed world (chi-square = 15.653, p < .001). This finding seconds those of Weaver and Wilhoit (1981) and Wilhoit and Weaver (1983). In addition, closer scrutiny shows that news concerning the Middle East and Africa was most laden with conflict, at 60 percent and 48 percent, respectively (chi-square = 32.703, p < .001). In regards to negativity in international news, these findings are similar to the general finding of Beaudoin and Thorson (2001).

Research Question 1 involved whether conflict resolution would be most common in stories concerning developed or developing nations. Conflict resolution was more common in coverage of the developing world. Conflict resolution was found in 36 percent of developing world stories, as compared to just 26 percent of stories focusing on developed nations (chi-square = 3.478, p < .062). Furthermore, in terms of total stories, conflict resolution was most common in the Middle East (28 percent) and Asia (25 percent), with only 4 percent in Africa. In terms of the percent of stories by region, however, the findings were somewhat different. The conflict resolution story rates were as follows: the Middle East, 60 percent; Eastern Europe, 37 percent; Russia and the former Soviet States, 29 percent; Asia, 28 percent; Western Europe, 21 percent; and Africa, 16 percent (chi-square = 30.086, p < .001). In other words, conflict was common in *Los Angeles Times* coverage of the Middle East and Africa, but conflict resolution rarely appeared in coverage of Africa.

Hypothesis 4 suggested that conflict stories would be handled in a more negative manner than conflict resolution stories. This hypothesis was supported in terms of the negative nature of conflict story headlines, hopefulness, and presumed reader impact. In terms of presumed impact, the conflict stories were more negative than other stories, 68 percent as compared to 42 percent (chi-square = 24.751, p < .001)—and more hopeless, 52 percent as compared to 23 percent (chi-square = 30.488, p < .001). In addition, the headlines for such stories were more negative than positive, 53 percent as compared to 31 percent (chi-square = 18.365, p < .001). The second part of the hypothesis, however, was not supported. Findings for story impact, hopefulness and headline were not significant for stories that dealt with conflict resolution. Thus, there were significant differences between conflict and non-conflict stories, but not between conflict resolution and non-conflict resolution stories.

Hypothesis 5 suggested that conflict resolution stories would be presented in a richer context (whether historical, social, economic, political or environmental) than conflict stories. The study did not support this hypothesis. For example, 94 percent of the conflict resolution stories had context (chi-square = 4.981, p < .026), as compared to 93 percent of conflict stories (chi-square = 5.855, p < .016). Both figures, however, are slightly above the overall international context mark of 88 percent in the Beaudoin and Thorson (2001) study.

Hypothesis 6 suggested that conflict stories in the *Los Angeles Times* would be presented as breaking news while conflict resolution stories would have greater depth. The study did not support this hypothesis. Conflict stories fell into the following story types: breaking news, 79 percent; features, 5 percent; commentaries,

12 percent; and editorials, 3 percent (chi-square = 14.513, p < .006). Much the same, peace stories fell into the following story types: breaking news, 73 percent; features, 7 percent; commentaries, 15 percent; and editorials, 5 percent (chi-square = 18.563, p < .001). Thus, figures were similar for both frames—as well as for the numbers for all international stories regardless of frame: breaking news, 73 percent; and feature stories, 13 percent.

Hypothesis 7 suggested that U.S. involvement would be common in both conflict and conflict resolution stories. The study offered support for this hypothesis. U.S. involvement was common in both conflict and conflict resolution stories. In terms of conflict, 47 percent of stories with U.S. involvement dealt with conflict, as compared to just 29 percent for stories that did not involve the United States (chi-square = 12.371, p < .001). In terms of conflict resolution, 44 percent of stories with U.S. involvement dealt with conflict resolution, as compared to just 24 percent for stories that did not involve the United States (chi-square = 15.741, p < .001). Thus, stories with U.S. involvement were more likely to deal with the topics of conflict and conflict resolution.

Hypothesis 8 suggested that international conflict and conflict resolution stories involving the United States would be more positive than other such stories. We begin with conflict resolution stories (chi-square = 15.741, p < .001). In terms of stories without U.S. involvement, 68 percent did not involve conflict resolution, while 46 percent did. In contrast, in terms of stories with U.S. involvement, 32 percent did not involve conflict resolution, while 54 percent did. Next, we look at conflict stories (chi-square = 12.371, p < .001). In terms of stories without U.S. involvement, 68 percent did not involve conflict, while 49 percent did. In contrast, in terms of stories with U.S. involvement, 32 percent did not involve conflict, while 51 percent did. In summary, this indicates that U.S. involvement was correlated with more positive news coverage. Thus, Hypothesis 8 is supported.

D. DISCUSSION AND CONCLUSIONS

Prior research had led us to believe that international news would be dominated by conflict, with most of it focusing on the developing world. In addition, previous studies suggested that the United States would be central to international news coverage, including stories about conflict and conflict resolution. In the current study, patterns of conflict and conflict resolution were examined in terms of a single prestige newspaper that had invested considerable resources in international reporting and had a high reputation for its journalistic coverage.

Surprisingly, it appears that conflict is not considerably more common than conflict resolution in terms of international coverage in the *Los Angeles Times*. This finding is especially impressive when considering the episodic nature of most newspaper reporting, a characteristic that would intuitively lend itself to a greater focus on conflict than conflict resolution. In contrast, it is clear that *Los*

Angeles Times coverage of the developing world is characterized by conflict to a greater degree. After all, conflict coverage was more prevalent in the developing world than in the developed world—and this was especially the case (by a 2-to-1 margin) when it came to Africa and the Middle East.

It is interesting here to compare the results of our content analysis findings to the global conflict findings of Wallensteen and Sollenberg (1997). Although the Wallensteen and Sollenberg study dealt with global conflict between 1989 and 1996, it could be argued that it provides a reasonable index of post-Cold War conflict patterns. Figures for conflict (1989–1996 vs. depiction in 1997–1998 news content) were as follows: Europe (17 percent vs. 20 percent); the Middle East (11 percent vs. 26 percent); Asia (29 percent vs. 31 percent); Africa (29 percent vs. 10 percent); and the Americas (13 percent vs. 12 percent). Thus, it appears that *Los Angeles Times* coverage properly represents Europe, Asia and the Americas—but overestimates conflict in the Middle East and underestimates it in Africa.

Conflict resolution was also more common in *Los Angeles Times* coverage of the developing world than that of the developed world. It is interesting to note that of the total number of conflict resolution stories, 25 percent focused on Asia and 28 percent on the Middle East—as compared to just 4 percent for Africa. This coverage suggests that although conflict is common in both the Middle East and Africa, resolution is far less common in Africa. Specifically, of the stories focusing on the Middle East, 60 percent referred to conflict resolution, while the figure for Africa was just 16 percent.

It is useful to return to the findings of Wallensteen and Sollenberg (1997). Figures for conflict resolution (1989–1996 vs. depiction in 1997–1998 news content) were as follows: Europe (16 percent vs. 16 percent), the Middle East (5 percent vs. 30 percent), Asia (5 percent vs. 36 percent), Africa (53 percent vs. 4 percent), and the Americas (21 percent vs. 13 percent). In terms of Wallensteen and Sollenberg's global peace index, it appears that coverage in the *Los Angeles Times* accurately portrays peace and conflict resolution only in Europe. Coverage appears to exaggerate conflict resolution efforts in the Middle East and Asia, while downplaying such efforts in the Americas and Africa. In Africa, for example, conflict resolution appears to be largely overlooked—even though more than half of global peace agreements between 1989 and 1996 were achieved in this region.

It is also important to look deeper into the prevalence of conflict and conflict resolution stories in the developing world. For example, our study demonstrated that 61 percent of all developing world stories dealt with either conflict and conflict resolution, as compared to just 40 percent for stories concerning the developed world. Thus, it appears that the *Los Angeles Times* frames the developing world in terms of conflict and conflict resolution—and, in doing so, disregards the breadth of life in such nations, a critique articulated earlier by Wilhoit and Weaver (1983).

The depiction of the developing world is more negative, as well. Conflict stories were more negative than general stories in terms of presumed overall impact, headline impact, and degree of hopefulness—findings that were also reflected in terms of general international coverage in the *Los Angeles Times* (Beaudoin & Thorson, 2001).

In addition, the study suggested strong U.S. involvement in *Los Angeles Times* coverage of international conflict and conflict resolution. These findings support previous research (e.g., Hicks & Gordon, 1974; Weaver & Wilhoit, 1981; Chang, Shoemaker & Brendlinger, 1987). Also, stories involving the United States—whether about conflict or conflict resolution—are significantly more positive than other stories.

Next, it is important to ponder what effects this coverage could be having on the American public—and, perhaps, on the world. Earlier, the effects of coverage were examined in terms of three streams of literature. First, prior research indicates that media coverage plays an important role in determining how people view the world (e.g., Gitlin, 1980; Hall, 1982; Carey, 1986; Carragee, 1991), especially when it comes to international affairs (Roach, 1993). As noted above, international news coverage in the *Los Angeles Times* appears to present a relatively balanced picture of the world (in terms of conflict and conflict resolution). Because *Los Angeles Times* coverage focused on both problems and solutions, Americans may hold a relatively balanced image of the world. In contrast, not only is *Los Angeles Times* coverage of conflict more negative in terms of the developing world (when compared to the developed world), but certain regions appear to bear the brunt of this skewed coverage. As a result, the newspaper's readers may view both Africa and the Middle East as consumed with conflict, but only the Middle East as concerned with achieving cessation to such hostility.

Second, the possible effects of *Los Angeles Times* international news coverage can be examined in terms of the concepts of *self* and *other*. Via previous research (e.g., Ross, 1977; White, 1970; Kelly & Michela, 1980; Shah, 1993), we would expect images of the United States to be more positive than images of various foreign nations. In the current study, we did not examine basic presentations of or references to the United States. We did, however, examine the nature of news stories that involved and did not involve the United States. Via a comparison of these two story types, we can see how international news in the *Los Angeles Times* appears to offer a glorified portrait of *self* at the expense of concocting a "demonized," negative image of other nations (Knightley, 1975; Ottosen, 1995). Simply put, international coverage is positive when the United States is involved, but negative when the United States is not involved. This gives support to the idea that the U.S. media may be unable to untangle the cultures and ideologies of other nations (Lynch & Effendi, 1964; Esposito, 1992) and, for this reason, may be a conduit for a dominant ideology (Carragee, 1991), one that focuses on *self* and ignores the values and concerns of other nations.

Third, the possible effects of *Los Angeles Times* international news coverage can be examined in terms of Zinnes' (1968) contention that a perception of international hostility can foment subsequent negativity in international relations. The seed to this cause-and-effect relationship would be international news coverage that emphasizes conflict, while neglecting conflict resolution. The current findings offer little support for this dramatic leap in terms of *Los Angeles Times* international news coverage. Such an expectation of aggression would not likely rise from the newspaper's balanced offering of conflict and conflict resolution. The coverage does not appear to be the type that would lead to the creation of a completely negative public perception of the world, nor to American governmental and military aggression toward other nations of the world.

1. Caveats

There are two main limitations that should be noted. First, because the study examines international news content in terms of only the *Los Angeles Times*, generalization of the current findings to other newspapers and other media outlets should be done only with caution. Second, it should be noted that reality occurs and varies by year. In 1997 and 1998 (the years of the current study), the world was relatively peaceful. The Cold War, with its innate sense of conflict, was years past, and the only critical global concern was the shifting relations between China and the world. This "passive" state of the world, however, seems counter to our finding that conflict coverage was more prevalent (36 percent) than had been demonstrated by previous research. In addition, at the time, as Wallensteen and Sollenberg (1996, 1997) pointed out, most conflict was in the developing world, which could explain our demonstration of higher figures for the developing world (53 percent) as compared to the developed world (31 percent). This evolving texture to conflict is important because international news coverage is determined by what happens in the world, not just by how it is covered. What is clear, though, is that international news was prioritized by the *Los Angeles Times*. This can be seen in two ways: 73 percent of the international news appeared in the front section and international news filled 19 percent of the paper's newshole.

2. Closing Remarks

How the mass media cover the world is of great importance. This study contends that unless the U.S. mass media want to foster inaccurate perceptions, news coverage of the developing world should be less conflict-oriented and more focused on other aspects of global life. It is clear, after all, that news stories should deal with more than war and polemics. The U.S. media should break from their cyclical, and almost ritualistic, coverage of the world and should focus on culture and convention, peace and passivism, not just conflict and chaos.

REFERENCES

Adams, J. B. (1964). A qualitative analysis of domestic and foreign news on the AP TA wire. *Gazette*, 10, 285–295.

Aggarwala, N. (1977). Third world news agency. Paper presented at a conference on the Third World and Press Freedom at the Edward R. Murrow Center for Public Diplomacy, Fletcher School of Law and Diplomacy, New York, May 12–13.

Arno, A. (1984). Communication, conflict, and story lines: The news media as actors in a cultural context. In A. Arno & W. Dissanayake (Eds.), *The news media in national and international conflict* (pp. 1–15). Boulder: Westview Press.

Augsberger, D. W. (1992). *Conflict mediation across cultures: Pathways and patterns*. Louisville, KY: Westminister/John Knox.

Beaudoin, C. E. & Thorson, E. (2001). *LA Times* offered as model for foreign news coverage. *Newspaper Research Journal, 22(1)*, 80–93.

Bonta, B. (1996). Conflict resolution among peace societies: The culture of peacefulness. *Journal of Peace Research, 33(4)*, 403–420.

Carey, J. (1986). The dark continent of American journalism. In R. K. Manoff & M. Schudson (Eds.), *Readings in the news* (pp. 146–196). New York: Pantheon.

Carragee, K. M. (1991). News and Ideology. *Journalism & Communication Monographs*. Columbia, SC: Association for Education in Journalism and Mass Communications.

Case, T. (1998). Newspapers. *Advertising Age*, April 20, 1998, S1.

Chang, T. K., Shoemaker, P. J. & Brendlinger, N. (1987). Determinants of international news coverage in the U.S. media. *Communication Research, 14*, 396–414.

Cohen, A. A., Adoni, H. & Bantz, C. R. (1990). *Social conflict and television news*. Newbury Park: Sage.

Eldridge, A. F. (1979). *Images of conflict*. New York: St. Martin's Press.

Entman, R. M. (1993). Framing: Toward clarification of fractured paradigm. *Journal of Communication, 43(4)*, 51–58.

Esposito, J. L. (1992). *The Islamic threat—Myth or reality*. New York & London: Oxford University Press.

Frederick, H. (1993). Communication, peace, and international law. In C. Roach (Ed.), *Communication and culture in war and peace* (pp. 216–251). Newbury Park: Sage.

Galtung, J. (1968). Peace. In D. Sills (Ed.), *International encyclopedia of social sciences*, (487–496). New York: Macmillan.

Galtung, J. & Ruge, M. H. (1965). The structure of foreign news. *Journal of Peace Research, 2(1)*, 64–85.

Gitlin, T. (1980). *The whole world is watching*. Berkeley: University of California Press.

Goodman, R. S. (1999). Prestige press coverage of US-China policy during the Cold War's collapse and post-Cold War years. *Gazette, 61(5)*, 391–410.

Hachten, W. (1996). *The world news prism* (4th Ed.). Ames: Iowa State University Press.

Hall, S. (1982). The rediscovery of 'ideology': Return of the repressed in media studies. In M. Gurevitch, T. Bennett, J. Curran & J. Woolacott (Eds.). *Culture, society and the media*, (pp. 56–90). London: Methuen.

Hicks, R. G. & Gordon, A. (1974). Foreign news content in Israeli and U.S. newspapers. *Journalism Quarterly, 51*, 639–644.

Jamieson, K. H. & Campbell, K. K. (1992). *The interplay of influence: News, advertising, politics, and the mass media* (3rd Ed.). Belmont, CA: Wadsworth.

Kelly, H. H. & Michela, J. L. (1980). Attribution theory and research. *Annual Review of Psychology, 31*, 457–501.

Kirat, M. & Weaver, D. (1984). Foreign news coverage in three wire services: A study of AP, UPI, and the nonaligned news agency pool. Paper presented at the annual meeting of the Association for Education in Journalism and Mass Communication, Gainesville, August.

Knauft, B. (1987). Reconsidering violence in simple human societies: Homicide among the Gebusit of New Guinea. *Current Anthropology, 28(4)*, 457–482.

Knightley, P. (1975). *The first casualty*. London: Deutsch.

Kosicki, G. M. (1993). Problems and opportunities in agenda-setting research. *Journal of Communication, 43(2)*, 100–127.

Lent, J. A. (1977). Foreign news in American media. *Journal of Communication, 27(1)*, 56–61.

Los Angeles Times 1997 Reader Survey. LA Times Marketing Research, 1997.

Luostarinen, H. (1989). Finnish Russophobia: The story of an enemy image. *Journal of Peace Research, 26(2)*, 123–137.

Lynch, M. D. & Effendi, A. (1964). Editorial treatment in the Arabic press: A comparative content analysis. *Public Opinion Quarterly, 41*, 430–432.

Mermin, J. (1996). Conflict in the sphere of consensus?: Critical reporting on the Panama invasion and the Gulf War. *Political Communication, 13*, 181–194.

Nader, L. (1991). Harmony models and the construction of law. In K. Avruch, P. W. Black & J. A. Scimecca (Eds.), *Conflict resolution: Cross-cultural perspectives* (pp. 41–59). New York: Greenwood.

Ottosen, R. (1991). The Gulf War with the media as hostage. *PRIO Report*, no. 4.

Ottosen, R. (1995). Enemy images and the journalistic process. *Journal of Peace Research, 32(1)*, 97–112.

Pan, Z. & Kosicki, G. M. (1993). Framing analysis: An approach to news discourse. *Political Communication, 10(1)*, 55–76.

Roach, C. (1993). Information and culture in war and peace: Overview. In C. Roach (Ed.), *Communication and culture in war and peace* (pp. 216–251). Newbury Park: Sage.

Ross, L. (1977). The intuitive psychologist and his shortcomings: Distortions in the attribution processes. In L. Berkowitz (Ed.), *Advances in experimental social psychology, 10*. New York: Academic Press.

Ross, M. H. (1993). *The culture of conflict: Interpretations and interests in comparative perspective*. New Haven, CT: Yale University Press.

Scott, W. (1955). Reliability and content analysis: The case of nominal scale coding. *Public Opinion Quarterly, 17(1)*, 281–287.

Shah, H. (1993). News and the "self-production of society"—Times of India coverage of caste conflict and job reservations in India. *Journalism Monographs, 142*, December.

Shoemaker, P. J., Chang, T. K. & Brendlinger, N. (1986). Deviance as a predictor off newsworthiness: Coverage of international events in the U.S. media. In M. L. McLaughlin (Ed.), *Communication Yearbook, 10* (pp. 348–365). Newbury Park, CA: Sage.

Tattarian, R. (1977). News flow in the Third World: Some problems and proposals. Paper presented at a conference on the Third World and Press Freedom at the Edward R. Murrow Center for Public Diplomacy, Fletcher School of Law and Diplomacy, New York, May 12–13.

Van Belle, D. A. (1997). Press freedom and the democratic peace. *Journal of Peace Research, 34(4)*, 405–414.

Van Belle, D. A. (1993). Domestic political imperatives and rational models of foreign policy decision-making. In D. Skidmore & V. M. Hudson (Eds.), *The limits of state autonomy: Societal groups and foreign policy formulation* (pp. 151–183). Boulder: Westview Press.

Wallensteen, P. & Sollenberg, M. (1997). Armed conflicts, conflict termination and peace agreements, 1989–96. *Journal of Peace Research, 34(3)*, 339–358.

Wallensteen, P. & Sollenberg, M. (1996). The end of international war? Armed conflict 1985–95. *Journal of Peace Research, 33(3)*, 353–370.

Weaver, D. & Wilhoit, G. C. (1981). Foreign news coverage in two U.S. wire services. *Journal of Communication, 31(2)*, 55–63.

Weaver, R. (1976). *Ideas have consequences*. Chicago: University of Chicago Press.

Wilhoit, G. C. & Weaver, D. (1983). Foreign news coverage in two U.S. wire services: An update. *Journal of Communication, 33*, 132–148.

Zinnes, D. A. (1968). The expression and perception of hostility in prewar crisis. In J. D. Singer (Ed.), *Quantitative international politics*. New York: Free Press.

APPENDIX

STORY DOMAINS

Art/Entertainment: concern art, dance, music, theater, vacations, travel, and restaurants.

Business: involve business dealings, commercial or industrial interests, and trade.

Culture: concerns culture, as in beliefs and thoughts, not the "high culture of art."

Crime: involves various crimes including murder, assault and car-jackings.

Economics: includes trends of economic markets, rises in stock, and market collapse.

Education: concerns formal education at all levels.

Environment: involves environmental issues, efforts and organizations.

Disaster/accidents: includes floods, hurricanes, and earthquakes.

Legal/courts: involves stories that deal with law, court cases, and judicial rulings.

Medicine: involves stories that focus on development of techniques to confront health concerns.

Military: includes military actions, plans and decisions.

Politics/government: includes all governmental dealings, elections and diplomacy.

Public Health: deals with population-based problems and epidemiology.

Religion: involves all forms of religion and how they can play a role in culture and other issues.

Science/technology: includes scientific discoveries and technological advancements.

Social/Human interest: concerns human interests and other socially oriented stories.

Social Unrest: involves forms of social protest including street protest, picketing, and rioting.

Transportation: includes all stories related to mass and individualized transit.

NEWS FRAMES

Advancement: involves development and progress—in terms of nation, group of individual.

Conflict/Rebellion: includes war, clash of nations or groups, and activities of rebel factions, etc.

Corruption: deals with stories involving immorality, such as illegal payments and faulty elections.

Democracy: concerns government by the people, majority rule, and elections.

Nuclear/arms race: involves the accumulation and testing of weapons and military supplies.

Race/ethnicity: involves groups defined by genetic histories and related issues.

Security Threat to United States: includes stories with foreign threat to the United States.

Sensationalism: involves the use of lurid or exaggerated, "tabloid-like" techniques.

Normalcy: deals with the calm and stable running of society and government.

Terrorism: involves the political use of violence or intimidation.

Violence: concerns abuse or injury, war, rape, and murder.

CHAPTER 4

RELATIONAL RIPENESS IN THE OSLO I AND OSLO II ISRAELI-PALESTINIAN NEGOTIATIONS

William A. Donohue and Gregory D. Hoobler

Anybody who thinks that serious negotiations can be held today in front of the media is wrong. Negotiations have never been conducted that way. In Camp David, too, a complete blackout was imposed on the talks whose intensity was unprecedented, not to mention all the contacts that preceded it.
—Israeli Prime Minister Yitzhak Rabin, August 11, 1993

Speaking in an interview broadcast on Israel Authority television less than five weeks before the secret Oslo negotiations culminated in a peace accord, Prime Minister Rabin here comments on the progress made in the "above the table" negotiations with Palestinian delegates in Washington, DC. This exasperation at the critical eye cast upon international peace negotiation hints at some of the critical issues surrounding the process of these talks. Diplomats in these situations are constrained not only by national security objectives, but also by public scrutiny through intense media attention. Diplomats and delegates are often called to issue public statements regarding the negotiation process that are directed at their constituency and are simultaneously examined by their negotiation partners and other members of the international community. This chapter examines how this public discourse creates a relational context surrounding the negotiation process that functions to cultivate or impede effective conflict management and resolution.

A. OVERVIEW

One of the ways to approach the "when to negotiate" question is from a ripeness perspective (see the most recent revision of such in Zartman, 2000). Ripeness suggests two conditions necessary but not sufficient for negotiations to take place. First, a situation should be perceived as a Mutually Hurting Stalemate (MHS) in order to bring parties to the table. Each should see the lack of negotiations as more costly than simply continuing to avoid them. A second primary element of ripeness is a Mutually Enhancing Opportunity (MEO). Conceptualized as the pull of an attractive outcome rather than the push of a painful stalemate, examples of the MEO suggested by Zartman (2000) include: a tiring rather than painful deadlock, view of perceived "victory" more cheaply through negotiation than less diplomatic means, or various "carrots" or enticements brought to the table by third parties. Zartman indicates that: "when an MEO is not developed in the negotiations, the negotiations remain truncated and unstable, even if a conflict management agreement to suspend violence is reached" (pp. 242–243).

This chapter seeks to provide an empirical foundation to the ripeness construct by assessing the kind of relational climate parties create as they move toward negotiations. If the relational climate expresses more affiliative messages and a greater desire for increased cooperation, then a mutually enhancing opportunity for productive substantive discussions might emerge. However, if the relational climate expresses more power messages, parties might deepen their sense of a mutually hurting stalemate. Relational climates are very dynamic and full of mixed messages. Parties often imbed affiliative messages within power messages requiring that negotiators develop the skills to sort through these messages and understand how they might define diplomatic conditions and opportunities. This goal of this chapter is to capture the dynamic nature of ripeness as individuals continuously construct the contexts surrounding negotiations.

To examine the empirical dimension of relational ripeness, the prenegotiation climate established between the Israelis and Palestinians prior to the Oslo I talks concluded in 1993 and the Oslo II talks concluded in 1995 are reviewed. Representatives of these two parties met secretly for many months in 1992 and 1993 to develop a framework for peace that was ultimately signed in Washington, DC, in 1993 termed the Oslo accords. Part of these accords called for parties to re-engage negotiations at some point in the future, which produced the Oslo II accords. While there is some consensus that ripeness led parties to produce the original Oslo accords, there was considerable political pressure to refine these accords and establish a more comprehensive and specific set of agreements.

During the period leading up to the negotiations, representatives from both parties gave several interviews, and wrote several editorials outlining their views on the issues. To compare the relational climates that surrounded both the Oslo I and Oslo II talks, the relational messages that parties communicated during these exchanges will be analyzed, beginning with a discussion of relational negotiation, which serves as the conceptual framework for this chapter.

B. RELATIONAL NEGOTIATION

The long-standing and internationally strategic nature of the Palestinian- Israeli dispute continues to keep Middle East conflict on the front page of the world's major media outlets, extending the media's tradition of making this a very public dispute. A unique feature of this public quality is that parties involved in negotiations often provide interviews for the media. These interviews, their accompanying editorials (print and electronic versions), publicly presented agreements, as well as other (often-violent) events that accompany these messages, continuously recreate the context within which negotiations occur. In effect, the negotiation's ecology is richly recorded and is commonly referenced by parties as they move forward in their deliberations both at the table and in caucus sessions.

Of particular interest is the manner in which these messages continue to redefine and renegotiate the relational parameters between the parties. As the original Oslo accords demonstrated quite clearly, relational issues such as interdependence (power) and affiliation are central to understanding the manner in which substantive negotiations progress or fail to progress. Recently, Donohue (1998) used Relational Order Theory (ROT) to track the relational context that evolved during the first Oslo negotiations held in 1992–93, which has served as a key framework for peace in the Middle East for several years. The Norwegian mediator patiently applied interpersonal and relational principles to help foster confidence-building and a constructive context for the talks. This same theoretical framework is used in this chapter to better understand the public relational context leading to the Oslo I accords in relation to what was occurring during the secret talks, and to compare this context to the Oslo II accords that were conducted in 1995.

This project is a preliminary step in a research agenda aimed at integrating relational communication strategies and theories into the study and practice of conflict negotiation processes. Attention in the conflict negotiation field has increased toward relational communication and management (e.g., Kelman, 1997) as a means of understanding how disputants reach for substantive agreement. For example, a readiness to negotiate in good faith, or state of "ripeness" (e.g., Zartman, 1989), entails a relationship between parties that is conducive to reevaluating the conditions of their conflict. Successful prenegotiation focuses on building positive relational exchange that may lead to the cessation of violence and to peace and reconcilliation (Saunders, 1996). The "Interactive Problem-Solving Approach" developed and implemented by Herbert Kelman primarily among Israeli and Palestinian parties (e.g., Kelman, 1996; Rouhana & Kelman, 1994) works along the premise that ongoing track II negotiations establish and reinforce relationships among participants. These programs offer important entry points to further develop the integration of relational communication strategies and principles into the field of conflict negotiation.

This chapter explores how one dimension of ripeness, the public context surrounding international negotiations, emerges through the process of relational framing as parties carry their issues to the public stage. Editorials and interviews from Israeli and Palestinian leaders during the periods leading up to the signing of both the Oslo I and the II treaties are examined and analyzed to determine how parties are defining the relational context as more affiliation oriented or more focused on power and domination and to "track" the kinds of relational frames that parties created throughout these two critical negotiation events. The social and political context in which both Oslo negotiations occurred are addressed in order to understand how the relational messages evolved.

C. THE OSLO I PROCESS

While the development of the Oslo I process is well documented (e.g., Corbin, 1994; King, 1994; Mazen, 1998), its breakthrough feature was its backchannel development and evolution. The secret negotiations began in late 1992 after a very intense set of informal diplomatic exchanges between representatives of both the Palestinians and Israelis. This process began with a group of Norwegian diplomats and academics facilitating communication between Israelis and the PLO about Middle East peace issues. Norwegian intermediaries led by Terje Larsen were able to facilitate unofficial meetings with informal representatives of both groups to see if secret, back-channel negotiations were possible. Through a deliberate process, these talks became sponsored negotiations, eventually supported from the highest levels of both the Israeli and Palestinian administrations. Against this backdrop of secret negotiations were the public negotiations that were making slow progress in Washington in the context of shifts of American political administrations and a variety of very public events in Israel. Thus, these events serve as the backdrop for the Palestinian and Israeli rhetoric that lead up to the Oslo I signing in Washington in August 1993.

D. THE OSLO II PROCESS

The Oslo II agreement was initialed in Egypt on September 24, 1995, and was officially signed by PLO Chairman Yasir Arafat and Israeli Prime Minister Yitzhak Rabin September 28, 1995, in Washington, DC, under the auspices of United States President Bill Clinton, at the same table in the White House where these parties first shook hands after signing the 1993 Oslo accord. The negotiated Oslo II agreement was the pivotal second stage of interim Palestinian autonomy, whereby both parties set terms for an Israeli military pullback from Palestinian cities and villages in the West Bank. It also made provisions for the transfer of autonomy to Arab residents in these areas and for elections of a Palestinian legislative council while also making security arrangements for Israeli settlements in central Hebron. This was the extension of the Declaration of Principles in the Oslo accord, which made detailed arrangements for the initial phase of Palestinian autonomy and Israeli military pullback. Oslo II was seen as a further step in the process of Israeli approval of an independent Palestinian state, a goal that remains unfulfilled.

Thus, comparing the Oslo I negotiations with the Oslo II events presents a unique opportunity to compare two negotiations that are often presented as having very different outcomes. The Oslo I accords was heralded as a breakthrough event in Palestinian-Israeli relations, since it forged a framework for peace. The

Oslo II accords, on the other hand, failed to meet the high expectations set by the success of the first event. Also, the first negotiations were secret while the second sessions were very public. Thus, we might expect to see some relational differences in the manner in which the ripeness construct emerges from the context of these two very different negotiations.

E. RELATIONAL ORDER THEORY

In Relational Order Theory (ROT), two main dimensions represent the interpersonal limits most associated with negotiation. The dimension of interdependence or power focuses on the degree to which parties influence or control one another. In contrast, the dimension of affiliation focuses on the degree to which parties communicate liking, trust, acceptance, and partnership. These two primary relational dimensions interact to define four relational orientations or frames: competition/aggression (high interdependence, low affiliation), isolationist peace (low affiliation, low interdependence), conditional peace (high affiliation, low interdependence), and unconditional peace (high affiliation, high interdependence) as explicated by Donohue (1998).

These frames offer a conceptual framework from which to examine the process of negotiations and international relations over time and to assess the communicative maneuvers of the primary and outside parties. In a short-term negotiation, such as a diplomatic summit or hostage negotiation, relational movement most often traverses only the interdependence dimension (Donohue 1998; Donohue & Roberto, 1993). Movement on the affiliation dimension is probably difficult in short time frames since issues like trust and liking generally develop slowly and cautiously. Accordingly, a longitudinal study of a greater span of time should allow for further test and possible extension of the ROT model.

The conclusion drawn by Donohue (1998) offered important lessons about the communication strategies implemented by intermediaries and the role ROT played in guiding the process of negotiation between hostile parties. One of the goals of this line of research is to trace the success or failure of ongoing negotiations in terms of these relational lessons as they are played out in the publicly available media context. Are there particular relational patterns that are publicly exhibited by parties that correspond to certain agreements or events that lead to agreements? Do parties appear to reciprocate relational proposals through the media that track progress in substantive negotiations?

In any communicative situation, including international conflict negotiation, the language used by parties "away from the table" functions to frame the context surrounding negotiations "at the table." Communicators make language choices that emphasize certain aspects of or attitudes toward an issue, while de-emphasizing others (Drake & Donohue, 1996). These linguistic choices, or "frames," in turn offer cues to other parties regarding the communicator's substantive, strategic, and/or relational dispositions. Use of language packed with images of control and domination or images of partnership and mutuality constitute a manner of framing the orientation of the communicators to the relationship with the party to whom the messages are directed. The ability of communicative frames to influence relational outcomes between parties in conflict relies upon the power of communication to create and maintain social reality (e.g., Berger & Luckman, 1966; Strauss, 1978; Weiner & Mehrabian, 1968). Particularly salient to conflict negotiation—especially an approach focusing on relational messages—is the way power and affiliation are framed away from the table to establish the negotiation context. These two dimensions are among the most elemental topics of relational messages (Burgoon & Hale, 1984). They are consistently identified as major elements of human psychological motivation, (Winter, 1993) and they help form the central elements of Relational Order Theory (Donohue, 1998).

1. Ripeness in Relational Order Theory

The relational dimension of ripeness denotes two points in which a "window of opportunity" exists to reduce tension(s) through negotiation and/or intervention. The original dimension of ripeness is described as the "Mutually Hurting Stalemate" (Zartman, 1989). At this point, the relationship is so bad that the parties see no better course of action than to seek conflict management, through bilateral action or external mediation. In other words, parties see little or no opportunity to meet their goals or objectives within the current trajectory of their conflict—they can do no worse than continuing down the same path so why not take a detour? In a relational sense, Relational Order Theory places this situation well within a frame of competition/aggression, but taken to an extreme such that although the parties view each other with antipathy, a mutual standing-down, "pulling away," or other form of reducing interdependence is desirable. This creates the readiness to engage in conflict reduction or management suggested by ripeness theory.

Relational Order Theory can also help develop the proposed second dimension of ripeness, the "Mutually Enhancing Opportunity" (Zartman, 2000). Rather than the MHS which "pushes" parties toward conflict de-escalation, the MEO serves to "pull" parties toward conflict management action by the appeal of an attractive outcome (Zartman, 2000). While this proposal very optimistically feeds into the desirable notion that crises of violent deadlock are not the only opportunity from which to intervene, there have been few examples of such cited in diplomacy literature and little theoretical explication. Viewed from Relational Order Theory, a MEO may develop as parties balance their relational frames between isolationist and conditional peace. If the possibility of extending cooperation, trust, and affiliation between parties does not exist, the decision to negotiate outside the purview of a MHS will likely meet with failure. This relational movement presents intervention efforts, a window of opportunity to help position or persuade the parties into a relational framework from which stable conflict management can be undertaken. The question to ask is then, how do external parties identify these propitious moments in which to intervene? One possible method looks at rhetorical language imagery.

2. Language Imagery

One manner of assessing communicators' use of power and affiliative messages to frame the negotiated relationship is through observing the motive imagery used in language. A "motive image" is "an action (past, present, future, or hypothetical), a wish, a concern, or some other internal state that is communicated" (Winter 1994, p. 4). While psychological literature is replete with examples of different techniques measuring individuals' motives, such as thematic apperception methods (e.g., Smith, 1992), it is not common to probe motive imagery in the context of negotiation. In a negotiation context the coding method can be applied to a collection of individuals representing a certain political party, agenda, or goal. Since political rhetoric is highly strategic, any collective, such as members of Rabin's cabinet and primary negotiators and Arafat's closest advisors and primary negotiators, should depict a fairly uniform representation of the power and affiliation orientation of each administration (see Winter, 1993, for further argument supporting the use of verbal productions of collectivities, institutions, and groups in such manner). Repeated findings support the pattern of power motivation being associated with war and violence with affiliation motives associated with peace (Winter 1973, 1980, 1991). Accordingly, power and affiliation motive imagery in language should offer information into the disposition of parties to enter into a conflict resolution process. From this perspective, the following questions, which focus only on the events leading up to the two Oslo agreements, are examined:

> RQ1: Do Israeli and Palestinian representatives differ in their use of language in terms of power and affiliation imagery prior to the Oslo I and Oslo II agreements?

> RQ2: Are there distinct patterns of power and affiliation motive image creation by both parties that correspond to unique events to each of the two negotiations (e.g., secret agreements in Oslo I or events such as bombings and riots, etc.)?

> RQ3: When translated into Relational Order Theory, do differences emerge in Palestinian and Israeli rhetoric regarding the kinds of relational frames speakers use?

F. METHODOLOGY

Documents in this study were collected from statements by official delegates or representatives from both parties who were in positions to directly influence the negotiation(s). These statements were released through widespread public media channels such as radio and television interviews, newspaper editorials, and governmental press releases. Documents were compiled form sources available through Lexis-Nexis Academic Universe.

Oslo I documents were compiled starting in January 1993 and running through September 13, 1993, the date of the signing of the peace plan. The six weeks prior to this date are somewhat favored in the document collection. A total of 30 Palestinian and 30 Israeli documents from this time period are examined. Oslo II documents were taken from the six-month period immediately preceeding the signing of the agreement on September 28, 1995, with a more intense focus on the three-month period directly leading up to the finalized negotiations as the most important window for the development of the relationship between the parties. In total, 20 documents from the Israeli side, and 18 from the Palestinian side were scored, with approximately equal representation of each along the linear timeline.

The documents were scored using a coding scheme developed by David Winter (1991; 1993; 1994). Originally developed as a measure power/affiliation psychological motivation (Winter, 1973), the measuring scheme was adapted for use in fiction, speeches, interview transcripts, and "almost any other kind of imaginative verbal material" (Winter, 1993, p. 533). Laboratory studies have supported the general premise of power motivation (Winter, 1973). Further, content-analytic methods of coding motivation for individuals have been successfully applied to groups, including countries, as well (Winter, 1991, 1992). Similar studies in political psychology have linked power and affiliation motivation to periods of war and peace respectively (Winter, 1973, 1991, 1993). We propose that the same premise should hold true for these motivations as seen in documentation that will reveal the relational frames that delegations or individuals are using in times of variable peace and hostility.

Text was scored for two of Winter's three dimensions: Power and Affiliation. Achievement was not scored because it is not central to the theoretical framework for the current study. The Winter (1994) coding method calls for Power to be scored according to six basic forms: (1) strong, forceful action(s) with impact upon another person or entity; (2) control or regulation, including "checking up on" or otherwise gathering information; (3) attempts to influence, persuade, convince, argue, etc., to affect others; (4) giving unsolicited help, advice, teaching, or support; (5) seeking to impress others, mention or concern over fame, prestige, or reputation; and (6) any strong emotional reaction, positive or negative, by one entity toward another. This method calls for Affiliation to be scored for four basic forms: (1) the expression of positive, friendly, or intimate feelings such as warmth, sharing, and mutuality; (2) sadness or other negative feeling about separation or loss of relation or wanting to restore relations; (3) affiliative or companionate activities; and (4) friendly, nurturant acts. The modification used for the current study allowed for each example of a motive image to be scored, regardless if it duplicated a motive image in an immediately preceding sentence or phrase.

For each document the totals for each motive was summed and divided by total number of sentences, representing a dimension of language/motive imagery intensity for each document through scores for Power Intensity and Affiliation Intensity. Graphical representations of these values along with statistical analyses provide the basis for deriving substantive conclusions. The mean level of power and affiliation intensity was computed across samples. In a frame analysis, any value above the mean was designated as "High," and any value below the mean was designated as "Low," with respect to the relational frame that is being proposed by the level of intensity reflected in the message.

G. RESULTS

The first research question of whether Israeli and Palestinian delegates and representatives differ in their use of language in terms of power and affiliation imagery in the months leading up to the 1993 Oslo I and the 1995 Oslo II accords is answered by calculating motive intensity scores by dividing the number of power or affiliation motive images in each document by the total number of sentences in that document to control for the length of the document. These data are presented in Tables 1 and 2, respectively. Table 1 reveals that in the nine months leading up to the Oslo I accords, Palestinians appeared to use language with slightly higher power intensity (m = .22, s = .17) than Israelis (m = .16 s = .11). However, the affiliation intensity scores were substantially lower than the power figures for both groups, but did not differ significantly between the Palestinians (m = .05 s = .11) and the Israelis (m = .06 s = .06). While these comparisons are complicated by the possible confounding effects of translation, the within-state comparisons pursuant to relational frame movement are not so affected and provide more interesting and practical data.

The data in Table 2 present the results for the six months preceding the Oslo II accords. Once again, the Palestinians displayed somewhat higher power intensity scores (m = .28 s = .21) than the Israelis (m = .26 s = .11) but the difference was clearly not significant. However, the Israelis displayed somewhat higher levels of affiliation in their rhetoric (m = .14 s = .11) than the Palestinian representatives (m = .06 s = .05), but these differences were not significant statistically.

More interesting perhaps than these overall motive images displayed through the rhetoric of both sides are the relational frames formed by the combination of power and affiliation images. Research Question 2 examines whether there are differences in the relational frames speakers use across the two groups. Recall that the low affiliation messages propose less constructive motives whereas the high affiliation messages often signal a desire for more constructive problem solving. High power messages combined with high affiliation propose even greater interest in moving toward one another whereas high power messages combined with low affiliation displays a highly confrontational motive. Table 3 reveals the patterns for the Israelis and Palestinians for both the Oslo I and Oslo II accords.

TABLE 1: Overall Power and Affiliation Coding and Frame Analysis for Oslo I

1993 (Oslo I)

Israeli Messages

Date	Power	Frame	Affil	Frame
6-Jan	0.2	high	0.067	high
15-Jan	0.28	high	0	low
21-Jan	0.193	high	0.064	high
3-Feb	0.28	high	0.08	high
4-Feb	0.033	low	0.067	high
11-Feb	0.4	high	0	low
9-Mar	0.222	high	0	low
15-Mar	0.091	low	0	low
30-Mar	0.325	high	0.026	low
8-Apr	0.109	low	0.016	low
13-Apr	0.111	low	0	low
22-Apr	0.179	high	0.026	low
6-May	0.074	low	0.096	high
14-May	0.091	low	0.121	high
23-May	0.118	low	0.059	low

Palestinian Messages

Date	Power	Frame	Affil	Frame
12-Jan	0.667	high	0	low
13-Jan	0.149	low	0.05	0
19-Jan	0	low	0.429	high
10-Feb	0.32	high	0	low
18-Feb	0.235	high	0	low
26-Feb	0.211	low	0	low
10-Mar	0.083	low	0	low
14-Mar	0.257	high	0	low
22-Mar	0.215	low	0	low
31-Mar	0.213	low	0.027	low
9-Apr	0.392	high	0.059	high
21-Apr	0.333	high	0.133	high
29-Apr	0.25	high	0.063	high
11-May	0.466	high	0	low
22-May	0.143	low	0	low

TABLE 1: *(continued)*

1993 (Oslo I)

Israeli Messages

Date	Power	Frame	Affil	Frame
10-Jun	0.161	low	0.107	high
19-Jun	0.053	low	0.026	low
22-Jun	0.5	high	0	low
4-Jul	0.077	low	0.077	high
9-Jul	0.065	low	0	low
22-Jul	0.16	0	0.04	low
3-Aug	0.125	low	0.125	high
8-Aug	0.091	low	0.091	high
11-Aug	0.172	high	0	low
25-Aug	0.091	low	0.136	high
28-Aug	0.125	low	0.125	high
7-Sep	0.133	low	0	low
12-Sep	0.095	low	0.024	low
13-Sep	0	low	0.162	high
13-Sep	0.226	high	0.226	high
	Power Intensity		Affiliation Intensity	
	M = .16 (SD = .11)		M = .06 (SD = .06)	

Palestinian Messages

Date	Power	Frame	Affil	Frame
23-May	0.241	high	0.017	low
12-Jun	0.077	low	0.077	high
15-Jun	0.589	high	0	low
30-Jun	0.055	low	0	low
16-Jul	0.096	low	0.058	high
20-Jul	0.125	low	0	low
9-Aug	0.133	low	0	low
13-Aug	0.538	high	0	low
17-Aug	0.032	low	0.032	low
21-Aug	0.098	low	0.011	low
26-Aug	0.15	low	0	low
31-Aug	0	low	0.4	high
2-Sep	0.182	low	0	low
7-Sep	0.077	low	0	low
13-Sep	0.2	low	0.1	high
	Power Intensity		Affiliation Intensity	
	M = .22 (SD = .17)		M = .05 (SD = .11)	

TABLE 2: Overall power and affiliation coding and frame analysis for Oslo II

1995 (Oslo II)

Israeli Messages

Date	Power	Frame	Affil	Frame
29-Apr	0.238	low	0.063	low
20-Jun	0.375	high	0	low
26-Jun	0.289	high	0.053	low
27-Jun	0.2	low	0.2	high
1-Jul	0.143	low	.143	high
4-Jul	0.308	high	0.154	high
5-Jul	0.182	low	0.455	high
12-Jul	0.183	low	0.183	high
24-Jul	0.385	high	0	low
24-Jul	0.471	high	0.196	high
28-Jul	0.442	high	0.077	low

Palestinian Messages

Date	Power	Frame	Affil	Frame
25-Apr	0.19	low	0.024	low
22-May	0.391	high	0.043	low
12-Jun	0.188	low	0.063	low
25-Jun	0.32	high	0.16	high
25-Jun	0.5	high	0	low
2-Jul	0	low	0.071	low
2-Jul	0.385	high	0.038	low
4-Jul	0.385	high	0.077	low
12-Jul	0.1	low	0	low
21-Jul	0.133	low	0.1	high
23-Jul	0.286	high	0.143	high

TABLE 2: *(continued)*

1995 (Oslo II)

Israeli Messages

Date	Power	Frame	Affil	Frame
11-Aug	0.308	high	0.192	high
18-Aug	0.115	low	0.027	low
21-Aug	0.375	high	0.125	high
27-Aug	0.333	high	0.143	high
6-Sep	0.22	low	0.093	low
13-Sep	0.111	low	0.333	high
24-Sep	0.268	low	0.161	high
26-Sep	0.214	low	0.071	high
28-Sep	0.111	low	0.111	high
	Power Intensity		Affiliation Intensity	
	M = .26 (SD = .11)		M = .14 (SD = .11)	

Palestinian Messages

Date	Power	Frame	Afil	Frame
7-Aug	0.194	low	0.129	high
15-Aug	0.231	low	0.154	high
23-Aug	0.971	high	0	low
7-Sep	0.138	low	0.069	low
17-Sep	0.318	high	0	low
22-Sep	0.067	low	0.033	low
25-Sep	0.286	high	0.024	low
	Power Intensity		Affiliation Intensity	
	M = .28 (SD = .21)		M = .06 (SD = .05)	

TABLE 3: Relational order findings for Oslo I and Oslo II

1993

High Affiliation	10 Frames	4 Frames
Low Affiliation	8 Frames	7 Frames
Israeli Frames:	Low Power	High Power

* one frame was at the mean for power and was low affiliation.

High Affiliation	5 Frames	3 Frames
Low Affiliation	13 Frames	8 Frames
Palestinian Frames:	Low Power	High Power

* one frame was low power and was at the mean for affiliation.

1995

High Affiliation	7 Frames	5 Frames
Low Affiliation	4 Frames	4 Frames
Israeli Frames:	Low Power	High Power

High Affiliation	3 Frames	2 Frames
Low Affiliation	6 Frames	7 Frames
Palestinian Frames:	Low Power	High Power

Remarkably, the data from Table 3 show about the same kinds of patterns from the months leading up to Oslo I as those preceding Oslo II. That is, the Israelis demonstrate a consistently higher ratio of high to low affiliation frames in the low power condition preceding both the Oslo I and Oslo II negotiations. However, both sides demonstrate about the same patterns in the high power frames that are dominated by low affiliation messages. Consistently, the Israelis appear more interested in establishing relational frames aimed at reaching across differences. However, when both sides cast their messages with high power it is rare that they combine them with high affiliation images.

What is surprising about these results is that differences between Oslo I and Oslo II are not seen in these overall patterns. Given the breakthrough nature of Oslo I, increases in affiliation on the Palestinian side, particularly in the low power condition as both sides reached across significant barriers to craft an agreement, were expected. Of course, the Oslo I process was not public and the rhetoric was publicly displayed perhaps in an attempt to portray business as usual.

However, the results in Table 3 are not time sensitive. The third research question asks whether there is a shift in relational frames from the first half to the second half of the negotiations leading up to the final agreement for both Oslo I and Oslo II. The data in Table 4 are intended to answer this question. For both negotiations, the data periods are split into time periods that correspond to both visible shifts in rhetorical frames and events "on the ground."

These data reveal some very interesting patterns associated with each of the negotiations. For example, in the Oslo I negotiations, there is a significant decrease in power intensity for both the Palestinians (m = .26 s = .17 in time 1 to m = .17 s = .18 in time 2; t(28) = 1.75, p < .05 (1-tailed) and the Israelis (m = .20 s = .11 in time 1 to m = .13 s = .11 in time 2; t(28) = 1.5, p < .10 (1-tailed) from the first to the second time period. In addition, the Israelis display a significant increase in the level of affiliation intensity from time one to time two (m = .03 s = .03 in time 1 to m = .08 s = .06 in time 2; t(28) = 2.5, p < .01 (1-tailed). The Palestinians did not increase their level of affiliation intensity, yet it remained steady from the first to the second time period (m = .05 s = .11).

Thus, the second time period in these Oslo I negotiations reflects a shift toward low power, high affiliation communication, and corresponds to the escalation of progress in the Oslo I negotiations that emerged in the Spring and Summer of 1993. The consistency of these trends for both groups suggests that they may have begun to recognize that Mutually Enhancing Opportunities were emerging at the secret bargaining tables in Oslo and that the public rhetoric ought to support these efforts.

However, the Oslo II negotiations were not secret, and there was significantly less correspondence between the relational frames displayed by each side. For example, Table 4 reveals that in the first time period the Israelis start with a series of high power/low affiliation messages, shift to low power/high affiliation messages, and then end with high power/low affilation frames leading up to the final agreement. The Palestinians demonstrate just the opposite patterns. They begin with low power/high affiliation messages, increase power in the second period, and significantly decrease power in the third period while increasing their affiliation messages. In other words, the relational coordination during the Oslo II negotiations was significantly less apparent than in the Oslo I negotiations.

Perhaps this lack of relational coordination stems from the evolution of specific events during the six-month period preceding the final agreement. For the Palestinian side, the first time period leads up to the interim agreement signed on July 4, the second period follows the interim agreement until Israel's closure of Palestinian establishments in Jerusalem on August 23, the third period follows the closures through the final agreement. While the differences in means are in

TABLE 4: Power and affiliation intensity shifts from Oslo I and Oslo II

1993—Israeli			
01/01/93–04/22/93		05/06/93–09/13/93	
Power Intensity	Power Intensity		
M = .20	SD = .11	M = .13	SD = .11
Affiliation Intensity		Affiliation Intensity	
M = .03	SD = .03	M = .08	SD = .06
1993—Palestinian			
01/01/93–05/23/93		06/12/93–9/13/93	
Power Intensity	Power Intensity		
M = .26	SD = .17	M = .17	SD = .18
Affiliation Intensity		Affiliation Intensity	
M = .05	SD = .11	M = .05	SD = .11

1995—Israeli					
04/25/95-07/04/95		07/12/95–08/15/95		08/23/95–09/25/95	
Power Intensity	Power Intensity		Power Intensity		
M = .28	SD = .17	M = .22	SD = .10	M = .35	SD = .34
Affiliation Intensity		Affiliation Intensity		Affiliation Intensity	
M = .06	SD = .08	M = .10	SD = .08	M = .03	SD = .03
1995—Palestinian					
04/25/95–07/04/95		07/12/95–08/15/95		08/23/95–09/25/95	
Power Intensity	Power Intensity		Power Intensity		
M = .24	SD = .09	M = .34	SD = .14	M = .23	SD = .10
Affiliation Intensity		Affiliation Intensity		Affiliation Intensity	
M = .16	SD = .14	M = .10	SD = .09	M = .15	SD = .09

the predicted direction, language use in the first period (PI: m = .28, s = .17; AI: m = .06, s = .08) was not statistically different from that of the second period (PI: m = .22, s = .10, t(11) = .79, n/s; AI: m = .10, s = .08, t(11) = .91, n/s). Between the second and third time periods, the increase in Power Intensity was noticeable but non-significant (m = .22, s = .10 compared to m = .35, s = .34, t(9) = .83, n/s). Meanwhile the decrease in Affiliation Intensity was marginally significant (m = .10, s = .08 compared to m = .03, s = .03, t(9) = 2.06, p < .10), allowing for a liberal significance standard considering the low statistical power of the test used for all Oslo II comparisons.

For the Israeli side, the first time period leads up to the bombing in Tel Aviv on July 24, the second period follows that bombing until the bus bomb in Jerusalem on August 21, the third period follows the final agreement. Between the first and second periods, Power Intensity increased significantly (m = .24, s = .09 to m = .34, s = .14; t(11) = 1.43, p < .10); and Affiliation Intensity showed a decrease but fell short of the test for significance (m = .16, s = .14 to m = .10, s = .09; t(11) = 1.0, n/s). Between the second and third time periods, there was again a significant change in Power Intensity, this time a decrease (m = .34, s = .14 to m = .23, s = .10; t(10) = 1.51, p < .10), and another non-significant change in Affiliation Intensity with an increase from m = .10 (s = .09) to m = .15 (s = .09), t(10) = .94, n/s.

H. DISCUSSION

The goal of this study was to compare the negotiation contexts preceding both the Oslo I and the Oslo II negotiations as revealed in the public rhetoric displayed by both groups as they moved closer to the final agreements. Did the relational conditions displayed in the rhetoric reflect ripeness for negotiation? The data provide an interesting view of the context surrounding these two negotiations.

The similarity in rhetorical and discourse pattern in the public media around the Oslo I and Oslo II accords is fairly consistent with our expectations entering this project. As the outcome(s) of the 1993 Oslo agreement has been viewed favorably—demonstrating a willingness to work together, mutual recognition, establishing a framework for future peace negotiations—compared to the relative failure in the Oslo II agreement, we expected that we would see a different pattern in language used. Relational ripeness suggested that a more affiliative tone should have been set in order to enter into a positive bargaining environment for the negotiators. The failure of an affiliative tone having been set requires a different look at the situation to explain the connection of the data to the outcome observed.

One explanation is the mutual "standing down" in the rhetoric of both parties seen in decreased levels of power intensity. Within a span of about five weeks in the period leading up to Oslo 1993, between May 6 and June 12 both parties demonstrated a move away from power rhetoric and dominance themes in their discourse. This mutual movement toward a more neutral or even at times somewhat positive tone reflects what may be seen as progress in the direction of making the development of a Mutually Enhancing Opportunity possible. This does not suggest that less hostile rhetoric *caused* a propitious negotiating moment to emerge, but rather that it helped foster a relational context in which a MEO might prevail.

This view also offers an explanation for the lack of ripeness that failed to emerge in the Oslo II process. The rhetoric immediately preceding the signed agreement lacks a synchronous movement—Israeli rhetoric softens while Palestinian rhetoric maintains a consistent degree of power intensity. This asynchronous movement does not demonstrate a contextual ripeness in which an MEO may develop, which was consistent with the failure retrospectively seen from Oslo II.

These exemplars demonstrate a method of offering a preliminary empirical foundation for the dimensions of ripeness viewed from a relational context using Relational Order Theory. The data presented here signify a relationship between Mutually Hurting Stalemates and Mutually Enhancing Opportunities as reflected in synchronous shifting of rhetoric away from intense hostility demonstrating a movement from a relational frame of competition/aggression toward isolationist peace. Beginning from approximately the same relational frames in 1993 and 1995, the Oslo I accord is preceded by a relational movement together and toward each other, whereas the Oslo II accord does not see the same movement together.

This ripeness evolution may have evolved partially from the secret nature of the 1992–1993 Oslo discussions and negotiations. Parties were not constrained by face needs to project toughness at the table, they were free to move toward one another. However, the 1995 negotiations were open to public scrutiny, meaning representatives from each party needed to use public rhetoric to manage their constituent relations. This management appears to have followed predictable role behavior: the Israelis, having control over resources, are freer to reach out with somewhat (although not overly) affiliative rhetoric. Since their constituents benefit from significantly better economic and human rights conditions, they are less threatened by a more moderate position taken by their political leadership. On the other hand, the PLO is consequently limited in their autonomous control over resources. This leads Arafat and others to assume the role of opposition where attacks and verbal hostility are typical behaviors—especially as they must manage their administration's position in a less stable administrative position. Their rhetoric must be inclusive of parties within their constituency that maintain a more extremist position. Thus the PLO may have benefited more directly from the secret negotiations in terms of being able to display a less power-oriented stance.

Contributing to the volatile nature of the context leading to the Oslo II negotiations were the effects of certain events. Interim agreements, terrorist attacks and political retribution had powerful and salient effects on the rhetoric on both sides. Along the timeline, an interim verbal agreement was reached on July 4, a suicide attacker detonated a bomb in Tel Aviv on July 24, an interim agreement was reached on August 11, and on August 21 a bus bombing in Jerusalem was followed on August 23 by the Israeli Ministerial Committee closing a number of Palestinian establishments in Jerusalem including Orient House. The pattern of relational frames of rhetoric from each party demonstrates the effect of these actions (Donohue & Hoobler, 2001).

In contrast, the events surrounding the Oslo I accords were responded to rhetorically in a very different manner. Where January and February 1993 held great progress in the secret Oslo channel, March brought great upheaval with a succession of shootings, bombing, and the sealing of the Gaza Strip by Israeli forces. Progress in Oslo talks is made in April and May seeming to begin the process of drawing the parties together (as identified by Donohue, 1998). With Uri Savir joining the group in late May—making the talks "official" on both sides—the parties begin to develop a deep bonding, demonstrated interdependence, trust, and respect. This period seems to have been the most crucial turning point for both parties during the 1993 Oslo process. The talks survived friction in July, likely aided by the relationship that had been developed between Abu Ala, Savir, and the mediation team led by Terje Larsen, culminating in a breakthrough negotiating session in mid-August.

These results carry implications for understanding the role of the negotiation context as it reveals a ripeness to negotiate, viewing the context of relationship management "away from the table" as influencing "ripeness" and negotiations "at the table." As indicated above one of the requirements for what may be perceived as a conflict "ripe" for negotiation is the perception of a mutually hurting stalemate. "Mutually hurting" can be conceived as including considerations of loss of life, public sense of peace and security, and economic pressures. While a variety of issues and pressures may influence the decision to seek an interim cease-fire or holding out for a definitive settlement (see for example Zartman & Touval, 1996), this issue is likely further complicated by relational considerations. If the conclusions drawn from Relational Order Theory hold true, then the manner in which public communication frames the relational context in which negotiations proceed should be added to the requirements for "ripeness." At some point, third parties might consider conditions that might allow a negotiated settlement to grow and endure. How parties frame their relationship through public communication can influence events at the table and, thus, bear observation and discussion.

Another dimension of the power-role issue is that of message strategies from the position of different power symmetries. By all indicators, including military armament, economic strength, and international political capital, Israel is the far more "powerful" state compared to Palestine. Seen from this power-role perspective, we are not surprised to see Israeli rhetoric demonstrating some degree of willingness to "reach out" to the Palestinian side while in comparison Palestinian rhetoric does not likewise demonstrate any considerable softening in tone that would suggest reaching out to the Israelis. This same pattern of low power-role parties using negative messages while bargaining with high power-role opponents is seen in other examples of low-high power-role bargaining and negotiations such as corporation versus labor union (Donohue, Dietz, Hamilton, 1984) and interpersonal negotiation (Levine & Boster, 2001). This runs contrary to strategies for optimal success for low-power parties. Levine and Boster reveal that the lone strong factor contributing to success in a low power condition was positively valenced messages. The apparent inability of low-power parties to utilize this strategy demonstrates the robust moderating effect of lower comparable power status while in a negotiating situation. Low-power parties perhaps see themselves as overly dependent upon the other party thus leading them to seek to rhetorically break from the other party as opposed to reaching out which may be construed as "giving in" to the more powerful party. If a low-power party is more dependent relative to the high-power party, the potential or likely divergence of interests will likely cause the low-power party to use contentious tactics to gain compliance from the high-power party (Pruitt & Rubin, 1986). This is not to say that such tactics are likely to be successful, rather that they reflect a strong situational predisposition. Other authors have identified tactics for low-power parties in power-asymmetric negotiations to gain bargaining leverage and advantage (e.g., Bacharach & Lawler, 1986; Pfetsch & Landau, 2000; Zartman & Rubin, 2000).

The question is to what extent are negotiation strategies constrained by rhetoric? Expressing messages indicative of more crisis-oriented frames appears to set the stage for a more hard-line competitive strategy. This strategy may seek to appeal more to constituents but may also constrain opportunities at the bargaining table. Managing one's constituency and less moderate factions within one's own administration are only two factors that would seem to set limits upon parties' ability to concede to making diplomatic concessions inherent in a relational frame of moving toward one another. This restriction of rhetorical freedom is further exacerbated by power-role expectations. In asymmetric negotiations, whereas high-power parties appear adequately empowered to propose a relational frame that reaches out to the other party, low-power parties perhaps do not share this same freedom. Whether the effect stems from decision-making biases encouraging distributive tactics or is an artifact of low-power parties seeking bargaining equality through tactical rhetoric, parties attempt to manage their relational power status. This suggests that parties are often strategically seeking power-role advantages through their management of relational-contextual features surrounding their conflict and negotiations. An asymmetrically higher power-role position empowers parties to covet their status and/or use that position to reach out to their opponent. An asymmetrically lower power-role position seems to effectively narrow a party's relational-contextual options, encouraging a defensive posture focused on distributive tactics. Viewed from a ripeness perspective, this suggests that in asymmetrical power situations, high-power parties need to engage the lower power party by promoting opportunities to reach out across the divide in a way that does not threaten the identity of the other party. When low-power parties are presented with a chance to engage that does not threaten their internal status among constituents or opposition factions, a mutually coming-together may be possible. This is seen in the secret Oslo negotiations in 1992–1993; the Palestinians were able to reach out to the Israelis without being undermined by less moderate factions within their state. This feature help to create a Mutually Enhancing Opportunity for both parties to explore the process of peace negotiations without the external pressures normally attributed to such talks. Oslo II in 1995 carried no such opportunities and accordingly a ripe moment was not achieved.

As these framing strategies are tracked, comparisons with negotiations from other periods will be assessed. For example, negotiations and various events following Oslo II have moved the Palestinians and Israelis into a different relational posture from the Oslo I achievement. Have the relational patterns displayed through the media shifted significantly following Oslo I and II and leading up to Camp David in 2000 in a manner that might predict current hostilities? The same kind of asynchronous power and affiliation shifts that preceded Oslo II given the failure of Camp David are expected. Also, issues will be tracked to determine if certain relational parameters follow particular substantive issues. It is quite likely that some issues are framed with more power-oriented language than others as attempts to capture a more comprehensive picture of relational order in this highly volatile conflict are made.

REFERENCES

Bacharach, S. B. & Lawler, E. J. (1986). Power dependence and power paradoxes in bargaining. *Negotiation Journal, 86*, 167–174.

Berger, P. & Luckman, T. (1966). *The social construction of reality.* Garden City, NY: Doubleday.

Burgoon, J. K. & Hale, J. L. (1984). The fundamental topoi of relational communication. *Communication Monographs, 51*, 193–214.

Corbin, J. (1994). *Gaza first.* London: Bloomsbury.

Donohue, W. A. (1991). *Communication, marital dispute and divorce mediation.* Hillsdale, NJ: Lawrence Erlbaum Associates.

Donohue, W. A. (1998). Managing equivocality and relational paradox in the Oslo peace negotiations. *Journal of Language and Social Psychology, 17*, 72–96.

Donohue, W. A., Dietz, M. E. & Hamilton, M. (1984). Coding naturalistic negotiation interaction. *Human Communication Research, 10*, 403–425.

Donohue, W. A. & Hoobler, G. D. (2001, June). *Plotting the continued course of Israeli-Palestinian negotiations from Oslo II (1995).* Paper presented at the International Association of Conflict Management Conference; Cergy, France.

Donohue, W. A., Ramesh, C., Kaufman G. & Smith, R. (1991). Crisis bargaining in intense conflict situations. *International Journal of Group Tensions. 21*, 131–154.

Donohue, W. A. & Roberto, A. J. (1993). Relational development as negotiated order in hostage negotiations. *Human Communication Research, 20*, 175–198.

Drake, L. E. & Donohue, W. A. (1996). Communicative framing theory in conflict resolution. *Communication Research, 23*, 297–322.

Druckman, D. (1997). Negotiating in the international context. In I. W. Zartman & J. L. Rasmussen (Eds.), *Peacemaking in international conflict* (pp. 81–123). Washington, DC: United States Institute of Peace Press.

Kelman, H. C. (1996). The interactive problem-solving approach. In C. A. Crocker, F. O. Hampson & P. Aall (Eds.), *Managing global chaos* (pp. 501–519). Washington, DC: United States Institute of Peace Press.

Kelman, H. C. (1997). Social-psychological dimensions of international conflict. In I. W. Zartman & J. L. Rasmussen (Eds.), *Peacemaking in international conflict* (pp. 191–237). Washington, DC: United States Institute of Peace.

King, J. (1994). *Handshake in Washington: The beginning of Middle East peace?* Reading, UK: Garnet.

Levine, T. R. & Boster, F. J. (2001). The effects of power and message variables on compliance. *Communication Monographs, 68*, 28–48.

Mazen, A. M. (1998). When settlement and resolution are in conflict: Searching for a mideast peace dividend. *Negotiation Journal, 14(4)*, 357–367.

Pfetsch, F. R. & Landau, A. (2000). Symmetry and asymmetry in international negotiations. *Peace Research Abstracts*, 38, 603-651.

Pruitt, D. G. & Rubin, J. Z. (1986). Escalation and stability. In *Social conflict: Escalation, stalemate, & settlement* (pp. 62–87). New York: Random House.

Rouhana, N. N. & Kelman, H. C. (1994). Promoting joint thinking in international conflicts: An Israeli-Palestinian continuing workshop. *Journal of Social Issues, 50*, 157–178.

Saunders, H. H. (1996). Prenegotiation and circum-negotiation: Arenas of the peace process. In C. A. Crocker, F. O. Hampson & P. Aall (Eds.), *Managing global chaos* (pp. 419–432). Washington, DC: United States Institute of Peace Press.

Smith, C. P. (Ed.). (1992). *Motivation and personality: Handbook of thematic content analysis*. New York: Cambridge University Press.

Strauss, A. (1978). *Negotiations: Varieties, contexts, processes, and social order*. San Francisco: Jossey-Bass.

Touval, S. (1995). Ethical dilemmas in international mediation. *Negotiation Journal, 11*, 333–337.

Touval, S. (2000). The impact of multiple power asymmetries on Israeli-Palestinian negotiations. In I. W. Zartman & J. Z. Rubin (Eds.), *Power and negotiation* (pp. 155–176). Ann Arbor, MI: University of Michigan Press.

Touval, S. & Zartman, I. W. (1985). Mediation in theory. In S. Touval & I. W. Zartman (Eds.), *International mediation in theory and practice*. Boulder, CO: Westview.

Weiner, M. & Mehrabian, A. (1968). *Language within language*. New York: Appleton-Century-Crofts.

Winter, D. G. (1973). *The power motive*. New York: Free Press.

Winter, D. G. (1980). Measuring the motive patterns of southern Africa political leaders at a distance. *Political Psychology, 2(2)*, 75–85.

Winter, D. G. (1991). Measuring personality at a distance: Development of an integrated system for scoring motives in running text. In A. J. Stewart, J. M. Healy, Jr. & D. J. Ozer (Eds.), *Perspectives in personality: Approached to understanding lives* (pp. 59–89). London: Jessica Kingsley.

Winter, D. G. (1992). Content analysis of achival productions, personal documents, and everyday verbal productions. In C. P. Smith (Ed.), *Motivation and personality: Handbook of thematic content analysis* (pp. 110–125). Cambridge: Cambridge University Press.

Winter, D. G. (1993). Power, affiliation, and war: Three tests of a motivational model. *Journal of Personality and Social Psychology, 65*, 532–545.

Winter, D. G. (1994). *Manual for scoring 'motive imagery' in running text*. Department of Psychology, University of Michigan, Ann Arbor: Author.

Zartman, I. W. (1989). *Ripe for resolution* (2nd ed.). New York: Oxford University Press.

Zartman, I. W. (2000). Ripeness: The hurting stalemate and beyond. In P. C. Stern & D. Druckman (Eds.), *International conflict resolution after the Cold War* (pp. 225–250). Washington, DC: National Academy Press.

Zartman, I. W. & Rubin, J. Z. (2000). Symmetry and asymmetry in negotiation. In I. W. Zartman & J. Z. Rubin (Eds.), *Power and negotiation* (pp. 271–293). Ann Arbor, MI: University of Michigan Press.

Zartman, I. W. & Touval, S. (1996). International mediation in the post-cold war era. In C. A. Crocker, F. O. Hampson & P. Aall (Eds.), *Managing global chaos* (pp. 445–461). Washington, DC: United States Institute of Peace Press.

CHAPTER 5

FRAMING INTERNATIONAL CONFLICTS IN ASIA: A COMPARATIVE ANALYSIS OF NEWS COVERAGE OF TOKDO

Young Chul Yoon and Gwangho E.

A. INTRODUCTION

The purpose of this study is to develop a framework for analyzing news coverage of international conflict, which will contribute to the understanding of the role of mass media in the process of international conflict. This study focuses on the way in which the conflict over the sovereignty of Tokdo (Takeshima in Japanese) is portrayed by the South Korean and the Japanese news media. The central questions to be raised are how the news coverage of Tokdo's issues differs between two nations, and what implications does the news coverage have on the diplomatic relationship between them.

Mass media are not objective messengers of information but active participants in forming international relations. As channels of international information flow, mass media are affected and affect the conflict. Therefore, mass media are part of the diplomatic process between two nations. Politicians and government officials actually derive their information from the mass media and signals through mass media to foreign counterparts, especially when two nations are involved in conflict. In addition to actual dialogue and negotiation between different nations, mass media provide an important route for government officials from different nations to communicate with eachother.

The news coverage of international conflict contributes to shaping the image of a foreign nation by providing information and symbols that can be used to change or reinforce attitude toward other nations. International conflict is often beyond direct experience for average people who depend upon mass media to know what is going on outside the home country. As Lippmann (1922) put it, "the world that we have to deal with politically is out of reach, out of sight, out of mind. It has to be explored, reported and imagined." Because most people tend to believe what the domestic news media say about foreign affairs, it is not particularly difficult for the media to distort the international reality and to manipulate public opinion of domestic people.

The conflict over the dominion of Tokdo has been one of the most controversial issues in the modern diplomatic history between South Korea and Japan. Both nations have seen this territorial dispute as critical to their national interests, and therefore argued that the island belonged to their own territories for decades. News media of the home country actively participated in the diplomatic friction by strongly supporting the position of the home government and harshly criticizing the counterpart. The mutual portrayals of South Korea and Japan by South Korean press and Japanese press reflected the mutual antagonism rooted in their historical experiences.

Thus, for the sake of this project, we will examine how the international conflict over the Tokdo issue affects the nature of news that the two countries receive about each other. Two questions are raised at this point. First, in what respect did the South Korean press and the Japanese press evaluate the Tokdo issue differently? Second, how did the different types of newspapers in both nations vary in their news coverage of Tokdo? Internal variations in the way the event is portrayed across newspapers published in each country will be explored.

B. THE TERRITORIAL CONFLICT OVER TOKDO

Tokdo, called Takeshima by Japanese people, consists of two islets with a combined area of 0.18 square kilometers. It is located 92 kilometers away from South Korea's Ulluong Island, while it is 160 kilometers from Japan's nearest island of Oki. It was first called Tokdo in 1881. The South Korean government proclaimed its sovereignty over the island on January 18, 1962, and has dispatched policemen to the island as guards since 1956.

The conflict over the disputed island between Japan and South Korea is nearly a century old. Both nations raised the jurisdiction issue occasionally, deteriorating the bilateral relationship between the two governments and diverting its people's attention outward from domestic issues.

The dispute flared up again in January 1996 when both South Korea and Japan prepared to claim a 200 nautical mile exclusive economic zone (EEZ) on the basis of the United Nations maritime treaty. On February 1, 1996, the Japanese government reportedly notified the South Korean government of its decision to promulgate the 200 mile EEZ, which would include the disputed island. In response to this movement, South Korea also made a firm decision to construct docking facilities on the island.

Japanese Foreign Minister Ikeda Euikihiko alleged that the island was part of his country's territories, and the construction of docking facilities on the island was an infringement of Japan's sovereignty. The South Korean government responded by claiming that the construction of docking facilities was a legitimate exercise of its sovereignty. While Japan criticized South Korea for violating its sovereignty, South Korea chided Japan for intervening in its domestic affairs. South Korea argued that the island was not a matter of bargaining between the two nations, because it clearly belonged to South Korea on the grounds of historical evidence and international laws that supported South Korea's position. It was also noted that a group of South Korean security guards has been posted on the island since 1956, implying that Japan has no other option.

On the other hand, Japan, relying on historical materials and its own interpretation of international laws, demanded that South Korea withdraw all personnel and remove facilities from the island. Japan has routinely dispatched coast guard ships to the nearby waters of Tokdo in a demonstration of its ownership of the island. As both sides continued to exchange the conflicting claims over Tokdo, the diplomatic relationship deteriorated. The territorial issue often turned into major diplomatic war between the two nations.

It was not until the South Korean government's announcement of the construction of docking facilities on the island that the Japanese press increased its news coverage of the Takeshima issue. The first story on this issue was carried by *Sankei* on the basis of dispatches by Yonhap (South Korean) news agency. The article said that South Korean workers started the construction of a harbor in Takeshima in accordance with the South Korean government's instruction. *Sankei* urged the Japanese government to take a strong protest against South Korea and to make an announcement to refute "the act of sovereignty invasion."

Other Japanese newspapers followed suit. This report was stimulating to Japanese readers and some Japanese politicians who were not even aware that South Korean guards have lived on Takeshima for decades. Reflecting the opinion climate demanding strong reaction against South Korea, the Japanese government raised the tone of criticism by referring to the construction of the harbor on the island as an "unforgivable act." Exchanges of harsh criticism against each other by newspapers of both nations followed, and the conflict between the two nations reached a climax in February 1996.

South Korea's Minister of Foreign Affairs advised that South Korea not become overly sensitive on this issue, because with South Koreans residing on Tokdo, it was in a much more advantageous position in the territorial dispute with Japan. Despite that advice, President Kim Young Sam outspokenly expressed his anger toward Japan. Canceling a meeting with Japanese politicians scheduled to visit the presidential office, he spoke on the phone with the commander of the garrison stationed on the island, encouraging him and his men. The South Korean news media understood this symbolic reaction by President Kim very well. Following the propaganda campaign criticizing Japan, they did not hesitate to reinforce the anti-Japanese news frame.

C. INTERNATIONAL CONFLICT AND NEWS FRAME

Many studies dealing with the news making process conclude that news media, far from conveying "value-free" or "ideology-free" objective reality, actively help to construct and reconstruct social reality by presenting a particular news frame. News frame is defined as "persistent patterns of cognition, interpretation, and presentation of selection emphasis, and exclusion, by which symbol-handlers routinely organize discourse, whether verbal or visual" (Gitlin, 1980). Gitlin (1980) also comments that "media frames, largely unspoken and unacknowledged, organize the world both for journalists who report it and, in some important degree, for us who rely on their reports." The concept of news frame has been employed by many media sociologists who examined the process of news making from the perspective of the social construction of reality well described by Berger and Luckman (1967). The construction and the existence of media frame (or news frame) can be explained at various levels.

Reporters unconsciously rely on their own values in writing news stories and absorb assumptions of the social world in which the news is embedded (White, 1950; Snider, 1967; Hackett, 1984). Gans (1979) notes that there is a set of common enduring values generally held by members of the American news media. The enduring values that intervene in news judgment are ethnocentrism, altruistic democracy, responsible capitalism, small-town pastoralism, individualism and so on. Anti-Japanese ideology is one of the enduring values shared by the South Korean journalists. The same thing can be said to the Japanese journalists even though it may be so to a lesser degree. This leads to the mutual negative news coverage of conflictual events between South Korea and Japan.

Not only the journalist's political disposition but also the organizational routine has much to do with the construction of news frame. Even the journalistic conventions of news writing, such as "objective reporting," functions as strategic rituals that reinforce the existing structure of power by favoring power institutions (Tuchman, 1978). News making is not random but patterned activities of reporters relying on news sources for a continuous supply of information (Sigal, 1973). Since news media seek efficient news sources who are authoritative and credible, they need to depend on government bureaucracies for news gathering and diffusing information that favor the government's position.

Fishman (1980) describes the process of the "bureaucratic subsidization of the news" in which the media are gatherers of news produced by government organizations. The government may withhold information and distort the reality to meet the public relations objectives. And reporters also need to establish good working relationships with government officials. There is an incentive to avoid publishing information which would aggravate the source and thus threaten the symbiotic source-reporter relationship. In these ways, news is shaped to become more supportive of the government. Thus, the information that finds its way to the media is generally harmonious with the position of the government in power. The beat system, which most media subscribe to in one form or another, is generally organized along the lines of government offices.

This is particularly so when news media report the international conflict in which national interest is deeply involved. A good deal of the information about international conflict used by news media comes from outputs generated by the foreign policy officials whose primary job is to promote the news frame suitable for realizing its foreign policy interests. Herman (1985) states that the functional bottom line of the "propaganda framework" in the United States is the mobilization of public support for the policies and actions of the American government. Herman charges that the officials in the Reagan administration were deciding how to best use international events to their advantage and ignoring the fact which might give positive effect on the Soviet Union. In a similar context, Yoon (1989) suggests that the South Korean newspapers continued to adopt the anti-communist news frame whenever they covered the conflict between South Korea and North Korea.

As long as journalists can easily reach a consensus on what is good for the home country and who is the enemy, they tend to offer a reflection of the government's interpretation of news events even without the government's attempt to control them. The press coverage of Tokdo is a case in point. Journalists in both South Korea and Japan, who share views on this diplomatic conflict with their home governments, don't think it unfair to advocate the home country and criticize the other side. Therefore, the news media of both nations have been writing in support of official positions of home governments, which fit well with the existing news frames that have portrayed the other side negatively for many decades. The news media tend to define international conflict by attempting to fit the incoming information into the existing frame that is culturally and ideologically familiar. Contradictory information is either ignored or rejected.

But the news frame on the antagonistic nation may shift as international political conditions vary over time. When the home government tries to improve its relationship with the counterpart, the news media may employ a less antagonistic frame. News media with varying political and cultural bases may react differently to the government's efforts to construct and reconstruct international reality, although they accept the assumption of the existing frame. The flexibility of news frame was illustrated by Wolfsfeld (1997) who analyzed the structural and cultural competition over the definition of news events occurring in the process of political conflict.

The inter-organizational relationship between the press and the government may affect the nature of news coverage of international conflict. The government-press relationship depends on how closely the press is connected with the government. There is an incentive for the government to give a favor to pro-government newspapers while discriminating against the anti-government newspapers. Some newspapers are more closely linked with the government than others. Given that news is the product of the interaction of two bureaucracies—one composed of journalists and the other of government news sources—differences in news coverage are found between pro-government papers and opposition papers.

Despite the existence of organizational imperatives which require reporters to rely on government sources, news media maintain relative autonomy to construct news frame tailoring their own ideological or political position to the extent in which it does not challenge the core assumption of foreign policy. While the foreign policy interest agreed upon by officials and journalists draw a boundary of what is permissible to publish, different types of newspapers may present diverse ideas and strategies to maximize foreign policy interest.

For example, as far as the Tokdo issue is concerned, the South Korean press will never criticize the anti-Japanese posture of the South Korean government and will not attempt to challenge the diplomatic authorities. The press will contribute to the maintenance of consent associated with the anti-Japanese ideology. But there may be room for news organizations to reflect their own perspectives within the limits in which the basic principle of foreign policy is not challenged. Although the anti-Japanese ideology will be dominant in the South Korean newspaper's coverage of the Tokdo issue, we may be able to find a certain amount of variation in news frames across different newspapers. The same thing can be expected in the Japanese case. So it would be interesting to see which nation allows a greater degree of variation in news frame of Tokdo-related conflict across newspapers.

D. CONFLICT MANAGEMENT AND MOBILIZATION OF PUBLIC OPINION

Media coverage of international events influence the public perception of the event, because mass media are the principal source of information for the audience. Many international conflicts center on disputes over news frames as each nation attempts to diffuse its own interpretation or idea of the conflict to the national and international public. Thus the conflict between two nations accompanies the competition over news frames which represent the national interest of each nation. Chang (1988) analyzes political symbols used in the news coverage of leading U.S. newspapers, and suggests that the dynamics of international conflict affects the symbolic representation of China in news coverage of U.S.-China policy.

When two nations conflict, news media of one nation may view its own state's policy or action in a positive image while portraying the enemy state's policy or action in a negative image. Thus the mutual perception of two adversarial nations tends to be similar. Negative stereotypes are held by citizens of both nations.

Uri Bronfenbrenner (1961) observed that the United States' perception of the Soviet Union during the Cold War were a "mirror image" of the Soviet Union's perception of the United States. He proposed five images constructed by citizens of both nations: First, they are the aggressors; second, their government exploits and deludes the people; third, the mass of their people are not really sympathetic to the regime; fourth, they cannot be trusted; fifth, their policy verges on madness.

These types of observations can be applied to other contexts where mutual antagonism has developed between two nations. The conflict on the dominion of Tokdo represents an excellent example in which the news media enthusiastically adopt news frame reflecting the home country's foreign policy interest. Following the propaganda framework set by the home government, the news media of South Korea and Japan played an important role in mobilizing patriotism, reinforcing the mutual antagonism which had already existed between two nations. As the news media continued to support the argument that the island belongs to each nation's territory, the international conflict between the two nations deepened.

Whenever it comes to the coverage of the Tokdo issue, the news frame adopted by the South Korean press was contradictory to that by the Japanese press. They exchanged criticism against one another for distorting the historical and judicial aspects of the island. Since the press coverage of each nation on the issue of Tokdo was based on the consensus of the national public, there has been little controversy among politicians and readers of the home country. As a result, it has been relatively easy for both governments to manipulate the international conflict.

One of the important functions of international conflict is to strengthen the domestic integration of national society. By creating news events that reinforce the existence of an external threat, the government can manage to shift news agenda from the domestic political strife to the international conflict which is directly related to national interest. The ability to shift the news agenda thus works favorably to the government in need of increasing internal solidarity. Coser's proposition (1956) that conflict with an external group increases internal group cohesion supports the theory that international conflict increases the degree of national integration.

One important point here is that the ruling government is in a situation to manipulate the news agenda by creating news events that easily lead to international conflict, which will be effective for strengthening social integration and political stability. This is particularly so in both South Korea and Japan where the symbiosis between reporters and government sources takes a unique form. The role of reporters' clubs attached to each government agency is important to understand the general pattern of news gathering in both nations. Reporters' club in the Ministry of Foreign Affairs works as an important news gathering mechanism by ensuring that government information related to the Tokdo issue is transmitted quickly to beat reporters. Reporters are supplied newsworthy information through reporters' clubs by government sources who also try to use them as a public relations instrument.

Public opinion toward the opponent nation can be thus mobilized by the government's management of news on the international conflict. The negative portrayal of the opponent nation by the home media can be widely diffused by official statements denouncing the opponent nation. This begs one to ask the question: If these processes are simultaneously occurring in both nations that conflict with each other, what are the consequences for international relations? With this question in mind, we will seek to examine news coverage of the Tokdo issue by South Korean and Japanese newspapers for evidence of this type of mutual construction of international imageries and perceptions.

E. METHOD

The purpose of this study was to analyze news content of newspapers in South Korea and Japan. Four newspapers from each nation, selected on the basis of their varying relationships with their respective governments and for their different ownership patterns, were analyzed. *Seoul Shinmun, Donga Ilbo, Chosun Ilbo*, and *Hangyoreh Shinmun* were selected in South Korea, and *Mainichi, Sankei, Yomiuri* and *Asahi Shinmun* from Japan. *Seoul Shinmun* is a government-owned paper that has been loyal to the policy line of the ruling government. *Donga* and *Chosun* are the two most popular and influential commercial newspapers that adopt a more market-oriented strategy. *Hangyoreh*, founded in 1988 by a group of anti-government journalists, maintains a critical stance against the government. Among the four Japanese newspapers, *Asahi* is known as the most critical against the Japanese government while *Sankei* is the least critical.

A quantitative content analysis was conducted to compare how the news event was reported by different newspapers in the two nations. News stories analyzed here were published from January 1 to June 30, 1996, when the conflict over the island had been culminated. Since this study attempts to find out the change of news frame as the conflict unfolds, all the stories that mentioned Tokdo were downloaded from the data base for analysis.

Eight hundred forty-four (844) news stories from South Korean newspapers and three hundred sixty-five (365) stories from Japanese newspapers were analyzed. The unit of analysis was each news story. Besides the descriptive nature of news coverage, various dimensions of news frame that we tried to identify were the origin of the news story, news source, news channel, types of evidence, editorial stance and the evaluation of conflict. Categories for each coding unit were obtained based on the pilot study. In the pilot study, a substantial degree of intercoder agreement was achieved for the application of the coding scheme. The coding scheme was developed to investigate how each newspaper framed news stories on the topics related to the conflict over the Tokdo issue between South Korea and Japan.

The coding procedure took place in two phases. Four coders, two for South Korean newspapers and two for Japanese newspapers, were permitted to confer with one another in order to resolve major coding disagreements. In this process, the coding guide has been modified so that it can be applied to the newspapers of both nations. Then each coder independently evaluated the news stories on the Tokdo issue.

F.   RESULTS OF CONTENT ANALYSIS

1.   Quantity of News Coverage

The eight newspapers examined in this study differed in the intensity of coverage on the Tokdo-related conflict between South Korea and Japan. The number of news stories published by *Chosun* (241) exceeded other South Korean newspapers. *Chosun* placed the highest news value on the Tokdo issue, and took the lead in launching the anti-Japanese media campaign.

News coverage by *Sankei* (142) was almost double those of the other three Japanese newspapers. Table 1 shows that about 40 percent of the stories covered by the four Japanese newspapers were supplied by *Sankei*. This suggests that *Sankei*, known as the most conservative newspaper in Japan, most actively participated in making the Tokdo issue a public agenda. As can been seen in Table 1, most of the stories (90 percent) were published in February and March 1996 when the conflict between the two nations culminated. The number of stories has decreased rapidly since May 1996, as both governments agree that it is not desirable for the two nations to aggravate the conflict between them.

The fact that the South Korean newspapers covered this event more frequently and more extensively than did the Japanese newspapers suggests that the South Korean press was placing greater emphasis on this issue than the Japanese press, and that the Tokdo issue was relatively less important to the Japanese readers. The Tokdo issue reminded South Korean people of the sense of humiliation related to the Japanese colonial rule over Korea, so they were deeply concerned about the territorial dispute with Japan. Thus the extensive press coverage, which included a great deal of criticism against Japan, was seen by South Korean readers as a natural and justifiable response.

TABLE 1: Distribution of News Stories Analyzed

Country / Month	Korea					Japan				
	Cho-sun	Dong-A	Seoul	Han-gyoreh	Total	Asahi	Yomi-uri	Mai-nich	San-Kei	Total
January	8 / 3.3%	4 / 2.0%	6 / 2.7%	5 / 2.7%	23 / 2.7%		1 / 1.3%	1 / 1.3	2 / 1.4%	4 / 1.1%
February	120 / 49.8%	93 / 47.4%	116 / 52.5%	104 / 55.9%	433 / 51.3%	43 / 61.4%	52 / 69.3%	44 / 56.4%	79 / 55.6%	218 / 59.7%
March	55 / 22.8%	54 / 27.6%	55 / 24.9%	38 / 20.4%	202 / 23.9%	18 / 25.7%	16 / 21.3%	13 / 16.7%	30 / 21.1%	77 / 21.1%
April	22 / 9.1%	22 / 11.2%	12 / 5.4%	11 / 5.9%	67 / 7.9%	5 / 7.1%	2 / 2.7%	14 / 18.0%	12 / 8.5%	33 / 9.0%
May	17 / 7.1%	11 / 5.6%	10 / 4.5%	9 / 4.8%	47 / 5.6%	2 / 2.9%	3 / 4.0%	5 / 6.4%	8 / 5.6%	18 / 4.9%
June	19 / 7.9%	12 / 6.1%	22 / 10.0%	19 / 10.2%	72 / 8.5%	2 / 2.9%	1 / 1.3%	1 / 1.3%	11 / 7.8%	15 / 4.1%
Total	241 / 100%	196 / 100%	221 / 100%	186 / 100%	844 / 100%	70 / 100%	75 / 100%	78 / 100%	142 / 100%	365 / 100%

2.   Types of News Stories

The comparison of news story types across the eight newspapers reveals differences within and between the two nations. Stories published by the South Korean newspapers tended to be scattered across various types such as straight news (46.4 percent), editorials and columns (11.3 percent), background news (26.8 percent), and letters from readers (7.5 percent). *Chosun* accounts for more than a half of the total number of "letters from readers."

Japanese newspapers were heavily dependent upon straight news (71.8 percent), while carrying a relatively small number of background news (9.6 percent). One of the interesting results was that the South Korean newspapers carried a large of number (63, 7.5 percent) of "letters from readers," while the Japanese newspapers published only 18 (4.9 percent) letters from readers. This suggests that the negative opinion toward the other side was more extensive and profound in South Korea. *Sankei* carried 16 editorials, and other Japanese newspapers wrote less than ten editorials on the Tokdo issue.

Table 2 suggests that the South Korean press was more active in problematizing the Tokdo issue, and more aggressive in molding public opinion on this issue than the Japanese press. Providing more opinion news and more background news, the South Korean press tried to give a full explanation of the news event. The significant discrepancy in the percentage of straight news between the two nations also reveals that the Japanese press was more inclined to write factual reports on the dispute.

3.   Origins of News Stories

It is important to know whether the news event was explained from the home nation's perspective or from the opponent nation's perspective. As shown in Table 3, more than half of the total stories of South Korean newspapers were supplied by domestic reporters. Only 19.2 percent of stories came from foreign correspondents. For the Japanese newspapers, 48.3 percent of stories were covered by domestic reporters, and 32.5 percent were written by foreign correspondents. It is interesting that the Japanese press relied more heavily on foreign correspondents than did the South Korean press. The fact that about half of 130 foreign correspondents in Seoul are from Japanese news organization explains to some extent how the Japanese press could publish so many stories written by correspondents.

4.   News Sources

Table 4 illustrates important differences in the newspapers' use of news sources. Sixty-three and six tenths (63.6) percent of Japanese stories used the Japanese government as a major source, while 43.5 percent of South Korean stories relied on its home government sources. Most of the stories using government officials as sources supported the home governments' official positions toward

TABLE 2: Types of News Stories

News Types	Korea					Japan				
	Cho-sun	Dong-A	Seoul	Han-gyoreh	Total	Asahi	Yomi-uri	Mai-nich	San-Kei	Total
Straight News	104 43.3%	107 54.6%	94 42.7%	86 46.0%	391 46.4%	55 78.6%	54 72.0%	52 66.7%	101 71.1%	262 71.8%
Editorial And Columns	34 14.2%	15 7.7%	28 12.8%	18 9.6%	95 11.3%	5 7.1%	8 10.7%	9 11.5%	16 11.3%	38 10.4%
Back-ground News	53 22.1%	49 25.0%	70 31.9%	54 28.8%	226 26.8%	5 7.2%	10 13.3%	8 10.3%	12 8.5%	35 9.6%
Letters From Readers	37 15.4%	8 4.1%	8 3.6%	10 5.3%	63 7.5%	4 5.7%	1 1.3%	4 5.1%	9 6.3%	18 4.9%
Interviews	6 2.5%	5 2.6%	4 1.8%	11 5.9%	26 3.1%		2 2.7%	2 2.6%		4 1.1%
Others	6 2.5%	12 6.1%	16 6.9%	8 4.3%	42 5.0%	1 1.4%		3 3.8%	4 2.8%	8 2.2%
Total	240 100%	196 100%	220 100%	187 100%	843 100%	70 100%	75 100%	78 100%	142 100%	365 100%

TABLE 3: Origins of News Stories

Origins \ Country	Korea					Japan				
	Cho-sun	Dong-A	Seoul	Han-gyoreh	Total	Asahi	Yomi-uri	Mai-nich	San-Kei	Total
Reporter	88 52.4%	82 57.7%	107 65.7%	86 60.5%	363 59.0%	33 49.3%	38 55.0%	33 55.0%	75 54.0%	179 51.2%
Correspondent	28 16.7%	33 23.2%	31 19.1%	26 18.3%	118 19.2%	27 40.3%	27 39.1%	26 35.1%	33 23.7%	113 32.5%
Foreign Press	8 4.8%	9 6.3%	11 6.8%	13 9.1%	42 5.0%	1 1.5%	3 4.3%	8 10.8%	17 12.2%	29 8.3%
Others	44 26.4%	18 12.6%	14 8.6%	17 11.9%	93 15.1%	6 9.1%	1 1.4%	7 9.5%	14 10.4%	28 8.1%
Total	168 100%	142 100%	163 100%	142 100%	615 100%	67 100%	69 100%	74 100%	139 100%	349 100%

TABLE 4: Types of News Sources

Country / News Sources	Korea					Japan				
	Cho-sun	Dong-A	Seoul	Han-gyoreh	Total	Asahi	Yomi-uri	Mai-nich	San-Kei	Total
Government Officials	58 39.5%	48 41.3%	71 50.1%	51 41.1%	228 43.5%	37 75.5%	29 54.7%	38 58.4%	74 65.5%	178 63.6%
Party/ Politician	10 6.8%	9 7.8%	15 10.8%	20 16.1%	54 10.3%	9 18.4%	13 24.5%	12 18.5%	16 14.2%	50 17.9%
Civic Organization	69 47.0%	52 44.9%	41 29.5%	43 34.7%	205 39.0%	1 2.0%	2 3.8%	6 9.2%	11 9.7%	20 7.1%
The press	4 2.7%	4 3.4%	7 5.0%	7 5.6%	22 4.1%	1 2.0%	8 15.1%	7 10.8%	10 8.8%	26 9.3%
Others	6 4.1%	3 2.6%	5 3.6%	3 2.4%	17 3.1%	1 2.0%	1 1.9%	2 3.0%	2 1.8%	6 2.1%
Total	147 100%	116 100%	139 100%	124 100%	526 100%	49 100%	53 100%	65 100%	113 100%	280 100%

the Tokdo issue. It was the government-owned *Seoul* (50.1 percent) that relied on the government sources most heavily among the four South Korean newspapers. As for the Japanese press, it was *Sankei* (65.5 percent) that was most dependent on the government sources. *Seoul* and *Sankei*, being more active than others in using government sources in their stories, maintained news frames reflecting the foreign policy interest of home government.

It was also interesting to note that the South Korean press was highly dependent on civic sector sources (39.0 percent), such as academic organizations, movement groups, and citizens, whereas the Japanese press was much less so (7.1 percent). Since South Korean readers could easily reach a consensus of national sovereignty over Tokdo, South Korean newspapers did not have to restrict news sources in the government circle. The South Korean press often interviewed protest groups that launched anti-Japanese rallies.

On the other hand, the lack of dependence on civic groups on the part of the Japanese press suggests that the opinions of average citizens were largely unsolicitated in the Japanese news coverage of the Tokdo issue. This can be interpreted as an effort by the Japanese press to manipulate public opinion in favor of the Japanese government's official position. Although this study did not attempt to examine the impact of press coverage upon the formation of public opinion, it might be said that the Japanese press led its readers, who did not know much about the Tokdo issue, to think about it.

The use of media organizations as news sources was more visible in the South Korean press coverage. This finding implies that the South Korean press actively sought news stories of foreign media that viewed this issue from perspectives favorable to South Korea.

5. News Channels

A related approach to examining the diversity of news sources is to investigate the channels of news. News channels, defined as the paths by which information reaches reporters, are classified into three categories (Sigal, 1973). Routine channels include official proceedings. Informal channels include nongovernmental proceedings such as leaks, background briefings, and news from non-government organizations (citizens). Enterprise channels include interviews conducted at the reporter's initiative, independent research involving books, historical data, and statistical data.

Table 5 illustrates the dominance of routine channels in the South Korean newspapers as opposed to the Japanese newspapers. *Seoul* and *Hangyoreh* reported more than 60 percent of the Tokdo-related stories through routine channels, while the other two newspapers reported less than 50 percent through routine channels. Informal news channels were rarely utilized by either the South Korean (2.3 percent) and Japanese press (9.0 percent). For the use of the enter-

TABLE 5: Use of different News Channels

News Channel	Korea					Japan				
	Cho-sun	Dong-A	Seoul	Han-gyoreh	Total	Asahi	Yomi-uri	Mai-nich	San-Kei	Total
Routine	62 42.5%	55 47.4%	85 60.7%	77 62.1%	279 53.0%	18 36.7%	22 41.5%	26 40.0%	49 40.5%	115 39.9%
Informal	3 2.1%	2 1.7%	4 2.9%	3 2.4%	12 2.3%	6 12.2%	6 11.3%	3 4.6%	11 9.1%	26 9.0%
Enter-prise	9 6.2%	12 10.3%	16 11.4%	12 9.7%	49 9.3%	3 6.1%	9 17.0%	12 18.5%	23 19.0%	47 16.3%
Not Applicable	72 49.3%	47 40.5%	35 25.0%	32 25.8%	186 35.4%	22 44.9%	16 30.2%	24 37.0%	38 31.4%	100 34.8%
Total	146 100%	116 100%	140 100%	124 100%	526 100%	49 100%	53 100%	65 100%	121 100%	288 100%

prise channels, the Japanese press was more active than the South Korean press. Again, *Sankei* was the leading Japanese newspaper using enterprise channels.

6. Presentation of Evidence

Newspapers of both nations presented different types of evidence to demonstrate that the island belongs to their own sovereignties. Comparison of how evidence was used in the stories reveals different patterns, as shown by Table 6. Historical evidence was utilized more often by the South Korean press (43.8 percent) than the Japanese press (23.9 percent). The use of evidences based on the international law and convention was notable in the news coverage of the Japanese press. The South Korean press, as compared to the Japanese press, was less enthusiastic in viewing this conflict as a legal issue. While the South Korean press tends to recognize Tokdo being an inherent part of the Korean territory, the Japanese report Tokdo as if it is subject to a territorial dispute that needs to be legally solved.

A significant gap was found in the use of public opinion. Thirty and six tenths (30.6) percent (116) of the stories carried by the South Korean press mentioned the public's evaluation that South Korea has the territorial right over Tokdo, while the Japanese press (*Sankei*) reported only three stories on the response of the Japanese public. This heavy reliance of the South Korean press on evidence obtained from the private sector indicates an attempt to mobilize public support, whereas such an intent was not as apparent on the part of the Japanese press.

7. Evaluation of the Conflict

South Korean newspapers held a predominantly negative view of Japan, although a small discrepancy among *Chosun, Donga, Seoul* and *Hangyoreh* was found. *Chosun* and *Donga*, both known as nationalistic papers, evaluated Japan's behavior as a distinctly negative act by leaders, and negative terminology such as "Japanese imperialism," "Japanese militarism," and "absurd remarks" was frequently used in the South Korean press.

The Japanese newspapers maintained a less negative position toward South Korea than the South Korean press did toward Japan. The proportion of unfavorable coverage of the opponent nation was higher in the South Korean press than the Japanese press. This suggests that the South Korean newspapers continued to frame the South Korea-Japan relationship from the perspective of anti-Japanese ideology widely shared by South Korean people. Seventy-six and five tenths (76.5) percent of South Korean news stories pointed out Japan as responsible for the conflict, and only 6.4 percent indicated South Korean to be responsible for it. But the Japanese press was divided when it came to the question of responsibility of the conflict. For example, *Mainichi* carried eight articles saying that Japan is responsible for intensifying the conflict, while *Sankei* released six articles blaming South Korea for the conflict (see Table 7).

TABLE 6: Types of Evidence used in Stories

Country	Korea					Japan				
Month	Cho-sun	Dong-A	Seoul	Han-gyoreh	Total	Asahi	Yomi-uri	Mai-nich	San-Kei	Total
Historical Evidence	40 36.0%	43 50.0%	57 51.9%	26 34.7%	166 43.8%		4 57.2%	3 21.4%	4 18.1%	11 23.9%
Convention Law	16 14.4%	7 8.1%	13 12.3%	10 13.3%	46 12.1%		2 28.6%	3 21.4%	2 9.1%	7 15.2%
Public Opinion	43 38.7%	29 33.7%	21 19.8%	23 30.7%	116 30.6%				3 13.6%	3 6.5%
Others	12 10.8%	7 8.1%	15 14.1%	16 21.2%	50 13.2%	3 100%	1 14.3%	8 57.2%	13 59.1%	25 54.4%
Total	111 100%	86 100%	106 100%	75 100%	378 100%	3 100%	7 100%	14 100%	22 100%	46 100%

TABLE 7: Responsibility of Conflict

Country / Responsibility	Korea					Japan				
	Cho-sun	Dong-A	Seoul	Han-gyoreh	Total	Asahi	Yomi-uri	Mai-nich	San-Kei	Total
Korea	5 8.1%		2 4.0%	5 11.6%	12 6.4%			1 1.3%	6 4.2%	7 1.9%
Japan	49 79.0%	29 90.6%	37 74.0%	28 65.1%	143 76.5%		1 1.3%	8 10.3%	2 1.4%	11 3.0%
Both	5 8.1%	3 9.3%	6 12.0%	8 18.6%	22 11.8%			1 1.3%	4 2.8%	5 1.4%
Others	3 4.8%		5 10.0%	2 4.6%	10 5.3%	70 100%	74 98.7%	68 86.9%	130 91.5%	342 93.7%
Total	62 100%	32 100%	50 100%	43 100%	187 100%	70 100%	75 100%	78 100%	142 100%	365 100%

TABLE 8: Actors for Conflict Management

Country / Actor	Korea					Japan				
	Cho-sun	Dong-A	Seoul	Han-gyoreh	Total	Asahi	Yomi-uri	Mai-nich	San-Kei	Total
Government	40 51.3%	18 51.4%	29 60.4%	21 36.8%	108 49.5%		1 100%	10 83.3%	17 81.0%	28 82.4%
Political Authority	1 1.3%			1 1.8%	2 0.9%			2 16.7%		2 5.9%
The Press			1 2.1%	1 1.8%	2 0.9%				2 9.5%	2 5.9%
Private Citizens	22 28.2%	5 14.3%	6 12.5%	18 31.5%	51 23.4%				2 9.5%	2 5.9%
Others	15 19.2%	12 34.3%	12 25.0%	16 28.1%	55 25.2%					
Total	78 100%	35 100%	48 100%	57 100%	218 100%		1 100%	12 100%	21 100%	34 100%

Both governments were mentioned as main actors that had the ability to resolve the conflict. The Japanese press had a tendency to rely on the government-level talk to decrease tension between the two nations. The South Korean press, despite its emphasis on the role of government, expected that the mutual efforts of private citizens would make a lot of difference in reducing the intensity of the conflict (see Table 8).

Newspapers also presented ways in which the conflict could be resolved. The editorial stance most strongly supported by the newspapers of both nations was that their home government should not give up their current positions. But the news coverage of the conflict solution revealed a notable difference. The South Korean press published more articles with an aggressive tone than the Japanese did. Twenty-two and nine tenths (22.9) percent of stories carried by the Japanese press implied negotiation and peaceful talks as a means to reduce the tension, while only 13.0 percent of stories by the South Korean press did so. The South Korean press was more inclined to propose an uncompromising policy in dealing with the conflict, referring more frequently to measures of punishment or protest against Japan (see Table 9).

8. Analysis of Editorials

A quantitative content analysis indicates that news coverage by the South Korean and the Japanese press reflected the foreign policy interest of each country, assuming Tokdo (Takeshima) as belonging to their own territories. Given the conflictual nature of territorial dispute between the two nations, this result is not surprising.

But the analysis of editorials enables us to examine internal differences across newspapers within each nation. Although the bottom line of editorial policy is to act in concert with the claim of territorial right by their home governments, each newspaper maintains a varying degree of autonomy to lay down its own editorial stand on how to view the nature of the conflict and how to deal with it.

The goal of foreign policy was never questioned, but the diplomatic tactics on particular issues were criticized by some newspapers. Newspapers operating in a given nation can present differing opinions on the various aspects of the diplomatic dispute. The qualitative analysis of editorials thus allows us to examine opinion diversity existing among newspapers in a given nation.

Opinion diversity was found to be greater in the Japanese press than in the South Korean press. South Korean newspapers had reached a consensus not only in the way of understanding the question of title to Tokdo but also in examining the underlying cause of the conflict. Upon the Japanese government's argument that Takeshima was legally incorporated into Japan on the basis of the legal announcement on January 1905, South Korean newspapers ran editorials pointing out the illegality of such an announcement on the ground that it was pro-

TABLE 9: Methods of Conflict Solution

Country / Method	Korea					Japan				
	Cho-sun	Dong-A	Seoul	Han-gyoreh	Total	Asahi	Yomi-uri	Mai-nich	San-Kei	Total
Straight News	9 11.5%	6 17.1%	9 19.2%	6 6.5%	30 11.9%				3 14.3%	3 8.6%
Editorial And Columns	29 37.2%	10 28.6%	8 17.0%	57 61.3%	104 41.1%		1 100%	3 23.1%	9 42.9%	13 37.1%
Back-ground News	11 14.1%	4 11.4%	9 19.1%	9 9.7%	33 13.0%			6 46.2%	2 9.5%	8 22.9%
Letters From Readers	2 2.6%	1 2.9%	1 2.1%	1 1.1%	5 2.0%			1 7.7%		1 2.9%
Interviews	2 2.6%	3 8.6%	8 17.0%		13 5.1%				1 4.8%	1 2.9%
Others	25 32.1%	11 31.4%	12 25.5%	20 21.5%	68 26.9%			3 23.1%	6 28.5%	9 25.7%
Total	78 100%	35 100%	47 100%	93 100%	253 100%		1 100%	13 100%	21 100%	35 100%

claimed when the Japanese imperial army had already occupied the Korean penin-sular and begun to exercise political control over Korea. According to the editor-ial coverage by the South Korean press, South Korea's territorial sovereignty over Tokdo has been an historical truth with ample evidence.

The issue was out of the question for South Korea. Therefore the question was rephrased by the South Korean press: Why did Japan bring up this issue at this particular time? Four South Korean newspapers reached a consensus on this question, too. It was viewed in union by the South Korean press that the real intention of the Japanese government was not to occupy the island, but to make it such a controversial issue to be solved by the international court. The basic atti-tude of the South Korean press was not to make the non-controversial issue con-troversial. Therefore, it argued that South Korea's protest against Japan be clear, strong and rational rather than too emotional. In the final stage of the conflict when the summit talks between the two nations sought ways to reduce the mutual antagonism, it was found that *Seoul Shinmun*, unlike other South Korean news-papers, weakened its negative editorial stance against Japan and emphasized the necessity of an amicable settlement of the dispute. The announcement that the 2002 World Cup Game would be co-hosted by South Korea and Japan created an atmosphere of reconciliation and cooperation and *Seoul Shinmun* swiftly responded to the shift of international environment. Other papers, however, main-tained the view that the government should make it clear that the Tokdo issue was not negotiable and not to confuse it with other issues.

The range of opinion diversity within the Japanese press system was found wider than that within the South Korean press system. Japanese newspapers pre-sented differing views on various issues of the Takeshima dispute. While *Sankei* and *Yomiuri* asked the Japanese government to persist in its dominion of Takeshima and to make a strong protest against the South Korean government which started the construction of docking facilities on the island, *Mainich* sug-gested its home government not to stimulate the negative sentiment of the South Korean people who had been inclined to relate the territorial dispute with the Japanese empire's colonial exploitation. *Asahi*, standing somewhere between *Sankei* and *Mainichi* in its editorial comment, wrote an editorial criticizing the overly sensitive reaction by the conservative Japanese politicians. While con-firming that Japan has sovereignty over Takeshima, *Asahi* pointed out that Japanese politicians had underestimated the deep-rooted anti-Japanese feeling widely shared by South Korean people.

It was between *Sankei* and *Mainichi* that the clearest difference in editorial view was found. *Sankei* carried articles with narrow-minded nationalism where it urged the Japanese government to follow a tough line in dealing with this issue and not to worry about the deterioration of the diplomatic relationship between the two nations. On the other hand, the editorial view published by *Mainichi* was more or less moderate, and it put greater emphasis on the peaceful relationship between the two nations than other Japanese papers did. Unlike *Sankei*, which tried to frame the Takeshima issue as a very serious news event associated with the infringement of national sovereignty, *Mainichi* viewed it as "technical mistake" made by some Japanese politicians who did not know much about the complicated situation of South Korean politics and underestimated the potential impact of such a sensitive issue on the South Korean people. *Mainichi* analyzed in an editorial that one of the reasons why so much news coverage of this territorial conflict was given by the South Korean press was that the ruling government intentionally mobilized the anti-Japanese public opinion with a view to attack one of the leading opposition leaders, Kim Jongpil, who has been known as a typical pro-Japanese politician.

The finding that the diversity in viewpoints published by the Japanese press was greater than that by the South Korean press has some important implications. First, it can be said that the Japanese press operates in a more pluralistic political environment that allows a greater degree of press autonomy. Japanese journalists with a more relative autonomy write more freely and comment on the conflict from diverse perspectives. Second, it may have to do with the climates of public opinion formed in each nation. The Tokdo issue has not been so much publicized in Japan as in South Korea. Since it has been the most significant public agenda during the period of conflict in South Korea, a strongly unified pubic opinion in favor of safeguarding Tokdo could be formed. However, the average Japanese readers have shown little concern over this issue. As a result, it can be said that the Japanese press has treated it as less critical than the South Korean press did.

Another interesting finding was that newspapers of both nations related the international conflict to the dynamics of political conflict within a nation. The strong repulsive attitude adopted by the Japanese government was understood by the South Korean press as a highly calculated diplomatic tactic to divert the public attention into an international issue rather than a domestic political battle and to mobilize conservatism as well as nationalism. A similar view was found in the Japanese press which pointed out that President Kim's blame on Japan was a political tactic to stimulate the anti-Japanese sentiment among the South Korean public and eventually to raise the popularity of the president.

In this context, *Yomiuri* carried an editorial mentioning that the South Korean government's strong protest was a calculated response to prepare for the forthcoming national assembly election in April 1996. Both governments were criticized by the press of the other side for their alleged attempt to divert the public attention from domestic conflict into the international conflict.

G. SUMMARY AND DISCUSSION

This study examined the characteristics of news coverage of the Tokdo issue of the South Korean and Japanese press to detect systemic differences in news presentation. During the period from January to June 1996, the conflict over

Tokdo has been the most sensitive diplomatic issue. As expected in the theoretical discussion, newspapers were basically sympathetic toward their home government in the coverage of the Tokdo issue. Considering the fact that mass media tend to depend on government officials for news supply, the news coverage in this period reflects the interest of foreign policy adopted by the home government.

The brief analysis of news stories was an attempt to show that newspapers differed in their pattern of news coverage of the conflict. First, the South Korean press was much more serious and active in reporting the Tokdo issue, and gave much more extensive coverage of the Tokdo issue than did the Japanese press. Thus, for the South Korean press, the Tokdo issue was the most important media item during that period. However, the news value given to the Tokdo conflict by the Japanese press was not as great. Even though both the South Korean and Japanese press condemned their counterpart, the intensity of their criticisms was different. Japanese papers' reaction was not as strong as that of the South Korean papers' reaction.

Second, the essential reason for difference in news coverage was that newspapers adopted different patterns of news source use for the coverage of South Korea-Japan relations. The South Korean press used news sources that were more diverse than the Japanese press. But this does not necessarily mean that the former reported the conflict with a more diverse perspective. Because there has been an enduring value, which is an anti-Japanese feeling shared by all the South Korean people, there was no question that Tokdo belonged to South Korea. Lacking such a firm national consensus, the Japanese press was found to be reluctant to rely on news sources other than government officials.

Third, news frames adopted by the South Korean press were more emotional and sensational than those adopted by the Japanese press. The South Korean press, calling statements made by high-ranking Japanese officials "absurd remarks," maintained an extremely negative tone toward Japan. Reaction by the Japanese press was not positive either. The result was the acceleration of mutual antagonism between the two nations. But the Japanese press reported more straight news and was seen as more "neutral" and less sensational. Mobilization of public support was much more notable in the news coverage of the South Korean press.

Fourth, newspapers of both nations employed different approaches to understanding the nature and solution of the conflict. While the Japanese press understood the conflict as an international issue to be settled by simply applying international law, the South Korean press adopted the view that no further negotiation with Japan was necessary to solve the conflict over the Tokdo issue. As a means to reduce the intense tension between the two sides, the South Korean press has a tendency to emphasize the importance of mutual understanding at the level of citizens, whereas the Japanese press does not.

Finally, the analysis of editorials reveals that the Japanese press presented more diverse views on this territorial conflict than the South Korea press did. The South Korean press made it clear that the Tokdo issue was not negotiable, while the Japanese newspapers were found to advocate the sovereignty of Takeshima with a differing degree of salience. The government-press relationship also explains how the press shifted editorial stance. The government-owned *Seoul Shinmun* quickly responded to the newly developed situation. As the decision to co-host the 2002 World Cup Game was announced, *Seoul Shinmun* immediately toned down the intensity of its negative evaluation of Japan.

To summarize, this study suggests that the propaganda framework works in the news coverage of Tokdo. Both nations reproduced and reinforced the "stereotype" of the opponent nation. The news coverage by both nations is biased in line with the prevailing view toward the other nation. Journalists appear to encode the Tokdo issue with the propaganda framework of each nation. As a result, the mutual misunderstanding and antagonism associated with the Tokdo issue is not likely to be reduced in the near future. The international conflict between South Korea and Japan is therefore managed and sometimes manipulated by the image-making process of the opponent nation, in which foreign policy officials and journalists actively participate.

REFERENCES

Berger, P. & T. Luckman, T. (1967). *The social construction of reality*. Garden City, NY: Anchor.

Bronfenbrenner, U. (1961). The mirror image in Soviet-American Relations: A social psychologist's report. *Journal of Social Issue, 17*, 46–56.

Chang, T. K. (1988). The news and U.S.-China policy: symbols in newspapers and documents. *Journalism Quarterly, 65*, 320–327.

Coser, L. (1956). *The functions of social conflict*. New York: Free Press.

Fishman, M. (1980). *Manufacturing the news*. Austin: University of Texas Press.

Gans, H. (1979). *Deciding what's news*. New York: Pantheon.

Gitlin, T. (1980). *The whole world is watching*. Berkeley: University of California Press.

Hackett, R. (1984). Decline of a paradigm: Bias and objectivity in new media studies. *Critical Studies in Mass Communication, 1*, 229–259.

Herman, E. S. (1985). Diversity of news: Marginalizing the opposition. *Journal of Communication*. Summer, 135–146.

Lippmann, W. (1922). *Public opinion*. New York: The Free Press.

Sigal, L. V. (1973). *Reporters and officials*. Lexington: Heath.

Snider, P. B. (1967). Mr. Gates' revisited: A 1966 version of the 1949 case study. *Journalism Quarterly, 44(3)*, 419–427.

Tuchman, G. (1978). *Making news*. New York: Free Press.

White, David M. (1950). The gatekeeper: A case study in the selection of news. *Journalism Quarterly 27*, 383–390.

Wolfsfeld, Gadi (1997). *Media and political conflict: News from Middle East*. Cambridge University Press.

Youngchul, Yoon (1989). *Political transition and press ideology in South Korea*. Unpublished Ph.D. thesis. University of Minnesota.

CHAPTER 6

FRAMING ENVIRONMENTAL CONFLICTS: THE EDWARDS AQUIFER DISPUTE

Linda L. Putnam

A. INTRODUCTION

Given that environmental decisions typically involve many individuals who hold diverse opinions on the issues, conflicts readily arise among groups, agencies, and institutions who have a vested stake in the decision. These differences have led to heated and often lengthy disputes that are not easily resolved, despite efforts to bring the parties together or to adjudicate the issues (Bingham, 1996; Crowfoot & Wondolleck, 1990). The purpose of this chapter is to examine the emergence of identity, characterization, and conflict frames revealed in newspaper coverage of the collapse of the Edwards Underground Water District. It poses the questions, how do the newspaper articles cast stakeholder identity and characterization in the early stages of the Edwards Aquifer dispute? What language is used in the coverage of these frames and how do descriptors of the dispute provide labels about the nature of the conflict itself? In particular, how do newspaper articles represent the issues of naming and blaming in this controversy? This study, then, employs language analysis to examine the identity and characterization frames in the Edwards Aquifer dispute and to explore the role of media in framing this environmental situation.

B. CONCEPTUAL FOUNDATION: THE FRAMING OF ENVIRONMENTAL DISPUTES

Gray's (1997) model of conflict framing forms the foundation for this research. Two of these frames, identity and characterization, form the foci for this study. In this chapter, framing refers to worldviews, interpretations of experiences, and perspectives that parties have on the situations they encounter. They can be both collective and individualistic; they help parties determine what is "figure," or the most salient features in a situation, and what is "ground," or least important elements. They provide participants with accounts for what is included and excluded, for ways of acting and reacting, and for interpreting the actions of other parties in the dispute. This definition of interaction is rooted in the social inter-

* This study was supported by the Hewlett Foundation, the Interdisciplinary Research Initiatives Program—TAMU Office of the Vice President for Research, and the Institute for Science, Technology, and Public Policy in the Bush School of Government and Public Service.

action among disputes and the way labels or naming of events reflects these social dynamics. Through framing, disputants provide interpretations of events, assess blame, and determine ownership of a conflict (Felstiner, Abel, Sarat, 1980–1981). Hence, this definition of framing differs from treating frames as cognitive models of judgment (Bazerman, 1983; Neale & Bazerman, 1991).

For this study, two types of framing will be examined: identity and characterization frames. Identity frames refer to language, statements, and phrases that reflect how stakeholders describe their own role in the conflict—who they are, what is important or central about their role as vested in the conflict. Characterization frames center on the way the disputants characterize other parties in the conflict. Since individuals have the potential to enact many different identities, (e.g., mother, professor, Girl Scout leader, Texan), the ones that surface in a conflict as central to the dispute are key to understanding the identification of stakeholder groups. In this study, for example, identity and characterization frames arise from the media's descriptions of disputants and from quotations that disputants make in newspaper articles to depict their own identity or to characterize the roles of other parties in the dispute. Identity frames also emanate from the way that the media aligns stakeholders with particular issues or positions or with other parties. Six categories of identity frames will be used to examine newspaper representations: occupational role, refers to a person's profession; societal role, refers to place in society (gender, mother, powerbroker, activist, victim); ethnic and cultural identity, refers to birth or subculture affiliation; place identity, refers to location; institutional identity, refers to organization/agency/or representative role; and interest-based identity, refers to issues and positions as a source of their involvement in the events. Characterization frames also fit into these six categories, but can be differentiated as positive or negative, depending on the language use to describe other participants. The overall question that guides this mini-study is how do the newspaper articles cast the identities of the disputants? Which identities surface as most salient in depicting stakeholders and in characterizing disputants in the conflict?

1. Intractable Disputes

Many environmental disputes remain mired in controversy, tied up in litigation, and/or riddled with long-standing tensions that defy resolution. Kriesberg (1993) and Burgess and Burgess (1997) refer to these types of disputes as intractable. Disputes that persist over long periods of time, and are not alleviated through either mediation or other consensus building efforts or by individual court actions, fall into the intractable category. Even disputes for which local consensus-building efforts were successful, may prove intractable in another locale or if these same issues are raised to a national level of debate. The evolution of such intractable disputes needs careful study (Kriesberg, 1993).

Burgess and Burgess (1997) identify a number of characteristics of intractable disputes including irreconcilable moral differences, high stakes distributional conflicts, pecking order conflicts, and zero-sum confrontations. Other descriptors of intractable disputes that surface in the literature are: escalation, polarization, casting issues in non-negotiable terms, obscure and often intangible costs, non-acceptance of settlements, series of unsuccessful interventions, and persistence over long periods of time (Putnam & Wondolleck, 2002). Most of these characteristics typify the Edwards Aquifer conflict. However, what is more interesting for this research project is not whether this conflict is viewed as intractable, but can we find elements of this intractability surfacing in the media coverage of the dispute? If so, which elements and how do they appear related to the identity and characterization frames that surface in these articles?

C.   MEDIA FRAMING OF SOCIAL AND ENVIRONMENTAL CONFLICTS

Mass media is a powerful institution in society. It is not simply a reflector or communication channel that plays back what it sees and hears. Rather the media makes the production of news its business. News production consists of reporters and editors who gather and assemble the process, stockholders and financial investors who contribute funds to the business, the marketplace that generates competition in news industry, and readers who consume the news. All are part of the production process (Douglas, 1992). Various models of media production cast different roles for the media in the coverage of social conflict (Arno & Dissanayaka, 1984; Bantz, 1985; Cohen, Adoni & Bantz, 1990; Douglas, 1992; Davison, 1974; Gilboa, 1998; Neuzil & Kovarik, 1996; Wolfsfeld, 1997). Several roles that emerge from the literature include: the media (1) as a powerful entity that tries to control the conflict; (2) as a biased participant who either defends or attacks the status quo; (3) as a third party "watchdog" who provides feedback to the public on local problems; (4) as a gatekeeper who sets agendas, filters issues, and accentuates other positions to maintain a balance of views; (5) as a mediator that builds consensus and manages community tensions; (6) as a corporate entity who celebrates conflicts and benefits through increased sales in covering conflicts. Thus, in its coverage of social conflict, the mass media serves a variety of roles, including, "interested bystander, advocate, legitimator, mediator, arbitrator, . . . truth-seeker, agenda-setter, watchdog, and guard dog" (Douglas, 1992). Although these roles differ depending on the type of dispute, nature and history of coverage, and audience/community of media coverage, what surfaces from this research is that the media is an active agent involved in the social construction of the public image of a conflict. The media frames the conflict, aids in identifying stakeholders and issues in a dispute, and shows how a conflict affects the status quo (Reese, Gandy & Grant, 2001).

Media framing has become a prominent area of mass media research in the past decade (Durham, 1998; Edelman, 1993; Entman, 1993; Iyengar, & Simon, 1993; Norris, 1995; Pan & Kosicki, 1993; Price, Tewksbury & Powers, 1997; Scheufele, 1999; Semetko & Valkenburg, 2000; Valkenburg, Semetko & de Vresse, 1999). Although connected to agenda-setting research, framing analysis examines how people talk and think about issues in the news (Pan & Kosicki,

1993). Media framing is selecting aspects of perceived reality to highlight or promote particular definitions and interpretations of situations (Entman, 1993). Thus, frames help convey, interpret, and evaluate information. Considerable work has been done on framing effects, particularly their risk perceptions, opinions of political institutions, and attributions of responsibility (Semetko & Valkenburg, 2000).

Work on types of media frames is growing and considers conflict a generic category of media framing (Cappella & Jamison, 1997; Patterson, 1993). This work has shown that complex political issues are often reduced to "overly simplistic conflicts" and that news of presidential campaigns are often framed in terms of conflict. Also, the more serious the newspaper, the more the media employs a conflict frame (Semetko & Valkenburg, 2000). However, most of the work on media use of conflict frames centers on the frequency of this frame type or on its effects. Few studies focus on how the conflict framing occurs in the media and how media framing can be merged with conflict framing to understand how social conflicts are presented in the media. In particular, research is needed to uncover the role of media framing in addressing environmental conflicts.

In the environmental arena, the media has played a strong agenda-setting role through heightening the public's awareness of environmental issues such as waste and pollution (Ader, 1995); through serving as a guard dog of society's dominant institutions (Corbett, 1992); through highlighting the dangers and consequences of global warming (McComas & Shanahan, 1999); and through framing environmental issues for the public (Davis, 1995). Research reveals that the media uses a utilitarian frame to report environmental issues in rural areas and employs a stewardship frame to present stories in urban newspapers (Corbett, 1992). Since media coverage of environmental issues is more likely to be controlled by technical experts, the official coverage in some communities minimizes the consequences of conflict and relegates disputes to a small number of powerful elites. Newspaper coverage of toxic waste is more likely in communities with only a moderate level of economic reliance on manufacturing than in locales with high or low economic dependence on this industry, suggesting that information about health risks from contaminators is filtered and framed for local readers (Griffin & Dunwoody, 1995).

On the issue of framing in the media, Davis (1995) examined the way news media frames environmental messages as either a gain or a loss frame, as affecting either current or future generations, and as taking less (conservation) or doing more (recycling). In a test of eight advertisements, the most persuasive environmental messages were cast in loss frames, ones that negatively impacted the people who failed to act. In a study of the logging controversy in California, Schlechtweg (1996) demonstrates how media framing sets up an binary logic that forms a cleavage between oppositional groups such as radicals and regular people and ecosystem and livelihood. The arguments of an environmental group with an alternative frame of reference fall outside the media frame and are not represented in the verbal text of the controversy. Other studies reveal that public relations agents and spokespeople for stakeholder organizations provide accounts aimed at shaping audience perceptions, especially when the controversy threatens the legitimacy of an organization (Elsbach, 1994). The most persuasive accounts of environmental controversies are those that acknowledge the problem and recognize institutional rather than technical characteristics that contribute to it. Justification is also a salient message strategy for framing adverse or "illegitimate" actions taken by environmental activists (Patterson & Allen, 1997).

These studies suggest that news coverage of environmental issues differs depending on the economic base in communities—one that is closely tied with status quo institutions. Media framing of environmental issues, then, aims to enhance the legitimacy of status quo organizations through acknowledging problems, justifying them, and recognizing the institutional factors that contribute to them. It also accentuates the conflict through creating binary frames that depict oppositional tensions in a complex, multiparty dispute. The research questions that stem from this literature review include: How is the media likely to frame identity and characterization frames in this controversy? How will media cast or label the dispute? What role will news media play in this controversy?

D. ENVIRONMENTAL CASE: THE EDWARDS AQUIFER DISPUTE

The environmental dispute selected for this study is the conflict over groundwater allocation in the Edwards Aquifer, located in the Texas Hill Country. The Edwards Aquifer is a unique underground limestone formation that stretches over 160 miles from south of Austin to west of San Antonio. The Aquifer is the sole source of drinking water for San Antonio; it provides irrigation for farming in six counties; it is the main water source for industry and recreational activities in three counties, and it is linked to five endangered species that live at its base— two types of salamanders, three types of fish. Since, in Texas, surface water belongs to the state and underground water is the property of landowners, the dispute about the Edwards Aquifer has been evolving for years, reaching its first big crescendo in 1990 with the dismantling of the Edwards Underground Water District and the ultimate rejection of the Regional Water Management Plan. This dispute evolved into multiple sanctions by state and federal agencies, four major court suites by the Sierra Club, and continued debates among stakeholders about private and public ownership as well as local and state rights (Foss, 1996; Wolff, 1997a, 1997b).

From a conflict scenario, the Edwards Aquifer is a classic case of the battle of the commons. However, the parties, not only disagree on the allocation and mode of distribution, but also, on the definition of the commons, who owns it, and who should govern it. Groundwater basin management, then, provides an excellent example of how competition among multiple users of limited, renewable common-pool resources can generate fierce, protracted conflicts both within and between communities (Blomquist, 1992; Ostrom, 1990; Ostrom, Gardner &

Walker, 1994). Thus, the primary issues in this dispute are fourfold: (1) the management of a scarce environmental resource limited by physical structure and used by many interdependent stakeholders; (2) the regulation of water allocation; (3) the effects of water shortage from excessive pumping on endangered species that live in the Aquifer and its associated springs; and (4) who should control this water resource and how should allocation and distribution be handled (Texas Water, 1993).

Since this conflict is so complex and covers such an extended period of time, the analysis of this dispute has been grouped into key events that stakeholders repeatedly identify as the major turning points in this conflict (Wolff, 1997a, 1997b; Votteler, 1998). This chapter focuses on the first of these key events, the demise of the Edwards Underground Water District. This dispute will be examined with an eye to media framing of stakeholder identity and characterization and with a focus on elements of intractability that surfaced in media statements about the conflict.

1. Description of the Edwards Underground Water District Scenario

The Edwards Underground Water District (EUWD) was sanctioned in 1959 by the Texas legislature to protect and conserve the Edwards Aquifer in the five-county area after the occurrence of the 1956 drought. Even though the District consisted of representatives from major users in each of the counties, it lacked the authority to limit pumping, or even require registering and metering of wells (Wolff, 1997a). However, in the years between 1970–1984, the EUWD built four small recharge dams over the Aquifer. At the same time, irrigation farming in the region increased dramatically; the U.S. Fish and Wildlife Service listed five species of fish as potentially endangered; the city of San Antonio rejected a plan to purchase water from the Canyon Reservoir; and pumping of water from the Edwards averaged 500,000 acre-feet per year. In 1984, the flow at Comal and San Marcos Springs reached critical levels during a brief drought.

In response to the drought, the city of San Antonio instituted a voluntary water rationing plan (Wood, 1988a). San Antonio Mayor Henry Cisneros along with EUWD Chair, Bobby Hasslocher, appointed a regional ad hoc committee to develop a water plan to govern the aquifer users in the five counties. After five years of negotiating, the committee reached consensus in 1987 on a policy to manage pumping so that annual volume of water taken from the aquifer did not exceed the average rainfall and stream percolation (Tolson, 1988; Wolff, 1997a, 1997b). They also agreed that the entire region should pay for the development of additional water sources, including a plan for reuse of wastewater and the development of new reservoirs and lakes. To reaffirm the decision, the San Antonio City Council approved the regional water plan and voted to construct the Applewhite reservoir on the Medina River in south Bexar County (Krausse, 1988). They sought support for the reservoir and the water plan among the farmers and ranchers in the western counties with the promise that there would not be pumping limits—if the farmers would not add irrigation wells. The Regional Water Management Plan was also approved by the Guadalupe-Blanco River Authority, the San Antonio River Authority, the Nueces River Authority in 1988 (Jensen, 1988). Finally, the EUDW approved the ad hoc regional water plan with a vote of nine to six (Tolson, 1988). All six of the representatives of the western counties voted against it. Despite the dissenting votes, the regional water plan was to be forwarded to the Texas Legislature as a recommended legal mandate (Tolson, 1988; Wolff, 1997a).

In the meantime, the farmers and ranchers in the western counties circulated a petition requesting that their representatives withdraw from the EUWD and develop their own underground water boards. After receiving signatures of 1,000 names on the petition, the western counties pulled out of the EUWD in January of 1989. Prior to this pull out, the EUWD voted in May of 1989 to delay legislation that would translate the Regional Water Plan into law; hence, the legislature adjourned without acting on an aquifer bill (Michaels & Lewis, 1989). In June of 1989, the EUWD voted to pull its bank deposits from the Uvalde State Bank and in January 1990, Uvalde and Medina counties held elections for Board members of their own underground water districts, which later were declared illegal (Wolff, 1997a).

The failure of the five-year negotiated Regional Water Management Plan and the withdrawal of the western counties from the EUWD became a type of "pseudo consensus without agreement." The ad hoc regional committee had brought together stakeholders who represented many different interests in this dispute, including competing interests of the farmers in the west, the spring flow advocates in the east, the industry and recreational users in the middle, and the local politicians interested in the growth of Baxter county (Tolson, 1988). They had hammered out a delicate, technical, and intricate agreement that San Antonio Mayor Cisneros termed, "the finest example of consensus building" (Tolson, 1988), yet there was no agreement. This chapter explores the newspaper coverage of this dispute as it relates to conflict and media framing of stakeholders, labeling of the conflict, and depictions of the intractability of the dispute.

2. Data Collection and Analysis

Newspaper articles on the Edwards Aquifer conflict were located using the NEWSBANK database; press clippings provided through the Texas Natural Resource Conservation Commission (TNRCC); and contributions from stakeholders interviewed in this study. NEWSBANK is a commercial service that indexes newspaper articles in 150 newspapers from all 50 states. Articles were identified through an electronic data search from 1975–1999 using key words, such as "Edwards Aquifer" and "Texas and Aquifer." NEWSBANK indexes only news articles and thus excludes letters to the editor, editorials, daily features, and other non-news items. Texas newspapers included in the NEWSBANK database were Houston Chronicle, the Dallas Morning News, Austin-American Statesman, the San Antonio Express News, and presses in local communities in the state. This search resulted in 122 articles, covering the period from 1988–1996.

The second method of locating newspaper coverage was through the database of TNRCC. TNRCC maintained a comprehensive file of newspaper coverage of articles related to their mission, e.g., reports of natural resources such as air, water, and soil. TNRCC staff scan all major Texas newspapers on a daily basis and has access to local newspaper coverage. This database produced 58 articles, primarily published in 1996–1997.

In addition to this source of newspaper articles, the researchers have interviewed 70 stakeholders in this dispute, including environmentalists; farmers and ranchers; city and state officials; local, regional, and state agencies; media personnel; spokespersons from business and industry; and mediators in this dispute. These people have provided us with copies of news stories, editorials, and letter to the editor that their agencies have collected. An additional 385 articles were collected from local, county, and regional newspapers. Of these articles 149 were editorials and letters to the editor.

For this particular mini-study, only the articles that covered the events surrounding the demise of the Edwards Underground Water District were included in the sample. Most of these 35 articles were published between 1988 and 1991, and 23 of these articles were news clippings that included aspects of framing. Editorials were not included in this analysis. The next stage was to examine each article and extract sentences and/or paragraphs that referred to individuals or stakeholder groups, that is, references that one group made about other stakeholders, references that the media made about any regions or groups, and any sentences that revealed ways the controversy was named, claimed, and/or blamed in the coverage. This data analysis drew from research on language analysis and focused on semantics (use of lexicon or vocabulary) for the six identity frames (see Cantrill & Oravec, 1996 for discourse analysis in environmental research), use of adjectives and adverbs to determine types of characterization, statements of interests and positions, and labels given to the controversy (what is this dispute about?). (See Putnam & Fairhurst, 2001, for a review of discourse analysis and organizations.)

In addition, the researchers examined statements that reflected the characteristics of intractable disputes through use of words that refer to: (1) non-acceptable agreements such as "non-negotiable demands," "stalemates," "talks have ceased;" (2) use of polarized language such as "versus," "we-them," "rivals," "pitted;" (3) references to escalation, "feud," "fighting," "storm" "legal battle;" and (4) comments on the length of the controversy, "months of talks," "long-term efforts." For this chapter, data analysis is qualitative and exploratory.

E. RESULTS OF EXPLORATORY INVESTIGATION

This section reports the identity and characterization frames of stakeholders that surface in the media, overviews references to the naming and blaming of the conflict, tracks elements of intractability that appear in the articles, and discusses the potential and shifting role of the media in this controversy.

1. Identity and Characterization Frames

In 1987–88 prior to the withdrawal of the western counties from the EUWD, newspapers cast *identity frames* through the lens of *prevailing interests of constituent groups*. For example, "the irrigation framers in Uvalde, Medina, and Bexar counties are opposed to giving up their traditional 'right of capture' under Texas law and all of the groundwater they can pump" (Krausse, 1988). For the farmers, identity was not occupation, or place, but one of holding to a belief in the sacred principle of "private property rights." San Antonio was cast as advocating pumping limitations as a strategy to gain leverage with voters for "an expensive and politically unpopular" reservoir construction program, and the major interests of Comal and Hays populations were the preservation of the springs and the recreational water parks that supported their growing tourism business (Krauss, 1988). Although these stakeholders were clearly linked to place or region in their identity, the media represented their involvement in this controversy as fundamentally interest-based. Interspersed with the interests of these stakeholders were the concerns of regional and state water agencies for impending droughts, dwindling water in the Aquifer, and the necessity to limit the pumping to a safe yield of 75 percent of the average annual recharge (Jensen, 1988).

These identity frames, however shifted as the controversy ensued. Newspaper articles began to cast the stakeholders into both *place and institutional identity* frames. Stakeholders were no longer referred to by names of counties or occupations, but by locations of western rural and eastern urban counties. Identity frames based on *place* reflected both the polarization of the conflict and the transformation of interests to location. "Efforts to control future aquifer use have split South-Central Texas users along urban and rural lines" (Gillman, 1989). One article, citing the Southwest Property Rights Association in Medina claimed that the Regional Water Management Plan favored the more populated eastern counties over the interests of rural users in the west (Collier, 1988). Or in another article, Senator Bill Sims of San Angelo asserted, "Urban areas have a greater need for the drought management plan than do rural communities" (Michaels & Lewis, 1989). Even though the farmers and irrigators took the lead in labeling their identities as rural, newspaper articles projected the conflict in these terms, "A regional committee of the EUWD rejected a proposed compromise between warring urban and rural factions on future use of the Edwards Aquifer" (Wood, 1988b).

Another form of identity began to surface immediately following the withdrawal of the western counties from the EUWD. Identity became linked to institutions, particular ones that could develop and implement rules for managing the Aquifer. The media depicted stakeholders as aligning with institutional allies, for example, the Guadalupe-Blanco River Authority who filed a lawsuit to declare the Edwards Aquifer an underground river subject to state regulation (Krause, 1989), the federal government who threatened to intervene (Crimmins, 1990e), and the Sierra Club who threatened to file an endangered species suit (Sierra Club, 1990). New splits developed among old allies in which EUWD members challenged San Antonio for "downplaying the problem" to preserve tourism and attract corporations (Crimmins, 1990a). U.S. Fish and Wildlife Services announced that they might take control of the Aquifer if Comal Springs dried up. San Antonio declared that "they are not willing to restrict themselves if everyone else is pumping like crazy" (Gillman, 1990).

Thus, the media's casting of identity frames shifted again as the naming of the dispute evolved from a "fragile consensus" (Krauss, 1988), to a battle between rural and urban interests (Wood & Fuentes, 1990), and to a struggle for exerting control (Crimmins, 1999b). The media cast both sides as blaming each other for the stalemate while they simultaneously depicted the conflict with descriptors of words, like "a revolt" (Wood, 1988), "a fight" (Crimmins, 1990b), and eventually "a takeover" (Bower, 1991a; Woods & Fuentes, 1990). The rural communities blamed the urbanites for poor planning and the urban constituents chided the rural counties for being demanding, unrealistic, and refusing to compromise (Gillman, 1990).

2. Intractability

Descriptors of intractability surfaced early in this controversy. Language patterns that depicted polarized conflict was evident in the way the media framed the identity of constituents as rural versus urban (Wood & Fuentes, 1990). Phrases such as, "warring urban and rural factions" "us against them," and "pitting" appeared in articles that discussed the pull out from the EUWD (Gillman, 1990). Conflict escalation was portrayed through phrases like, "fighting for water"(Michaels & Lewis, 1989; Wood & Fuentes, 1990) "storm brewing in the west" (Wood, 1988), "battle to regulate" (Bower, 1991a), "Edwards comes under assault" (Aquifer, 1991),"latest shots in the regional water battle (Wood & Fuentes, 1990)," "feuding interests" (Crimmins, 1990d), "scuttled by intense fighting" (Michaels & Lewis, 1989), "face off," "raucous five hour hearing" (Bower, 1991a), and "surrendering water rights" (Gillman, 1989)

Although these terms depicted a level of escalation that moved from "talking about compromise," to treating the controversy as a "battle" with "nuclear options" (Gillman, 1990) and "political bombshells" (Wood & Fuentes, 1990), the conflict escalation seemed secondary to the ways that the articles framed intractability. Particularly their focus on ultimatums issued by both sides and continual reports of "failed plans" "hitting dead ends" (Crimmins, 1990a), "another impasse" "stymied efforts" (Collier, 1990), "killed the chances for the task force to succeed" (Bower, 1989) and "talks that cease" (Crimmins, 1990a), cast an image of the controversy as stalemated and hopeless. Quoting ultimatums such as Maurice Rimkus from Uvalde, "If you aren't going to fight for your water, then there ain't nothing worth fighting for" (Wood, 1988) "If it is a choice between our rights and the springs going down the tubes, let them go down the tubes" (Krausse, 1988). "We'll [the Uvalde delegation] will fight them all the way, even if we have to mortgage the family milk cow (Wood, 1988). "A lot of them [farmers] see it [the aquifer] the way they see gun control—you can have my water when you peel my cold, dead hand off my pump. Its that level of emotion," said Mr. Stagner, a San Antonio consultant (Gillman, 1990).

Moreover, although this particular event had ensued for only several years, newspaper articles depicted the conflict as "enduring" with such phrases as, "the last episode of a long-running dispute between rural and urban users" (Wood & Fuentes, 1990), "threats to sue are cries of blackmail in this long-running dispute," (Bower, 1991a) and "months of talk" (Crimmins, 1990b). Thus, even before the Edwards dispute reached volatile levels, the controversy was framed as stalled and hopeless. These depictions of intractability appeared immediately after the EUWD vote on the Regional Water Management Plan and became descriptors of the conflict during the polarization stage. In the aftermath of the pull out, these descriptors set the stage for mediation and for the legal battles that followed from this event.

3. Media Role in the EUWD Controversy

By relying exclusively on the content of the newspaper articles, it is difficult to determine what role the media plays in this controversy. However, an examination of the balance of coverage in these articles, partisanship of papers, and stance on issues in the articles suggests that the media did not function as a biased participant, nor a gatekeeper, consensus builder, or mediator. Overall, the media seems to assume the role of *tertius gaudens*, referring to the third party, outsider, who rejoices (Douglas, 1992). Arno and Dissanayke (1984) borrow this term from Simmel (1950) to discuss the structural logics of the third party when two are in conflict. The third party possesses autonomy and can, as a free agent, pursue its own narrow interests. The media needs societal conflict to function; and it profits from the continuation of conflict. To the extent that it acts in its own self-interest, and profits from it, it rejoices (Douglas, 1992, p. 268). In this exploratory study, the media seems to function as a storyteller that cast the scene, characters, and motives of an evolving melodrama. Its story is a tale of intractability, one that may or may not characterize the incidents as they occurred in 1988. However, the tale itself has become legend, one that contemporary players often recite.

4. Limitations and Future Directions

Given that this study is rooted in historical events, it may be very difficult to determine if the media's depiction of this early controversy parallels stakeholders' views of these events. Clearly, alternative sources of data are necessary to make projections about the way that stakeholders viewed these events and how stakeholder frames compared with media frames. This study is also limited in that the majority of articles on the EUWD were published in major newspapers and the UPI wire service. Our sample from newspapers published in the rural western counties did not contain many articles that date back to 1988–1990. Hence, differences between newspaper coverage in rural and urban areas could not be examined for this particular event, but will be explored for the other major events in this dispute.

However, this particular study is interesting from the way that the media framed institutional and environmental issues. Several observations can serve as insights for continued research. Of particular note, institutional frames surfaced when the media saw agencies as critical players in the disputes and when the identities of stakeholders became allied with agency interests. In this particular event, the environmental issues in the conflict were the shortage and rationing of water, the drying up of the springs, the potential threat to endangered species, a plan to register and permit wells, and a goal of pumping to a safe yield of 75 percent of the annual recharge. These issues, however, while presented early in the framing of the controversy, became lost as the media focused on the conflict itself. Thus, one concern for environmental reporters and media coverage of conflict is how to frame a dispute as it evolves from one stage to the next. By centering on a play-by-play analysis of the controversy, media coverage may inadvertently contribute to escalating a conflict through casting the issues as intractable.

What is important in this line of work is to see the media as a critical player in a complex, multifaceted dispute. Since the parties in this conflict are separated geographically and organizationally, media framing plays a very important role in documenting events, representing environmental concerns to the public, and forming images of the nature of a dispute.

REFERENCES

Ader, C. (1995). A longitudinal study of agenda setting for the issue of environmental pollution. *Journalism & Mass Communication Quarterly, 72(2)*, 300–311.

Aquifer 'river' ruling comes under assault; Hall suggests looking toward Canyon Lake. (1991, May 6). *San Antonio Express-News*, pp. 1A–2A.

Arno, A. & Dissanayke, W. (1984). *The news media in national and international conflict*. Boulder: Westview Publishers.

Bantz, C. R. (1985). News organizations: Conflict as a crafted cultural norm. *Communication, 8*, 225–244.

Bazerman, M. H. (1983). A critical look at rationality of negotiator judgment. *American Behavioral Scientist, 27*, 211–228.

Bingham, G. (1996). The growth of the environmental dispute resolution field. In G. Bingham, *Resolving environmental disputes: a decade of experience*. (pp. 13–63). Washington, D.C.: The Conservation Foundation.

Blomquist, W. (1992). Dividing the waters: *Governing groundwater in southern California*. San Francisco: Institute for Contemporary Studies.

Bower, T. (1991a, May 6). Aquifer 'river' ruling comes under assault; Lawmaker vows to thwart panel. *San Antonio Express-News*, p. 1A, 4A.

Bower, T. (1991b, May 12). Water chief blasts city on Applewhite, *San Antonio Express-News*, p. A4.

Burgess, H. & Burgess, G. (1997, March). *Constructive confrontation: A transformative approach to intractable conflicts*. Paper presented to the Conference on Environmental Conflict Resolution in the West, Tuscon, AZ.

Cantrill, J. G. & Oravec, C. L. (1996). *The symbolic earth: Discourse and our creation of the environment*. University of Kentucky Press.

Cappella, J. & Jamieson, K. (1997). *Spiral of cynicism*. New York: Oxford University Press.

Cohen, A. A., Adoni, H. & Bantz, C. R. (1990). *Social conflict and television news*. Newbury Park: Sage Publications.

Collier, B. (1988, November 2). Troubles for the Edwards regional management plan. *Houston Chronicle*, p. C7–C8.

Collier, B. (1990, February 25). Edwards in for a dry spell. *Austin American-Statesman*, p. B7.

Corbett, J. B. (1992). Rural and urban newspaper coverage of wildlife: Conflict, community and bureaucracy. *Journalism Quarterly, 69(4)*, 929–937.

Crimmins, P. (1990a, June 23). Regional plan for aquifer at dead end. *The San Antonio Light*, p. A3.

Crimmins, P. (1990b, June 28). Federal officials to look into aquifer situation. *The San Antonio Light*, p. A4.

Crimmins, P. (1990c, July 3). Aquifer negotiators float regional emergency plan. *Houston Chronicle*, p. B10.

Crimmins, P. (1990d, July 7). Agreement surfacing on acquifer plan. *The San Antonio Light*, p. A6.

Crimmins, P. (1990e, July 10). Limitation plan for aquifer doesn't hold water with U.S. *The San Antonio Light*, p. A3.

Crimmins, P. (1990f, November 2). New plan for aquifer surfaces; 'Breakthrough' offer is made to buy water from Medina Lake. *The San Antonio Light*, p. A1.

Crimmins, P. (1991, March 9). Hopes for agreement dry up as aquifer talks apparently end. *The San Antonio Light*, p. A1.

Crowfoot, J. E. & Wondolleck, J. M. (1990). *Environmental disputes: Community involvement in conflict resolution*. Washington, D.C.: Island Press.

Davis, J. J. (1995). The effects of message framing on response to environmental communications. *Journalism & Mass Communication Quarterly, 72(2)*, 285–299.

Davison, W. P. (1974). *Mass media and conflict resolution*. New York: Praeger.

Douglas, S. U. (1992). Negotiation audiences: The role of mass media. In L. L. Putnam & M. E. Roloff (Eds.). *Communication and negotiation* (pp. 250–272). Newbury Park, CA: Sage Publications.

Durham, F. D. (1998). News Frames as social narratives: TWA Flight 800. *Journal of Communication, 48(4)*, 100–117.

Edelman, M. (1993). Contestable categories and public opinion. *Political Communication, 10*, 231–242.

Entman, R. (1993). Framing: Toward clarification of a fractured paradigm. *Journal of Communication, 43(4)*, 51–58.

Elsbach, K. D. (1994). Managing organizational legitimacy in the California cattle industry: The construction and effectiveness of verbal accounts. *Administrative Science Quarterly, 39*, 57–78.

Felstiner, W. L. F., Abel, R. L. & Sarat, A. (1980–1981). The emergence and transformation of disputes: Naming, blaming, claiming. *Law and Society Review, 15*, 631–654.

Foss, M. G. (1996). "Whiskey is for drinking, water is for fighting over!" A case study analysis of the dispute concerning the Edwards Aquifer water supply. Unpublished manuscript, Texas A&M University.

Gilboa, E. (1998). Media diplomacy: Conceptual divergence and applications. *The Harvard International Journal of Press/Politics, 3*, 56–75.

Gillman, T. J. (1989, May 18). Compromise efforts for aquifer fail. *Dallas Morning News*, pp. A10, A11.

Gillman, T. J. (1990, August 19). Rural, urban interests collide over precious underground resource. *The Dallas Morning News*, p. B8.

Griffin, R. J. & Dunwoody, S. (1995). Impacts of information subsidies and community structure on local press coverage of environmental contamination. *Journalism & Mass Communication Quarterly, 72(2)*, 271–284.

Gray, B. (1997). Framing and reframing of intractable environmental disputes. In R. J. Lewicki, R. J. Bies & B. H. Sheppard (Eds.), *Research on Negotiation in Organizations, 6*, 163–188.

Iyengar, S. & Simon, A. (1993). News coverage of the Gulf crisis and public opinion: A study of agenda-setting, priming, and framing. *Communication Research, 20*, 365–383.

Jensen, R. (1988). A new approach to regional Water Management; Two plans are developed to manage and protect the Edwards Aquifer. *Texas Water Resources, 14*, 1–6.

Krausse, H. (1989, June 3). Edwards Aquifer water level sinking to near-record low. *Austin American-Statesman*, p. A1.

Krausse, H. (1988, July 24). San Antonio strengthens effort to protect aquifer. *Austin American-Statesman*, p. B3.

Kriesberg, L. (1993). Intractable conflicts. *Peace Review, 5(4)*, 417–421.

Kriesberg, L., Northrup, T. A. & Thorson, S. J. (Eds.), *Intractable conflicts and their transformation*. (pp. 13–24). Syracuse: Syracuse University Press.

McComas, K. & Shanahan, J. (1999). Telling stories about global climate change: Measuring the impact of narratives on issue cycles. *Communication Research, 26(1)*, 30–57.

Michaels, J. & Lewis, J. (1989, May 28). Mayor fears worst, pushes for aquifer legislation. *The San Antonio Light*, p. A4.

Neale, M. A. & Bazerman, M. H. (1991). *Cognition and rationality in negotiation*. New York: Free Press.

Neuzil, M. & Kovarik, W. (1996). *Mass media and environmental conflict: America's green crusades*. Thousand Oaks: Sage.

Norris, P. (1995). The restless searchlight: Network news framing of the post-cold war world. *Political Communication, 12*, 357–370.

Ostrom, E. (1990). *Governing the commons: The evolution of institutions for collective action*. New York: Cambridge University Press.

Ostrom, E., Gardner, R. & Walker, J. (1994). *Rules, games, and common-pool resources*. Ann Arbor, MI: University of Michigan Press.

Pan, Z. & Kosicki, G. M. (1993). Framing analysis: An approach to news discourse. *Political Communication, 10*, 59–79.

Patternson, T. (1993). *Out of order*. New York: Knopf.

Patterson, J. D. & Allen, M. W. (1997). Accounting for your actions: How stakeholders respond to the strategic communication of environmental activist organizations. *Journal of Applied Communication Research, 25*, 293–316.

Price, V., Tewksbury, D. & Powers, E. (1997). Switching trains of thought: The impact of news frames on readers' cognitive responses. *Communication Research, 24*, 481–506.

Putnam, L. L. & Fairhurst, G. T. (2001). Discourse analysis in organizations. In F. M. Jablin and L. L. Putnam (Eds.), *The New Handbook of Organizational Communication* (pp. 78–136). Newbury Park, CA: Sage.

Reese, S. D., Gandy, O. H. & Grant, A. E. (Eds.), (2001). *Framing public life: Perspectives on media and our understanding of the social world*. Hillsdale, NJ: Lawrence Erlbaum Associates, Inc.

Schlechtweg, H. P. (1996). Media frames and environmental discourse: The case of "Focus: Logjam." In J. G. Cantrill & C. L. Oravec (Eds.), *The symbolic Earth: Discourse and our creation of the environment* (pp. 257–277). Louisville, KY: University of Kentucky Press.

Scheufele, D. A. (1999). Framing as a theory of media effects. *Journal of Communication, 49(1)*, 103–122.

Semetko, H. A. & Valkenburg, P. M. (2000). Framing European politics: A content analysis of press and television news. *Journal of Communication, 50(2)*, 93–109.

Sierra Club enters water dispute. (1990, April 18). *Houston Chronicle*, p. A4.

Simmel, G. (1950). *The Sociology of George Simmel* (K. H. Wolff, Ed.). Glencoe, IL: Free Press.

Texas Water Resources Institute. (1993). Legislature agrees on compromise to manage Edwards Aquifer. *Texas Water Resources, 19(3)*, 1–13.

Tolson, M. (1988, July 29). Regional water plan approved by council. *The San Antonio Light*, pp. A1, A6.

Valkenburg, P. M., Semetko, H. A. & de Vreese, C. (1999). The effect of news frames on readers' recall and thoughts. *Communication Research, 26*, 550–568.

Votteler, T. H. (1998). The little fish that roared: The Endangered Species Act, State groundwater law, and private property rights collide over the Texas Edwards Aquifer. *Environmental Law, 28(4)*, 845–879.

Wolff, N. (1997a). Water Wars—I. *Mayor; An Inside View of San Antonio Politics, 1981–1995*. (pp. 65–77). San Antonio, TX: San Antonio Express-News.

Wolff, N. (1997b). Water Wars—II. *Mayor; An Inside View of San Antonio Politics*. (pp. 369–395). San Antonio, TX: San Antonio Express-News.

Wolfsfeld, G. (1997). *Media and political conflict: News from the Middle East*. Cambridge: Cambridge University Press.

Wood, J. (1988a, June 25). EUWD, city prepares water rationing plea. *San Antonio Express-News*, p. A4.

Wood, J. (1988b, November 15). Uvalde farmers to fight proposed legislation, *San Antonio Express News*, p. A7.

Wood, J. & Fuentes, D. R. (1990, June 30). South Texans ready to fight for aquifer. *San Antonio Express-News*, pp. A3–A8.

PART II. MEDIA AND POLICY

CHAPTER 7

SOURCES, THE MEDIA AND THE REPORTING OF CONFLICT

Howard Tumber

A. INTRODUCTION

Recent work on the empirical sociology of news production and journalism has concentrated on or re-emphasised the role of sources in the "manufacture" of news. One of the most interesting developments has been an examination of the relationship between different sources—"official" and "non-official" and between sources and the media. In the past, a vast majority of research into the sociology of news sources tended to be "media centric" and failed to examine the source-media relationship from the sources viewpoint. The important role of official sources in government and civil service in shaping and framing the news agenda through the interaction with journalists is generally acknowledged by most empirical studies of news production (Schlesinger & Tumber, 1994, p. 22).

Source-media analyses have become an important element in understanding the kinds of news we receive. The part played by sources in the media production process has been explored recently in various different representations including crime, the environment, politics, business and war and conflict (*cf.* Schlesinger & Tumber, 1994; Ericson *et al.*, 1989; Anderson, 1997; Bennett, 1990; Tumber, 1993b; Hallin, 1986; Miller, 1993). In their study of the criminal justice arena, Schlesinger and Tumber (1994) set out to analyze the behavior of political actors and their role as news sources.—"Crucial to the study of news sources are the relations between the media and the exercise of political and ideological power, especially, but not exclusively, by central social institutions that seek to define and manage the flow of information in contested fields of discourse" (1994, p. 16). The principle of Wolfsfeld's (1997a, 1997b) political contest model appears to adopt a similar position, namely that "the best way to understand the role of the press in politics is to view the competition over the news media as part of a larger and more significant contest for political control" (1997b, p. 30).[1]

---

[1] Despite the use of different conceptual terms, Wolfsfeld's ideas on the role of the Israeli media in the Oslo Peace process makes the comparison with studies carried out on domestic policy such as the criminal justice system a useful exercise in understanding how source behavior occurs.

One aspect of the theoretical debate about sources centers on questions of "primary definition." To what extent do official sources maintain a structured access to the media by means of their dominant positions in power? There are a number of problems in the concept of "primary definition," a general formulation of the social production of news put forward by Stuart Hall and his colleagues (1978). Hall *et al.* maintain that media statements are grounded in "objective" and "authoritative statements from sources" accredited by virtue of their institutional power and position. They argue that the nature of news production inevitably leads to a "systematically structured *over-accessing* to the media of those in powerful and privileged institutional positions. The result of the structured preference given by the media to the opinions of the powerful is that these 'spokesmen' become what we call the *primary definers* of topics. This then allows the institutional definers to "establish the initial definition or *primary interpretation* of the topic in question. This interpretation then 'commands the field' in all subsequent treatment and sets the terms of reference within which all further coverage takes place" (Hall *et al.*, 1978, pp. 58–59, see also Schlesinger & Tumber, 1994, p. 17).

While acknowledging the political and economic constraints that undoubtedly limit access to the news media, it is important to recognize the resistances to domination and ideological competition, and the competitive strategies for media attention employed by news sources situated outside the centers of power (1994, p. 16).

Of the criticisms of "primary definition" made by Schlesinger and Tumber, three are particularly appropriate to this discussion. First is the absence of account in primary definition of the possible contention between official sources in attempting to influence the construction of news stories. For example, conflict between members of the same government or between government and the military. Second is the overstating of the passivity of the media. Primary definition is seen as moving uniformly from power centers to the media. No account is taken within the concept of the occasions when the "media may themselves take the initiative in the definitional process by challenging the so-called primary definers and forcing them to respond" (1994, p. 19). Investigative journalism is the prime example of this, digging out scandals inside government, exploiting leaks by dissident figures and forcing out "undesired and unintended official responses" (1994, p. 19). Third, the conception of "primary definition" is characterized as possessing a lack of curiosity about the way sources may "engage in ideological conflict prior to, or contemporaneous with, the appearance of 'definitions' in the media." In effect the concept rules out any analysis of the process of negotiation concerning questions of policy that may occur prior to the emergence of primary definitions (1994, p. 20).

There is no doubt that the views and interests of authoritative sources are generally promoted by the operation of news organizations and the practice of journalism but "because the conception of 'primary definition' resolves the question of source power on the basis of structuralist assumptions, it closes off any engagement with the dynamic processes of contestation in a field of discourse." (Schlesinger & Tumber, 1994, p. 20–21)

The studies by Schlesinger and Tumber and by Hall and his colleagues involved empirically researched areas of domestic policy within the criminal justice arena in Britain, although the theoretical formulations are intended to apply to other fields as well. A closely related study is the three-volume work by Richard Ericson and his colleagues who investigated the reporting of crime and deviance in Toronto (see, in particular, Ericson *et al.*, 1989). They argue that a more complex arrangement exists than one of uncontested dominance of the news agenda by well-endowed sources. While acknowledging that authoritative sources attempt, usually successfully, to manage the flow of information to the new media, "their room for manoeuvre varies according to the institutions setting in which any given set of source-media relations take place" (Schlesinger & Tumber, 1994, p. 32, Ericson *et al.*, 1989, p. 378).

The concern with the role of sources has not been confined to the area of criminal justice alone. A similar attempt to analyze the source-media relationship has been a feature of the empirical sociology of the media for decades but the emphasis has been from the journalists' perspective rather than the source. Interestingly, some of the recent work on war and conflict has provided some insights into the source-media relationship. The concern with censorship, propaganda and information management has characterized much of the work. But while censorship in the reporting of domestic policy has not featured as prominently as that of foreign engagement, information management and political public relations *have* been a significant aspect of government political behavior over the last two decades. In Britain a growing professionalization of expertise in the management of public information emerged during the Thatcher administration in Britain (Tumber, 1993a).

One explanation often put forward by governments and institutions to account for changes in public opinion and the reduction in public support for their particular policies is that the "message is not getting accross." One of the principal features of recent change has been the move from a reactive mode of behavior to a proactive one involving the increasing use of long-term promotional strategies by governments, political parties, institutions and corporate interests to promote their image and influence policy making (Tumber, 1995, p. 511). The culture of promotionalism has taken over many areas of public life. For government the break down of party identification and partisanship has led politicians to turn increasingly to political consultants and public relations advisors to get themselves elected and once in office continued to employ these spin doctors and professional communicators to promote themselves and maintain public approval for their policies. Information management has thus pervaded all aspects of government behavior whether it is directed towards domestic or foreign policy (Wernick 1991, p. 135; Berkman & Kitch, 1986, p. 147).

B. WAR AND CONFLICT

Recent studies on war and conflict provide a fruitful field for exploring the conjunction between the formulations discussed earlier in the studies on criminal justice and those considered in research on international conflict. In his study of the U.S. media and the Vietnam war (Hallin, 1986) argued that the way the media report events is closely tied to the degree of consensus among the political elite, the "sphere of consensus" as he labels it. Hallin's view contrasts with the conservative analysis of the media as "anti-establishment" institutions which were undermining the authority of governing institutions (Hallin, 1994, p. 11) The explanation for the media" "volte face" in its support for the war was grounded in the "commitment to the ideology and the routines of objective journalism"; up to 1967 there was relatively little disagreement among the policy elite and reflecting this official viewpoint did not "seem to violate the norms of objective journalism" (1994, pp. 52–53).

The gradual breaking down of the national security consensus and the Cold War ideology among the political elite, together with the concern over the conduct of the war, was reflected in the coverage by the news media. The media was able to respond to the growing strains and divisions within the foreign policy elite by producing far higher amounts of critical news coverage "without abandoning objective journalism for some activist and anti-establishment conception of their role." As opposition to the war moved into the mainstream, the news media reflected this movement of debate into "the sphere of legitimate controversy." The media reflect the prevailing pattern of political debate: "when consensus is strong, they tend to stay within the limits of the political discussion it defines; when it begins to break down, coverage becomes increasingly critical and diverse in the viewpoints it represents, and increasingly difficult for officials to control" (1994, p. 55).

One response from officials to the emergence of critical coverage of international conflict is to increase censorship and attack news organizations for their "unpatriotic" behavior. The latter corresponds to "flak," the fourth filter of Herman and Chomsky's propaganda model (1994). In these cases the media may be regularly assailed, threatened and "corrected" (often by govenment) in order to try and contain any deviations from the established line (1994, pp. 26–28). During the Falklands conflict, for example, attacks were made on the BBC, the Guardian and the Daily Mirror by the government, conservative MPs and sections of the press for their supposedly unpatriotic coverage at a time when questions began to form over the problems that could arise should a long campaign develop in the Falklands. While fulfilling an important element of tactical advantage, the attacks on media organizations during the Falklands campaign could also be interpreted as "part of a more far-reaching effort to loosen the liberal intelligentsia's grip on public symbolic life by neo-conservatives eager to settle permanently the cultural landscape in their own market-dominated image" (Morrison & Tumber,

1988, p. 354).[2] Similarly, the imposition of censorship in Northern Ireland can be viewed as part of a wider set of relationships concerning the flow of sensitive information between the media and the "secret state" (Schlesinger, 1987, p. xxiii).

The "flak" exhibited by the government towards sections of the media during the Falklands conflict bore a striking similarity to the challenges made on broadcasters over current affairs programs about Northern Ireland.

Incidents of censorship and attacks on news organizations by the British government directed predominantly towards current affairs and documentary programs on Northern Ireland have been a feature of the last 30 years. The list of affected news and current affairs programs is too long to detail here[3] but overt and manifest government censorship reached its height in 1988 when Douglas Hurd, the Home Secretary banned the broadcasting of the voices of members of proscribed organizations by the terrestrial television and radio stations. The ban led to the ridiculous sight of television images of Sinn Fein representatives having their voices dubbed by actors (see Henderson *et al.*, 1990).[4]

It is evident that, as policy agreement moves from the "sphere of consensus" to the "sphere of legitimate controversy," governments and administrations become concerned at the possible loss of the news agenda. Censorship and flak consequently become prominent features of their response to the increase in media activity as journalists begin to question government statements and become more sensitive to other official and non-official viewpoints (Hallin, 1994, p. 71; see also Morrison & Tumber, 1988, p. 228).

---

[2] The 1980s signalled a transformation in the broadcasting environment with repeated challenges to the BBC over its method of funding and to the Independent Television terrestrial companies over their restrictive practices. It was the desire of the Conservative government to implement change and challenge the current public service system that some viewed as underlining the attacks on broadcasters over their coverage of the Falklands conflict and Northern Ireland.

[3] Highlights include a BBC *Tonight* (1979) interview with a representative of the Irish National Liberation Army that resulted in representations being made to the BBC by government ministers, opposition spokesmen and questions in Parliament. A BBC *Panorama* program (1980) (not transmitted) containing film of an IRA roadblock in Carrickmore, which led to denunciations of the BBC in Parliament. *At the Edge of the Union* (1985) an episode of The BBC *Real Lives* documentary series that included an interview with a leading member of Sinn Fein. Intensive pressure from the Home Secretary was put on the BBC to ban the program. This caused a split within the BBC when its Govenors acceded to the governments' request. *Death on the Rock* (1988) a program in Thames Television's *This Week* series investigating the shooting dead of suspected IRA terrorists by the SAS in Gibraltar. The program resulted in interventions by the Prime Minister and Foreign Secretary. For detailed accounts of these important episodes, *see* Schlesinger 1978; Schlesinger *et al.*, 1983; Bolton, 1990; Rolston, 1991; Miller, 1994).

[4] Carruthers (1995, 1996) examines a number of examples of propaganda and censorship in British colonial wars during this period showing that the British governments' attitude to and actions regarding the media and terrorism, from the end of the first World War to the present time, have a degree of consistency.

A similar formulation of source behavior to account for press-government relations is Bennett's (1990) "indexing hypothesis": "Mass media news professionals, from the boardroom to the beat, tend to 'index' the range of voices and viewpoints in both news and editorials according to the range of views expressed in mainstream government debate about a given topic" (1990, p. 106). According to the hypothesis, non-official sources only appear in news stories when their opinions are "already emerging in official circles." The possibility of contention between official sources is acknowledged and this is sometimes reflected in the news media, but when that institutional opposition collapses, even if public opinion is opposed to a particular policy, the volume of opposition in news and editorials is indexed accordingly. In effect the news media revert to the established line at the expense of the democratic ideal (1990, p. 113). Even in the Watergate scandal, the classic case of investigative journalism, Bennett contends that the story was "indexed according to the more pronounced political decisions and definitions offered up" by official sources (1990, p. 124). Bennett argues that normative pressures to use the hypothesis are so strong that the press will report a story within a consensus framework even knowing that policy opponents exist but may have been silenced through the corruption of the democratic process (1996, p. 377).[5]

In exploring the coverage of three military interventions that won bipartisan support in Washington, Mermin (1996) concurs with the indexing hypothesis but adds an amendment to the effect that the major media are doing something to maintain the illusion of fulfilling the journalistic ideals of balance and objectivity. What the news media present as subject to question and debate "is the *ability of the government to achieve the goals it has set*. When there is no policy debate in Washington, reporters may offer critical analysis *inside the terms of the apparently settled policy debate*, finding a critical angle in the possibility that existing policy on its own terms might not work" (1996, p. 182).

Focussing on this "critical angle" helps to explain the perception among politicians and business leaders, that American journalists are overly independent and critical of government and also illustrates that there is a significant element of present-day conflict in the news. Some journalism can find conflicting possibilities in the effectiveness of the government of achieving its own goals but "does not present the policy decision that set those goals in the first place as open to critical analysis and debate" (Mermin, 1996, p. 182). This view offers an explanation of the "Vietnam syndrome," the belief that the media lost the war and the battle for public opinion. The "lessons" of Vietnam were incorporated, by the

---

5 Bennett cites an incident of the reporting of Reagan's policy on Nicaragua in 1986, on the eve of the election, when Democrat opposition to the administration line was silenced in the face of a "red scare" dirty tricks campaign run by the White House. Bennett reports that the mainstream press told the story through a policy consensus framework rather than to continue to report the serious doubts of the now politically neutered opponents (1996, p. 377).

British government and military, in their formulation and implementation of information policy during the Falklands conflict. These policies were further developed by U.S. officials in dealing with the media during the invasions of Panama and Grenada, and honed to a higher degree in co-ordinating the effort in the Gulf War and subsequently in Kosovo and Afghanistan. (See Hallin, 1986; Morrison & Tumber, 1988; Mowlana *et al.*, 1992; Bennett & Paletz, 1994.)

To fulfil the idea of independent, balanced coverage when official sources are united behind a particular policy, journalists attempt to fill the void "by finding conflicting possibilities in the efforts of officials to achieve the goals they have set" (Mermin, 1996, p. 191). In cases concerning the effectiveness of government policy, the reader-viewer is a spectator to the "political game" with the tools to predict whether the leadership is likely to win or lose; whereas the focus of policy formulation views the reader-viewer as a citizen with the tools to deliberate on the soundness of the President's decision (1996, p. 191). When there is consensus therefore, in the policy formulation, the vigilant reporting may rest solely on the effectiveness and the politics of the policy's execution. Mermin does not see his argument as contradicting the indexing hypothesis. Rather "seeing the critical angle that is covered may help to account for the conviction of journalists that they offer independent, balanced reporting, and the view of politicians that the media are highly critical, perceptions the indexing hypothesis does not convincingly explain" (1996, p. 189).

Mermin sees his amendment as strengthening the indexing hypothesis particularly in the area of foreign policy where most of the work on indexing has been conducted. His view is that in the realm of foreign policy the use of governmental sources will predominate strengthening the indexing affect. The question of how generalizable the findings may be to domestic policy remains but the likelihood is that non-governmental sources are consulted on domestic issues with alternate opinions represented more frequently (1996, p. 191).

C. NORTHERN IRELAND

Before suggesting a further conceptual development concerning the reporting of conflict, I want to look at some aspects of the initial press coverage of Northern Ireland in May 1997.

One of Tony Blair's first acts on becoming Prime Minister after his sweeping landslide victory in the May 1, 1997, elections in the U.K. was to arrange a meeting with his fellow Irish Prime Minister, John Bruton. This signalled a new wave of optimism about the peace process reflected in the way that the news media portrayed the meeting. Headlines such as "Bruton's Hope After No. 10 Talks" (*The Guardian 9.5.97*). The story, written by the Guardian's chief political correspondent reported the meeting at 10 Downing Street, was phrased in fairly optimistic tones, stressing the huge parliamentary majority that Blair now enjoys. An editorial on the same day in *The Guardian*, while bemoaning the fact that the Northern

Irish electorate had voted along traditional sectarian lines as usual, did signal some optimism that the Labour government, having such a large majority, might be able to move the peace process forward but stated the usual obstacles and problems that would inevitably have to be overcome should real progress hope to be made.

Shortly after this meeting in London, Tony Blair paid a visit to Northern Ireland on May 16, 1997, his first visit anywhere outside England and made a speech in Belfast. The positive tone was again reflected in the national daily British press the following day (May 17, 1997). All the "quality" broadsheet newspapers led their front pages with the story:—"Blair takes gamble for Ulster peace," *The Times*; "Blair offers a fresh start for Irish peace, *The Independent*; "Blair bids to Break Ulster deadlock," *The Daily Telegraph*; "Blair seeks progress on Ulster peace," *Financial Times*; and echoing Munich in 1938, "Peace in their time?," *The Guardian*.

The optimistic tone was a feature of the stories as well as the headlines. *The Times* wrote "Hopes rose last night that Mr Blair may have kick started the faltering peace talks." The article contrasted Blair's stance on wasting "little time in inviting Sinn Fein to the multi-party talks" with that of John Major's position, "who faced a barrage of criticism from nationalists when he waited three months after the 1994 IRA cease-fire before allowing Sinn Fein to join 'exploratory talks' with officials." Inside on the "politics and government" pages, *The Times* had a picture of Blair in Northern Ireland with a caption underneath: "Tony Blair in Armagh during his visit to Northern Ireland yesterday, where he attempted to kick-start the faltering peace process" (p. 14). *The Financial Times* carried the same picture on its front page but with the caption: "Tony Blair greets well-wishers in Armagh yesterday on his first prime ministerial visit to Ulster." The FT also included a piece, on its inside pages, commenting on Blair's speech. *The Independent* quoted John Hume, the leader of the nationalist Social and Democratic Labour Party saying that "people owed Blair a 'debt of gratitude'" and that "he had 'delivered the most comprehensive speech made by any Prime Minister in the last 25 years of our Troubles'." *The Telegraph* provided extracts of Blair's speech in addition to its main story that included quotes from the Prime Minister.

The editorials, at least in their headlines, endorsed the hopes of the front-page political stories. "Blair's Brave Start" stated *The Times*. *The Independent* placed its leader on the front page: "The Moment is ripe for the Brave." "Blair's Irish touch" headed *The Telegraph's* editorial that began by providing transatlantic comparisons of the first flush of electoral victory: "Rather like a new American president descending on an aircraft carrier, this visit to the province symbolised the gravity of the burdens of state that now fall upon his shoulders." Not normally a supporter of Labour administrations, *The Telegraph* in its leader went on to praise Mr Blair's "promising sureness of touch." The general sentiment of all the editorials was that Blair has the authority to move the peace process forward building on the momentum of Major's administration which, in its early stages, had achieved some progress but recently had allowed the momentum to stagnate. They all urged the Republicans, once again, to call a cease-fire and join the talks: "grasp the olive branch or face the consequences" *The Times*; "Are the Provos brave enough to seize it?" *The Independent*.

The Telegraph was more pessimistic stating that the ". . . northern national-ists were becoming greener" and shed doubt on Blair's contention "that everyone now supports the principle of consent." *The Telegraph's* piece ended by intimat-ing splits within the new administration, questioning the role of Mo Mowlem, Blair's new Northern Ireland Secretary, and suggesting that he "keep a careful eye on her in the months to come." *The Guardian* editorial was headed "A new open-ing in Belfast—will Blair's frankness pay off" and while praising Blair's perfor-mance and gestures to date, ended on a note of caution about the IRA's reaction: ". . . If the considered response is more positive, then Mr Blair may be on the verge of facilitating the breakthrough which Mr Major strove for but fumbled. If it is negative or, as we have come to expect, simply evasive, then it is hard to be optimistic about the immediate future of Northern Ireland in spite of Mr Blair's assured debut there." The *Financial Times* left no doubt as to what it saw as the key element. "Calling Sinn Fein's bluff" was the title of its leader and reiterated the point that ". . . The only remaining obstacle to republicanism's inclusion (in the talks) is its own violence." All the editorials mentioned the assurances to the unionists and the retention of a permanent veto.

The mid-market and tabloid press carried the story on their inside pages. *The Express*, optimistic in tone, headlined its report "Blair offers Ulster the hand of peace" beneath the same picture as the one in the *Financial Times* and *The Times* but with the caption "Welcome: The Prime Minister shakes hands with well-wish-ers in Armagh during a visit designed to stress the importance he attaches to peace in Ulster" (p. 9). The *Daily Mail* was more direct with its headline "Blair's last-chance offer to Sinn Fein" and in the story suggested that Blair was making "a marked policy shift" in appealing to Sinn Fein to ". . . come in from the cold and help work towards a permanent terrorist cease-fire" (p. 2).

The tabloid *Sun* headed its report "Blair There's a Will There's a Way" (p. 2). The story likened Blair to a pop idol "'Pop star' Tony brings new hope to Ulster" and in an editorial entitled "Good feeling" quoted from Blair's speech "'The set-tlement train is leaving,' he told Sinn Fein and the IRA. 'I want you on that train. But it is leaving anyway, and I will not allow it to wait for you.' What a refresh-ing difference after the dithering of Mr Wait And See (John Major). All aboard the Blair express we're enjoying the ride." (p. 6). *The Mirror* spread the story over one and a half pages, used six pictures of Blair's visit to Northern Ireland and headlined "Tony Blair Wows Crowds Who Yearn For Peace." Whereas all the other papers concentrated on Blair's speech, *The Mirror* described his visit to Ulster and his rapturous reception from the ordinary people who he met in the streets and shops. A separate piece reporting the speech and entitled "PM Lifts Talks Ban" was also included in *The Mirror's* coverage. *The Mirror's* leader called Blair the "Bold New Champion of Peace." The editorial line went further than the other papers in its willingness to allow Sinn Fein in to the "fold." (p. 6).

Discussion of possible solutions or further progress to the intractable problems of Northern Ireland were undoubtedly caught up in the general euphoria sweeping Britain that a new era had begun after 18 years of Conservative rule. It was the *Daily Mail*, the most hysterical newspaper opponent of New Labour during the election campaign that provided the most perceptive editorial.[6] Headed "Mr Blair should be wary of the cheers" it stated, "Tony Blair can hardly have been surprised by the ecstatic cheers which welcomed him to Northern Ireland yesterday. For the past two weeks he has been greeted with enthusiasm and genuine excitement wherever he goes. Few Prime Ministers have ever swept into office on such a high tide of public expectation." Eschewing churlishness, the leader explained the euphoria over Blair and praised the way the new government had behaved "in a way that puts the do-nothing Tories to shame." It warned, though, that expectations may be "running unrealistically high" and that even if it avoided all mistakes, "it still has tough and inevitable unpopular decisions to take. The sense of let down could be all the more painful" (p. 10).

Governments with big parliamentary majorities normally have a better chance of making progress on policy implementation and execution. Blair's position then was similar to the position of the Thatcher government in the mid-1980s that enjoyed a 144 seat majority after the election in 1983. The Conservative government, at the time, was able to secure the Anglo-Irish Agreement, incorporating greater ties with the Irish government over the governance of Northern Ireland. In response the media usually reflect the optimistic noises that emanate from government after securing a huge majority.

Before the election of the (New) Labour government in 1997, the most recent defining phase of journalistic behaviour occurred during the period from the time of the Hume-Adams initiative in September 1993 until the Canary Wharf bomb in London's docklands in February 1996 effectively ending the IRA cease-fire. The emergence of the peace initiatives caught journalists unaware and the anti-terrorism paradigm, existing for the last 26 years in Northern Ireland and reflected in the media reporting of the conflict, was in crisis. From a position that "terrorism" especially republican terrorism was the cause of the conflict, and the only way forward for peace was to defeat the IRA, the British government now regarded Sinn Fein as having "a legitimate electoral mandate" and at some point should have a place at the negotiating table (Miller & Mclaughlin, 1996, p. 436).

---

6 The entire front page of the *Daily Mail* April 30, 1997, the day before polling, carried a picture of the Union Jack with the words: "There is a terrible danger that the British people, drugged by the seductive mantra 'It's time for a change,' are stumbling, eyes glazed, into an election that could undo 1,000 years of our nation's history."

Miller and Mclaughlin argue that the media reporting of the peace process between September 1993 and May 1994, which included the revelations that officials of the British government had been engaged in secret contacts with members of Sinn Fein, exhibited a "lack of perspective." Slavishly following the government line without acknowledging the possible "spin" on events is difficult to defend especially when the government was caught misleading the media and the public. "Either the government is engaged in an honest attempt to progress the peace process by political propaganda and news management or they are engaged in information management and propaganda to cover up their duplicity" (1996, p. 436). The British media defended the government for its "principled" line even as it moved towards further negotiations with "terrorists." Should the peace process advance any further, other shifts in government positions will be framed in a similar way by the news media. "One day soon, with barely a ripple, we might find that British opinion, journalism and political culture has been radically changed" (1996, p. 436).

Since 1969 most news stories about Northern Ireland were conflict related with violence the main ingredient (cf. Elliot, 1977; Schlesinger, 1987). Official sources in Northern Ireland have operated a dual strategy with regard to media coverage. As well as painting Northern Ireland as a battle zone where violence is endemic, the Northern Ireland Office, on occasions, has pointed to the positive aspects of the province and the "spirited resolve" of its people (Miller, 1993, p. 395). The concentration on violence by the news media therefore is not a simple reflection of the dominant definitions of the conflict by authoritative sources. While the "terrorism" coverage is framed within the "official" government position, "those same sources are still not able to secure the prominence they would like for stories about the 'other side' of life in Northern Ireland." The 'good news' part of British strategy meets with *relatively* little success in the news media.[7] Case studies of the news reporting of Northern Ireland have shown that breakdowns of official government policy and public relations sometimes occur. This is especially interesting in the case of Northern Ireland because of the belief that "official" sources totally dominate the news agenda and that opposition or alternative sources are unable to intervene with much success in the public sphere (1993, p. 397).

---

[7] The attitude of the Northern Ireland Information Service, the propaganda arm of the British government, adopted a different strategy when dealing with the population in Northern Ireland to the audience back in Britain. One reason why the journalists in Northern Ireland were not given the same priority by the NIIS was the relative unimportance and considered lack of influence of the media they represented. The Press in Northern Ireland was seen as being part of the problem too. The main reason for this attitude was the view that the Northern Ireland newspapers were sectarian both in their editorial policy and amongst their readership. It was believed that the key objectives of British information policy, such as contextualising and re-legitimizing terrorism were less likely to have a productive outcome among the Belfast newspapers. One reason suggested for this was the Belfast newspapers closeness to the "Troubles" and both their awareness and willingness to articulate the mini-context of terrorism (Bromley, 1997).

Applying Mermin's amendment to the reporting of Northern Ireland, the bipartisan political approach of the two main political parties in Britain to the Northern Ireland conflict suggests that much of the "critical gaze" lies within the judgment of policy execution. Certainly the reporting of the peace process in the latter part of Major's administration which focused on the breakdown of talks and Major's reliance on the Ulster Unionist MPs for parliamentary survival, might "fit" the idea of "conflict in the sphere of consensus." An important question though, is when do the news media begin to offer this questioning of the policy goals. If it occurs immediately then presumably "indexing" is in operation. Does a honeymoon period of critical abstinence on policy effectiveness exist in the national media? If so, how long Blair's lasts on Northern Ireland remains an empirically researchable question. The difficulty of testing Mermin's "critical gaze" is that support for a particular policy is often bound up with general support for a government. Once this dissipates then all policy goals may be subjected to journalistic criticism irrespective of whether there is a breakdown in the "sphere of consensus." If the honeymoon continues then the news media may eschew offering critical analysis of policy execution inside the bipartisan consensus. The size of the electoral mandate may also act as a break on media criticism.

The case of John Major's government is an interesting one. It could be argued that for four and a half years from September 1992 following "Black Wednesday"[8] when the government lost most of its credibility, the majority of policy goals were questioned through media coverage. It may also be the case that scandal may envelop a government to the extent that all policy is subjected to journalistic criticism.

A further point is the effect on public opinion. As long as the policy upon which war is fought is accepted as correct, news reports or pictures while disturbing will not necessarily weaken support for the war or possess the power of social disruption. "It is only if genuine questioning of policy is taking place, sufficient to enquire over the legitimacy of the exercise, that news, indeed all news, even battle victories, becomes bad news" (Morrison & Tumber, 1988, p. 349). This is the problem for governments posed by current affairs and documentary programs. "News can become an articulator of concern when the images presented interact with other information that questions the validity of policy. It is current affairs, with its tradition of challenge and discussion, the airing of opin-

---

8   Black Wednesday, September 16, 1972, was the day Britain suspended sterling membership of the ERM (European exchange rate mechanism). Sterling opened that day under intense pressure and despite Bank of England attempts, by buying pounds with reserves of foreign currency to push up the rate, the pound remained under pressure. Despite raising interest rates to 12 percent and then 15 percent the Treasury realized the position was hopeless. The financial markets assumed devaluation. By the end of the week the pound had fallen 6 percent below the old ERM floor. The Conservatives, always seen as the party best able to manage the economy, lost credibility from that point and were unable to garner public opinion throughout the next four and a half years up to the election of May 1997 when they suffered a landslide defeat.

ion and dissenting voices, which has the capability, of assembling pictures shown by the news into a different framework of reception" (1988, p. 349).

In the context of Northern Ireland, the key moments of tension arising out of media-government relations have been disagreements over documentary programs and current affairs television. In attempting to provide a theoretical framework to comprehend representation of policy whether it is of formulation or execution, account must be taken of the difference in that representation between news and current affairs. This is not a point discussed at length by Hallin, Bennett or Mermin.

It is not always clear when a government or President's honeymoon dissipates. In the case of New Labour in Britain, the final six months of 1998 may come to be interpreted as the beginning of the end of the press honeymoon with Blair. But like former President Clinton's opinion poll ratings in the United States, New Labour remained the most popular mid-term government since records began despite being enmeshed in media-reported scandal.[9] What is required is a window of opportunity to test whether the critical gaze over policy execution begins in earnest if support for the government seriously declines and, secondly, if an acknowledged post-honeymoon period evolves among the public whether policy formulation becomes unpacted in media coverage.

Mermin's amendment to the indexing hypothesis would suggest that coverage of policies enjoying bipartisan support receive some critical comment on policy execution. In some cases though and Northern Ireland is one, even policy execution may avoid the critical gaze not just for "honeymoon" reasons but also because of the strong bipartisanship of the policy. This may change because, as of December 2001, the opposition Conservative Party is planning to drop its bipartisan approach to the Northern Ireland conflict.

The announcement or presentation of peace agreements enjoys a honeymoon period with the media. The Good Friday Agreement of April 10, 1998 received very positive coverage in the national media. The media love a peace deal especially the excitement of all night negotiations culminating in a signing and shak-

---

[9] The (New) Labour government, first elected May 1997, had to deal with a number of media reported scandals including the revelations about the private life of the Foreign Secretary, Robin Cook; the resignation of the Secretary of State for Trade and Industry, Peter Mandelson and Treasury Minister Geoffrey Robinson over a controversial house loan; the resignation of the Welsh Secretary, Ron Davies amid accusations of gay sex after being mugged in London; the exposure of adultery by Tourism Minister, Janet Anderson; the charges of electoral fraud by Labour MPs, Fiona Jones and Mohammad Sarwar; the resignation of Ministerial aide Derek Draper amidst allegations of cash for gaining access to ministers and influencing decisions— known as lobbygate; the admission of the Agriculture Secretary that he was gay; and the revelation that the boss of Formula One, Bernie Ecclestone, had donated £1million to the Labour Party before the election and once elected the Labour government ruled out banning tobacco advertising in grand prix motor racing.

ing of hands. Television screens live coverage of the "event," and, in the past, often changed established schedules to provide coverage. As Dayan and Katz (1992) describe about special media events "they are *interruptions* of routine; they intervene in the normal flow of broadcasting and our lives. Like the holidays that halt everyday routines, television events propose exceptional things to think about, to witness, and to do. Regular broadcasting is suspended and preempted as we are guided by a series of special announcements and preludes that transform daily life into something special and, upon the conclusion of the events are guide back again" (1992, p. 5). The role of the media may be celebratory and may not only be a forum for the celebrations but also play an active part in them (Wolfsfeld, 1997c, p. 5). Whilst acknowledging Dayan and Katz's main sentiments, the advent of all news networks such as CNN, Sky News, BBC World and BBC 24 in the broadcasting landscape means that big news events are not "interruptions" on these channels in the same way as previously. Many of the "old" broadcasters don't even cover some of these events live. The House of Representatives impeachment debate and vote against President Clinton was not shown live by any of the five British terrestrial channels. In contrast CNN, Sky News and BBC 24 had full coverage. CNN split the screen to enable coverage of the bombing of Iraq alongside the impeachment vote. The press plays their part in these events with "historic" photos and special editions.

In Northern Ireland optimism in the past over the IRA ceasefire and later the Good Friday Agreement was led by the media who caught a "mood" of peace emanating from the Middle East Oslo agreement and the relatively peaceful demise of apartheid in South Africa. But as many previous studies of news have shown, the media like events and not processes, so that when negotiations become protracted or flounder, reporting resorts to the usual routines and lack of interest. In the case of the Middle East "The continual use of hyberbole turned the peace process into a melodrama designed to move the audience from ectasy to despair. Israelis were constantly given the impression that either peace had arrived or that the process was about to explode" (Wolfsfeld, 1997c, p. 74).

D. DISCUSSION AND CONCLUSIONS

Conflict is an essential ingredient of news and discussion of the role of the media in conflict resolution has ranged from realist approaches to conflict (Arno, 1984, pp. 229–239) to prescriptive measures for international communications organizations and the news media (Phillips Davison, 1974). Tehranian (1996) proposes structural pluralism in media ownership as the most effective approach to widening the public sphere for democratic discourse and for introducing balance and equality into the coverage of conflict (1996, p. 5). Vincent (1997) points to his own work with Galtung that the issues are not bipolar and that the solution may exist outside of an either/or mentality (1997, p. 2) An editorial in *Media Development* called for journalists to educate the public about the "merits of peace by demythologising warspeak and exposing the many proponents of conflict—government spin doctors, military apologists and supporters of the arms trade" (1996, p. 4). Similarly, Scott (1997) calls for the education of public opinion by the news media about the reality and causes of humanitarian crises. Further, he argues for increased dialogue between policy makers, humanitarian organizations and the media to publicize the real effectiveness of international responses without the latter sacrificing their watchdog role (1997, p. 10).

Bennett, as well, argues that reporting can only change if an independent press returns ready to exercise independent judgment (1990, p. 124). How this can be achieved poses considerable problems requiring a complete transformation of current media ownership and journalistic practices and education. Normative ideals, particularly in regard to conflict resolution remain just that, far removed from working practices.

In the interim the work on sources informs the way that policy is formulated and the manner in which the media frames it. The recent explorations of source behavior help to understand how communicative action takes place within the contemporary public sphere. By developing conceptual frameworks and understanding the strategies and tactics employed by actors in pursuit of certain goals aimed at affecting public attitudes we can gain insight into the role of the media in the reporting of conflict.

REFERENCES

Anderson, A. (1987). *Media, culture and the environment.* London: UCL Press.
Arno, A. (1984). The News Media As Third Parties in National and International Conflict. In Arno, A. & Dissanayake, W., (Eds.) *The News Media in National and International Conflict* (pp. 229–238). Boulder: Westview Press.
Bennett, W. L. (1990). Toward a Theory of Press-State Relations in the United States. *Journal of Communication, 40,* 103–125.
Bennett, W. L. (1996). An Introduction to Journalism Norms and Representation of Politics. *Political Communication, 4(13),* 373–384.
Bennett, W. L. & Paletz, D. (1994). *Taken By Storm.* Chicago: University of Chicago Press.
Berkman, R. & Kitch, L. W. (1986). *Politics in the Media Age.* New York: McGraw Hill.
Bolton, R. (1990). *Death on the Rock and Other Stories.* London: W. H. Allen.
Bromley, M. (1997). Writing Terrorism out of the story. In O'Day (Ed.) *Political Violence in Northern Ireland: Conflict and Resolution* (pp. 133–151). London: Praeger.
Carruthers, S. L. (1995). *Winning Hearts and Minds.* London: Leicester University Press.
Carruthers, S. L. (1996). Reporting terrorism. In Stewart, I. & Carruthers, S. L. (Eds.). *War Culture and the Media* (pp. 101–129). Trowbridge: Flicks Books.
Dayan, D. & Katz, E. (1992). *Media Events.* Cambridge, Mass.: Harvard University Press.
Elliot, P. (1997). "Reporting Northern Ireland. In *Ethnicity and the Media.* Paris: Unesco.
Ericson, R. V., Baranek, P. M. & Chan, J. B. L. (1989). *Negotiating Control.* Milton Keynes: Open University Press.
Hall, S., Critcher, C., Jefferson, T. Clarke, J. & Roberts, B. (1978). *Policing the Crisis.* London: Macmillan.
Hallin, D. (1986). *The Uncensored War.* New York: Oxford University Press.
Hallin, D. (1994). *We Keep America On Top Of The World.* London: Routledge.
Henderson, L. Miller, D. & Reilly, J. (1990). *Speak No Evil: The British Broadcasting Ban, the Media and the Conflict in Ireland.* Glasgow University Media Group.
Herman, E. & Chomsky, N. (1994). *Manufacturing Consent.* London: Vintage.
Media Development (1996) editorial 4, 2.

Mermin, J. (1996). "Conflict in the Sphere of Consensus? Critical Reporting on the panama Invasion and the Gulf War, *Political Communication, 13(2)*, 181–194.

Miller, D. (1993). Official Sources and "primary defintion": the case of Northern Ireland. *Media Culture and Society, 15(3)*, 385–406.

Miller, D. (1994). *Don't Mention The War*. London: Pluto Press.

Miller, D. & McLaughlin, G. (1996). Reporting the Peace in Ireland. In Rolston, B. & Miller, D., *War and Words*. Belfast: Beyond the Pale Publications.

Morrison, D. & Tumber, H. (1988). *Journalist at War*. London: Sage.

Mowlana, H., Gerbner, G. & Schiller, H. (1992). *Triumph of the Image*. Boulder: Westview Press.

Phillips Davison, W. (1974). *Mass Communication and Conflict Resolution*. New York: Praeger.

Rolston, B. (Ed.) (1991). *The Media and Northern Ireland: Covering the Troubles*. London: Macmillan.

Schlesinger, P. (1987). *Putting Reality Together*. London: Methuen.

Schlesinger P., Murdock, G. & Elliot, P. (1983). *Televising "Terrorism."* London: Comedia.

Schlesinger P. & Tumber, H. (1994). *Reporting Crime: The Media Politics of Criminal Justice*. Oxford: Oxford University Press.

Scott, C. (1997). The humanitarian response to war: who are the drivers, policy-makers, aid agencies or the media?, *Intermedia, 25(1)*, 8–10.

Tehranian, M. (1996). Communication and conflict. *Media Development, 4*, 3–5.

Tumber, H. (1993a). Taming The Truth: Government Information Policy. *British Journalism Review, 4*, 1.

Tumber, H. (1993b). Selling Scandal: Business and the Media, *Media Culture and Society, 15(3)*, 345–362.

Tumber, H. (1995). "Marketing Maastrict" The EU and News Management, *Media Culture and Society, 17*, 511–519.

Vincent, R. C. (1997). *The "troubles" as portrayed in four Irish newspapers*. Paper presented at the International Conference on Media and politics, Brussels, February.

Wernick, A. (1991). *Promotional Culture*. London: Sage.

Wolfsfeld, G. (1997a). *Media and political conflict: News from the Middle East*. Cambridge, U.K.: Cambridge University Press.

Wolfsfeld, G. (1997b). Fair Weather Friends: The Varying Role of the News Media in the Arab-Israeli Peace Process, *Political Communication, 14(1)*, Jan.–Mar. 29–48.

Wolfsfeld, G. (1997c). *Constructing News About Peace*. Tel Aviv: The Tami Steinmetz Center for Peace Research Tel Aviv University.

CHAPTER 8

AN EXPLORATORY MODEL OF MEDIA-GOVERNMENT RELATIONS IN INTERNATIONAL CRISES: U.S. INVOLVEMENT IN BOSNIA 1992–1995

Yaeli Bloch and Sam Lehman-Wilzig

A. INTRODUCTION

Several studies have looked into the relationship between media and government, but there is no consensus as to the nature of such a relationship (Robinson, 2000; Wood & Peake, 1998; Bennett, 1997; Mowlana, 1996; Reese, 1991; Entman, 1991; Rogers & Dearing, 1988). However, even those who argue that the media do not have overwhelming influence, still agree that it is not insignificant. The issue has become even more salient in the contemporary period with the advent of advanced mass communication technologies along with major changes in the arena of international relations.

Unfortunately, regarding the connection between foreign policymaking and the mass media, a large lacuna exists. More research has been undertaken dealing specifically with war and the mass media, but less is available regarding the role of the mass media in foreign policy decision making during *peacetime*. Even more specifically, almost nothing exists on the topic of foreign policy *crisis management* and the media—despite the large number of such IR phenomena in the contemporary era (Malek, 1996).

Thus, the present study is a pioneering work that will offer a comprehensive model connecting the media's role and government foreign policy in an IR crisis.* It will apply a familiar theory from the field of IR (division of crisis phases) to the developing discipline of mass communication research, in order to achieve a better understanding of the media's different ways of functioning in a time of international crisis. The model is applied to an international crisis in which we found significant links between crisis phase and press positions/arguments, as

---

* An earlier version of this paper was presented at the annual convention of the International Studies Association, Chicago, February 2001.

well as types of argument put forth by the government. The study concludes with a discussion of the results and suggestions for future research.

B.   THEORETICAL FRAMEWORK: THE MODEL'S COMPONENTS

1.   Media—Functions and Roles

Over the years, the question of media roles has elicited an outpouring of research (Lasswell, 1948; Siebert *et al.*, 1956; Lee, 1977; Wright, 1985; McQuail, 1992; Hindell, 1995). There are several specific questions related to the overall issue of general journalistic coverage (Wolfsfeld, 1993) that one can apply to the foreign policy domain. First, in which circumstances and conditions do the media act independently in covering political conflict? Second, is there a tendency on the media's part to take a stand or is balanced neutrality the norm (Wolfsfeld, 1997)? Third, if the media do take sides, *which arguments*—economic, security/world-order, domestic politics, or humanitarian—tend to be put forward by the columnists?

This leads to the question of *framing*, whereby the journalists "package" the information in such a way as to present a specific reality that can influence public opinion (Wolfsfeld, 1997; Entman, 1991; Entman & Rojecki, 1993; Pan & Kosicki, 1993; Gamson & Herzog, 1999; Gitlin, 1977; Tuchman, 1978). Such packaging usually involves a broad range of subjects, all of whom are presented from the same *weltanschauung*, thereby limiting the full panoply of public discourse. As a result of such framing, not only is the issue presented in a "pre-set" fashion, familiar to the public and therefore "understandable" (Eliders & Luter, 2000; Gamson & Herzog, 1999; Durham, 1998; Norris, 1997), but the very *meaning* of the news is changed (Schefele, 1999; Kuypers, 1997; Putnam *et al.*, 1996; Neuman, *et al.*, 1992; Entman, 1991). Fourth and finally, how do the media "create" (through selection) and produce the news (Wolfsfeld, 1993)? Does drama take precedence over substance, thereby perhaps focusing more on easily reportable stories rather than complex ones, exciting items instead of more mundane issues?

These questions lead ineluctably to the complex issue of media influence on the political actors. Here one can discern three broad functions.

(1) Independence/Major Influence: Several analysts believe that the media are a major factor in the foreign policy decision-making process. This approach is supported by the journalists involved and is found mostly among media scholars with a "practical" bent, i.e., those focusing on the mass media and less on IR and political science (Malek & Wiegand, 1996). To be sure, one must distinguish between two aspects here: media independence and media influence (Wolfsfeld, 1997). The two do not necessarily go together, so that showing journalistic independence still demands proof of significant influence on the behavior of the actors or the conflict's evolution (Wolfsfeld,

1993). A possible lesser (albeit still "strong") type of direct influence is the media's ability to determine the public agenda (Mowlana, 1996). By playing up—or down—events, the media can influence the amount of pressure that policy makers feel to respond to foreign threats.

(2) Indirect (Passive) Influence: Other scholars view the media as pawns in the political process, manipulated by the political leadership for its own purposes. Malek and Wiegand (1996) use the term "passive" to describe this media function; by so doing they do not mean to suggest that the media have influence but rather that such influence is not a product of the media's own initiative but rather as a powerful tool in the hands of others (Mowlana, 1996).

(3) Lack of Influence/Neutrality: This approach takes a middle position, albeit with a wide range of views among the scholars. The central argument here is that neither the politicians nor the media are manipulative of each other or public opinion (Malek & Wiegand, 1996)—in short, the media's coverage of foreign policy crises does not influence the decision makers nor public opinion (Wolfsfeld, 1993).

Within these disparate approaches one can delineate four different types of media roles connected to foreign policymaking as well as to public opinion formation. First, the media as observer standing apart from the conflict; second, as commentator, verbally/textually responding to the actor's moves; third, as actor, playing a more active role as one of the conflict's "players"; finally, as catalyst of change, i.e., playing a central and highly influential role. However, these roles have not been fleshed out in the research literature and there is a need for further theorizing and empirical testing (Rivenburgh, 1996)—especially regarding times of crisis. The reason for this is that heretofore the analysis of the media's role has been overly general, not taking into account the phases of foreign crises or the mutability of the media's role depending on circumstances in the field.

The need for more in-depth categorization and analysis of media/government relations has become especially pronounced over the past two decades with the huge expansion of the electronic media and the increased amounts of information flowing from the field. Another factor behind the increased importance of the mass media is related to the satiated and highly educated democratic public at large that no longer can be easily railroaded into supporting war. Thus, democratic governments are more dependent on public opinion (Mueller, 1994; Powlick, 1995), which itself is (at least) partly dependent on its major source of information—the mass media (Graber, 1984; Graber, 1996).

Consequently, several experts recommend pursuing different research strategies. The present study attempts to integrate most of the research questions into an exploratory model: examining foreign policy and newspaper framework; dealing with national interests in international event coverage; relating to the different types of media functions; all of this in addition to the central goal of assessing the extent to which the press responds differently to government foreign policy decision-making and overseas crisis management.

The model is applied to an international crisis, for as noted earlier, very little work has been done on press-government relations during such a politically stressful period. It is precisely during such a period that the ability of the media to influence public opinion, highly dependent on it as a main source for information, is the greatest (Powlick & Kats, 1998; Paletz & Entman, 1991).

2. Media—Government Relations

Democratic regimes have a tendency to bask in the myth of a free press, but even in "open societies" the media serve the polity's control apparatus, consciously or not. On the one hand, most media organizations expect their representatives to cover government actions (Grossman & Kumar, 1981), in one way or another (see above). On the other hand, the universal temptation exists for governments to manipulate and control the media—especially true during crisis periods.

The amount and type of governmental supervision and control over the media depend in large part on the political/mass communications philosophy of each country at distinct points in time. Overall, the research literature has centered on five main, general, politico-philosophical approaches (Siebert et al., 1956; McQuail, 1992). We shall focus here on the two that are relevant to the model:[1]

(A) In the *libertarian* philosophy of government/press relations, also called the Free Press theory (a normative approach), the mass media best serve the public as an aggressive, independent, adversarial "watchdog" on government actions. This approach assumes a high level of competition between the media themselves, tending to decrease editorial supervision of journalistic practice as well as leading to denial of "public education" as a prominent journalistic role (Serfaty, 1991).

(B) While the media might be formally and legally free, politico-cultural constraints can render its output highly supportive of the government. This approach can best be categorized as *mobilization* (an empirical approach), whereby the media view their task more in terms of supporting the authorities and reinforcing the national consensus. This is most widely found among developing nations (even democratic ones, e.g., Israel during its first few decades), but it is also not unusual to see such "self-mobilized journalism"

---

[1] The three other approaches are: Social-Responsibility (located between the abovementioned two), Authoritarian and the Totalitarian. For elaboration, *see* Siebert et al. (1956), Hutchins (1947) and McQuail (1992).

during times of crisis among otherwise libertarian-minded media in a "rally-round-the-flag" mentality (however temporary). Indeed, previous studies have found that most domestic mass media support national foreign policy aims and goals, especially when the national interest is threatened, thereby acting as a source of "national integration" (Russet, 1990), i.e., a unifying force behind government decisions and actions (Holsti, 1996; Rivenburgh, 1996). One must note, however, that it is hard to find in the literature a clear definition of what we here call the "self-mobilized media." Moreover, it is not always clear *for whom* the media are mobilized: the constitutional regime, state, government, specific interest groups (even if this entails the majority against a minority, a la Japanese concentration camps on the West Coast during World War II)? It seems that the two main roles of the press within this approach are, on the one hand, "rally-round-the-flag," i.e., socio-national consensus-building, and on the other, "government support" for policies and decisions in the conduct of the crisis.

3.   Government—International Crises

In the research literature, one can find definitions of "international crisis" at various levels: macro-objective and micro-subjective. In general, one can posit that from a (macro) systems perspective a crisis entails an event constituting a drastic change that influences and destabilizes the international system (Young, 1968). From a (micro) psychological perspective, we accept Brecher's definition of crisis as a situation perceived by policymakers as threatening their values and interests, leaving them little time to respond, and involving a high probability of violence (Brecher & Wilkenfeld, 1989).

The present study also follows Brecher's (1993) categorization of four international crisis phases:

(1) *Onset*, the pre-crisis period typified by change in the intensity of disruption between two or more states and of threat perception by at least one of them;

(2) *Escalation*, in which perceptions of time pressure and heightened war likelihood are added to more acute threat perception. On the micro-level, increased time pressure adds to the feeling of maximal threat;

(3) *De-escalation*, characterized by reduction in hostile interactions leading to accommodation and crisis termination; and

(4) *Impact*, occurring in the post-crisis period, which includes the consequences of a crisis. We omitted this phase from the model because our study focuses on the roles of the media and government *during* a crisis and not afterwards.

C. EXPLORATORY MODEL OF MEDIA-GOVERNMENT RELATIONS IN INTERNATIONAL CRISES

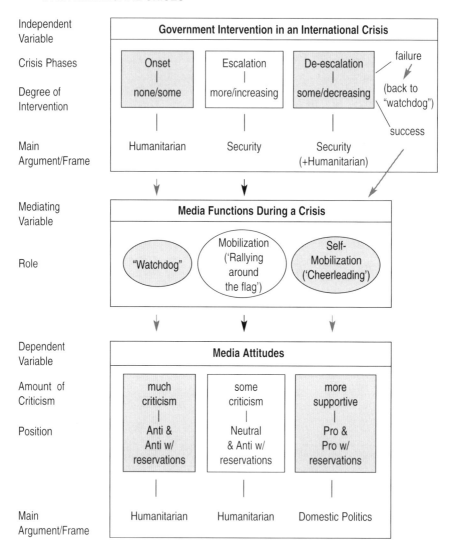

In the model, government interventionist foreign policy is the independent variable while media attitudes constitute the dependent variable, itself mediated by the media's conception of its functional role.

The model illustrates that each particular phase (marked in a different shade) has its own media function. In the Onset phase the media function primarily as a barking "watchdog," opposed to the government's natural inclination to do what is in its own best political (not necessarily *national*) interest. In the Escalation phase the media begin to play a "mobilization" role, rallying the public around the flag and in support of government policy. The third phase, De-escalation, that terminates the crisis, may end in failure or success. In the case of failure, the media return to their watchdog function. In the case of success or interpreted success, the media move toward a role that can best be described as "cheerleading." One can view this as a matter of "self-mobilization" to aid the authorities in garnering political support or as jumping on-board a successful campaign (one might even argue that the media are emotionally "swept away" by government success).

However, it is not enough just to match a function with a crisis phase; we also need to know what are the basic media attitudes (in each phase) regarding each function. To do that, we have distinguished among five types of argumentation (frames), and also compared them with governmental arguments for each crisis phase. As can be seen at the bottom of the model's first square, in the first crisis phase the media and the government both employ humanitarian arguments, but the media criticize the government's line of reasoning (in favor of self-restraint). In the second phase, the media are still using primarily humanitarian arguments, but the specific positions are more neutral. The government, however, prefers security justifications. In the third phase, the media become more supportive of governmental policy and therefore the media's arguments deal mostly with domestic political ramifications. In this phase, the government uses a combination of security and humanitarian arguments.

After presenting the various parts of this integrative model, the results are applied to the Bosnian case (1992–1995). The Bosnian crisis was a product of the ongoing Yugoslavian conflict that turned into a crisis and then escalated into outright war (Brecher & Wilkenfeld, 1997). This crisis was chosen because it was one of the first *extended* and *complex* crises that American foreign policy makers had to deal with since the demise of the Soviet Union (Woodward, 1995). As the world's sole superpower since the breakup of the Soviet empire in the late 1980s, the United States has had difficulty defining its international interests and central role in the new international (dis)order (Hass, 1999). The Bosnian case study can serve as an exemplar for understanding foreign policy in the post-Cold War era. One should note that the Bosnian crisis was largely ethnic in character—precisely the type of conflict on the increase in the post-Cold War era—with direct influence on the degree of superpower intervention as well as on media coverage.

D. RESEARCH DESIGN

The period under study was June 1991 until November 1995. We first mapped all the significant events of the crisis (Reuters, 1995; Keesing's 1992–1994)—105 specific dates. Then we selected only those in which the United States was mentioned (initiating or reacting)—23 main events that formed the core sample of the study. In order to examine the positions and compare the arguments of the media and the government, we performed a qualitative and quantitative content analysis of commentary and editorial articles published in two elite newspapers: the *New York Times* (hereafter, *NYT*) and the *Washington Post* (*WP*). The press was chosen because it constituted one of the most influential institutions in society (Vincent, 2000), which most of the public still depends on as a main source of information (Taylor, 2000). These specific newspapers were selected because they are incontestably the main elite press sources for America's foreign policy decision makers (Denham, 1997; Malek, 1996; Merrill, 1995). Both have extensive resources for overseas information gathering and analysis, and are noted for their independence and critical stands on the issues (Van Belle, 2000; Denham, 1997; Grosswiler, 1996; Negrine, 1989; Karetzky, 1986; Ferre, 1980; Weiss, 1974). Editorial and commentary articles were chosen because they present to the public the newspaper's opinion in overt fashion (Mermin, 1999; Denham, 1997; Peh & Melkote, 1991), thus constituting the readership's main source of foreign policymaking information (Mowlana, 1996). Moreover, the decision makers tend to view issues dealt with on these pages as being important and so at least necessitating an official response (Grosswiller, 1996).

The same type of analysis was carried out for all Presidential Documents (hereafter PD) and State Department press releases (hereafter SD), together providing a uniform documented source of official foreign policy statements by the President and other decision makers (Malek, 1996). All the publications (press and government) were examined during the 23 specific periods under scrutiny— an entire week before and after each main event, in order to ensure that all relevant material would be included.[2] Thirty-nine (39) such items were identified in *NYT* and 60 in *WP*, in addition to 61 SD releases and 37 PD—overall 197 items: 99 of the press and 98 of the government.

The study included several scales and categories, of which two are directly relevant to the model: (1) the main position taken in the article (pro, pro with reservations, neutral, anti with reservations, anti); and (2) the type of argument/frame (security and world order, economic, humanitarian, domestic politics, or combination of these).[3] These scales were designed to enable intra-government comparison (between PD and SD), intra-press comparison (*NYT and WP*), and government/press comparisons as a whole. They were further divided into the first three central crises phases as delineated earlier (Brecher, 1993). The "Onset" phase included four dates, from April 6, 1992, to February 1, 1993, during which the U.S. did not offer to intervene diplomatically or militarily. The "Escalation" phase included 16 dates from February 10, 1993 (when the U.S. offered to lend its diplomatic services for finding a peaceful solution to the Bosnian crisis) until

---

2   We had intended to compare the Bush and Clinton administrations, but it turned out that only three of the 23 periods occurred during Bush's tenure.

3   As the research has a qualitative component, we tested for inter-coder reliability regarding the scoring of the study's items (*WP*, *NYT*, SD and PD). For the variable "Position" the correlation between the primary and backup coding is .934 (p = .006), and for the variable "Argument" the cross-tabulation between them is $x^2 = .001$. It is usually preferable to check correlation, but on a categorical variable we need to perform cross-tabulation.

June 1994. The third phase ("De-escalation") included three dates running from October 5, 1995, until Nov. 21, 1995 (Dayton Agreement).

E. FINDINGS

While the study was based on two newspapers and two government institutions, we found (unsurprisingly) that a high Pearson correlation exists (p = 0.043; r = 42.5 percent) between the two newspapers' coverage, and an even higher correlation was found between the SD and PD (p = 0.007; r = 54.7 percent). In other words, as the *NYT* reports increased/decreased so did those of the *WP*; the same held true for the White House and the State Department's press releases. As a result, when making comparisons, we will henceforth refer to them as two 'groups' and not as individual actors.

As we see from Graph #1, we found a high (0.363) and significant (p = .05) association between the press's position and the crises phases, as illustrated in the model. From Graph #1, we can see that during the "Onset" phase, the percentage of completely negative columns was very high (54 percent) with another 23 percent largely negative (77 percent altogether). During this phase not one single column was unequivocally supportive of government policy regarding the Bosnian crisis. During the "Escalation" phase we still found a large number of critical columns (37.8 percent) but much lower in comparison to the first period. Neutral positions increased (to 24 percent) but still did not overtake policy criticism. For the first time a few totally supportive opinions were voiced (3 percent). Overall, the press's critique of government policy declined significantly—especially as this phase of the conflict evolved, i.e., the later the date in the phase, the less critical and more neutral/supportive the press's position became regarding Administration policy. During the "De-escalation" phase leading up to the 1995 Dayton

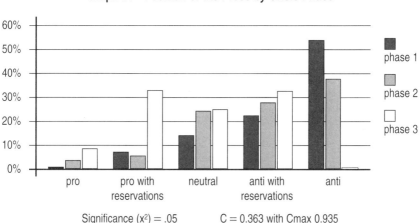

Graph #1—*Position of the Press by Crisis Phase*

Agreement, ending the crisis, the press is quite supportive of the government's handling of the situation. No unequivocally critical opinions whatsoever were voiced in the two papers during this period! On the other hand, the completely supportive columns rose by 300 percent; so did partly supportive opinions (33.3 percent). Overall, during this period the number of positive opinions expressed (39.6 percent) was greater than the negative ones (33.3 percent).

Graph #2—*Type of Argument of the Press by Crisis Phase*

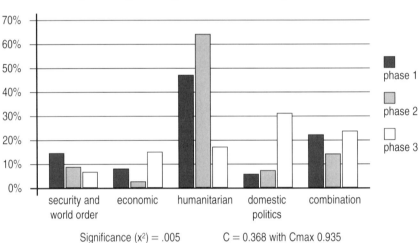

Significance (x^2) = .005   C = 0.368 with Cmax 0.935

As is obvious from Graphs #2 and #3, a high (0.368) and significant (p = .05) association was found between the press's type of argument and the crisis phase. From Graph #2, we can see that there was a marked relative increase (of 40 percent) in humanitarian arguments found in the press from phase 1 (46.2 percent) to phase 2 (64.9 percent). The "De-escalation" phase was marked by a significant relative increase (of more than 300 percent) in domestic-political arguments (33.3 percent of the total) compared to the previous crisis phase, mostly at the expense of humanitarian arguments (16.7 percent). Economic (16.7 percent) arguments also increased somewhat.

A very high (0.415) and significant (p = .009) association was found between the government's types of argument and the crisis phase. We can see clearly from Graph #3, that during phase 1, PD and SD arguments were heavily humanitarian (57.1 percent) and military (28.6 percent) oriented. During the Escalation phase, security and world-order arguments dominated all others (66.2 percent), while the humanitarian argument plummeted to only 13.5 percent of the total. Regarding the "De-escalation" phase, security arguments by the government dropped by about half (30 percent) and the humanitarian arguments increased to 20 percent with another 40 percent being a combination of the two.

Graph #3—*Type of Argument of the Government by Crisis Phase*

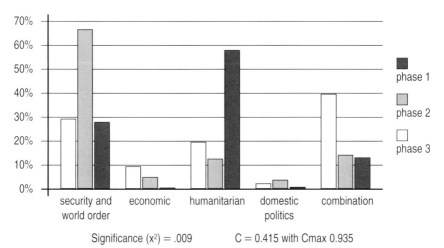

Significance (x²) = .009   C = 0.415 with Cmax 0.935

F.   FINDINGS: APPLYING THE MODEL

After presenting the data in light of the press's positions as well as government/press arguments, it is time to illustrate our model for a more inclusive exposition of the inter-relationship between the two actors during each phase of the crisis.

Phase 1: This "Onset" Phase was marked by lack of government intervention, based on the Administration's assessment that the civil war was an internal Yugoslavian problem with little impact on Europe as a whole. This marginalization of the conflict was also based on American public opinion—while sympathetic to the victimized Bosnians, was not ready to commit troops to a complex overseas affair. The language of the Administration (when it deigned to mention the conflict altogether) was couched in humanitarian terms—partly as a reflection of public opinion and perhaps as well as preparation for later intervention.

One main factor behind the Administration's heavily humanitarian argumentation is America's self-perceived role as torchbearer of liberal democracy and human rights around the world. With hundreds of thousands of people being killed, raped and banished from their homes in the heart of Europe, the U.S. could not easily ignore the victims' plight. We might even assume that towards the end of this early period, the Clinton foreign policy makers were obviously priming the public in a way similar to the elite press. Along somewhat the same lines one can understand the not insignificant use of security arguments as well. As the world's "policeman," the U.S. could not allow havoc to occur within Europe without such inaction having far-reaching effects on its ability to threaten military intervention elsewhere around the world. For if not in the Balkans (the trigger for World War I), then where else would military intervention be justified? The Bosnian crisis soon became defined as a symbol of U.S. foreign policy (Daalder, 2000; Banks & Strussman, 1999; Danner, 1997, p. 58) and, as such, the declared policy had to back up its morality with a big security stick as well.

One can note here possible press influence on the foreign policymakers. Those in charge of foreign policy within any American Administration are known to assiduously read the elite press—whether in organized synopsis form (the President's daily packet) or in normal fashion. In our present case, the emphasis and continuing use of humanitarian arguments by the elite press probably had an effect on those in charge of explaining U.S. foreign policy. This of course does not necessarily mean that those decision makers had already internalized the depth of the humanitarian tragedy unfolding in Bosnia (or the need to actively do something about it), but at least on an exhortative level they were mouthing the same line emanating from the press.

Although also using humanitarian arguments, the press was highly critical of such isolationism. In such an ongoing terrible conflict and public opinion vacuum, the press has little reason to support government policy of non-involvement. This is in line with Malek's findings (1996) regarding the Iran-Iraq War that was not perceived by the American public as being something critical to the national interest. His study did not divide the war into periods as we do here, but it is instructive to note that overall almost two-thirds of the *NYT*'s editorials were critical of Administration policy during that earlier war.

Our case study is a clear example of the fact that *type* of argument does not correlate with the *position* taken on the issue.[4] One of the reasons for this lack of symmetry is that journalists do not have the same political constraints that normally bind politicians (i.e., republican party neo-isolationism, generally apathetic public opinion, etc.). Add to this the elite press's general libertarian, barking "watchdog" function as opposed to any government's natural inclination to do what is in its own best political (not necessarily *national*) interest, and it is not hard to understand the disparity between the two sides on either argument or position. As we saw earlier, the professional literature does not relate to the types of arguments put forward by the press over the course of the crisis's phases. Thus, our explanations are a first attempt to deal with the question, although Malek's study (1996) suggests at least one explanation. America is a multi-cultural country of immigrants that can only keep its social order intact through an ethos of ethno-cultural tolerance. As such, it has a particular sensitivity to ethnic strife. Moreover, the elite press in the United States (certainly the *NYT* and the *WP*) has a liberal orientation. In addition, American foreign policy for most of the country's history has been highly "moralistic" in tone (if not in fact), as a way of "excusing" the occasional forays into interventionism much against the nation's

---

4 Statistical tests (chi squre, contingency coefficient) of "type of argument" and "position taken" showed that any correlation between the two were not significant.

deeply ingrained isolationist tradition, existing as far back as Washington's Farewell Address—in contrast to the more "Realpolitik" tradition of Continental Europe (France, Germany). Thus, it is not surprising that if the elite press calls for an interventionist policy in any foreign crisis, it does so with the only type of argument that could move public opinion away from its reflexive isolationist stance. And the closer such foreign policy comes to interventionism, the more numerous the press's humanitarian arguments will tend to be. One might even view the increase from phase 1 to phase 2 as a move from "priming the public" (raising issues) to "influencing the public" (mobilizing public opinion to pressure/support government interventionism).

Phase 2: At this point in the crisis ("Escalation"), the Administration began to get involved in the Bosnian crisis, using primarily security/world-order arguments.

A few possible explanations could account for this. First, Bosnia was not the first nor was it the only civil war in the contemporary era where ethnic-humanitarian considerations were palpable. Somalia, Rwanda, Congo, Eritrea, Sudan, and a host of others were no less bloody than Bosnia; the humanitarian argument by itself could not justify interventionism in Bosnia when it did not lead to American "policing" elsewhere. From a geo-political standpoint, though, Bosnia was a clearer case for the American public and the strategic security argument (and world-order) could be more easily made—especially when America's closest allies (the European Union) were in need of help. After all, the "limited" Bosnian civil war could very easily turn into an "unlimited" conflict undermining 50 years of European efforts to solidify national borders—not to mention offering a precedent for insurgencies elsewhere around the world to remake national borders, as President Clinton himself noted during his visit to Bosnia.

Second, the nature of the "audience" differs between the government and the press. Whereas the latter address themselves mostly to the domestic public and the government, once getting officially involved in the conflict the Administration had a wider audience (world public opinion), extending to overseas allied governments, the "other side," and other organizations involved in the crisis (e.g., the UN's Security Council which must approve American military intervention overseas). The latter are swayed far more by Realpolitik argumentation than by humanitarian concerns, especially coming from the one superpower whose military weight can make a difference in almost any civil war crisis.

The elite press, in counterpoint, placed its emphasis on humanitarian needs, albeit with reduced criticism of Administration policy, once it became clear that the latter was tending toward the desired interventionism. Thus the press mobilized itself, and actually played more of a "national integration" role than a traditional "watchdog" function, rallying the public around the flag and in support of Administration policy. This function probably lies in the fact of diplomatic/military interventionism itself. Once the country becomes directly involved in a foreign policy crisis, the papers' official position becomes supportive of the official line (Grosswiler, 1996). We believe that this is due to public opinion which "awakens" to the issue but is not yet fully aware of the nuances (or potential complications) of interventionism, so that the dominant reflexive response is "rally-round-the-flag" which even the elite press are somewhat loath to completely counter. As a result, the media's role becomes more one of "national integration" and the watchdog begins to take a long nap.

Phase 3: The "De-escalation" period was marked by the increasing perception (and fact) of Administration foreign policy success in bringing the combatants to the negotiating table after three and a half years of combat. At this juncture the government brought forth security/world-order as well as humanitarian arguments in a sort of platform for the future.

This reflects the government's attempt to ensure that its underlying foreign policy message would be clearly understood: with the rise of ethnic conflict in the post-Soviet period, the U.S. will not hesitate to use its diplomatic and military power to ensure that humanitarian travesties do not occur. In this third phase, the Administration actually moved away from arguments to *convince* the public (domestic and foreign), focusing instead on reiterations as to what its policy was designed to do during the Bosnian crisis in particular and elsewhere in the future in general.

The press, for its part, became even more supportive—it too tended to move over to *ex post facto* commentary, and for the first time devoted more space to *retrospective* analysis of domestic ramifications than in *prospective* pontificating about what the Administration should do from here on out. This can be described as a further move away from its "watchdog" function toward a self-mobilization (cheerleading) role—either to aid the authorities in garnering political support and/or to jump on board a successful campaign.

Why? First, the Administration's foreign policy was obviously succeeding. Second, the prestige of the United States was on the line here—and not just that of the Clinton Administration—so that the public's "rally-round-the-flag" mentality continued apace, albeit with less of a military slant and more of a feeling of national pride and status in the eyes of the world. As a result, the elite press "self-mobilized" to support a policy that by now had become relatively bi-partisan and thus "American" in the widest sense of the word. Thus, we do not consider it an exaggeration to call this the "cheerleading" role of the press—either consciously (rationally supporting real success) or subconsciously (emotionally identifying with the prestige of one's country).

What accounts for this overall change? Several explanations are possible, none mutually exclusive. At the point where the humanitarian problems were lessening in Bosnia and the sides were ready to sit together on the negotiation table, there was little objective reason to continue emphasizing the issue. Moreover, by the third phase the Administration's policy was obviously progressing success-fully so that the elite press no longer saw its function as being "advisory" (offer-ing suggestions what to do) but rather "evaluatory" (commenting on the implications of such policy). In this regard, of course, there was little to evaluate in terms of "saving lives" but much to say regarding the domestic political rami-fications of the Administrations' crisis management as a whole. This explains the increase in economic and security/world-order editorials/columns as well. As a result of the fact that this phase took place close to the start of the 1996 Presidential election campaign, it was only natural for the press pundits to shift gears into a mode of discourse relevant to the political reality at hand.

Of course, this journalistic approach is probably only relevant in the case of foreign policy *success*, for had the result been failure it is highly likely that the press would have reverted in this third phase to its more traditional critical watch-dog role, as the model shows. In any case, given the dearth of research dealing with the "theory" of journalistic "self-mobilization," we wish to posit here two different types. The first emphasizes the need for socio-political cohesion while the crisis continues. This is more a "national" goal than a "political" one, playing on patriotic themes. For example, Stephen Rosenfeld wrote in an op-ed piece in the *WP* (Nov. 24, 1995) after the signing of the Dayton Agreement: "To hear the gifted advocate, Vice President Al Gore, struggling to win support for the Administration's Bosnia venture is to realize this debate is less about foreign pol-icy 'interests' than about the very definition of being American." The second type of "self-mobilization" is more specifically political—support for the Admini-stration's policies. In the case of Bosnia, the first occurred in phase 2 to some extent, while the second was found in phase 3.

G. DISCUSSION AND CONCLUSIONS

This study offered a comprehensive look at the inter-relationship between the press and the government during an international crisis. A distinction must be made between the two types of phenomena that were under scrutiny. First, the *positions* of the press regarding administration policy. Here we are on firmer ground in arguing that the press almost always reacts to government (in)action, so that the relationship is mostly uni-directional. "Mostly," because the policy makers do read the elite press and may be swayed at times in two ways: either they worry that public opinion is being influenced by the press's position or the arguments offered by the press may in and of themselves be persuasive. The sec-ond element that we scrutinized was the *type of argument/framing* used by both sides. In this case, the inter-relationship is probably more of a two-way street, i.e., the arguments/types of framing proffered by the press (e.g., humanitarian, mili-tary, etc.) could just as easily influence the policy makers as the latter's declara-tions may influence the journalists.

The contribution of this research is both theoretical and practical.

Theoretically, we have presented an original, integrated model combining theories from different fields (IR and mass communications), in order to explain the relationship between the media and the government during an international crisis. In so doing, we hope to have made clearer the functioning of the press in foreign policy making—especially during a crisis period, where virtually very little research has been undertaken heretofore. The model was applied to a case study, and the findings support our contention that the media react to the government's foreign policy in a way that changes the "politico-philosophical" role of the press over the crisis's various phases.

On the practical side, we offered several explanations for the press's functioning during the crisis phases, in the hope that journalism practitioners and students will more clearly understand the important role that the media can play in foreign policy in order to improve the media's coverage and analysis of international crises—not to mention enabling foreign policy makers to better handle public opinion and improve their dealings with the press, especially regarding ethnic conflicts which seem to dominate the international arena at the turn of the millenium.

Regarding the case study itself, since the time of the Vietnam War the U.S. has had strong reservations about military intervention abroad, because it feared negative reaction in the media and public opinion. This had been even more constraining regarding humanitarian military intervention, which was difficult to justify in terms of clear national interest. One of the most interesting conclusions emerging from the present case study is that the elite-press actually helped to articulate a rationale for humanitarian, military intervention. The government, however, was not sufficiently aware of this; had it been, the leading policy makers might have taken more decisive action and much sooner.

Nevertheless, the comprehensive model presented here was examined regarding one case study, so that its validation requires future research. Future studies might look into other case studies with other elements: *different* types of *democratic* regimes; *totalitarian* or *authoritarian* regimes; *short-term* crisis; *small state's* foreign policy; a similar case which resulted in *foreign policy failure* (with emphasis on the role of the press in phase 3); *other media*, e.g., popular press, electronic media; or even *correlating* the model to *actual public opinion*; etc.

The present study is an attempt to create an exploratory model that can explain (and after further refinement, perhaps predict) the inter-relations between media and government during international crises. Although the central focus was on the impact of foreign policy on press attitudes, our model and concomitant analysis also included the various philosophies of the press's role in a democracy, the differences between types of argument in the administration and the press at various phases of the crisis, and several thoughts regarding the nature and direction of mutual influence between these two central actors in the foreign policymaking drama. Much work is yet to be done. We believe, however, that the present study is an important first step along the road to a better understanding of what has become a critical subject in both mass media and international relations studies.

REFERENCES

Banks, W. C. & Straussman, J. D. (1999). A New Imperial Presidency? Insights from U.S. Involvement in Bosnia. In Caraley, D. J. (Ed.), *The New American Interventionism: Lessons from Successes and Failures* (pp. 39–62). New York: Columbia University Press.

Bennett, L. W. (1997). Toward a Theory of Press-State Relations in the United States. *Journal of Communication, 40*, 103–125.

Brecher, M. (1993). *Crises in World Politics*. USA: Pergamon Press.

Brecher, M. & Wilkenfeld, J. (1989). *Crisis, Conflict and Instability*. UK: Pergamon Press.

Brecher, M. & Wilkenfeld, J. (1997). *A Study of Crisis*. Michigan: The University of Michigan Press.

Daalder, I. H. (2000). *Getting to Dayton: The Making of America's Bosnia Policy*. Washington: Brookings Institute.

Danner, M. (1997). The US and the Yugoslav Catastrophe. *The New York Review of Books*, Nov. 20, 56–64.

Denham, B. E. (1997). Anonymous Attribution during Two Periods of Military Conflict: Using Logistic Regression to Study Veiled Sources in American Newspapers. *Journalism & Mass Communication Quarterly, 74, 3*, 565–578.

Durham, F. D. (1998). News Frames as Social Narratives: TWT Flight 800. *Journal of Communication, 48, 4*, 100–117.

Eliders, C. & Luter, A. (2000). Germany at War: Competing Framing Strategies in German Public Discourse. *European Journal of Communication, 15, 3*, 415–428.

Entman, Robert M. (1991). Framing U.S. Coverage of International News: Contrasts in Narratives of the KAL and Iran Air Incidents. *Journal of Communication, 41, 4*, 6–27.

Entman, R. M. (1993). Framing: Towards Clarification of a Fractured Paradigm. *Journal of Communication, 43, 4*, 51–58.

Entman, R. M. & Rojecki, A. (1993). Freezing Out the Public: Elite and Media Framing of the U.S. Anti-Nuclear Movement. *Political Communication, 10, 2*, 155–173.

Ferre, J. P. (1980). Denominational Biases in the American Press. *Review of Religious Research, 21, 3*, 276–283.

Gamson, W. & Herzog, H. (1999). Living with Contradictions: The Taken-for-Granted in Israeli Political Discourse. *Political Psychology, 20, 2*, 247–266.

Gitlin, T. (1977). Spotlight and Shadows: Television and the Culture of Politics. *College English*, 790–798.

Graber, D. A. (1984). *Mass Media and American Politics*. Chicago: CQ.

Graber, D. A. (1996). The "New" Media and Politics: What Does the Future Hold? *PS: Political Science & Politics xxix, 1*, March, 33–36.

Grossman, M. B. & Kumar, M. J. (1981). *Portraying the President*. USA: The Johns Hopkins University.

Grosswiler, P. (1996). The Impact of Media and Images on Foreign Policy: Elite U.S. Newspaper Editorial Coverage of Surviving Communist Countries in the Post-Cold War Era. In A. Malek (Ed.), *News Media & Foreign Relations* (pp. 195–210). New-Jersey: Ablex Publishing Corporation.

Hackett, R. A. (1996). The Press and Foreign Policy Dissent: The Case of the Gulf War. In Malek, A. (ed.), *News Media & Foreign Relations* (pp. 141–160). New Jersey: Ablex Publishing Corporation.

Hass, R. N. (1999). *The Reluctant Sheriff*. New York: Brookings Institution Press.

Hindell, K. (1995). The Influence of Media on Foreign Policy. *International Relations, 12*, 73–84.

Holsti, O. R. (1996). *Public Opinion and American Foreign Policy*. Michigan: The University of Michigan Press.

Hutchins, W. E. (1947). *Freedom of the Press. A Framework of Principles*. Chicago: University of Chicago Press.

Karetzky, S. (1986). *The Media War Against Israel*. New York: Steimatzky & Shapolsky.

(1992). *Keesing's Record of World Events, 38*, Roger East (Ed.). London: Longman, 38832–33, 38848–50, 38970–91, 39012–13, 39035–37, 39102–103, 39149–50, 39197–98, 39240.

(1993). *Keesing's Record of World Events, 39*, Roger East (Ed.). London: Longman, 39277–79, 39327, 39374–75, 39425–27, 39469–70, 39516–19, 39563–65, 39603–606.

(1994). *Keesing's Record of World Events, 40*, Roger East (Ed.). London: Longman, 39870–72, 39925–27, 40071–73.

Kuypers, J. A. (1997). *Presidential Crisis Rhetoric and the Press in the Post-Cold War World*. Westport, Connecticut: Prager.

Lasswell, H. D. (1948). The Structure and Function of Communication in Society. In L. Bryson (Ed.), *The Communication of Ideas* (pp. 37–51). New York: Harper.

Lee, J. R. (1977). Rallying around the Flag: Foreign Policy Events and Presidential Popularity. *Presidential Studies Quarterly*, Fall, 252–256.

Malek, A. (1996). 'New York Times' Editorial Position and U.S. Foreign Policy: The Case of Iran Revisited. In A. Malek (ed.), *News Media & Foreign Relations* (pp. 224–245). New Jersey: Ablex Publishing Corporation.

Malek, A. & Wiegand, K. E. (1996). News Media and Foreign Policy: An Integrated Review. In A. Malek (Ed.), *News Media & Foreign Relations* (pp. 3–28). New Jersey: Ablex Publishing Corporation.

McQuail, D. (1992). *Mass Communication Theory: An Introduction* (2nd ed.). London: Sage.

Mermin, J. (1999). *Debating War and Peace*. New Jersey: Princeton University Press.

Merrill, J. C. (1995). *Global Journalism*. New York: Longman.

Mowlana, H. (1996). The Media and Foreign Policy: A Framework of Analysis. In A. Malek (Ed.), *News Media & Foreign Relations* (pp. 29–42). New Jersey: Ablex Publishing Corporation.

Mueller, J. E. (1994). *Policy and Opinion in the Gulf War*. Chicago: University of Chicago.

Negrine, R. M. (1989). *Politics and Mass Media in Britain*. London: Routledge.

Neuman, R.W., Just, M.R. & Crigler, A.N. (1992). *Common Knowledge: News and the Construction of Political Meaning*. Chicago: University of Chicago Press.

Norris, P. (1997). *Politics and the Press*. London: Lynne Rienner Publishers.

Pan, Z. & Kosicki, G. M. (1993). Framing Analysis: An Approach to News Discourse. *Political Communication, 10, 1*, 55–75.

Paletz, D. L. & Entman, R. M. (1991). *Media, Power, Politics*. New York: The Free Press.

Peh, D. & Melkote, S. R. (1991). Bias in Newpaper Reporting: A Content Analysis of the Coverage of Korean Airlines and Iran Airbus Shootings in the U.S. Elite Press. *Gazette, 47*, 59–78.

Powlick, P. J. (1995). The Sources of Public Opinion for American Foreign Policy Officials. *International Studies Quarterly, 39*, 427–451.

Powlick, P. J. & Katz, A. Z. (1998). Defining the American Public Opinion/ Foreign Policy News. *Mershon International Studies Review, 42*, 29–61.

Putnam, L. L., Philips, N. & Chapman, P. (1996). Metaphors of Communication and Organization. In S. H. Clegg, C. Hardy & W. R. Nord, W. R (Eds.), *Handbook of Organization Studies* (pp. 375–408). Thousand Oaks, California: Sage.

Reese, S. D. (1991). Setting the Media's Agenda: A Power Balance Perspective. In J. A. Anderson (Ed.), *Communication Yearbook/14* (pp. 308–341). USA: Sage.

Reuters (1995). Major Events in Former Yugoslavia [Hebrew]. *Haaretz* (Nov. 24), 2A.

Rivenburgh, N. (1996). Social Identification and Media Coverage of Foreign Relations. In A. Malek (Ed.), *News Media & Foreign Relations* (pp. 79–94). New Jersey: Ablex Publishing Corporation.

Robinson, P. (2000). The Policy-Media Interaction Model: Measuring Media Power during Humanitarian Crisis. *Journal of Peace Research, 37, 5*, 613–633.

Rogers, E. M. & Dearing, J. W. (1988). Agenda-Setting Research: Where Has It Been, Where Is It Going. In J. A. Anderson (Ed.), *Communication Yearbook/11* (pp. 555–594). USA: Sage.

Rosenfeld, S. (1995). The American Response. *Washington Post*, Nov. 24.

Russet, B. (1990). *Controlling the Sword*. Cambridge, MA: Harvard University Press.

Scheufele, D. A. (1999). Framing as a Theory of Media Effects. *Journal of Communication, 49, 1*, 103–122.

Serfaty, S. (1991). The Media and Foreign Policy. In S. Serfaty (Ed.), *The Media and Foreign Policy* (pp. 1–16). New York: St. Martin's Press.

Siebert, F. *et al.* (1956). *Four Theories of the Press.* Urbana: University of Illinois Press.

Taylor, P. M. (2000). The Media and Kosovo Conflict—Introduction. *European Journal of Communication, 15, 3*, 293–297.

Tuchman, G. (1978). *Making News: a Study in the Construction of Reality.* New York: Free Press.

Van Belle, D. A. (2000). *Press Freedom and Global Politics.* Westport, CT: Praeger.

Vincent, R. C. (2000). A Narrative Analysis of US Press Coverage of Slobodan Milosevic and the Serbs in Kosovo. *European Journal of Communication, 15, 3*, 321–344.

Weiss, C. H. (1974). What America's Leaders Read. *Public Opinion Quarterly, XXXVIII, 1*, 1–22.

Wolfsfeld, G. (1993). The Role of the News Media in Unequal Political Conflicts: From the Intifada to the Gulf War and Back Again. *Research Paper R-8* (pp. 1–21). USA: Harvard College.

Wolfsfeld, G. (1997). *Media and Political Conflict.* Cambridge: Cambridge University Press.

Wood, B. D. & Peake, J. S. (1998). The Dynamics of Foreign Policy Agenda Setting. *American Political Science Review, 92, 1*, 173–184.

Woodward, S. (1995). *Balkans Tragedy: Chaos and Dissolution after the Cold War.* Washington, DC: Brookings.

Wright, C. R. (1985). *Mass Communication: A Sociological Perspective* (2nd ed.). New York: Random House.

Young, O. R. (1968). *The Politics of Force.* New Jersey: Princeton University.

CHAPTER 9

GLOBAL TELEVISION AND CONFLICT RESOLUTION: DEFINING THE LIMITS OF THE CNN EFFECT

Piers Robinson

A. INTRODUCTION

Dramatic news media coverage of suffering people is widely understood to profoundly impact upon Western responses to "distant" war. Intervention in Northern Iraq in 1991 and Somalia in 1992–1993 is claimed to have been the result of media pressure, the so-called CNN effect. Currently however, the precise link between media coverage and third-party intervention in war is the subject of controversy. Although intuitively appealing, the argument that media coverage forces intervention has been countered in two studies (Gowing, 1994; Strobel, 1997) arguing media impact on the policy process is at best limited. Yet even those skeptical of a CNN effect argue that at times news media coverage plays a key role in shaping policy responses (Gowing, 1994, pp. 38–84; Strobel, 1997, pp. 127–209).[1]

While the significance of the CNN effect remains controversial, scant attention is paid to both the type of policy response media coverage provokes and the consequence of that policy for any given war.[2] In terms of conflict resolution, an important development of the 1990s was the increased willingness of Western powers to act as third-party interveners, and to use force, during civil war. Intervention takes one of three forms. First intervention may be aimed at securing humanitarian objectives by either consensual or coercive means. Such action does not contribute to the resolution of a conflict, only to the mitigation of its worst effects. An example of humanitarian intervention is the initial deployment of U.S. troops in Somalia who were mandated to use force in order to ensure the delivery of food aid. Second, military action may be taken to force one or more warring parties to settle for peace. A recent example of such action is the NATO operation Allied Force in Kosovo initiated in order to enforce Serb compliance

---

[1] For a review of the literature on the CNN effect, *see* Robinson (1999).

[2] For an initial speculative examination of the types of policy media coverage might effect, *see* Steve Livingston (1997).

with U.S. goals. Third, involvement can take the form of a peace-building operation where force is used to ensure compliance with a settlement. The ongoing operations in Bosnia (SFOR, initially IFOR) and Kosovo (KFOR) are two examples of peace-building operations. It is important to note the last two coercive forms of intervention extend the concept of conflict resolution beyond traditional concerns with non-coercive "arbitration, bargaining . . . negotiation, . . . [and] mediation etc." (Hoffman, 1992, p. 263). Whether or not coercive means should be considered a part of conflict resolution (as opposed to the lesser goal of conflict management) is a contested issue and it is necessary to clarify my position at the outset. In this chapter conflict resolution is understood as a complete and equitable political settlement that deals with all underlying tensions that exist between parties. However, it is also assumed here that, in order to achieve conflict resolution, coercive means might have to be employed at some stage. Accordingly, military intervention to end war is understood as being at one end of a continuum of policies, ranging from coercion to arbitration, all of which might be necessary to resolve a conflict.[3] For those working in the field of conflict resolution we need to understand the type of intervention media coverage causes. Two questions are at stake. First, is the CNN effect limited to humanitarian action? Second, can media coverage cause direct military intervention in order to end a conflict? It is important to note at the outset that the focus of inquiry is the impact of media upon forcible intervention (defined as the threat or use of force) aimed at conflict resolution and not other non-military responses such as diplomatic engagement (e.g., brokering peace talks). By examining the case of the 1992–1995 war in Bosnia I will offer an answer as to whether the CNN effect can trigger military intervention aimed at ending war, or alternatively, is limited to causing narrowly prescribed humanitarian action.

1. Bosnia

The 1992–1995 Bosnian conflict is a useful case against which to examine the effects of media coverage upon forcible intervention in war. The war received sustained coverage from the Western media and apparently triggered the three types of intervention listed above. For the bulk of the conflict Western intervention was spearheaded by a humanitarian operation UNPROFOR (United Nations Protection Force) designed to both contain the conflict and mitigate its worst effects on civilians but not resolve the war. The operation was largely consensual but did occasionally resort to the use of force. By the summer of 1995, with U.S. leadership, the Western response took on a more forceful character. By late August a sustained bombing campaign, in tandem with a major U.S. diplomatic effort, was initiated.[4] For many it was the "aggressive deployment of NATO airpower against the Bosnian Serbs [that] made the crucial difference and . . . had

---

[3] *See* Andrew Williams (1999, p. 83) for a brief discussion of this issue.

[4] A key component in the military action was the newly deployed European Rapid Reaction force.

this happened earlier, the war would have been brought to a close sooner" (Neville-Jones, 1996–1997).[5] Within weeks the Dayton peace agreement was signed and a peace-building operation, IFOR, was in place.

The aim here is to identify the potential of media coverage regarding conflict resolution focusing upon whether or not media might trigger military intervention aimed at ending war. We therefore need to identify if media coverage was a causal factor in shifting policy from a non-coercive humanitarian operation (UNPROFOR), toward a policy of direct military intervention that, many argue, helped end the war. In order to do this I first detail the events leading up to U.S. military (and diplomatic) engagement in Bosnia. Having identified the decision period regarding the military lead, a model is used to assess media influence. The bombing campaign that resulted from the military lead is considered next, focusing upon whether it played a decisive role in ending the war. I conclude that while media coverage triggered narrowly prescribed humanitarian action, it was not sufficient to force a decisive intervention aimed at ending the war. Using these findings to elaborate upon a more general thesis put forward by Michael Barnett (1996), I conclude that military intervention in Bosnia represented a form of image management. Governments were pressured to intervene but only in response to atrocities that attracted widespread media coverage and even then only in a limited fashion. This finding fits a wider pattern of Western responses to "distant" war and raises an important question of how to force governments, concerned primarily with image management, to pursue long-term conflict resolution policies. On this issue the chapter concludes with a consideration of how improved media coverage of war might cause Western governments to take conflict resolution more seriously.

2.   U.S. Military Engagement in Bosnia

By spring 1995 the war in Bosnia was entering its closing stages. In terms of the international response, the U.S. continued to avoid direct engagement in the war, leaving instead the British and French governments in command. In terms of the geo-strategic situation, Bosnian Serb nationalists possessed 70 percent of Bosnian territory but were diplomatically and militarily isolated. Supported by the United States, the Croatian army had retrained and rearmed since 1994 and successfully demonstrated their military capability in May 1995 when Operation Flash captured Sector West in Western Slavonia. The formation of a military alliance between the Muslim-Croat Federation and the Republic of Croatia coupled with Serbian President Milosevic's increasing unwillingness to offer support compounded the Bosnian Serb nationalists' isolation.

---

[5] For accounts that highlight the importance of U.S. military engagement, see Daalder (2000), Gow (1997, pp. 278–279), Holbrooke (1998), Malcolm (1996, p. 266), Sharp (1997–1998, p. 113).

From a position of weakness Bosnian Serb nationalists accelerated an aggressive policy of subjecting UN "safe areas" to attack. As a result limited NATO air strikes were authorized. In response Bosnian Serb nationalists took UNPROFOR personnel hostage. Humiliated by the hostage taking, a debate broke "out within the Western alliance over whether or not to stay in Bosnia" (Holbrooke, 1998, p. 65; Christopher, 1998, p. 348). Importantly, the U.S. had committed itself to the NATO extraction plan Determined Effort that required the deployment of U.S. ground troops to cover an UNPROFOR withdrawal (Christopher, 1998, p. 348; Daalder, 2000, pp. 56–61; Holbrooke, 1998, pp. 66–67). By all accounts this was considered a bad option (Christopher, 1998, p. 348; Holbrooke, 1998, p. 66). Facing the unwelcome possibility of an UNPROFOR withdrawal sucking U.S. ground troops into Bosnia, Anthony Lake (National Security Advisor to the Clinton administration) began creating a policy alternative for Clinton (Woodward, 1996, pp. 254–260; Loza, 1996, p. 38). Lake "proposed two parallel actions: the strengthening of UNPROFOR and the launching of an American peace initiative-both to be supported by a decisive threat of NATO air strikes" (Loza, 1996, p. 38). Lake's policy became known as the end game strategy. At this point in time U.S. policy toward Bosnia was clearly under review. However, as Holbrooke (1998, p. 68) describes, "events in Bosnia were moving faster than the policy-review process in Washington. As the Administration deliberated, the Bosnian Serbs attacked. This time their action would go down in history."

The fall of the UN "safe area" in Srebrenica on and around July 11, the ensuing massacre of around 8,000 inhabitants and the displacement of its remaining population, marked a turning point for the U.S. response to the war in Bosnia. In the following days the Western alliance fell into disarray. On French television Chirac derided the U.S. and British for failing to support action to retake Srebrenica: "I owe it to the truth to say that up until now the contacts the French government has made have not been positive. I deplore that. For the moment, we are alone."[6] Prime Minister John Major publicly opposed Chirac's demands. According to Holbrooke (1998, p. 70), "Everywhere one turned, there was a sense of confusion in the face of Bosnian Serb brutality." A flurry of diplomatic activity accompanied a series of high level meetings while Clinton contacted President Chirac, Chancellor Kohl and Prime Minister Major.[7] U.S. policy was rapidly being transformed to adopt a more forceful posture. By July 23, two days after the London Conference on Bosnia had been convened; the United States threatened any further violation of "safe areas" with actions at "unprecedented levels."[8] The immediate concern here was to deter an attack on the Gorazde "safe area"

---

[6]   Chirac cited in Ann Devroy & William Drozdiak, "Clinton Agrees to Plan Defense of Safe Areas, French Seek help in Shoring up UN Effort," *Washington Post*, July 15 1995, A17.

[7]   White House Press Statement (WHPS) July 13, 1995; White House Press Briefing (WHPB) July 13, 1995; WHPB July 14, 1995; WHPB July 18, 1995; WHPBs and WHPSs available on line at http://www.whitehouse.gov.

[8]   WHPS July 23, 1995.

(Holbrooke, 1998, p. 72; Christopher, 1998, p. 348) but the threat was extended to include attacks on any "safe areas" including Sarajevo. With a robust policy in place, the United States took the necessary measures to enable a forceful military response. On July 26 the North Atlantic Council met in Brussels to "work out the command and control arrangements"[9] and, after "two firm phone conversations" (Christopher, 1998, p. 348) between Warren Christopher and Boutros-Ghali, the dual key arrangement was terminated by handing military control from the UN over to NATO. By the end of July officials presented Milosevic and Mladic (Bosnian Serb nationalist military leader) with a list of targets NATO would bomb the next time a "safe area" was attacked (Sharp, 1997–1998, p. 112) (The threat to use force was to be finally realized in late August after a mortar bombing of a Sarajevo market place). Within two weeks the U.S. also initiated a diplomatic effort following a Croatian offensive to retake the Krajina region.[10] On August 10 Clinton declared:

> This is an important moment in Bosnia, and it could be a moment of real promise. Because of the military actions of the last few days, the situation on the ground has changed . . . I think its time we should try to make a move to make peace.[11]

As Holbrooke notes (1998, p. 73), the Croatian offensive altered the "diplomatic landscape" and placed Bosnian Serb nationalists in a position of weakness. All in all, within a month of the fall of Srebrenica, U.S. policy had shifted from a four and a half-year avoidance of the war in Bosnia to close military and diplomatic engagement.

3. Measuring Media Impact on U.S. Military Leadership in Bosnia

If the fall of Srebrenica represented a turning point regarding the use of force, which in turn is widely held to have played a crucial role in ending the war, what impact did media coverage have on this policy change? In order to examine the impact of the media on intervention decisions a policy-media interaction model was applied to this period.[12] The model was developed, in part, from recent research by Gowing (1994) and Strobel (1997). The model posits that media influence on policy occurs when there exists (1) policy uncertainty (Gowing, 1994, p. 38, Strobel, 1997, p. 219) and (2) extensive and critically framed media coverage. In this situation, uncertain of what to do and without a clearly defined policy line with which to counter critical media coverage, policy makers can be

---

[9] WHPB July 26, 1995.

[10] *Strategic Survey* (1996–1997) and Holbrooke (1998, p. 74).

[11] White House Press Conference (WHPC) Aug. 10, 1995. WHPCs available on line at http://www.whitehouse.gov.

[12] For full details of the model and its application to this case, *see* Robinson (2000).

forced to respond to media driven public pressure or the fear of *potential* negative public reaction to government inaction. Alternatively, when policy makers are set on a particular course of action (i.e., there is policy certainty), critical media coverage is unlikely to influence policy. Instead policy makers are more likely to work harder to promote their chosen course of action through press briefings and public announcements. In this situation the media tends to reflect elite decisions and helps to build support for them (Hallin, 1986; Bennett, 1990; Herman & Chomsky, 1988). Hence in the case of U.S. military leadership in Bosnia, if media were a factor in causing the intervention, we would expect to observe critical media framing and policy uncertainty preceding the decision to intervene. Alternatively, the U.S. executive might have been intent on intervening for some other reason. If this was the case, we would expect to observe a certain policy line being fed to the media after a decision to intervene and supportively framed media coverage.

4.   Media Framing and Policy Uncertainty Following the Fall of Srebrenica

The media treated the fall of Srebrenica as an event of pre-eminent importance devoting extensive coverage to the story.[13] Every day the *Washington Post* and the *New York Times* ran at least one front page article on Bosnia while CBS treated the fall as the key news story between July 11 and 14 allocating it to the leading headline slot. The media not only focused upon events in Bosnia but also framed coverage in a way that both empathized with the plight of refugees from Srebrenica and was deeply critical of U.S. policy toward Bosnia. For example press coverage contained emotive descriptors such as "mass of wailing humanity," "dazed," "weeping" and "trail of tears." Also the population of Srebrenica were repeatedly referred to as refugees, people, women, elderly and children. These are empathizing labels which encourage identification with the plight of the refugees and emphasize their status as victims. An example of an empathy framed article can be seen in the following exert:

> Rousted from their homes by conquering Serb soldiers, the refugees formed a trail of tears stretching through north eastern Bosnia from the outskirts of Srebrenica, 10 miles from the Serbian border, to this once-thriving industrial city 40 miles to the north. Frantic mothers searched desperately for their babies . . . Officials said an elderly woman died of heat exhaustion.[14]

References to Western policy contained critical descriptors such as "doing too little too late," "absence of will," "impotence," one "humiliation after another" and

---

[13]   Full details regarding the framing analysis can be found in Robinson (2000) and Robinson (2002 in press).

[14]   John Pomfret, "Serbs Force Thousands of Muslims on Harrowing Journey," *Washington Post*, July 14 1995, A01.

"sickly." In addition, the words fail, withdraw and end were repeatedly used in reference to the UN mission and Western policy which created an impression of Western failure throughout the media coverage. An example of such critical framed coverage can be seen in the following exert from an opinion editorial by Charles Gati:

> After the fall of the U.N.-declared "safe zone" in eastern Bosnia, American politicians should be asked to repeat at least four of their favorite cliches and half-truths to the displaced people of Srebrenica—or to recant. First, they should say "never again," or concede that words alone cannot help the refugees nor erase the memory of the dead—nor stop the fanatics bent on creating a Greater Serbia. President Clinton, please go to see the people of Srebrenica. Tell them "never again" was meant for domestic consumption; you didn't really mean what you said. For Srebrenica is safe for thugs only. The 42,000 civilians of the city, mostly refugees now, should fend for themselves.[15]

Overall it was found that the vast bulk of reports were framed in such a way. Western policy was heavily criticized for having failed to prevent the fall of Srebrenica and coverage highlighted the plight of the refugees expelled from Srebrenica.

In terms of policy certainty, an analysis of U.S. executive press briefings revealed policy uncertainty over whether or not greater force would be used to defend the threatened Gorazde "safe area." For example, on July 13 a State Department spokesperson stated:

> I think there are two factors at work. One is that the United Nations and the troop-contributing countries have got to make a fundamental decision—whether they will use military force or military strategy to try to either regain what has been lost or to protect what may be lost. That is a very important question, one that has not yet been fully answered.[16]

Also, according to both Holbrooke (1998, p. 72) and Christopher (1998, p. 348), one of the key decisions made during the days following the fall of Srebrenica was the decision to *draw a line* at Gorazde and respond with decisive force to further attacks on UN safe areas. Clearly this decision would have been under discussion in the days leading up to it therefore indicating that policy was uncertain during this period in that no final decision had been made regarding the use of force.

---

[15] Charles Gati, "Tell It To Srebrenica," *Washington Post*, July 13, 1995, A25.

[16] State Department Press Briefing (SDPB) July 13, 1995. SDPBs available on line at http://www.secretary.state.gov.

B. ASSESSING MEDIA INFLUENCE

By emphasising the failure of the West, and empathizing with the expelled population of Srebrenica, news media coverage was of a critical "do something" nature. This critical coverage took place alongside policy uncertainty when U.S. policy makers were unsure whether or not any further violations of UN "safe areas," specifically an attack on the Gorazde "safe area," should be responded to with the use of force. The theoretical insight provided by the policy-media model indicates policy makers would have been under pressure to respond to the critical and emotive news media coverage. Deciding to "draw a line" at Gorazde provided a response to the critical "do something" media coverage, preventing both more unwelcome images of displaced refugees and further criticisms of Western policy. An account by Woodward of the events in question supports this inference and indicates media coverage being a factor during policy deliberations. In a foreign policy meeting on July 17 Clinton is quoted as stating "We have a war by *CNN*. Our position is unsustainable, it's killing the US position of strength in the world" (*emphasis added* Woodward, 1996, p. 261). Also, In the Oval office on July 18, Gore is quoted as stating "The worst solution would be to acquiesce to genocide . . . and allow the rape of another city [Gorazde] AND more refugees . . . But we can't ignore the images either, . . . My 21-year-old daughter asked about that picture (in the *Washington Post* of a Muslim woman who hung herself following the Serb assault) . . . What am I supposed to tell her? Why is this happening and we're not doing anything . . . Acquiescence is not an option.' (Woodward, 1996, pp. 262–263). Overall, while other factors were likely to have played a part in motivating U.S. leadership,[17] both the policy-media interaction model and other accounts indicate that media coverage, combined with policy uncertainty is likely to have been a factor in causing U.S. military leadership in Bosnia.

At this point it is worthwhile differentiating between the diplomatic initiative of early August and the military lead in July. The diplomatic effort represented a concerted effort on behalf of the U.S. to seek an end to the war, albeit taking advantage of the Croatian offensive that was rapidly changing the geo-strategic balance. The military lead, as we have seen, was aimed primarily at averting the fall of Gorazde (and more generally to enforce UN directives). In terms of U.S. engagement in Bosnia during summer 1995 we therefore have two relatively distinct policies being pursued, one aimed at using diplomacy to end the war, the other aimed at using force to prevent further violations of UN directives.[18] If the military lead was aimed at achieving such relatively limited objectives, the question raised is precisely how important was the military dimension of the U.S. lead

---

[17] Other factors identified as important during this period include the desire to avoid a humiliating U.S. backed withdrawal from Bosnia, U.S. and Western credibility and pressure from congress. For a full discussion of these alternative/additional factors and their relative significance in this case, *see* Robinson (2002 in press).

[18] For a detailed analysis of the policy process during this period, *see* Daalder (2000), Holbrooke (1998) and Robinson (2001).

with respect to the ending of the war. An analysis of the bombing campaign offers further insights into this question.

1. Operation Deliberate Force: Humanitarian Action Aimed at Ending the Siege of Sarajevo and not a Decisive Military Intervention to End the War[19]

The threat to use force was finally realized in late August when a widely televised mortar bombing of the Sarajevo "safe area" triggered Operation Deliberate Force. The bombing campaign also ran hand in hand with furious diplomatic activity conducted by Richard Holbrooke and preceded major Croatian and Bosnian government offensives. By the end of September a cease-fire had been agreed to and, within weeks, the Dayton peace negotiations had been initiated. For many Operation Deliberate Force played a key role in ending the Bosnian war (e.g. Gow, 1997, pp. 278–279; Malcolm, 1996, p. 266; Neville-Jones, 1996–1997; Sharp, 1997–1998, p. 113). Holbrooke's (1998, p. 104) personal account also highlights the importance of the bombing campaign in furthering his negotiating efforts. If these accounts are correct, given the earlier finding of media influence, there might be grounds for arguing that media coverage was a factor in triggering a military intervention which in turn played a key role in ending the war. In order to assess such an analysis we need to answer two key questions. First, was the bombing campaign a strategic attempt at forcing the war to an end? Second, even if the bombing campaign was not designed as such, did it in any case play a major role in ending the war?

Regarding the first question, Operation Deliberate Force began as a response to a violation of the UN "safe area" of Sarajevo and was suspended, on September 14, when an agreement was reached to withdraw Bosnian Serb nationalist heavy weaponry from around the city.[20] This suspension was followed by a 144-hour deadline for the removal of the weaponry.[21] By September 21 the deadline had expired, NATO was satisfied the Bosnian Serb nationalists had withdrawn heavy weaponry, and the air strikes were stopped indefinitely. As such, the bombing served primarily to achieve a narrowly prescribed humanitarian objective (ending the siege of Sarajevo) and not a strategic goal of forcing an end to the war. The fact that the bombing was not part of an orchestrated attempt to end the war is also supported by Holbrooke's (1998, p. 104) account:

[A]lmost everyone came to believe that the bombing had been part of a master plan. But in fact in none of the discussions prior to our mission had we

---

[19]   *See* Robinson (2001) For a more detailed analysis of the role of Operation Deliberate Force and the ending of the war in Bosnia, in particular Daalder (2000) and Holbrooke' (1998) claim that the bombing was a key factor.

[20]   SDPB, Sept. 14, 1995; Department of Defense Background Briefing (DDBB), Sept. 18, 1995. DDBB available on line at http://www/defenselink.mil/news.

[21]   DDPB, Sept. 18, 1995.

considered bombing as part of a negotiating strategy . . . but it simply did not happen that way. It took an outrageous Bosnian Serb action to trigger Operation Deliberate Force.

Hence if media coverage was a factor in moving the U.S. towards intervention, this action was clearly not aimed at forcing an end to the war. Even if this was the case, did the bombing play a key role in ending the war? The evidence here is unclear but it would seem that the bombing was a marginal factor in ending the war.

First, Bosnian Serb nationalist co-operation had been secured *before* Operation Deliberate Force. On August 29 the Bosnian Serb Assembly agreed to support the Contact Group plan.[22] On the evening of the 29th the leaders of the Bosnian Serb nationalists and Serbia met and agreed a joint negotiating team[23] which included Bosnian Serb leader Karadzic and Mladic. These events occurred prior to Operation Deliberate Force that started at midnight August 29–30.[24] Holbrooke (1998, pp. 105–106) identifies this agreement, handed to him as a note by Milosevic (later to become known as the Patriarch Paper) as a "real breakthrough" indicating "genuine negotiations were about to begin." Interestingly Holbrooke (1998, pp. 104–105) implies the agreement was a result of the bombing. As we have seen, the agreement was made prior to the bombing, therefore making Holbrooke's interpretation of events problematic. While the bombing would have undoubtedly increased the pressure on the Bosnian Serb nationalists to continue negotiating, the fact that they had already agreed to enter negotiations makes problematic the idea that the bombing was decisive in this respect. Interestingly, consistent with the argument made here, most of Holbrooke's (1998, pp. 119–152) discussion and indeed evidence, regarding the importance of the NATO bombing relates to negotiations to lift the siege of Sarajevo rather than the broader peace negotiations.[25]

Second, Operation Deliberate Force might have served to help the military defeat of the Bosnian Serb nationalists during major Croatian and Bosnian offensives in September. However, these offensives started on September 11[26] and were

---

[22] BBC *Summary of World Broadcasts* (*SWBs*), Aug. 31, 1995, EE/2396 C/10. *SWBs* available via the BBC Written Archives Centre, Reading nr. London.

[22] *SWB*, Sept. 1, 1995, EE/2397 C/9.

[23] *SWB*, Sept. 1, 1995, EE/2397 C/9.

[24] *SWB*, Aug. 31, 1995, EE/2396 C/5.

[25] The only direct evidence Holbrooke regarding the bombing being crucial vis-à-vis the broader peace negotiations was that Bosnian President Izetbegovic linked acceptance of general principles to a resumption of the bombing after it had been halted in early September (Holbrooke, 1998, pp. 131–134).

[26] *Strategic Survey*, (1996–1997) A Fragile Peace for Bosnia, 134.

largely complete by September 17.[27] As Operation Deliberate Force started on August 30 and ended on the September 14, with a conditional suspension of bombing, the overlap between the NATO action and the Bosnian and Croatian offensives was minimal. Even during the three to four days between September 11 and 14, when Operation Deliberate Force may have provided close air support to the Bosnian and Croatian forces, there is no evidence this occurred. The bombing campaign did serve to soften up the Bosnian Serb nationalist forces by attacking command and communication targets. To this extent, the bombing helped the offensives underway. But set against this is the fact that the Bosnian and Croatian governments were already in a position to defeat the Bosnian Serb nationalists as evidenced by the successes of Operations Flash and Storm earlier in the year. Indeed, the September offensives were responsible for forcing Bosnian Serb nationalists out of 20 percent of Bosnian territory, thereby returning the territorial division of the country to the 51/49 percent split demanded by the Contact Group plan (which formed the basis of the U.S. diplomatic effort). NATO air power undoubtedly played a part, but it is unlikely to have been a decisive factor in the ground war.

In short, Operation Deliberate Force did not represent a conscious attempt to bring the war in Bosnia to an end. Rather it was primarily aimed at the enforcement of UN directives pertaining to Sarajevo. As such the operation represented a shift from a non-coercive to a coercive "humanitarian" intervention rather than a strategic attempt to force an end to the war. Moreover, the idea that the U.S. military action played a decisive role in ending the war is made problematic because (1) Bosnian Serb nationalist cooperation with the peace process had been secured prior to the bombing, and (2) the Bosnian Serb nationalists were facing military defeat at the hand of Croatian and Bosnian government forces. U.S. diplomacy undoubtedly played a major role in securing the peace, but given the above points, it stretches credibility to argue Operation Deliberate Force represented some kind of decisive military intervention to end the war.

2.   Media Coverage and Intervention in Bosnia: An Exercise in Image Management?

The foregoing analysis indicates that media coverage did play a part in pushing the U.S. to intervene militarily in Bosnia during 1995. However, Operation Deliberate Force was primarily aimed at achieving humanitarian objectives rather than forcing an end to the war. Does this finding fit a wider pattern of Western responses (military and other) to the war in Bosnia? An analysis by Michael Barnett (U.S. Mission to the UN, 1994) is helpful here. Barnett develops a substantial critique of the inadequacy of the Western response to the war in Bosnia. He argues that governments, perceiving no vital interest in the former Yugoslavia, but unable to totally disregard the ethnic cleansing, sought to find "a middle road

---

[27]   *SWB*, Sept. 25, 1995, EE/2419 A/9.

between disengagement and involvement" (Barnett, 1996, p. 150). Hence, from Barnett's perspective, Western governments were forced to provide some kind of response to the war but sought to avoid substantive involvement. Barnett (1996, p. 151) writes:

> The United Nations had the authority to enforce these resolutions and pro-tect civilians: it could use "all necessary means." Yet these mandates were intermittently implemented at best, and, at worst, ethnic cleansing, war crimes, and other atrocities were carried out by Serbs in full view of the United Nations without much response.

Barnett (1996, p. 155) goes on to note, consistent with the case study find-ings here, that at times Western governments did attempt more forceful interven-tions but only "after the Serbs launched a well-publicized attack against civilians."

Combining Barnett's critique with the research here, we can discern a pattern vis-à-vis Western responses to Bosnia. Policy was set against substantive inter-vention aimed at ending the conflict. As Gowing (1996, p. 83) puts it "As in Bosnia, their fundamental long-term strategy was to engage in low-risk, low-cost, minimalist policies that gave the impression of a full engagement when the polit-ical will was anything but." However, during periods of policy uncertainty, when widely televised atrocities brought into question the adequacy of the Western response to the war in Bosnia, Western governments were moved to "do some-thing." This often took the form of a threat to use force such as after the shelling of Sarajevo or the fall of Srebrenica. At other times Western governments responded with non-military policies such as the creation of safe areas. But these policies and responses did not represent attempts at forcing an end to the war. As such, military intervention represented a kind of image management or, as Barnett (1996, p. 155) puts it, an attempt to "retrieve . . . [the] reputation" of Western gov-ernments. The summer of 1995 did witness an important and substantial U.S. mil-itary and diplomatic engagement in the war. But the military dimension was still primarily designed to achieve humanitarian objectives rather than bring the war to an end. More critically Barnett (1996, p. 155) argues that "the real threat unleashed by the Serbian attack on Srebrenica was to the 'integrity of the mis-sion' suggesting that the increasing NATO engagement in Bosnia was designed to 'rescue reputation and not to protect civilians'." Ultimately, what marked the significant change in 1995 was the willingness to properly enforce UN directives that had only been sporadically enforced before. In terms of our interest here, at no point during the four and a half year war in Bosnia was media coverage able to force Western governments to forcibly intervene and bring the war in Bosnia to an end.

3. The CNN Effect Triggering Humanitarian Action not Conflict Resolution

The question posed at the start of this chapter asked whether media coverage, the so-called CNN effect, was capable of pushing Western governments to intervene militarily in order to end war. The case study of U.S. military intervention in Bosnia 1995 indicates that media coverage did indeed influence Western military responses, but that these responses had limited humanitarian objectives. Even the major and sustained intervention of late summer 1995 was primarily aimed at lifting the siege of Sarajevo as opposed to forcing an end to the war. Hence, for those seeking to understand the potential of news media coverage with regard to conflict resolution, the case of Bosnia indicates that the CNN effect is unlikely to promote the kind of decisive military intervention that is sometimes required to end a conflict[28] (although media might still influence diplomatic engagement as an approach to resolving a conflict).[29]

The findings here fit with a broader pattern of Western responses, whether media influenced or not, to war during the 1990s.[30] Intervention in Northern Iraq in 1991 to protect the Kurds from the brutal retribution of Saddam Hussein provided limited security and prevented Kurds from starving, but little attempt was made to force a long term political settlement for Kurds. In Somalia, the U.S. was willing to deploy ground troops but only in support of food aid delivery. When the operation staggered toward forcing an end to the conflict (by attempting to capture the warlord Aideed), U.S. casualties gave Clinton a reason to withdraw U.S. troops from Somalia. The case of the Western response to the genocide in Rwanda, 1994 follows a similar pattern. In April 1994, when the genocide started, Western governments deflected pressure to intervene and media reports emphasized the supposed tribal and confused nature of the conflict (Livingston, 1999; Robinson, 2002 forthcoming). Consequently the international community failed to intervene when the genocide could have been prevented. By the summer of 1994, emotive media coverage of people suffering in the refugee camps, defined the crisis, not as one of tribal conflict, but rather as a humanitarian crisis that demanded intervention (Livingston, 1999). The U.S. obliged and troops were deployed as part of a feed and water operation. Media coverage was able to trigger humanitarian action, but not action aimed at resolving the underlying political and military situation. Operation Allied force in Kosovo is a possible departure from this pattern in that military action would appear to have been used to force an end to the civil war. Quite what role media coverage played in triggering this response requires investigation. It should be noted however that extensive media coverage followed the decision to bomb and is therefore unlikely to have been a

---

[28] *See* Jakobsen (2000) for a critique of media influence in which he argues the CNN effect is "probably more of a hindrance than a help for Western conflict management as the general level" (Jakobsen, 2000, p. 141).

[29] A further factor that might curtail, although not decisively, the utility of the CNN effect with regard to conflict resolution point is that the effect is likely to be limited to influencing air power not ground troop intervention (Robinson, 2002 in press). With respect to ground troop intervention the body bag effect (fear of casualties and their impact on public opinion) overrides immediate media pressure to intervene (Robinson, 2002 in press).

[30] *See* Robinson (2002 in press) for a case study comparison of 1990s interventions and the role of media.

key factor in triggering this intervention. Indeed, Alexander Vershbow (US Ambassdor to NATO) notes: "I don't think it (media) made a big difference . . . I think from the outset . . . my government was seized by the political and regional consequences [of the crisis] . . . and with protecting our investment in Bosnia."[31]

Are there any explanations for why media impact, so widely argued to profoundly impact upon Western responses to distant wars, should be so inadequate with regard conflict resolution? Two points are of note. First, Western governments, and indeed most others, are extremely reluctant to become involved in conflicts where there is no perceived national interest. The associated doctrine of non-intervention in the internal affairs of states is a powerful realist belief that inhibits Western policy makers from embarking upon what some dismiss as the foreign policy of Mother Teresa. Policy makers are therefore unlikely to act of their own volition during "distant" crises. Rather some kind of external pressure is required for them to act. When policy makers are forced to respond, the desire is to minimize the extent of involvement. As we have seen in the case of the Western response to the war in Bosnia instances of forceful intervention are driven by the need for image management when widely publicized atrocities force governments to act. But any such action was never sufficient to force an end to the war. In short, policy makers seek to adopt policies that, while responding to the demand of media coverage, do not draw them into costly and unwanted engagements.

How then can those seeking conflict resolution put greater pressure on governments concerned largely with image management. One possible answer lies within media reporting itself. It is important to note here that it is not merely the reluctance of Western governments that stifles the possibility of conflict resolution policies being pursued. Media coverage itself is often inadequate. On one level, the news values that inform editorial and journalistic practice means that substantive media reporting tends to be confined to dramatic incidents that in turn hold press attention for short periods. By focusing upon the dramatic, reporting often ignores the underlying political and social complexities of a war. The limited attention span of media reporting does little to encourage the kind of long-term response required to settle and then resolve a conflict. Perhaps more importantly, journalists often frame reports in a way that defines war as a "humanitarian" crisis. The coverage of Srebrenica documented here highlighted the plight of refugees, and also that of Western failure, but primarily defined events as a humanitarian crisis. This, in itself, is not greatly problematic, but the failure to also relay the political and military context is. The image of suffering people pressures only for a humanitarian response, not a concerted attempt to resolve the broader political and military situation. At this point it is worth discerning three possible frames of reference available to journalists during reporting of the war in Bosnia (and indeed most other wars). The first is the frame of ancient ethnic hatred and the equal responsibility of all sides for the violence. As David Campbell (1998, pp. 53–54) argues:

---

[31] Interview with author Mar. 1, 2001.

News reports have repeatedly spoken of the way in which "Serbs savor ancient hatreds," how "Balkan hatreds defy centuries of outside meddling," the way the end of the Cold war has seen a "conflict born of old grievances" such that "the contagion" of "Europe's new tribalism should infect us all."

As noted above, Steven Livingston identified a similar frame of reference during the 1994 genocide in Rwanda when the international community failed to respond. At times, as we have seen in this chapter, media coverage adopts an empathizing frame, highlighting the suffering of the individual and often criticizing governments for not intervening. A third possible frame of reference, one that was not present in the vast bulk of reporting in Bosnia, was also available. As Eric Herring (1997) argues, the war in Bosnia could have been interpreted as a war between citizens committed to a multicultural Bosnia Herzegovina and nationalist committed to its destruction. In terms of potential effects, the first *tribal* framing does not pressure governments to intervene and tends to justify non-intervention on the grounds that nothing can be done to end supposedly ancient hatreds. The second empathizing frame, with its focus upon the suffering of individuals, pressures for humanitarian action to relieve suffering but not a determined effort to resolve the underlying political and military situation. In the case of the 1992–1995 war in Bosnia, the third type of framing would have pressured for a more substantive involvement in particular from Western government that are themselves committed to multicultural ideals. On this point it is interesting to note the prevalence of the multicultural discourse in the statements of Western leaders during Operation Allied Force in Kosovo. To a large extent it would appear that Western leaders justified this war in terms of maintaining an ethnically diverse Kosovo. To this extent, this particular framing of the crisis served to enable substantial and decisive military intervention in order to force an end to the conflict. Whether or not extensive media coverage of the war in Bosnia framed along similar lines would have helped force Western leaders to decisively intervene is open to debate. But such coverage would have made it difficult for Western leaders to justify the limited "humanitarian" involvement that actually occurred.

To conclude, evidence does point to media coverage having the power to facilitate Western responses to war. But such responses are limited to humanitarian objectives rather than concerted attempts to force an end to war. For those seeking action to achieve conflict resolution such policies are inadequate. Western governments are likely, in the main, to continue to seek to avoid military intervention in order to resolve war (Kosovo suggests a possible departure from this norm.) However, the media might be able to play a greater role if reporting moved beyond "humanitarian" frames of reference, that promote narrowly prescribed humanitarian, toward reporting that at least attempts to deal with the underlying political and military dimensions of a conflict. Such framing has greater potential to force decisive intervention that can end war thereby beginning the long process toward conflict resolution.

REFERENCES

Barnett, M. C. (1996). The Politics of Indifference. In T. Cushman & S. G. Mestrovic (Eds.), *This Time We Knew* (pp. 148–162). New York: New York University Press.

Bennett, W. C. (1990). Toward a Theory of Press-State Relations in the United States. *Journal of Communication*.

Campbell, D. (1998). *National Deconstruction: Violence, Identity and Justice in Bosnia*. London and Minneapolis: University of Minnesota Press.

Christopher, W. (1998). *In the Stream of History*. Stanford, California: Stanford University Press.

Daalder, I. (2000). *Getting to Dayton: The Making of America's Bosnia Policy*. Washington, D.C.: Brookings Institution Press.

Gow, J. (1997). *Triumph of the Lack of Will*. London: Hurst and Company.

Gowing, N. (1994). Real-time Television Coverage of Armed Conflicts and Diplomatic Crises: Does it pressure or Distort Foreign policy Decisions, Working Paper 94-1, The Joan Shorenstein Barone Center on the Press, Politics and Public Policy. Harvard: President and Fellows of Harvard College.

Gowing, N. (1996). Real time TV Coverage from War. In J. Gow, R. Paterson & A. Preston (Eds.), *Bosnia By Television*. London: British film Institute Publishing.

Hallin, D. (1986). *The Uncensored War: The Media and Vietnam* (Berkley: University of California Press).

Herman, E, & Chomsky, N. (1988). *Manufacturing Consent: the Political Economy of the Media*, New York: Pantheon.

Herring, E. (1997). An Uneven Killing Field: The Manufacture of Consent for the Arms Embargo on Bosnia-Herzegovina. In M. Evans (Ed.), *Aspects of Statehood and Institutionalism in Contemporary Europe* (pp. 159–182). Aldershot: Dartmouth.

Hoffman, M. (1992). Third Party Mediation and Conflict-Resolution in the Post-Cold War World. In J. Baylis & N. J. Rengger (Eds.), *Dilemmas of World Politics*. Oxford: Clarendon Press.

Holbrooke, R. (1998). *To End a War*. New York: Random House.

Jakobsen, P. V. (2000). Counter Point: Focus on the CNN Effect Misses the Point: The Real Media Impact on Conflict Management is Invisible and Indirect. *Journal of Peace Research, 37, 2*, 131–143.

Livingston, S. (1997). Clarifying the CNN Effect: an examination of media effects according to type of military intervention. Research Paper R-18. The

Joan Shorenstein Barone Center on the Press, Politics and Public Policy. Harvard: President and Fellows of Harvard College.

Livingston, S. (1999). US Coverage of Rwanda. In H. Adelman & A. Suhrke (Eds.), *The Path of a Genocide* (pp. 122–156). London and New Brunswick: Transaction Publishers.

Loza, T. (1996). From Hostages to Hostiles. *War Report*, July 43, 28–38.

Malcolm, N. (1996). *Bosnia: A Short History*. London: Macmillan.

Neville-Jones, P. (1996–1997). Dayton, IFOR and Alliance Relations in Bosnia. *Survival*. Winter 38, 1.

Robinson, P. (1999). The CNN Effect: can the news media drive foreign policy?. *Review of International Studies, 25, 2*, 301–309.

Robinson, P. (2000). The Policy-media Interaction Model: Measuring Media Power During Humanitarian Crisis, *Journal of Peace Research, 37, 5*, 625–645.

Robinson, P. (2001). Misperception in Foreign Policy Making: Operation Deliberate Force and the Ending of War in Bosnia, *Civil Wars* 19, 115–126.

Robinson, P. (2002 *in press*). *The CNN effect: The myth of news, foreign policy and humanitarian crisis.* Routledge: London and New York.

Sharp, J. M. O. (1997–1998). Dayton Report Card. *International Security, 22, 3*, 101–137.

Strategic Survey (1995–1996). A fragile Peace for Bosnia, International Institute for Strategic Studies, London: Oxford University Press.

Strobel, W. (1997). *Late Breaking Foreign Policy*. Washington. DC: United States Institute of Peace.

Williams, A. (1999). Conflict Resolution after the Cold war: the Case of Moldova. *Review of International Studies, 25*, 71–86.

Woodward, R. (1996). *The Choice*. New York: Simon and Schuster.

CHAPTER 10

MEDIA DIPLOMACY IN THE ARAB-ISRAELI CONFLICT

Eytan Gilboa

A. INTRODUCTION

In the last 25 years the news media has played significant roles in Arab-Israeli negotiations. Policymakers and negotiators used the media for various positive and negative purposes, although occasionally they neutralized coverage by conducting secret or closed-door diplomacy (Gilboa, 1998a; 2000a, pp. 546–552). Negative uses include propaganda and incitement for violence and hate. Positive uses include mediation, reconciliation and mobilization of public support for negotiations and peace agreements. The main purpose of this chapter is to demonstrate how leaders, officials and even journalists have employed the media in an effort to advance Arab-Israeli negotiations. It also explores professional and ethical problems involved in these uses. Media utilization in Arab-Israeli negotiations is analyzed in this chapter through joint application of negotiation and communication theories. The presentation is organized around selected significant elements of negotiation in international conflicts including signaling, confidence building, mediation, bridging, and promotion of negotiations and agreements.

Theories of international negotiation emphasize the significance of "pre-negotiation" stages, the role of "third parties," and "track-two diplomacy."[1] In the pre-negotiation stage, the sides explore the advantages and shortcomings of a specific negotiation process and make a decision—based on information received from the other party and other domestic and external considerations—on whether to enter formal negotiations. Signaling intentions and conditions and building confidence are significant factors throughout negotiation processes but are more critical at the pre-negotiation stage. Policymakers can use the media along other channels to signal intentions and to build confidence (Arno, 1984). These uses of the media have been defined as "media diplomacy" (Gilboa, 1998b). This chapter demonstrates how Secretary of State Henry Kissinger first used media diplomacy in his 1973–1974 mediation efforts and how Israeli and Arab leaders and negotiators followed him.

---

[1] On international negotiation and mediation, *see* Zartman & Rasmussen (1997), and Berton, Kimura & Zartman (1999). On pre-negotiation, *see* Stein (1989), and on "multi-track" diplomacy, *see* Diamond & McDonald (1996).

Sometimes, third parties are needed to help enemies begin negotiations: these can be formal representatives of superpowers, neutral states, international and global organizations, or ordinary individuals, who facilitate negotiations by talking to parties in conflict and persuading them to consider negotiation as a viable option. Third parties are particularly helpful in the pre-negotiation stage. "Track-two diplomacy" refers to unofficial mediators and informal forms of negotiation. It is possible and useful to view journalists acting independently as "third parties," pursuing "track two diplomacy" particularly in "pre-negotiation stages." These uses of the media have been defined as "media-broker diplomacy" (Gilboa, 2000b, pp. 298–302). This chapter examines several examples of prominent television journalists performing this role in Arab-Israeli negotiations including Walter Cronkite and Ted Koppel.

As this chapter explores media utilization in Arab-Israeli negotiations, it is necessary to distinguish among four separate peace processes defined mostly in geopolitical and chronological terms.[2] Following the historic visit of President Anwar Sadat in Jerusalem, Israel and Egypt began serious peace negotiations in 1977 and signed a peace agreement in March 1979. After the 1991 Gulf War, the United States initiated and started in Madrid Spain a process involving Israel and all its immediate Arab neighbors: Egypt, Syria, Lebanon, Jordan and the Palestinians. This effort was slow to produce any significant results and was replaced in 1993 by three separate although somewhat related processes between Israel and three of its neighbors: the Palestinians, Jordan, and Syria.

During 1993, Israel and the organization representing the Palestinians, the Palestine Liberation Organization (PLO), conducted secret negotiations in Oslo that produced a major breakthrough, a mutual recognition agreement and a declaration of principles for further negotiations. From September 1993 to October 1998 Israel and the Palestinian Authority reached several interim agreements, but in 2000 Yasser Arafat, the Palestinian Authority Chairman, rejected President Clinton's proposal for a permanent peace agreement and subsequently the Palestinians began a campaign of violence and terror against Israel. Following a relatively short period of negotiations, Israel and Jordan concluded a peace agreement in 1994. Israeli and Syrian negotiators held several significant meetings between 1992 and 2000 but didn't reach any agreements.

In terms of both Israeli and Arab public opinion, the Israeli-Egyptian and the Israeli-Jordanian peace processes were conducted on the basis of relatively wide domestic consensus, while the Israeli-Palestinian and the Israeli-Syrian processes were highly controversial. The news media played significant roles in all the Arab-Israeli peace processes but more so in the controversial ones. This chapter analyzes media utilization in Arab-Israeli negotiations in the following order and

---

[2] For recent comprehensive works on Arab-Israeli negotiations see Eisenberg & Caplan (1998), Savir (1998), Kleiman (2000), and Quandt (2001).

specific Arab-Israeli peacemaking processes: media diplomacy is applied to Kissinger's mediation in the Israeli-Egyptian process, signaling is applied to the Israeli-Syrian negotiations, while mediating appears in the Israeli-Egyptian context. Bridging and building confidence is applied to the Israeli-Palestinian process, and the final function, promoting negotiations and agreements, is applied to all the Arab-Israeli peace processes.

B. INITIATING MEDIA DIPLOMACY

Although President Nixon's National Security Adviser and Secretary of State Henry Kissinger devoted little attention to the media in his public statements, memoirs, and books, including the one he wrote on diplomacy (1994), he is probably the inventor of modern media diplomacy. "Kissinger's assiduous quest for favorable coverage was not merely a craving of his ego" wrote Isaacson (1992, p. 576), "it was also a way to further his foreign policy." Following the 1973 Arab-Israeli war, Kissinger perfected the use of the media for signaling and pressure purposes during his famous and highly successful "shuttle diplomacy." His relentless efforts to achieve disengagement and interim agreements between Israel and her neighbors, Egypt and Syria, included the extensive use of senior American correspondents aboard his plane, who became known as "Kissinger 14." Sensing the growing power of television and sound-bites, Kissinger gave special attention to the television reporters accompanying him: Marvin Kalb of CBS, Ted Koppel of ABC, and Richard Valeriani of NBC.

Kissinger was able to develop an intimate relationship with the correspondents aboard his plane. He gave them background reports, information and leaks mostly intended to amplify his status and position in the negotiations, extricate concessions from the negotiating parties, and break deadlocks. Ironically, perhaps, the correspondents knew more about his plans and tactics than the U.S. ambassadors in the places he visited. They also became instant sources of information on Kissinger's activities for local journalists, policymakers, and diplomats. On the other hand, as Koppel acknowledged, he and his colleagues couldn't reach the other participants in the process simply because of time and regime constraints: "We would get up at 5:30 or 6:00 in the morning, fly over to Damascus and sit in the lobby because we weren't allowed to go anywhere else until we were ready to get back on the plane" (Kalb, Koppel, & Scali, 1982, p. 42). At that point the reporters were completely dependent on Kissinger for information on what happened during his visit.

In Israel, where journalists enjoyed free movement and free access to politicians and negotiators, Kissinger employed another tactic. He would time the landing of his plane just before the deadline of the accompanying correspondents. Consequently, they had no time to check facts with Israeli and Arab leaders and negotiators, and the stories they filed were solely based on what Kissinger told them. In more critical cases he would land in Israel on a Friday afternoon, when, due to the Sabbath, Israeli leaders and journalists do not conduct official business. He would say, for example, in a press conference, that during his last meeting with an Arab leader like Sadat all the problems had been settled, and it was now up to the Israeli cabinet to say yes (Patir, 1997). Although, in many cases this kind of statement was incorrect or misleading, it was quite effective in getting concessions from Israel. Israel responded to Kissinger's media manipulations by creating for the first time a new position: Communication Adviser to the Prime Minister. Kissinger didn't like this competition and at one time asked Prime Minister Yitzhak Rabin to fire his newly appointed communication adviser.

The intimate relationship Kissinger developed with the correspondents on his plane was natural and understandable. However, it also raises several journalistic dilemmas and problems (Isaacson, 1992, p. 573). The correspondents became too dependent on one source whom they could not afford to antagonize (Seib, 1997, p. 85). His manipulations challenged both the diplomatic correspondents and the consumers of their reports. In talking to correspondents, he distinguished and switched back and forth between different categories of briefings: "background," "deep background" and "off the record." Sometimes quotes were directly attributed to the Secretary of State, at other times to the "senior official." Kissinger also appeared in person at airport welcoming ceremonies and in official press conferences. On the plane he would make one statement and in public a different one, and Koppel used to ask himself "whether what I had said quoting a 'senior State Department official' or what the Secretary of State himself was saying was going to get the greater weight?" (Kalb, Koppel, & Scali, 1982, p. 42).

The diplomatic correspondents also developed a stake in Kissinger's success, and the stardom status they acquired inside and outside the media depended on his achievements. As Americans, they naturally supported a diplomatic effort, which if successful, could have restored American prestige and status in world politics, particularly after the traumatic failure in Vietnam. Furthermore, because Kissinger pursued a noble cause in trying to prevent the resumption of Arab-Israeli violence, the correspondents enthusiastically supported his mission. Finally, Kissinger was a master of diplomatic maneuvers and the reporters could not help but admire his skills and exceptional talent. Marvin and Bernard Kalb (1974) and Valeriani (1979) even wrote books enthusiastically documenting their experiences with him. Yet, the correspondents' stakes in Kissinger's success could have compromised their journalistic integrity by allowing the Secretary of State to manipulate them for his diplomatic goals.

Since the Kissinger era all U.S. secretaries of state have been extensively involved in Arab-Israeli negotiations and they, like him, often used the media to enhance their influence over decisions and events. Israeli and Arab leaders have also learned from him how to employ the media in negotiations.

C. SIGNALING

The argument suggested by Wood (1992, p. 235) that when politicians wish to mediate they use diplomatic channels, secure and private, and when they wish to confront they use open forms of mass communication requires substantial modification. Policymakers usually prefer secret negotiations but in the absence of direct channels of communication, or when one side is unsure how the other would react to conditions for negotiations or to proposals for conflict resolution, officials use the media, with or without attribution, to send signals and messages to leaders of rival states and non-state actors. State Department spokesperson Nicholas Burns (1996, pp. 12–13) admitted: "We use the briefings to send messages to foreign governments about our foreign policy. For example, I sometimes read carefully calibrated statements to communicate with the governments with which we have no diplomatic relations: Iraq, Iran, Libya and North Korea." He explained that "given the concentration of journalists in Washington and our position in the world, the United States is uniquely situated to use television to our best advantage, with our friends as well as with our adversaries."

During grave international crises or when all diplomatic channels are severed the media provide the only channel for communication and negotiation between the rival actors. During the first phase of 1979–1981 Iranian Hostage Crisis, the United States communicated with the terrorists holding the hostages exclusively through the media (Larson, 1986). A similar case occurred in the 1985 hijacking of a TWA jetliner to Beirut (Gilboa, 1990). During the 1990–1991 Gulf War, Bush and Saddam Hussein hurled messages back and forth via the global news networks. Tom Shales of the *Washington Post* called this channel a "de facto hotline" between Washington and Baghdad (cited in Newsom, 1996, p. 96).

Using the media without attribution to sources is particularly efficient when policymakers wish to fly a "trial balloon." They can avoid embarrassment and disassociate themselves from an idea that may receive a negative response. Leaders use reliable third parties to secretly explore intentions of the other side, but sometimes simultaneously they also use the media to support the secret exchanges and to further indicate that their approach is serious. In recent years, leaders more frequently use global communication to deliver messages intended to alter an image or to open a new page. They pursue signaling through press conferences, interviews, leaks, and attitudes toward journalists of the other side.

Israeli and Arab leaders have extensively used the media to send signals. Of all the negotiations Israel conducted with its neighbors, those with Syria were the most difficult and complicated (Rabinovich, 1998; Cobban, 1999). Syria's leader Hafez el-Assad opposed any direct talks because he felt they would grant Israel recognition and legitimacy. Syria also presented a pre-condition for negotiations: an Israeli commitment to withdraw from the Golan Heights, a strategic area taken from Syria in the 1967 Six Day War. Israel rejected this demand and said the territorial issue cannot be separated from other significant issues including normalization and security arrangements. The two countries used only limited secret channels to exchange messages and therefore occasionally needed the media to openly send signals.

In September 1993, Israel and PLO signed an historic Declaration of Principles designed to produce Israeli-Palestinian negotiations and eventually a peace agreement. Israel wanted to use this opportunity to begin negotiations also with Syria. During a visit to the United States in November 1993, Rabin spoke at the National Press Club in Washington in front of an audience that included journalists and ambassadors from Arab countries. While criticizing the Syrian attacks on the Israeli-PLO accord, he also invited Assad to join the peace process: "I believe that in secret negotiations, far away from the media attention, it would be possible to deal with questions related to the depth of withdrawal and the essence of peace" (*Yediot Aharonoth*, Israel, November 17, 1993, p. 2). As if to further underline the purpose of his statement, following additional Israeli unofficial briefings, on the next day the Israeli media wrote that Rabin sent a message to Syria: "Would tell in secret negotiations how far Israel would be willing to withdraw in the Golan Heights."

Sometimes attitudes towards journalists of the other side send an important signal. Assad and his Foreign Minister Farouq al-Shara have accumulated an interesting record in approaching Israeli reporters. In the 1991 Madrid Peace Conference, where Israeli and Syrian officials met for the first time in decades to explore conflict resolution, Shara's spokesman carefully picked out non-Israeli reporters to ask questions at a news conference. Thomas Friedman (1991) of the *New York Times* called Shara's performance "chilling" and added: "Any notion that Syria had come to Madrid because of 'new thinking' or for any other purpose than to make peace with Washington, was dispelled by his performance."

In an effort to promote Israeli-Syrian negotiations President Clinton met Assad in Geneva in January 1994 (Rabinovich, 1998, pp. 128–130). The main purpose of the meeting was to obtain from Assad a public statement of interest in peace. In a press conference, Clinton said that Assad indeed promised to normalize relations with Israel. However, Assad himself did not make any public comment on this issue, even in response to a question directed to him by an American journalist. For the first time Syrian television broadcast live the press conference from Geneva, including Clinton's interpretation of Assad normalization commitment, but Assad did not allow Israeli reporters to participate in the press conference. When U.S. envoy Dennis Ross flew to Jerusalem to brief Rabin on the results of the meeting and said Assad opened a new page in the peace process, Rabin responded that he could not see any and that the boycotting of the Israeli press was inconsistent with the statement Clinton made on Assad's commitment to normalize relations.

In September 1994, however, Shara sent a different signal. He answered for the first time a question by an Israeli reporter at a press conference in London and later gave a first-ever interview to Israeli television (Rabinovich, 1998, pp. 159–160). Although he gave the interview only under American pressure and what he said was disappointing to Israel, Syria's new attitude toward Israeli journalists was seen as a possible attempt by Syria to build confidence required for peace with Israel. All the efforts to achieve Israeli-Syrian peace at that time and afterwards failed, and no wonder that on July 5, 2001, the same Syrian foreign minister appeared in London but reverted back to old negative practices when he refused to answer questions by an Israeli reporter, thus indicating again the unwillingness of Syria to negotiate with Israel. A month later he exhibited the same negative behavior at the UN infamous conference on racism held in Durban, South Africa. Thus, attitudes toward journalists of the other side have become a barometer of Syrian interest in conflict resolution.

D. MEDIATING

While discussing the globalization of electronic journalism, Gurevitch noted the new role of journalists as "international political brokers" (1991, pp. 187–188). He cited the examples of Walter Cronkite from CBS News who helped to arrange the historic visit of Sadat to Jerusalem and television news anchors who rushed to interview Saddam Hussein in Baghdad during the days preceding the 1991 Persian Gulf War. These examples argues Gurevitch, suggest that globalized television "may launch reportorial initiatives that tend to blur the distinction between the roles of reporters and diplomats." This typically occurs when reporters slid during interviews, almost imperceptibly, into the roles of advocates, as if representing their own government, and negotiators, exploring with their interviewee avenues for resolving the crisis. Cronkite's role in the initial critical stage of the Israeli-Egyptian peace process is a classic case of journalists turning international mediators.

On November 9, 1977, Sadat told the Egyptian parliament that he was ready to travel to the ends of earth, even to the Israeli Knesset (parliament), if that would help prevent a single Egyptian soldier from being killed or wounded in battle. Israeli Prime Minister Begin responded with an open invitation to Sadat, but the prospects for such a breakthrough in Arab-Israeli relations were at least unclear and further clarifications were needed. In the absence of a direct channel of communication between the sides, the media stepped in as a "go between" for Israel and Egypt. Sadat's new policy and Begin's immediate response attracted the attention of the American media and the three major television networks scrambled to interview Sadat and Begin. Walter Conkite won the battle.

On the morning of November 14, 1977, Cronkite interviewed Sadat, who confirmed his plan to go to Jerusalem (Cronkite, 1996, pp. 312–317). Cronkite asked what would Sadat need to go and the answer was just a "proper invitation" from Israel. When Cronkite asked how soon could he go, Sadat answered "[in] the earliest time possible." Cronkite took the initiative by suggesting a possible time table: "that could be, say, within a week?" to which Sadat responded "you can say that, yes." Even before this interview ended, Cronkite's producer searched for Begin and located him six hours later. Cronkite told Begin the results of his conversation with Sadat, and Begin responded: "tell him he's got an invitation." This reaction, "*tell him . . . ,*" shows that Begin perceived Cronkite as a mediator and not just as a journalist. Cronkite recalled that he pressed Begin for details, and Begin said he would make a statement to the Knesset the following day and would talk to the U.S. Ambassador to Israel about the forwarding of the invitation. When Cronkite informed Begin that Sadat might arrive within a week, Begin said he would postpone a scheduled visit to Britain.

The CBS Evening News of November 14, 1977, opened with the pictures of Sadat and Begin on a split screen behind Cronkite who declared that "now all obstacles appear to have been removed for peace discussion in Jerusalem between Egyptian President Sadat and Israeli Prime Minister Begin." The pictures created the impression that Cronkite had actually sat down with Sadat and Begin and mediated the visit to Jerusalem. Sadat arrived in Jerusalem five days after the broadcast. The papers unanimously praised Cronkite. In his *New York Times* column (November 17, 1977), titled "Cronkite Diplomacy," William Safire wrote: "when Egyptian president Sadat first proposed his trip to Jerusalem, the Carter administration fretted and dithered. It took Walter Cronkite of CBS, placing an electronic hand on the backs of Israel and Egypt, to bring them together." In her *New York Post* column (November 17, 1977) Mary McGrory wrote: "Americans are delighted to have Walter Cronkite as their Secretary of State."

At the time, Cronkite did not share the overwhelming enthusiastic praise for his role: "I don't think a journalist should become involved in high-level diplomacy," he stated in *Time* magazine's November 28, 1977, issue. "Maybe we (at CBS) were catalysts. But then, maybe they would have gotten together without us." In his recently published memoirs Cronkite offered, for the first time, new details about his role and put it in both historical and professional context. But even 20 years after the event, he was still not sure how to characterize his role.

Cronkite responded to some critics who argued that he overstepped the bounds of journalistic propriety in the Sadat-Begin case by claiming that he did not believe Sadat would really go to Jerusalem and that he only wanted to "knock down the speculation over the visit" (1996, p. 316). But the lack of motivation or planning to engage in diplomacy does not mean that the reporter was not performing a diplomatic role. Cronkite testified that he was aware of the historic opportunity he was handling. On the interview with Sadat he wrote, "suddenly I was trying to put the ribbon around a much bigger story." During the interview with Begin, he felt that the Israeli Prime Minister "did not believe this was all for real," and he pressed Begin to come up with details on the visit.

In other parts of his autobiography and in different contexts, Cronkite did acknowledge his diplomatic role and distinguished between unintended planning and results: "A problem with the anchor's exalted position is the tendency for her or him to slide from observer to player. Sometimes this is the unintended result of a purely journalistic exercise, such as our Sadat-Begin interviews . . . the important point is that television journalism, in this case at least, speeded up the process, brought it into the open, removed a lot of possibly obstructionist middlemen, and made it difficult for principals to renege on their very public agreement" (1996, p. 354). Any professional diplomat would have been very proud of achievements like these.

Cronkite even argued that negotiations through television may be more effective than negotiations between professional diplomats: "television as a means of communication between heads of state outside the stodgy bureaucratic channels may be one of its great contributions. Professional diplomats may differ because it is their ox that is being gored" (1996, p. 355). In the concluding pages of his book, once again he wrote about the role of television in writing history, and one of his examples for television impact was the Israeli-Egyptian peace that "resulted from the meeting of Anwar Sadat and Menachem Begin that was partly brought about by the separate interviews with them on the CBS Evening News" (1996, p. 383).

Cronkite did not plan a mediation role in Israeli-Egyptian relations but was spontaneously drawn in. He was aware of his actions and his questions and activities went far beyond the normal course of journalistic interviews. His interviews produced an agreement between Sadat and Begin on a visit to Jerusalem within a week from the date of the interviews. Furthermore, of the several reporters involved in the story, only Cronkite was able to get Sadat to state his willingness to go to Jerusalem within a week.

Cronkite's mediation raises a professional dilemma. As in the case of Kissinger's "shuttle diplomacy," journalists may have an interest in the success of the diplomatic move they help to initiate. Furthermore, Cronkite had achieved a preferred status during Sadat's visit. He and Barbara Walters from ABC News were the only American journalists allowed to board Sadat's plane on his way from Cairo to Jerusalem. Thus, after helping to arrange Sadat's visit, and being already partly rewarded for that role, Cronkite could have had a stake in the results of the visit, and a question could have been raised as to the possible effects of his diplomatic role on his daily reporting and editing of the CBS Evening News, before, during and immediately after the visit.

A much less known but not less ambitious attempt of a journalist to mediate in the Arab-Israeli conflict occurred in March–April 2000, when the British correspondent Patrick Seale offered a plan to break the deadlock in Israeli-Syrian negotiations. Seale was Assad's biographer (1988) and was known for his excellent relations with the Syrian president. Assad used Seale to send messages about his negotiating positions and intentions. For example, during a critical round of negotiations in May 1993, Seale published an interview with Assad in the London based Arabic-language newspaper *al-Wasat* (May 10, pp. 12–20) and in the *New York Times* (May 11, p. A21). The interview presented new significant ideas (Rabinovich, 1998, pp. 96–97).

It seems that in March 2000 Seale assumed a more ambitious role. He traveled between Jerusalem and Damascus, met and conducted talks with Assad and Israeli politicians, and developed a proposal to break the deadlock and to end the Israeli-Syrian conflict. (Davis, 2000). On April 17, he published his plan in the London based Arabic daily *Al-Hayat* as an open letter to the leaders of the two countries. The article was cited and extensively discussed in the Israeli media. Seale wrote that Syria must display "clear evidence of a change of heart toward Israel," while "Israel must recognize that the June 4, 1967 line is the best and only possible boundary between two proud states anxious to be good neighbors." He even criticized Assad: "the way you go about it sometimes seems to send a contrary signal. You may need to consider changing the manner in which you address your Israeli negotiating partner." Seale's proposal was received in Israel with considerable suspicion, but the Justice Minster Yossi Beilin called upon Assad's heir-apparent, Bashar Assad to seriously consider the proposal. Seale's initiative however, failed to produce the intended breakthrough. Unlike Sadat, Assad lacked the courage and determination needed to reach peace, and Seale lacked the professional prestige Cronkite enjoyed in 1977. Furthermore, as a representative of the printed press he couldn't attract even a fraction of the attention Cronkite drew in his capacity as a world known television news anchor.

E.   BRIDGING AND BUILDING CONFIDENCE

The media may help to create bridges among enemies and build confidence needed to open negotiations. This function typically occurs when representatives of rival sides are brought together on the air for discussions of the issues dividing them. It is more likely to happen when there is no formal third party helping enemies to engage in conflict resolution. A well-known and respected journalist associated with a highly regarded program has a better chance of successfully performing this function. Ted Koppel assumed this role in *Nightline* (Newsom, 1996, p. 96). *Nightline*'s motto: "bringing people together who are worlds apart" reveals the program's self-declared mission. Observers have agreed: "What else is *Nightline* but an electronic negotiating table with the anchor bringing combatants together, searching for answers, probing for common ground? Koppel may never get Kissinger's old job, but he is already television's Secretary of State" (Alter, 1987, p. 50). Koppel, as noted earlier, was one of the selected correspondents accompanying Kissinger on his diplomatic travels, and was exposed to his uses of the media to advance negotiations.

A series of special programs that *Nightline* broadcast in April 1988 from Israel was credited with facilitating significant steps toward conflict resolution

(Koppel & Gibson, 1996, pp. 95–117). Koppel brought together representatives of Israel and Palestinians affiliated with the PLO on one stage for the first time. Both sides were mainly interested in talking to the moderator and in influencing American and world public opinion, and not in a meaningful dialogue. The Palestinians even insisted on placing a wall on the stage between themselves and the Israeli participants. Regardless of the initial motivation of the rival sides, Koppel pursued classic means of successful pre-negotiation by bestowing credibility and legitimizing the participants, empowering and equalizing the parties, and providing direct communication (Botes, 1997). These means helped to realize goals of pre-negotiation including the removal of psychological barriers to negotiation, eliminating mutual dehumanization and demonization, defining the conflict as a mutual problem, considering negotiation as a viable option to resolve the conflict, cultivating domestic support for negotiation, and emphasizing the need to open official negotiations.

Senior American policymakers were divided on the contributions of *Nightline* to conflict resolution in general and to Arab-Israeli peacemaking in particular (O'Heffernan, 1991, p. 52). Harold Saunders, a former Assistant Secretary of State, who was intensively involved in American mediation in the Arab-Israeli conflict, said that "television diplomacy generally hinders foreign policy. If you take *Nightline*, etc., I don't think those dialogues are particularly useful because they are not very well prepared." He explained that the participants were engaged in debates and scoring points instead of "learning how to handle sensitive issues creatively." Phyllis Oakely, a State Department Spokeswoman, however, argued that "the Koppel Arab-Israeli show was well done. It was useful in presenting the passions of both sides and how difficult it is to make an agreement." A scholar and a high level foreign policy official in Republican administrations Richard Haass made a similar observation, adding that the program "helped at the margins. And that's not bad. A lot of history happens at the margins."

An Israeli communication scholar (Loshitzky, 1991) argued that the Israeli-Palestinian *Nightline* series was a meta-televisual dialogue and not a serious realistic dialogue. But the Israeli and Palestinian participants disagreed with her and the American critics of the program. They said the program was a significant diplomatic event pushing them toward official direct negotiation. Hanan Ashrawi (1995, pp. 48–50), a Palestinian representative, wrote that "the show broke barriers. It made acceptable the idea of an encounter between Palestinians and Israelis." Ehud Olmert, an Israeli representative, commented: "there was this sense that this was more than just a TV show, that this was a political event, an international event, that TV had become more than just a technical instrument" (Koppel & Gibson, 1996, p. 116). A few years later, Israel and the PLO conducted official indirect talks in Washington and direct secret talks in Oslo, leading to a major breakthrough in Israeli-Palestinian relations.

Twelve years later, in October 2000, following the eruption of the second Palestinian *Intifada*, Koppel and *Nightline* returned to Jerusalem, hoping, perhaps, to repeat the successful experience of the 1988 broadcasts. He even invited to this town meeting three participants from the 1988 series, one Israeli, Ehud Olmert, now the Mayor of Jerusalem, and two Palestinians: Hanan Ashrawi, now a Palestinian official Spokesperson, and Saeb Erekat, now an official Palestinian negotiator. This time, the Palestinians didn't insist on placing a wall between the two sides, but the program failed to produce any meaningful dialogue. The participants were angry and yelling at the same time forcing Koppel to ask them to show courtesy to each other. The expected dialogue failed to materialize and at one point Koppel even said "I surrender" (Sontag, 2000).

One Israeli participant, Member of the Knesset Naomi Chazan, explained later that what was happening at the program was a microcosm of what's was going on in the area and that trust had broken down terribly and horrifically. But in order to achieve bridging and confidence building, the program had to depart from reality and to engage the participants in a constructive dialogue. In October 2000, Koppel was unable to facilitate this outcome and repeat his 1988 success, although as noted by the *New York Times* reporter covering the event, during this period of violence he was the only American to engineer any kind of talks between the two sides. Perhaps, the choice of participants on both sides wasn't successful, and the timing and flames on the ground were too prohibitive for successful bridging and confidence building of the kind the program produced in 1988.

F. PROMOTING NEGOTIATIONS AND AGREEMENTS

"Media events," spectacular celebrations of peacemaking, may help to promote negotiations and mobilize public support for agreements. This media contribution is particularly critical in situations where the respective societies are highly suspicious of each other and have been educated for years to believe that the other side is only interested in violence and war. Israeli and Arab leaders as well as American mediators have recognized this media potential to move societies from hostile relations to peacemaking. Media events are broadcast live, organized outside the media, pre-planned, and presented with reverence and ceremony (Dayan & Katz, 1992, pp. 4–9). Live coverage of media events interrupts scheduled broadcasting and attracts wide audiences around the world. Dayan and Katz (1992, pp. 204–205) identify several direct effects of media events on diplomacy: (1) trivializing the role of ambassadors, (2) breaking diplomatic deadlocks and creating a climate conducive to negotiations, and (3) creating a favorable climate for sealing an accord. The distinction between the last two effects is significant because media events can be used at the onset of negotiations to build confidence and facilitate negotiations, or at the end of negotiations to mobilize public support for an agreement that has already been achieved.

There is also an intermediary effect that occurs in the interim: when officials use media events to cultivate public support for a peace process *after* the conclusion of the initial phase but *before* moving on to the next phase. This typically appears in cases where a breakthrough has been achieved, but the sides still have a long way to go before translating a declaration of principles into a permanent legal peace agreement. Such an intermediary effect can help in mobilizing sufficient public support inside the societies involved for the next phase in the negotiations. All three effects of media events gained vivid expression in chapters of Arab-Israeli peacemaking.

Sadat's historic visit to Jerusalem in November 1977, and the 1991 Madrid Peace Conference demonstrate the initial effect of using a media event to facilitate negotiations. The signing ceremonies of three major documents represent the intermediary effect: the Camp David Accords of September 1978, the PLO-Israel Declaration of Principles of September 1993, and the Israel-Jordan Washington Declaration of July 1994. The signing ceremonies of two peace treaties demonstrate the "sealing effect" of media events: the Israeli-Egyptian Peace Treaty of March 1979, and the Israeli-Jordanian Peace Treaty of October 1994. Three of these media events were selected for analysis and interpretation in this chapter: Sadat's visit in Jerusalem, the Madrid Peace Conference, and the signing of the Israel-PLO Declaration of Principles.

Sadat's visit in Jerusalem was one of the most spectacular media events in the post -World War Two era. It also provided the initial impetus for scholarly interest in media events. For the first time in Arab-Israeli history, an Arab leader of the most important Arab country recognized Israel, visited Jerusalem, and offered direct negotiations toward comprehensive Arab-Israeli peace (Stein, 1999). The visit was an electronic extravaganza (Bagnied & Schneider, 1982; Gilboa, 1987, pp. 90–93). About 2,000 reporters, including 580 Americans, followed every move of Sadat in Jerusalem. During the visit, the evening news on the American networks originated from Jerusalem and almost two-thirds of the editions were devoted to the visit. Typical characterizations of the visit were "historic," "breakthrough," "stunning," "daring venture," bold gamble," and "momentous visit." Harry Reasoner of ABC called it a "sheer drama of pictures," and John O'Connor (1977) of the *New York Times* added that the drama continued "as various network commentators rattled on about boggled minds, astonished ears and startled eyes, the images alone-moving and even thrilling-told all."

While Sadat's visit was highly successful and eventually produced Israeli-Egyptian peace agreement, an American sponsored media event in 1991 was much less successful. The United States wished to exploit the window of opportunity created by the end of the Cold War and the defeat of Saddam Hussein in the 1991 Gulf War to renew the frozen Arab-Israeli peace process. The two sides, however, were reluctant to begin negotiations under the terms suggested by the United States. The Arabs demanded to jointly negotiate with Israel in an international peace conference, while the latter preferred separate bi-lateral negotiations with each Arab country. The United States offered a compromise: a ceremonial opening in an international conference followed by bilateral negotiations (Bentsur, 2001, pp. 117–128). Under heavy American pressure the two sides accepted the compromise and the historic Royal Palace in Madrid was selected as the site for the opening international conference. The conference was significant because it brought for the first time Syrians and Palestinians into direct negotiations with Israelis. The declared purpose of the talks was to produce a comprehensive peace agreement. The two sides however, exhibited strong reservations about the process and behaved as if they were forced to attend the meeting.

The United States planned to use the Madrid conference as a major platform to overcome the mistrust and reservations of Arabs and Israelis. American officials soon labeled the event "the largest peace conference held since Versailles." Presidents George Bush and Mikhail Gorbachev opened the conference on October 30, 1991 with messages of hope and encouragement. Most of the major American and global networks sent their anchors to Madrid to broadcasted the event. About 4,500 journalists from all over the world covered the conference. But Arab and Israeli representatives were very suspicious, cold and reserved and refused even to shake hands. Secretary of State James Baker suggested that they were merely posturing for the cameras, but Robert Fisk (1991) of the London newspaper *The Independent* disagreed: "Watching the faces at the T-shaped table—sullen, watchful, suspicious, occasionally images of suppressed fury-it was clear that they really hated each other." In this case the media event did not work with either the sides to the conflict or with American and world public opinion. Apparently, media events cannot work in the absence of minimal cooperation among the adversaries.

Following the conference in Madrid, the sides moved to Washington for bilateral negotiations but were unable to make any progress. Israel and the PLO decided to break the impasse via secret negotiations in Oslo, far away from the camera lights of the pressing Washington press corps. These negotiations yielded an agreement for mutual recognition—a major historical breakthrough. President Bill Clinton invited Prime Minister Yitzhak Rabin and PLO Chairman Arafat to sign the accords at a ceremony on the White House lawn. He wanted an extravagant ceremony to compensate for the exclusion of the United States from the secret diplomacy in Oslo, and for his failures particularly in foreign affairs. Israel and the PLO however, perceived the event as an opportunity to mobilize support for the accords among their respective skeptical peoples, and to assure quick approval and effective implementation.

American officials named the ceremony an "an historic day" and invited 3,000 people to the White House lawn including well-known personalities, and even used meta-communication methods loaded with symbols including the table used by Begin and Sadat to sign the 1978 Camp David Agreements. All these were designed to produce a major media event that would be broadcast live to the entire world, would present a clear support of the entire international community for the Agreement, and would strengthen the peace process and move it beyond the point of no return. The contents of the speeches delivered during the ceremony, the famous handshake between Rabin and Arafat and the positive responses to the ceremony coming from all over the world fulfilled the expectations of all the participants from the event.

Analysis of Arab-Israeli media events reveals advantages as well as shortcomings. They certainly confirm legitimacy on negotiations and agreements and help to mobilize public support for peacemaking. On the other hand, by definition, media events have to be spectacular thereby creating high expectations for rapid and efficient progress toward peace. But as recent Arab-Israeli peace processes demonstrate, even following breakthroughs, difficult and long negotiations are needed to conclude agreements. The gap between the promise of media events and the actual results often create disappointments and confusion. Media events are not always successful, as was the case in the Madrid conference, and such ploys become far less effective when employed too frequently and the ground-breaking effect becomes diluted (Liebes & Katz, 1997). Finally, politicians and officials fully control media events in a way that could undermine balanced and realistic assessment of the events and their consequences.

G. CONCLUSIONS

Media utilization in peacemaking is complicated and problematic. Even before summarizing the Arab-Israeli experience, it should be noted that international negotiation in a highly complex and difficult conflict, such as the Arab-Israeli conflict, usually moves up and down and there are many moments and stages of stalemate and frustration. During these stages, policymakers and negotiators often use the media to bitterly attack and criticize each other as well as mediators. This chapter, however, focused on media utilization designed to positively influence significant negotiation elements including signaling, mediation, bridging, confidence building, and promotion of negotiations and agreements. Even so, as the dysfunction element of the functional communication theory suggests, there might be situations where the intention of those using the media had been positive but the results were either negative or mixed, as was the case in the Madrid media event.

The evidence presented here shows that in Arab-Israeli talks the media functioned both as a tool in the hands of policymakers, and as an autonomous independent actor. Policymakers, like Kissinger, used and manipulated the media to pressure negotiators; leaders such as Rabin and Assad used the media to exchange signals, and American, Arab, and Israeli leaders employed the media to mobilize public support for negotiations and agreements. On the other hand, Journalists including Cronkite, Koppel, and Seale, took the initiative and became, at least temporarily, mediators in the conflict.

This chapter shows that contrary to popular myths, leaders and policymakers have learned how to use the power of the media, particularly of global television, to advance negotiation and peacemaking. However, it is clear that media utilization should be carefully pursued. Signaling might be confusing, if reporters of the other side are excluded from a press conference designed to build confidence. Media events aren't always successful, and are likely to fail if several participants have no interest in negotiations. And even if all the participants collaborate to produce a spectacular media event, they may create too high expectations that may lead to a dangerous gap between peace promises and results.

Even if the media are used to achieve highly desirable goals such as reconciliation and peace, the findings in this chapter raise serious practical, professional, and ethical questions. It is assumed that the main duty of the media is to present objective, reliable and accurate information on events and processes. It is doubtful if this function can be adequately fulfilled if reporters entirely depend on one source, such as Kissinger, who made a deliberate effort to ensure that he would be the only source for the coverage of his diplomacy. It is also doubtful whether the public receives adequate information on negotiating difficulties, when leaders fully control media events and relegate journalists to secondary insignificant roles.

The thought of journalists turning mediators is indeed intriguing. If parties to a conflict can't make progress on their own and if no "third parties" are around, why would journalists be prevented from conducting mediation and constructive diplomacy. The frequent counter argument is that journalists are supposed to cover events, not to create them. It could be argued that journalists assume mediation and bridging roles spontaneously. Cronkite did not preplan a diplomatic role but was drawn into one. Koppel, however, clearly initiated television electronic town meetings between rivals on *Nightline*. The problem is that when journalists become players in a negotiation process, they don't suspend their professional reporting and coverage of the process. In fact, they become players due to their professional standing and work. Yet, as players they develop an interest in the outcome and this may compromise their coverage of the process. Both leaders and journalists must be extremely cautious in using the media to advance peacemaking processes.

REFERENCES

Alter, J. (1987, June 15). America's Q & A Man. *Newsweek*, pp. 50–53, 55–56.

Arno, A. (1984). The News Media As Third Parties in National and International Conflict. In A. Arno & W. Dissanayake (Eds.), *The News Media in National and International Conflict* (pp. 229–238). Boulder, CO: Westview.

Ashrawi, H. (1995). *This Side of Peace: A Personal Account.* New York: Simon and Schuster.

Bagnied, M. & Schneider, S. (1982). Sadat Goes to Jerusalem: Televised Images, Themes, and Agenda. In W. Adams (Ed.), *Television Coverage of the Middle East* (pp. 53–66). Norwood, NJ: Ablex.

Bentsur, E. (2000). *Making Peace: A First Hand Account of the Arab-Israeli Peace Process.* Wesport, CT: Praeger.

Berton, P., Kimura, H. & Zartman, W. I. (Eds.) (1999). *International Negotiation.* Basingstoke: Macmillan.

Botes, J. (1997). Media Roles in Conflict Resolution: A Comparison Between Television Moderators and Conventional Moderators. Doctoral Dissertation, Institute for Conflict Analysis and Resolution, George Mason University.

Burns, N. (1996). Talking to the World about American Foreign Policy. *The Harvard International Journal of Press/Politic, 1*, 10–14.

Cobban, H. (1999). *The Israeli-Syrian Peace Talks.* Washington, D.C.: U.S. Institute of Peace Press.

Cronkite, W. (1996). *A Reporter's Life.* New York: Random House.

Davis, D. (2000, April 18). Seale asks Barak, Assad to Resume Talks. *Jerusalem Post*, p. 3.

Dayan, D. & Katz, E. (1992). *Media Events: The Live Broadcasting of History.* Cambridge, MA: Harvard University Press.

Diamond, L. & McDonald, J. (1996). *Multi-track Diplomacy: A Systems Approach to Peace.* 3rd edition. West Hartford, CT: Kumarian Press.

Eisenberg, L. Z. & Caplan, N. (1998). *Negotiating Arab-Israeli Peace.* Bloomington, IN: Indiana University Press.

Fisk, R. (1991, November 2). Middle East Conference: The Peace Conference that Spoke about War. *The Independent* (London), p. 12.

Friedman, T. (1991, November 3). Amid Histrionics, Arabs and Israelis Team Up to Lose an Opportunity. *New York Times*, p. 4/1.

Gilboa, E. (1987). *American Public Opinion Toward Israel and the Arab-Israeli Conflict.* Lexington, MA: Lexington Books.

Gilboa, E. (1990). Effects of Televised Presidential Addresses on Public Opinion:

President Reagan and Terrorism in the Middle East. *Presidential Studies Quarterly, XX*, 43–53.

Gilboa, E. (1998a). Secret Diplomacy in the Television Age. *Gazette: The International Journal for Communication Studies, 60*, 211–225.

Gilboa, E. (1998b). Media Diplomacy: Conceptual Divergence and Applications. *The Harvard International Journal of Press/Politics, 3*, 56–75.

Gilboa, E. (2000a). Media Coverage of International Negotiation: A Taxonomy of Levels and Effects. *International Negotiation, 5*, 543–568.

Gilboa, E. (2000b). Mass Communication and Diplomacy: A Theoretical Framework. *Communication Theory, 10*, 275–309.

Gurevitch, M. (1991). The Globalization of Electronic Journalism. In J. Curran, & M. Gurevitch, (Eds.), *Mass Media and Society* (pp. 178–193). London: Edward Arnold.

Isaacson, W. (1992). *Kissinger: A Biography*. New York: Simon and Schuster.

Kalb, M. & Kalb, B. (1974). *Kissinger*. Boston: Little, Brown.

Kalb, M., Koppel, T. & Scali, J. (1982). The Networks and Foreign News Coverage. *The Washington Quarterly, 5*, 39–51.

Klieman, A. (2000). *Compromising Palestine: A Guide to Final Status Negotiations*. New York: Columbia University Press.

Kissinger, H. (1994). *Diplomacy*. New York: Simon and Schuster.

Koppel, T. & Gibson, K. (1996). *Nightline: History in the Making and the Making of Television*. New York: Times Books.

Larson, J. (1986). Television and U.S. Foreign Policy: The Case of the Iran Hostage Crisis. *Journal of Communication, 36*, 108–130.

Liebes, T. & Katz, E. (1997). Staging Peace: Televised Ceremonies of Reconciliation. *The Communication Review, 2*, 235–257.

Loshitzky, Y. (1991). The Intifada As a Meta-Televisual Dialogue. *Media, Culture and Society, 13*, 557–571.

Newsom, D. (1996). *The Public Dimension of Foreign Policy*. Bloomington, IN: Indiana University Press.

O'Connor, J. (1977, November 22). TV: Symbolic Event is Highlighted by 'Sheer Drama of Pictures.' *New York Times*, p. 17.

O'Heffernan, P. (1991). *Mass Media and American Foreign Policy: Insider Perspectives on Global Journalism and the Foreign Policy Process*. Norwood, NJ: Ablex.

Patir, D. (1997, May 13). The Spokesman in Central Political Evens of the Peace Process. Lecture delivered at the symposium Spokesmanship in the Service of Peace in the Middle East. Bar-Ilan University, Israel.

Quandt, W. (2001). *Peace Process: American Diplomacy and The Arab-Israeli Conflict since 1967*. Washington, D.C.: Brookings Institution Press & Berkeley: University of California Press.

Rabinovich, I. (1998). *The Brink of Peace: The Israeli-Syrian Negotiations*. Princeton, NJ: Princeton University Press.

Savir, U. (1998). *The Process*. New York: Vintage Books.

Seale, P. (1988). *Asad of Syria*. London: I. B. Taurus.

Seib, P. M. (1997). *Headline Diplomacy: How News Coverage Affects Foreign Policy*. Westport, CT: Praeger.

Sontag, D. (2000, October 11). Whose Holy Land? The Town Meeting. *New York Times*, p. 10A.

Stein, J. (Ed.) (1989). *Getting to the Table: The Processes of International Prenegotiation*. Baltimore: Johns Hopkins University Press.

Stein, K. (1999). *Heroic Diplomacy*. New York: Routledge.

Valeriani, R. (1979). *Travels with Henry*. Boston: Houghton Mifflin.

Wood, J. (1992). *A History of International Broadcasting*. London: Peter Peregrinus.

Zartman, I. W. & Rasmussen, J. L. (Eds.) (1997). *Peacemaking in International Conflict: Methods and Techniques*. Washington, D.C.: U.S. Institute of Peace Press.

CHAPTER 11

THE RUSSIAN MEDIA ROLE IN THE CONFLICTS IN AFGHANISTAN AND CHECHNYA: A CASE STUDY OF MEDIA COVERAGE BY *IZVESTIA*

Olga V. Malinkina and Douglas M. McLeod

A. INTRODUCTION

This chapter examines the role of the media in the resolution of conflicts in Afghanistan (1979–1988) and Chechnya (1994–1996). In the interim between these two conflicts, Russia experienced sweeping social, political, and ideological reforms that drastically altered its role as one of the major players in such conflicts. The changes initiated under Mikhail Gorbachev's policies of *perestroika* and *glasnost* permeated all aspects of Russian society. One of the most visible manifestations of these changes is found when examining the mass media. Prior to the onset of the reforms, Soviet media were centrally controlled by the Communist Party leadership. Under this system, no media criticism of Soviet policies was permitted. In the wake of the reforms, Russian media were partially privatized and given much greater latitude to criticize the Russian system. This is important to the process of conflict resolution, because under their newfound freedom, Russian media put pressure on government officials to bring a swift resolution to conflicts and to minimize casualties. In turn, media pressure may stimulate public opinion and public actions to further influence the Russian government. Such media and public pressure were non-existent under the Soviet system.

B. HISTORICAL OVERVIEW OF THE CONFLICTS

1. The Conflict in Afghanistan

In the waning days of 1979, the Soviet Union entered a conflict that would endure for ten years. The Soviet Union sent military experts and weapons to Afghanistan to stabilize the country against a growing rebel presence with ties to Pakistan, a U.S. ally. The Soviets claimed that their presence was at the invitation of Afghan President Hafizullah Amin; however, the intervention ultimately secured the position of communist leader Babrak Karmal as Amin's replacement. Soon, the Soviet presence in Afghanistan escalated into a large-scale military operation, which fueled the emergence of previously dormant opposition from Islamic parties. What Soviet leaders assumed would be a brief action to install a compliant government, became a prolonged engagement as the rebels received financial and military assistance from Pakistan, the U.S. and China (Kakar, 1995). The decade of conflict led to thousands of deaths and injuries on both sides. On a global scale, the conflict resulted in the U.S. boycott of the Moscow Summer Olympics in 1980, and the Soviet boycott of the 1984 Los Angeles Olympics in retaliation.

As casualties accumulated, Soviet resolve weakened and troops were withdrawn. At the end of 1989, the Soviet Union reversed its policy in Afghanistan by declaring the Soviet invasion unconstitutional. In this about face, the Soviet Supreme Council admitted to a political and military mistake by stipulating that the decision to invade Afghanistan "was made by a small circle of people in violation of the Soviet constitution, according to which such matters belong to the jurisdiction of the higher state bodies" (Kakar, 1995, p. 74).

2. The Conflict in Chechnya

Chechnya is part of the Caucasus region on the Russian side of the border with Georgia. It is one of the most varied areas of the world in terms of its ethnic and linguistic composition (Gaal & De Waal, 1997; Gammer, 1995). In total, about 70 aboriginal ethnic groups populate the Caucasus, speaking languages belonging to three different linguistic families (Turkic, Iranian, and Ibero-Caucasian). During Soviet rule, the Caucasus area was divided among the four union republics of Armenia, Georgia, Azerbaijan, and the Russian Federation as part of a "gerrymandering" strategy to break up cultural groups and exacerbate divisions within the area, contributing to the conflicts that persist today. Local connections were discouraged in favor of vertical connections to Moscow. According to Gammer (1995), three cultural characteristics of the Caucasus people have contributed to fragmentation in the area: (1) zealous vigilance over personal and group freedoms, including the rejection of authority external to the kin-group, (2) the warrior tradition, and (3) vicious blood feuds that have persisted for generations. Unifying factors in the area have been Islam (the majority of people are Sunni Muslims) and a history of conflict with Russia (Gaal & De Waal, 1997; Gökay, 1998).

The disintegration of the Soviet Union resulted in the intensification of several conflicts in the Caucasus region, including the renewal of a long-standing conflict between Russia and Chechnya. In the Northern Caucasus, Moscow is still regarded by the locals as an "old empire in a new guise" (Gammer, 1995, p. 171). Moscow has maintained control of the area for strategic and economic reasons, as well as for the fear of encouraging a domino effect in other areas of the Russian Republic. Prior to the development of the Chechen conflict, there were three other conflicts in the Northern Caucasus: in North Ossetia, in Dagestan, and in Georgia. Chechens fought in support of their neighbors against Russia in all three conflicts. The tensions between the Chechens and the Russians have surfaced periodically since the Russian expansion in 1785 (Gaal & De Waal, 1997; Gammer, 1995; Gökay, 1998; Lieven, 1998). Joseph Stalin ordered the deportation of the 400,000 Chechens to Kazakhstan in 1944 (Flemming, 1998). Their houses and land were turned over to Russians; those who were deported faced starvation and disease for 13 years until they were allowed to return (Gaal & De Waal, 1997; Lieven, 1998). This episode left a painful memory in the minds of many Chechens (Flemming, 1998).

The specific episode of the Chechen-Russian conflict under study in this chapter was rekindled in 1991 by the Chechen declaration of independence from Russia. Russian President Boris Yeltsin decreed that this action was illegal and launched an economic blockade and media campaign against Chechnya (Gammer, 1995). For three years (1991–1994), Russia ignored the Chechen parliament's declaration of independence. In December of 1994, after several weeks of intensive debates in the Russian parliament that mainly protested military involvement in Chechnya, Russian troops entered Grozny, the Chechen capital. President Yeltsin's prediction that the Chechens would surrender within a few hours never materialized. The Russian-Chechen War lasted almost two years and cost more than 30,000 Russian and Chechen lives (Gaal & De Waal, 1997; Lieven, 1998). Both parties signed a peace agreement in the summer of 1996.

3. Differences Between Afghanistan and Chechnya

One might argue that the conflict in Chechnya is hardly comparable to the Afghan conflict. Indeed, there are many obvious differences. To begin with, Afghanistan was outside the boundaries of the Soviet Union. By definition, this was an international conflict prior to the reaction of countries opposed to the Soviet action. By contrast, Chechnya is part of Russia in the post-Soviet era. Defenders of the Russian action would argue that this was a domestic conflict. However, critics would point out that Chechnya declared its independence from Russia; though Russia never recognized this independence and in fact sent in troops to prevent it. Earlier in the decade numerous former Soviet republics had asserted their own independence from the Soviet Union, raising the possibility of an independent Chechnya. So at some level, both conflicts involved the struggle for autonomy against a larger power.

Another difference is in the volume and tenor of international reaction, which was considerably milder for the Chechen conflict. It is probable that the Chechen conflict would have received greater international condemnation by the U.S. and its allies had this conflict taken place ten years prior when foreign policies were determined by the Cold War framework; in the 1990s, these countries had a vested interest in the success of the Yeltsin government. With an eye on avoiding Cold War animosities and keeping the markets of Eastern Europe open, Western nations have become far less vocal in their criticism of the Russian leadership. In part, this could account for the lower volume of international condemnation of Russian actions in Chechnya relative to the reaction to Afghanistan.

Ultimately, the conflict in Chechnya never developed into the scale of the conflict in Afghanistan, despite the lower level of pressure from the international community. The case can be made that Afghanistan was the Soviet Union's Vietnam—a prolonged and costly foray into the affairs of another country in the name of halting tampering from parties on the other side of the Cold War. Clearly, the Chechen conflict lacked the scope, duration and global dimensions of the Afghan conflict. It is contention of this chapter that among the many forces that have kept a lid on the Chechen conflict is the emergence of a Russian media critical of the actions of the Russian government. In essence, media such as *Izvestia* have given a voice and confidence to internal opposition within the Russian power elite; it has also given a voice to public opposition. In fact, the Chechen view of the conflict was given virtually equal time to the Russian point of view. Perhaps then, the Russian media played a role in keeping the Afghan and Chechen conflicts from being more directly comparable.

4. Social Change in Russia

In analyzing the role that the Soviet/Russian media played in the two conflicts, it is essential to take into account the dramatic social change that occurred in Russia in the interim between the conflicts. The changes ostensibly began with the ascendancy of Mikhail Gorbachev to the post of Secretary General of the Communist Party. The reforms that Gorbachev set in motion brought an end to the 40-year Cold War between the Soviet Union and the West. Gorbachev's policy of *perestroika* was the underlying principle guiding the process of change in many different realms of Soviet society including economic reform, democratization, *glasnost* and foreign policy (Lane, 1992).

Economic reforms, referred to as *uskorenie* (rapid growth), included a plan for the modernization of industries, investment in new technologies, the introduction of new techniques in the industrial sector, and increased resources devoted to consumer production (Jones, 1989). Ultimately, the system was transformed from a centralized, planned economy into a privatized, market-driven economy, with a greater presence of private ownership and foreign investment.

In addition to economic reforms, there were radical changes in the sociopolitical sphere as well, including a move toward democratization and decentralized decision making. As part of this change, an effort was made to encourage pluralism of opinions, a new concept for Soviet society accustomed to party dogma and decrees. Pluralism was extended to greater tolerance for dissent and the creation of independent political parties. New democratic freedoms were extended to the Russian people including freedom of speech, the right to association, the right to run for office and elect leaders, and a greater responsiveness to people's needs by the government. Individual rights, freedoms and responsibilities were given unprecedented emphasis in the new Soviet society (Lane, 1992)

Glasnost was the cornerstone of Gorbachev's policy of social change. It initiated a new spirit of openness, public criticism and access to information. It brought about a reduction in the centralized, top-down, state-controlled flow of information. In Gorbachev's view, the mass media, "rather than being merely a conduit for the transmission of government policies, have the responsibility to articulate a spontaneously expressed range of views" (Lane, 1992, p. 14). *Glasnost* led to the establishment of private media organizations that were no longer under the direct control of government ownership and censorship.

Gorbachev stressed new approaches to Soviet foreign policy and a reemphasis away from global issues toward domestic concerns (Hough, 1989; Marantz, 1989). One of Gorbachev's major changes was a more pragmatic, less ideological approach to global problems. He also made a commitment to reduce the threat of nuclear conflicts. He emphasized global interdependence and a more cooperative orientation to addressing global issues such as environmental degradation, resource scarcity, terrorism, and drug trafficking. Finally, he reduced the Soviet military commitment to a more defensive, "reasonable sufficiency." Some of the more visible manifestations of Gorbachev's changes were: the Soviet withdrawal from Eastern Europe, the destruction of the Berlin Wall, the abandonment of SS-20 missiles, an intermediate-range nuclear forces treaty, and the withdrawal of troops from Afghanistan and public admission of a flawed policy.

5. Changes to the Russian Media System

Gorbachev's reforms had a profound effect on Russian media. Ownership of the media was privatized. Media profits were no longer directed to the coffers of the Communist Party. Direct censorship by the government has become less pervasive and practiced on a consensual rather than coercive basis (Androunas, 1991; Androunas, 1993). The function of the media also shifted from promoting ideological uniformity to providing information to the public. The nature of the government's power over Russian media changed as well. No longer engaged in direct control, the government resorted to less direct controls over the mass media (Jensen, 1993).

6. Changes to *Izvestia*

Izvestia was founded in 1917 as the newspaper of the Petrograd Council of Workers, Soldiers and Peasants (Vachnadze, 1992). Under the direction of Nikita Khrushchev's son-in-law, Alexei Adjubei, *Izvestia* became the most powerful newspaper in the Soviet Union. Relative to *Pravda, Izvestia* has had greater content diversity, including feature news stories on family life, sports and entertainment. After the attempted coup against Yeltsin in 1991, the journalists of *Izvestia* requested the registration of the newspaper as an independent joint-stock company, freeing it from a relationship with the Supreme Soviet. This request was ignored by the speaker of the Soviet parliament, prompting the newspaper to file a lawsuit. Today, *Izvestia* has been successful in securing independence.

C. MASS MEDIA AND CONFLICT RESOLUTION

1. The Political Contest Model

This study follows Wolfsfeld's assertion that the "best way to understand the role of the news media in politics is to view the competition over the news media as part of larger contest among political antagonists for political control" (Wolfsfeld, 1997, p. 3). According to the Political Contest Model (Wolfsfeld, 1997), the political process is more likely to have influence on the media than the media on the political process. Similarly, political power is more likely to translate into power over the media, than is control of the media likely to produce political influence. Moreover, the media are more likely to react to the unfolding events than to initiate them. However, the media can magnify political successes and failures, help to set the public agenda, serve as an independent advocate for victims and mobilize third parties into a conflict.

The level at which authorities control the political environment is one of the key variables determining the role of the news media in political conflicts. When authorities dominate the political environment, the news media find it difficult to play an independent role. The role of the news media varies based on the political context of the conflict, the resources, skills, and political power of the players involved, the existing relationship between the press and each antagonist, the state of the public opinion, and the ability of the journalists to gain access to what is happening in the field. Wolfsfeld's model looks at the competition between the antagonists along structural and cultural dimensions. The structural dimension assesses the extent of mutual dependence between the antagonists and the media to determine the power of each player in the conflict. The cultural dimension focuses on media's framing of the conflict based on the norms, beliefs and routines prevalent in the society (Wolfsfeld, 1997).

The authorities' degree of control over the political environment determines whether the news media will play an independent role in a political conflict. When the authorities are forced to react to events instead of instigate them, it suggests that others are framing the media's agenda. Losing the initiative in a conflict weakens political control over news coverage of the conflict. As Wolfsfeld noted, "those who control the situation have little problem controlling the news" (Wolfsfeld, 1997, p. 29). The media's ability to set the public agenda is important especially for the opposition, who depend on the media to achieve political goals. The weaker side in the conflict must find ways of bringing third parties into the conflict on its side to create more equal balance of power. Information is the chief commodity being exchanged between the opponents; those who have control over information have control over the conflict.

During political conflicts, governments often employ censorship in the form of denying access or accreditation to journalists, expelling them or shutting down press agencies. Wolfsfeld (1997) emphasized that greater access for reporters to the front lines increases the level of journalistic independence. Another potential source of the journalistic independence in reporting the political conflict is rooted in the existence of various factions within a government promoting different frames about the conflict. It is difficult to control an information environment full of choices. Media independence primarily refers to independence from authorities (Wolfsfeld, 1997).

One of the major reasons challengers, or a weaker side in the conflict, depend on the media to achieve their goals, is the media's ability to set the public agenda, and lower the political standing power of powerful authorities, which in turn could upset the balance of power. When the authorities are portrayed as incompetent, cruel or dispassionate, it diminishes their level of political status and power. In such situations, "the authorities become more vulnerable to attack, the news media more willing to carry out such attacks" (Wolfsfeld, 1997, p. 68).

Wolfsfeld (1997) believes that the news media play the most independent role when they act as "advocates of the underdog by amplifying the claims of challengers against the authorities" (p. 69). In these situations, the authorities find themselves "in an uphill battle for legitimacy." When the media concentrate on injustice and innocent victims frames in their coverage of the conflict, the underlying theme of the coverage is that "something must be done" to remedy the situation (Wolfsfeld, 1997, p. 70). When the third-party intervention becomes a real possibility, a convincing shift in the balance of power has occurred. News media have an influence on the conflict if challengers receive a significant amount of space and time in major news media, and if the media sympathize with the challengers' cause.

Wolfsfeld's model specifies three factors that assess the independence of the news media in conflict coverage: (a) use of exclusively official sources for information; (b) appearance of non-official stories and frames in the coverage of the conflict; and (c) frustration or anger of the authorities due to the coverage they are receiving (Wolfsfeld, 1997). Media coverage of the Afghan and Chechen conflicts will be examined based on these important components.

2. Parties in the Conflict

In Afghanistan, the major parties were the Soviet government, which instigated the intervention and throughout the conflict adhered to the official version of military, political and cultural assistance to the new revolutionary Afghan regime. The Soviet military served as the obedient "right arm" of the government, and did not really play an independent role in the political arena of the conflict. The Afghan government led by Babrak Karmal was important, although not as an independent player, totally relying on Soviet support. The U.S. and other Western countries were important actors in the Afghan conflict accusing the Soviet Union of outright aggression against the sovereign country, demanding unconditional troop withdrawal, and imposing international sanctions in political, economic and cultural spheres.

The palette of key players was more diverse in the Chechen conflict, including the leaders of the Russian government and military, the leaders of the Russian opposition, Chechen officials and field commanders, and finally leaders of the Moscow-backed Chechen government. One of the characteristics of the Chechen conflict that distinguishes it from the Afghanistan conflict was the emergence of division within the Russian power structure. It was alleged that the Russian Air Force deliberately disobeyed Yeltsin's orders of ceasefire. Two days prior to the Russian assault on Grozny, Minister of Defense Pavel Grachev publicly denied on Russian TV that troops would storm the Chechen capital (O'Ballance, 1997). During the first days of the assault on Grozny, Russian soldiers complained in television interviews that they had been given hardly any orders, and had lost contact with their commanders shortly after the storming began. The command structure of the military campaign degenerated to such a degree, that it was not clear who was in actual command (O'Ballance, 1997).

3. Internal Opposition

In Afghanistan, the Soviet media framed internal opposition to the Soviet invasion as imperialist incursions on the newly established revolutionary regime. The financial basis of this opposition was provided by the U.S. and other Western countries. Until the late 1980s, internal Soviet opposition to the intervention in Afghanistan, whatever opposition existed, was not made public.

In the conflict with Chechnya, senior Russian generals criticized the launching of the operation. Georgi Kondratyev, a deputy defense minister, declared that the Chechen problem could not be solved by military means (O'Ballance, 1997). General Eduard Vorobyov, deputy commander of the Russian ground forces refused to assume command of the forces in Chechnya and resigned, blaming Minister of Defense Pavel Grachev for lacking courage to present facts to Yeltsin (O'Ballance, 1997). Popular Russian general Alexander Lebed called the Russian storming of Grozny "foolish" and blamed the Russian government for using young soldiers with no combat training. Deputy Defense Minister Boris Gromov, a veteran of the Afghanistan conflict, criticized the "barbaric methods" used in the assault on Chechnya and resigned from the military in protest of the Russian intervention (Curran, Hill & Kostritsyna, 1997). Prominent political figures such as former Prime Minister Yegor Gaidar, *Yabloko* leader Grigory Yavlinsky, former President of the Soviet Union Mikhail Gorbachev spoke out strongly against the war and urged the government to seek an immediate political solution (Curran, Hill & Kostritsyna, 1997; Lieven, 1998; O'Ballance, 1997). Russian Human Rights Commissioner Sergei Kovalev, with other members of the Russian parliament, issued an appeal to President Yeltsin to stop the "massacre" of civilians with indiscriminate bombing, to halt combat and start negotiations (Curran, Hill & Kostritsyna, 1997). Sergei Kovalev, despite his removal from the position as Human Rights Comissioner by Yeltsin, remained one of the most resolute and outspoken opponents of the Russian invasion of Chechnya. He has repeatedly criticized the West for ignoring the war in Chechnya due to its vested interest in Yeltsin's government.

4. International Pressure

The Soviet invasion of Afghanistan was under international scrutiny throughout the entirety of the conflict. The U.S. and other major Western countries did everything in their power to urge the Soviet Union to withdraw its troops from Afghanistan. The measures included a UN declaration condemning the Soviet intervention and demanding unconditional immediate troop withdrawal from the Afghan territory, an economic embargo and a boycott of the 1980 Olympic Games in Moscow.

The international community was not nearly as vocal during the Russian intervention of Chechnya. Although several countries including the United States, France and Germany, expressed concern over civilian casualties in Chechnya, no concrete actions were taken to persuade Russia to end the warfare. The Chechen problem was conveniently considered to be a domestic issue, not requiring international interference. In spite of Chechen appeals to the international community for assistance, the West preferred to maintain good relations with Yeltsin's government, rather than deal with the uncomfortable issues of the Chechen claims for independence and the Russian military operations that were resulting in civilian casualties.

The Red Cross alleged that a "massacre of 250 people occurred at the taking of village Samaski by Russian troops" (O'Ballance, 1997, p. 206). The respected French medical group, *Medecins Sans Frontières* (Doctors without Borders), issued a rare direct appeal to the G7 leaders, citing heinous abuses of human rights in Chechnya and alleging that the Russian assault on the secessionist republic was among the most bloody that the organization had witnessed anywhere in the world (Curran, Hill & Kostritsyna, 1997). The Organization for Security and Cooperation in Europe (OSCE), which in April 1995 established a permanent mission in Chechnya after heavy diplomatic pressure from Western Europe and the United States, was criticized for not doing enough to raise the issue of atrocities committed by the Russian troops (Lieven, 1998).

5. Public Opinion

During the Soviet intervention in Afghanistan, public opinion was reported to be unanimously supportive of the Soviet actions. The Soviet news media carried out reports from numerous Soviet towns and villages alleging support from workers, farmers, and students to the Soviet troops in Afghanistan and accusing the imperialist West of sinister intentions to suffocate the revolution in Afghanistan. In the public's eye, the Soviet Union's assistance to the struggling Afghanistan, proved that Russia was a good friend and neighbor, and the only stronghold against the expansionistic West.

In Chechnya, Yeltsin's popularity rating plummeted in response to the violent assault on Grozny (O'Ballance, 1997). Opinion polls showed growing anger with the incompetence of the Russian authorities (Lieven, 1998, p. 125). In 1995, only one year before presidential elections and just months to parliamentary elections, authorities could not ignore public discontent with the ongoing Chechen war. In March 1996, opinion polls for the first time revealed that a majority of the population (52 percent) was in favor of an unconditional pullout of Russian forces from Chechnya (Smith, 1996). By the time of the presidential elections in the summer of 1996, Chechnya had become the number one issue of the presidential agenda.

6.   Mass Media

The Soviet news coverage of the Afghan conflict was attuned to the Soviet official view on the intervention. Newspapers were full of stories featuring Afghan peasants, students or workers praising the revolution for giving equal rights to men and women in education and employment, and the Soviet Union for its continuous assistance in the construction of schools and roads. Western accusations of Soviet brutality and the use of unacceptable military tactics such as the poisoning of wells were firmly refuted as propaganda techniques aimed to discredit the Soviet Union's true intentions. Media coverage relied solely on official sources of information. Very few journalists were allowed access to the frontlines, and even then they could only report an officially approved and censored version of the events. Foreign journalists were denied access to information, and U.S. correspondents were expelled from Afghanistan.

In Chechnya the situation was completely different. The Russian media, formerly an obedient extension of the Communist Party, emerged as a truly independent entity (Knezys & Sedlickas, 1999). All observers of the Chechen events agree that Russian media coverage was controversial, challenging the official accounts of the events, and being remarkably critical of Russian authorities. Lieven (1998) called NTV's (Independent Television Channel) coverage of Chechen war "ferociously critical and deeply embarrassing" to the Russian authorities. O'Ballance (1997) referred to Chechen war as a "TV war with television camera teams in forward position amid shooting and shelling, often relying pictures as they were happening" (p. 161).

In the beginning of January 1995, just a few days after unsuccessful and bloody Russian assault on the Chechen capital of Grozny, the director of All Russian State TV station was dismissed after broadcasting stories about the devastation in Grozny, and the director of NTV was warned that unless his policy of showing live battle scenes changed, his station license would be revoked (O'Ballance, 1997). No further official action ever followed. NTV continued its criticism of Russian political authorities and the Russian military.

Lieven (1998) noted that the lack of a press policy in Chechnya was just one of many features of Russian military disorganization. He argues that most of the time the frontlines in Chechnya were easily accessible and Russian soldiers at the posts were friendly to journalists. The lack of the press policy was manifested in the public acknowledgement by head of the FSK (Federal Counter-Intelligence Service) Sergei Stepashin that the "Russian administration has lost the information war" (Lieven, 1998, p. 120). Stepashin emphasized that Chechen Minister of Information Mauvladi Udugov constantly released information to the media, while Russian authorities pushed journalists away and failed to deliver information to the public. The gap between the optimistic official pronouncements and the grim experiences of Russian soldiers in Chechnya portrayed in the media added to the demoralization and anger of the troops (Lieven, 1998). He noted that the "ineffectiveness of internal military propaganda is another result of the excess of propaganda under the Soviet rule, and the gap between rhetoric and reality, which became apparent to the troops in Afghanistan" (p. 121).

While reporting the conflict in Chechnya, the Russian media emerged as a conduit of information between the two opposing sides. During the hostage-taking crisis in Budennovsk, negotiations between Russian Prime Minister Chernomyrdin and a leader of the Chechen insurgents, Shamil Basaev, were televised live.

Russian authorities often received information about new Chechen initiatives from the media. The Russian public was able to obtain the Chechen interpretation of the course of the operation, as well as an account of casualties and devastation, which Russian officials tended to underestimate. The media closely covered hostage-taking crisis in Budennovsk, reporting disorganization, confusion and lack of discipline among Russian troops. Several journalists including Valeri Yakov of *Izvestia* volunteered to travel with Chechen militants back to Chechnya as a live shield. After the agreement between Chernomyrdin and Basaev was reached, the Chechens were promised a safe way home. When a journalist, Natalya Alyakina, was shot and killed by a Russian soldier in the confusion, the Interior Ministry had to excuse the tragedy with the emotional reaction of Russian troops to the plight of hostages (O'Ballance, 1997).

7. Framing of the Conflict

In Afghanistan, the Soviet version of the military and political assistance requested by the Afghan government prevailed. In Chechnya, due to a variety of sources of information available to the public, there were contradicting versions of the outbreak of the war, as well as different interpretations of the major events of the conflict. Russian military authorities thought that the initial show of force would be sufficient to get the Chechens to surrender. It was a grave miscalculation. Hundreds of armed people came to Grozny to support the Chechen leader Johar Dudaev, who promised to turn Chechnya into a "second Afghanistan" if military force was used against him (O'Ballance, 1997). As the conflict progressed, the Russian military showed no signs of slackening their offensive, while the Chechens showed no sign of surrender or fading morale. The ferocity of Russian attacks, innumerous cases of Russian brutalization of the Chechen civilians, and the torture and murder of Chechen prisoners of war appalled both the Russian and Western publics (Lieven, 1998). The Russian military operation exhibited remarkable disorganization, lack of control and ill preparedness. Reports of mutiny and abandonment of their positions by Russian military complaining of lack of food, orders and insufficient weaponry were common (O'Ballance, 1997).

8. The Dynamics of Conflict Resolution

The Soviet intervention in Afghanistan came to an end with the ascent of Mikhail Gorbachev to power and the introduction of reform policies. In the process, the Soviet invasion was acknowledged to be a mistake and the troops were finally pulled out in 1989.

The development of the Russian-Chechen war included several major phases; each was characterized by an unforeseen crisis with bloody showdowns between Russian and Chechen forces, leading to civilian casualties. Prior to the Russian invasion, negotiations were conducted behind the scenes by Russian operatives to try to persuade Chechnya to suspend its 1991 declaration of independence and to sign a bilateral treaty of power-sharing and autonomy, similar to the one signed between Russia and the Republic of Tatarstan in February 1994 (Allison & Hill, 1997).

Allison and Hill (1997) described the peace process in Chechnya as "successive failed attempts to end the war by diplomatic means and a series of negotiations conducted against the backdrop of ongoing military conflict" (p. 1). Indeed, it seemed that Russian authorities made an effort to resolve the Chechen problem with political means only when they were forced to the negotiation table by the violent Chechen actions.

In March 1995, Dudaev suggested negotiations with Moscow to reach a settlement to the war. Meanwhile, Russia attempted to subjugate Dudaev's strongholds using military force. In one of those raids, Russian troops sealed off the small Chechen town of Samashki and shelled it with heavy bombing. Press and international workers were not allowed at the front. Reports of civilian deaths by international aid groups ranged from several hundreds to a thousand in the four-day assault. In retaliation, the Chechen field commander Shamil Basaev led an attack on the Russian town Budennovsk, where close to 2,000 people were taken hostage in the local hospital. In exchange for their release, gunmen demanded the withdrawal of Russian troops from Chechnya. The Russians attempted to seize the hospital and failed miserably, leaving several hostages dead or wounded. Subsequently, Russian Prime Minister Victor Chernomyrdin negotiated the release of the hostages in exchange for a ceasefire by Russian military forces in Chechnya. The negotiations, which took place over the telephone, were broadcast on national TV.

Basaev's raid demonstrated that the Chechens were determined and capable of taking the war outside Chechnya's borders. It also proved that Russia was extremely vulnerable to such attacks. Moscow, propelled by the events in Budennovsk, concluded a peace accord on July 30, 1995 with a provision for a ceasefire and a gradual withdrawal of Russian troops from Chechnya. However, by the fall of 1995, the accord disintegrated into further rounds of fighting and mutual recriminations. The situation further deteriorated after Salman Raduev's hostage-taking raid on the village of Kizlyar in neighboring Dagestan in January 1996. A military confrontation on the border of Pervomaiskoye, which resulted in the deaths of hostages and Russian soldiers, from which most of the Chechen militants escaped further strained Russian-Chechen relations (Allison & Hill, 1997).

By the Spring of 1996, with the Russian presidential campaign not far away, the war in Chechnya had become a primary campaign issue for Yeltsin. In an attempt to improve Yeltsin's record low ratings, a major peace initiative was announced with the intention of bringing peace before the June 1996 elections. Yeltsin's peace proved to be a smokescreen with Russian military strikes intensifying around the time of Yeltsin's announcement of his peace initiatives (Lieven, 1998). Around the time of elections, a combination of diplomatic maneuvers and a press blackout succeeded in diverting public attention from the Chechen war.

Throughout June and July of 1996, Moscow continued the dual policy of negotiations accompanied by massive military actions aimed at defeating Chechen forces and establishing the Moscow-backed government. It took another well-orchestrated raid by the Chechens in August of 1996, on the day of Yeltsin's inauguration, to create conditions for the major change. The raid resulted in the seizure of three major Chechen cities occupied by Russian troops. The Chechen raid demonstrated that Russian forces were incapable of defeating the Chechens even when the Russians were prepared to pay a high cost (Allison & Hill, 1997). Russia was left with the dilemma of whether to start the war all over again or surrender in return for peace (Lieven, 1997).

Finally, in a series of secret meetings between Alexander Lebed, newly appointed Secretary of the Russian Security Council, and Aslan Maskhadov, the chief Chechen official (Dudaev died from the Russian rocket attack in April 1996) signed an agreement, which later became the cornerstone for the withdrawal of Russian troops from Chechnya (Lieven, 1998). The issue of Chechen independence was postponed for a five-year period. In spite of Lebed's subsequent dismissal, the peace accord stayed unchanged.

9. The Role of the Media in the Conflict Process

Returning to Wolfsfeld's (1997) factors for assessing media independence, we now turn to examining the role of the media in the two conflicts. First, Wolfsfeld asserts that a key factor is the extent to which the news media use exclusively official sources for information. In covering the Afghan conflict, the Soviet media used only official sources of information. No story could be submitted for publication or broadcast without censorship and approval of the authorities. In Chechnya, official sources were used mostly for the purpose of getting an official view on the events. Alternative sources such as Chechen commanders, Chechen civilians, Russian soldiers and leaders of Russian political and military elite were the most frequent sources of information in the Russian media. The inability of Russian authorities to prevent journalists from getting to the frontlines, and the lack of an explicit press policy during the conflict, simplified the media's efforts to gather objective information (Knezys & Sedlickas, 1999).

Second, Wolfsfeld (1997) says that it is important to consider the extent to which non-official stories and frames appear in the coverage of the conflict. In their coverage of the Afghan invasion, the Soviet media produced only officially sanctioned stories. No dissent or interpretation of the events was permitted. In Chechnya, non-official frames prevailed. An "innocent victims" frame provided human interest to the plight of Chechen civilians trapped in the midst of the fierce fighting. The stories brought public attention to the condition of Russian soldiers: untrained, hungry, frightened and forgotten by the authorities. The readiness of the Chechen Minister of Information Mauvladi Udugov to render the Chechen slant on the unfolding events provided the Russian media with a continuous interpretation of the events by the opposing side.

Third, Wolfsfeld (1997) identifies the factor of the extent to which the authorities appear to be frustrated or angered by the coverage they are receiving. Soviet authorities in Afghanistan did not receive negative coverage; thus they were not frustrated with the media. In Chechnya, Russian authorities publicly admitted defeat in the information war, as evidenced by their inability to restrain journalists from getting to the front and broadcasting extremely critical and embarrassing information. The fact that Yeltsin dismissed the director of the major television station for its shocking live coverage of the Russian's brutal assault on Grozny, is the evidence in itself of the media's independence from the control by authorities.

Wolfsfeld (1997) believed that although it is difficult to isolate the role of the media when a shift in official policy occurs, there is no reason to deny it. In Chechnya, the Russian media proved to be an invaluable resource of information on the conflict, providing a platform for voicing opinions to various parties in the conflict. For the first time, the Russian media provided an objective view on the Chechen war and the atrocities carried out by the Russian troops against the innocent Chechen civilians, thus amplifying the Chechen claims against Russian authorities (Knezys & Sedlickas, 1999). The Russian media pressured authorities to find a peaceful solution to the Chechen problem emphasizing low morale and disorganization among the troops, a lack of coordination among Russian generals, and a fast growing discontent among the Russian public to the actions undertaken by the authorities.

Media became an advocate for thousands of wounded and dead children, elderly left in the devastated Chechen cities, and Russian soldiers abandoned in Chechen captivity or in the ruins of Grozny. The Russian media's continuous theme of devastation and despair brought to Chechnya by the Russian invasion eventually helped to rectify the situation, when the Russian-Chechen peace agreement was signed.

D. *IZVESTIA*'S COVERAGE OF AFGHANISTAN AND CHECHNYA

1. Methods of Analysis

Both quantitative and qualitative approaches were used to analyze *Izvestia's* coverage of the Afghan and Chechen conflicts. *Izvestia* published a total of 485 articles on the Afghan conflict from December of 1979 through April of 1985 (the date of Gorbachev's appointment to the Secretary General of the Communist Party). From November of 1994 through August of 1996 (the official signing of the peace agreement), *Izvestia* published 589 articles. Sixty articles from each conflict were randomly sampled for analysis. Three coders, fluent in Russian, performed the quantitative part of the analysis. Among the quantitative indicators isolated were: the article's valence toward the intervention, the role of the Soviet/Russian government, the role of the Soviet/Russian military, and the role of the Afghan/Chechen rebels, all judged as being positive, neutral or negative. It was also noted whether the articles dealt with the devastation that resulted from the conflicts. To assess the reliability of the coding, one third of the articles were analyzed by more than one coder. The Krippendorff's Alpha intercoder agreement coefficients for the variables reported are as follows: .97 for the valence toward the intervention, .99 for the role of the Soviet/Russian government, .98 for the role of the Soviet/Russian military, .96 for the role of the Afghan/Chechen rebels, and .94 for whether the article dealt with devastation.

2. Criticism of Soviet/Russian Institutions and Conflict Policies

Coverage of the Chechen conflict was significantly more critical of the intervention policy than it was for the Afghanistan conflict (Table 1). For Afghanistan, the mean of 2.25 (on a scale ranging from 1 to 3) was on the positive side of neutral. For the Chechen conflict, coverage was actually on the negative side of neutral (1.70). The Chechen coverage was also significantly more critical than the Afghan coverage of the Russian government (1.61 to 3.00) and the Russian military (1.63 to 3.00). These results indicate that there was no criticism of either the Russian government or military for Afghanistan. For Chechnya, the evaluations were on the negative side of neutral. Similarly, there were significant differences in the characterizations of the rebel forces (1.00 for the Afghan rebels and 2.13 for the Chechen rebels). All representations of the Afghan rebels were negative, whereas the characterizations of the Chechen rebels were on the positive side of neutral.

Coverage of the Afghanistan conflict was extremely one-sided, supporting the Soviet intervention as an action taken to maintain peace and stability in Afghanistan. One article reporting a speech by Babrak Karmal noted that he emphasized "sincere and timely international Soviet assistance. Soviet support and solidarity with Afghan people helped us to resist the imperialist attacks" (Kondrashov, 1981, p. 5). In another interview, Karmal thanked the Soviet Union for its "brotherly assistance and support." He noted that "cordial relations between neighboring countries received a greater development of the interests of people of the two countries, interests of the whole world and security of the region" (*Izvestia*, 1980, p. 4). At another press conference Babrak Karmal accentuated that "if Afghanistan did not have the Soviet Union on its side, our country could have lost its independence. We are grateful to the Soviet military support" (Ilyinski, 1980, p. 4).

TABLE 1. T-test for differences in coverage of the Afghanistan and Chechen conflicts by *Izvestia*.

Content Variable	Mean	S.D.	df	t-value	p
Valence of Coverage of the Intervention Policy			118	4.55	.000
Afghanistan (n = 60)	2.25	.68			
Chechnya (n = 60)	1.70	.65			
Role of the Soviet/Russian Government			71	8.90	.000
Afghanistan (n = 16)	3.00	.00			
Chechnya	1.61	.61			
Role of the Soviet/Russian Military			43	2.35	.001
Afghanistan (n = 1)	3.00	.00			
Chechnya (n = 44)	1.61	.57			
Role of the Afghan/Chechen Rebels			71	−11.53	.000
Afghanistan (n = 34)	1.00	.00			
Chechnya (n = 39)	2.13	.57			

Note: 60 Izvestia articles were sampled for each conflict. Not all articles commented on the role of the Soviet/Russian government and military, and the Afghan/Chechen rebels. As such, many of the n's are less than 60. When these elements were mentioned, coders rated the article as being positive (3), neutral (2), or negative (1).

Referring to the Soviet assistance to Afghanistan, Brezhnev noted that "We only did our duty responding to the request made by the Afghan government. We have done it in full compliance with the Soviet-Afghan Friendship agreement and the UN declaration. No one should doubt it" (Ilyinski, 1980, p. 4).

Criticism of Russian officials and the intervention policy was quite apparent and took a variety of forms in *Izvestia*'s coverage. President Yeltsin was criticized for letting the Chechen conflict get out of hand, "Yeltsin is too late to take control of the situation with his own hands" (Kononenko, 1995, p. 1). Another article portrayed Yeltsin as being pressured by his close circle of advisors to undertake military actions and ignore possibilities for a negotiated, peaceful solution (Stepovoy, 1994).

Izvestia articles blamed the Russian leadership for the conflict. One article quoted a Chechen volunteer, "Russian officials are to blame for the situation. All we want is freedom" (Gritchin, 1994, p.1). Another article said that, "Russian intentions to demolish a small village are the intentions of maniacs" (Konovalov & Serdukov, 1995, p. 4). Two days later, another article stated, "Federal troops claim to bring peace and order to Chechnya. So far they have caused only devastation, death and despair. Chechens and Russians living in Grozny condemn Russian military attacks" (Konovalov, 1995, p. 4). The leadership was also blamed for trying to spread the conflict into Dagestan, "What the Russian government has done in Pervomayskoe is impossible to comprehend. It seemed that Moscow intentionally attempted to involve Dagestan into the armed conflict" (Rotar, 1996, p. 1).

Another article quoted Sergei Kovalev, a Russian Human Rights Commissioner as accusing officials in Moscow of being "bloody liars." Kovalev also called for the "complete withdrawal of the troops, the acknowledgment of criminal activities against civilians, and the punishment of Russian officials responsible for the outbreak of the conflict" (Zheludkov & Mostovschikov, 1994, p. 2).

Izvestia drew attention to the incompetence of the Russian military. One article stated that, "Political and military maneuvers in Chechnya lack logic" (12-7-94, p. 2). It questioned the military leadership by asking, "Who was planning an attack on Grozny, only to see it fail so miserably? Who trained Russian tank operators so that they surrender without firing a single shot?" (12-7-94, p. 2). Another article evaluated the role of Russian military generals in the attack on Grozny by blasting the "idiotic organization of the attack" and criticized "the betrayal and the indifference of the generals to the fate of the wounded and dead soldiers on the streets" (1-16-95, p. 2). Another article noted that the Russian military leadership compared unfavorably to the Chechen military, "In contrast with Russian military units, the Chechens don't have a problem with commanders trying to trip each other up" (Yakov, 1996a, p. 2).

Izvestia charged that the Russian leadership failed to uphold promises, "In spite of the peace declaration signed by the highest levels of power, the bloodshed in Chechnya continues" (Mamaladze, 1996, p. 1). Leaders were also criticized for their treatment of captives, "Hostages were put through filtration camps where they had no food or water. Their documents were taken away from them and never returned. Even Chechen hostage takers treated their captives better. Some of the prisoners [taken by the Russians] were written off as people assisting the guerillas, and no one listened to their side of the story" (Yakov, 1996b, p. 2).

Izvestia was on several occasions skeptical of the claims made by the Russian authorities. One author calls the Russian suspicion that the Chechens intend to hide heavy weaponry and equipment in a small mountainous village as "complete idiocy" (Konovalov, 1995, p. 4). Another example is found in an article claiming that "the myths that Dudaev (the Chechen leader) bombs his own capital to ignite hatred against Russians among the city's populations are ridiculous" (Zheludkov & Mostovschikov, 1994, p. 2).

Articles in *Izvestia* were vocal in their criticism of Russian officials for blocking the process of peace negotiations. Long before the end of the conflict, one article charged that "Russian generals intend to intensify military assaults on Grozny and would not even consider the possibility of negotiations" (1-2-95, p. 1). Toward the end of the conflict, another article criticized on Russian official for blocking negotiations, "Doku Zavgaev is the leading opponent of open negotiations. He did everything in his power to end the negotiations, including the declaration that the Chechen military leaders are criminals at large and signing orders for their arrest. He maintains that one cannot conduct negotiations with criminals" (Yakov, 1996b, p. 2).

Izvestia also criticized the Russian negotiators, "There is no hope of achieving peace with a delegation lead by Stepashin, head of the FSB [Federal Security Service], the organization responsible for the attack on Grozny. . . . People untainted by the blood that was shed should head the negotiations. Alexander Lebed, who promised his voters to stop the Chechen war could be such a person. Unfortunately, right now he prefers to listen to others' opinions instead of personally looking into the situation" (Yakov, 1996b, p. 2). Four days later, another article reiterated the criticisms of the Russian negotiators, "The secrecy surrounding the peace negotiations between A. Lebed and A. Maskhadov is easy to explain. There are powerful people on both sides of the conflict who are interested in the continuation of the war. Hopefully, civilian lives will turn out to be more important than the pride of those in the power" (Yakov, 1996c, p. 1). Ten days later, another article stated that, "Some of the Russian officers look at the peace initiatives with skepticism. They are angry and wish for complete and irrevocable victory, but could not explain how they would achieve it without the massive extermination of the Chechen people" (Lotovkin, 1996, p. 2).

3. Evidence of Human Casualties and Economic Devastation Attributable to the Conflict

Afghan coverage referred to devastation and human casualties resulting from actions instigated by the U.S. and it allies. No mention of the brutal methods used by the Soviets against the civilians opposing the new Afghan regime appeared in the Soviet press. The examples of remarks alluding to the savage techniques used by the imperialist enemies of the democratic Afghanistan, are plentiful. For instance, the Minister of the Interior of DRA (Democratic Republic of Afghanistan) accused the "criminals from the U.S. agencies in gas poisoning thousands of Afghan students in Kabul" (*Izvestia*, 1982, p. 4). Babrak Karmal claimed that "American imperialists, Peking hegemonists, and local reactionary groups train and send assassins and thieves to our country, to plant fear and uncertainty among civilian population" (*Izvestia*, 1982, p. 4). Another article blamed "enemies of the Afghanistan that with the help of hired assassins and bandits, terrorists and diversants lead an undeclared war against young republic aiming at its isolation and suffocation" (Kondrashov, 1981, p. 5). *Izvestia* published personal accounts of the Afghan refugees returned to their homes from Pakistan that referred to poverty and horrifying persecutions of the civilians in refugee camps they called "hell" (Rashidov, 1981, p. 4).

Table 2 shows that there was a dramatic increase in *Izvestia*'s coverage of devastation caused by the conflict ($t = -4.29$, $df = 188$, $p < .001$). Only 20 percent of the articles on Afghanistan paid attention to devastation, whereas 80 percent of the articles on Chechnya covered devastation.

Izvestia's coverage of the Chechen conflict was not shy about detailing casualties and devastation. For instance, one article noted that, "People are getting killed in Chechnya by the dozens everyday. But it seems that everyone except the relatives of the dead got used to the continuous nightmare" (Yakov, 1995, p. 1). Several articles described an incident in which a village was destroyed and

---

TABLE 2. T-test for the differences in *Izvestia*'s coverage of the devastation caused by the conflicts in Afghanistan and Chechnya.

Content Variable	Mean	S.D.	df	t-value	p
Coverage of the Devastation			118	−4.29	.000
Afghanistan (n = 60)	.20	.58			
Chechnya (n = 60)	.80	.92			

Note: These figures indicate that 20 percent of the articles covered the devastation caused by the Afghanistan conflict, whereas 80 percent of the articles covered the devastation caused by the Chechen conflict.

charged the Russian military with committing war atrocities. "The Russian military made the decision to destroy the village whose inhabitants had been taken hostage by the Chechen guerrillas. The military falsified data regarding the actual number of people taken hostage. This was a terrible betrayal of the hostages by the Russian military leaders" (Yakov, 1996b, p. 2). Another article noted that, "It was not the Chechen insurgents but the Russian troops who were destroying villages with innocent civilians trapped in their homes. . . . Civilians were furious with Russian troops that destroyed their village, showed a lack of care for the fate of the hostages, and allowed the Chechen guerillas to escape" (Rotar, 1996, p. 2).

E. CONCLUSION

Throughout the 1994–1996 war between Russia and Chechnya, *Izvestia* served as a source of critical evaluation of official Russian actions. Its coverage was a force that applied pressure to the Russian government for a swift and peaceful resolution to the conflict. This is in stark contrast to the role that *Izvestia* played during the Afghanistan conflict, where it provided the official line of the Soviet ruling authority. This entailed virtually unwavering support for the Soviet intervention. While it is difficult to estimate the impact that this coverage had on policy, there are a number of paths through which its influence could have manifested itself. In the post-Soviet era, a critical press is a new factor in the equation of power. First, coverage could have influenced policymakers directly, shaping their actions by applying pressure for conflict resolution. Second, the changes to the Russian media system permitted *Izvestia* to be able to provide a platform for criticism within the Russian leadership. Third, *Izvestia* provided a voice for the Chechens to make their viewpoints known in Russia, and among the Russian elite. Fourth, the coverage in *Izvestia* may have stimulated and encouraged dissent within the larger Russian public. What is clear is that the operating environment for the Russian government has changed dramatically, and the Russian media are now an important part of that operating environment. Within this new context, the Russian government has been hesitant to engage in a prolonged conflict along the lines of what happened in Afghanistan.

As this chapter was nearing completion, the second war in Chechnya, or as officials prefer to call it, an anti-terrorist operation, had been going on for over two years. This new conflict had been sparked in the late summer of 1999 by two Chechen incursions into the neighboring republic of Dagestan and a series of apartment building bombings in Moscow and other Russian cities that killed more than 300 people, and resulted in a new eruption of fierce fighting between the Russian military and the Chechen rebels. Although, Chechen president Aslan Maskhadov categorically denied the Chechen role in the bombings and promised to crack down on Islamic rebels operating out of Chechen territory in exchange for the withdrawal of Russian troops and adherence to the conditions of the 1996 peace agreement, then Prime Minister Vladimir Putin chose to ignore promises made in 1996 and proceed with military operations.

The situation has continued to escalate. Russia launched intense air strikes and moved thousands of ground troops into Chechnya. In the first few months, the situation developed rapidly, stirred by public support in the wake of the apartment building bombings and the anticipation of a speedy resolution. Russian officials, Putin in particular, played the Chechen card in order to gain political support.

What Russian officials, both military and civilian, seem to learn very well was the lesson of media control. Journalists were no longer permitted access to the frontlines, to interview the Chechens or the freedom to cover events as they pleased. Information is once again subjected to scrupulous control by the authorities. Journalists refusing to play by the rules were refused access to information. Criticism of official policy and operations in Chechnya has become extremely limited with the dissolution of the sole influential independent TV channel (NTV) in the Spring of 2001. Human rights abuses continue to mount with very little done to remedy the situation.

Western governments and international organizations have appealed on numerous occasions to the Russian government to resolve the Chechen problem by political means. But after the September 11th terrorist attacks in the United States, pressure on Russia to resolve the Chechen situation by peaceful means has dissipated as a result of potential connections between Chechnya and Osama bin Laden's Al Qaeda network. So Russia once again finds itself in a stalemate in Chechnya. It cannot win the war in Chechnya. The Chechens are determined to fight to the death, while Russia does not want to endure casualties. And it cannot make peace with terrorists and admit another defeat. One thing is clear, Russian media do not represent the force for conflict resolution that they did from 1994 to 1996.

REFERENCES

Allison, G. & Hill, F. (1997). Preface. In D. Curran, F. Hill. & E. Kostritsyna (Eds.) *The search for peace in Chechnya: A sourcebook 1994–1996* (pp. 1–4). Cambridge, MA: Harvard University.

Androunas, E. (1991). Mass media: Stereotypes and structure. In E. E. Dennis, G. Gerbner,. & Y. N. Zassoursky (Eds.) *Beyond the Cold War: Soviet and American media images* (pp. 84–90). Newbury Park: Sage.

Androunas, E. (1993). *Soviet media in transition: Structural and economic alternatives.* Westport, CT: Praeger.

Bowen, G. L. (1989). Presidential action in public opinion about U.S. Nicaraguan policy: Limits to the 'Rally Round the Flag' Syndrome. *PS: Political Science and Politics, 22*, 793–800.

Curran, D., Hill, F. & Kostritsyna, E. (1997). *The search for peace in Chechnya: A sourcebook 1994–1996.* Cambridge, MA: Harvard University.

Flemming, W. (1998). The deportation of the Chechen and Ingush peoples: A critical examination. In B. Fowkes (Ed.), *Russia and Chechnia: The permanent crisis.* (pp. 25–64). New York: St. Martin's Press.

Full agreement in opinions. (1980, October 10). *Izvestia*, p. 4.

Gaal, C. & De Waal, T. (1997). *Chechnya: A small victorious war.* London: Pan Books.

Gammer, M. (1995). Unity, diversity and conflict in the Northern Caucasus. In Y. Ro'I (Ed.) *Muslim Eurasia: Conflicting legacies* (pp. 163–186). London: Frank Cass.

Gökay, B. (1998). The long standing Russian and Soviet debate over Sheikh Shamil: Anti-imperialist hero or counter-revolutionary cleric? In B. Fowkes (Ed.), *Russia and Chechnia: The permanent crisis.* (pp. 25–64). New York: St. Martin's Press.

Gritchin, N. (1995, January 6). The city is lit by the fires and rockets. *Izvestia*, p. 1.

Gritchin, N. (1994, December 2). The ultimatum is over. What is next? *Izvestia*, p. 1.

Guarantee of progress. (1982, September 7). *Izvestia*, p. 4.

Hough, J. F. (1989). The domestic politics of foreign policy. In C. G. Jacobsen (Ed.). *Soviet foreign policy* (pp. 3–18). New York: St. Martins Press.

Ilyinski, M. (1980, September 9). Solidarity and support. *Izvestia*, p. 4.

Irrevocable proof. (1982, March 2). *Izvestia*, p. 4.

Jensen, L. (1993). The press and power in the Russian federation. *Journal of International Affairs, 47*, 97–122.

Jones, D. R. (1989). Domestic and economic aspects of Gorbechev's foreign policy. In C. G. Jacobsen (Ed.) *Soviet foreign policy* (pp. 32–53). New York: St. Martin's Press.

Kakar, M. H. (1995). *Afghanistan: The Soviet invasion and the Afghan response 1979–1982*. Berkeley, CA: University of California Press.

Knezys, S. & Sedlickas, R. (1999). *The war in Chechnya*. College Station: Texas A&M University Press.

Kondrashov, V. (1981, April 28). To break reactionary intentions. *Izvestia*, p. 5.

Kononenko, V. (1995, January 12). There is a growing understanding in Kremlin that not everything cannot be resolved by force. *Izvestia*, p. 1.

Konovalov, V. (1995, January 21). Help to the refugees is brought only by the volunteers. *Izvestia*, p. 4.

Konovalov, V. & Serdukov, Mi. (1995, January 19). Guerrilla warfare in Chechnya is not far away. *Izvestia*, p. 1.

Lane, D. (1992). *Soviet society under perestroika*. London: Routledge.

Lieven, A. (1998). *Chechnya: Tombstone of Russian power*. New Haven, CT: Yale University Press.

Litovkin, V. & Urigashvili, B. (1996, August 23). When Lebed is in Grozny—war stops. *Izvestia*, p. 2.

Mamaladze, T. (1996, June 1). Today is June 1: End of the war? *Izvestia*, p. 1.

Marantz, P. (1989). Gorbachev's "new thinking" about East-West relations: Causes and consequences. In C. G. Jacobsen (Ed.) *Soviet foreign policy* (pp. 18–32). New York: St. Martin's Press.

McLeod, D. M., Eveland, W. P. Jr. & Signorielli, N. (1994). Conflict and public opinion: Rallying effects of the Persian Gulf War. *Journalism Quarterly, 71*, 20–31.

Mueller, J. E. (1970). Presidential popularity from Truman to Johnson. *American Political Science Review, 64*, 18–34.

O'Ballance, E. (1997). *Wars in the Caucasus, 1990–1995*. London: Macmillan Press.

Rashidov, K. (1981, February 19). We returned from hell. *Izvestia*, p. 4.

Rotar, I. (1996, January 23). Residents of Pervomaiskoye returning to their burned homes are bewildered and infuriated. *Izvestia*, p. 1.

Smith, M. A. (1996). *A chronology of the Chechen conflict*. Conflict Studies Research Center, v. 2, p. 15.

Stepovoy, A. (1994, December 1). North Caucasus and the language of the ultimatum. *Izvestia*, p. 2.

Vachnadze, G. (1992). *Secrets of journalism in Russia*. Commack, NY: Nova Science Publishers Inc.

Vyzhutovich, V. (1994, December 7). Right "arm of Moscow" does not know what the left is up to. *Izvestia*, p. 2.

Wolfsfeld, G. (1997). *Media and Political Conflict: News from the Middle East*. New York: Cambridge University Press.

Yakov, V. (1995, May 26). Difficult beginning of the negotiations to stop a conveyer of death. *Izvestia*, p. 1.

Yakov, V. (1996a, August 9). Grozny. Two days of feebleness: Federal authorities lost one more round of the Chechen war. *Izvestia*, p. 1.

Yakov, V. (1996b, January 20). Operation in Pervomaiskoye. *Izvestia*, p. 1.

Yakov, V. (1996c, August 13). Will the war end with a night meeting between Lebed and Maskhadov. *Izvestia*, p. 1.

Zheludkov, A. & Mostovschikov, S. (1994, December 30). One day of the life of human rights activists in Grozny. *Izvestia*, p. 2.

CHAPTER 12

EFFECTS OF AMBIGUOUS POLICIES ON MEDIA COVERAGE OF FOREIGN CONFLICTS: THE CASES OF ERITREA AND SOUTHERN SUDAN

Meseret Chekol Reta

A. INTRODUCTION

This chapter aims at examining media performance at a time when U.S. policymakers are uncertain of what position to take in a foreign conflict situation that affects U.S. national interest. It departs from the argument that while Herman and Chomsky's propaganda model may serve as an explanatory tool for U.S. media coverage of foreign conflicts within the context of the Cold War, it is unable to address those conflicts that leave U.S. policymakers uncertain as to what position to take. Thus, a policy uncertainty model is developed in this chapter to explain media reporting of such scenarios. The model is tested using the Eritrean and Southern Sudan conflicts as case studies.

The study is quantitative in approach, employing systematic sampling and chi-square test methods. The data revealed in only one of four test cases a relationship between uncertainty and neutrality of coverage, hence marginally supporting the first hypothesis. But no relationship was found between uncertainty of U.S. foreign policymakers and source diversity, hence lending no support for the second hypothesis. Based on these findings, the researcher concludes that the impact of uncertainty of U.S. policymakers on media coverage of a foreign conflict is minimal. At the same time, however, the data confirm that dichotomous treatment of U.S. media in their coverage of foreign conflicts is not to the level that Herman and Chomsky suggest in their propaganda model.

Finally, the significance of the study lies in three areas:

(1) It develops a model to explain international scenarios which the propaganda model could not; namely, conflicts which U.S. foreign policymakers are uncertain of what position to take.

(2) It presents a compelling critique of the propaganda model from a new perspective.

(3) Although the data minimally support the hypotheses formulated here, the study makes a significant contribution in guiding further research by concretely suggesting new hypotheses as well as new methodological approaches.

B. THE RESEARCH PROBLEM

In 1988 Herman and Chomsky published a book entitled *Manufacturing Consent*. In this elaborate work, the two authors provide an explanation of the modus operandi of the U.S. media through their propaganda model. The premise of the propaganda model is that the press is dependent on, and therefore reflective of, the dominant power structure. More specifically, it posits that the media serve to mobilize support for the special interest groups that dominate the state and the private sector; namely, government officials and top business leaders. Through both coercion and consensus, the dominant elite are able to fix frames of reference and agendas, as well as to exclude undesirable facts from public scrutiny (Herman & Chomsky, 1988, p. xiv). That way, the dominant elite through the media "manufacture consent" of the people.

Thus, within the realm of dominance theory, the propaganda model draws its explanatory power particularly from the Gramscian theory of hegemony. The media like the church and educational system are key agents through which hegemony is constructed, exercised and maintained. On the other hand, the propaganda model operates within a conflict framework when it comes to foreign news reporting. Herman and Chomsky assert that in foreign news reporting in particular, the media tend to treat events (and issues) taking place in a given country based on U.S. policy toward the regime of that country. They present a compelling argument along this line by introducing two notions of dichotomized treatment by the media: one, anti-communism as a national religion and control mechanism, and the other, "worthy" and "unworthy" victims. Both notions operate within the dichotomy of "friendly" versus "unfriendly" (or "client" versus "enemy") states or regimes. This dichotomization may also be extended to political groups like rebel movements.

The first notion advances the argument that communist nations, groups or individuals associated with any given event are always presented in an unfavorable light. Particularly in a political or military conflict between a communist nation or faction and a non-communist one, communists are always treated as villains—unjust, brutal, and enemy of the people, even if they have popular support. By contrast, the non-communists are portrayed as struggling for democracy and freedom of the people, regardless of their political practices or human rights records. They provide a number of detailed case studies along this "them" and "us" dichotomy: the Sandanistas versus the Contras in Nicaragua, the guerrillas in El Salvador versus the right-wing government, and the conflict in Guatemala between the left-wing Mayan Indians and the right-wing government — to name a few.

The second notion, "worthy and unworthy victims," presents a scenario in which similar negative events taking place in countries whose regimes hold contrasting relations with the United States are reported with different levels of intensity. Undesirable acts in a communist or "enemy" country are highly emphasized, repeated, and reinforced in order to show the cruelty of the system. Thus, according to the propaganda model, victims of such acts in an "enemy" state are "worthy" victims. On the other hand, similar atrocities or other evil acts by a "friendly" or "client" regime or dissident group are humanized, marginalized, or even given some kind of favorable excuse. This is to show that such regimes or groups and the political system they represent are not inherently evil. Therefore, victims of such an act by the "friendly" regime are considered "unworthy" victims. Herman and Chomsky illustrate this point of dichotomized treatment by contrasting the level of intensity of coverage given by the U.S. elite media to the murder of Father Popieluszko in Communist Poland in 1984, on one hand, and the murder of a total of more than 100 religious dissidents by Pro-U.S. regimes in Central America during the same period. The authors conclude that such contrastive coverage is a result of the subservience of the U.S. media to the dominant agenda—in this case, U.S. foreign policy.

While the propaganda model presents a powerful explanation of the media as reflectors of U.S. policy in foreign news coverage, it still suffers from three fundamental shortcomings:

(1) It was developed in a Cold War mindset, hence operating only within the framework of the East-West conflict. Thus, it is historically bound. A model must at best be able to explain phenomena beyond a specific historical period.

(2) The propaganda model presents an absolutist view of the anti-communist bias of the media. By doing so, it fails to consider the times when the media changed their characterization of some communist countries in the wake of a policy change by the U.S. government toward those countries. A good example is China. Until the early 1970s, U.S. foreign policy toward China was hostile, marked by references such as "Red China" and "Communist China." Such references were also widely used by the media. But upon the Nixon Administration's adoption of a "one China" policy in the early 1970s, negative references toward Communist China were dropped, and references denoting the legal identity of China began to be used. The media followed suit: not only did they drop the negative references, but they also minimized critical reporting of China as a whole (Chang, 1990; Chang, 1993). Indeed, the China scenario

demonstrates that to U.S. foreign policy (hence to the media), prag-
matism based on political realism outweighs American bitterness
against the dogma of communist ideology.

(3) Because of its extreme focus on the East-West conflict, the propaganda model ignores political scenarios around the world where the
U.S. holds no definite position or is uncertain about what policy, if
any, it might adopt. Good examples are the Eritrean conflict in
Ethiopia, the civil war in Sudan, and the secessionist war in Sri
Lanka. Thus a model addressing policy uncertainty is needed to
explain political scenarios that the propaganda model has been
unable to explain because of its confinement to East-West conflicts.

In this research, then, we shall take as our case studies the Eritrean conflict
in Ethiopia during the imperial and communist regimes (1962–1991) and the second round of the Southern Sudan conflict, which has outlived several regimes
since its inception in 1983. We present the significance of these two case studies
as follows: While U.S. policy was clear toward the friendly imperial regime and
the hostile communist government of Ethiopia, its position on the war in the
northern province of Eritrea between the government and the rebels was uncertain during both regimes. For one thing, the U.S. was not sure what the consequence of the independence of Eritrea would eventually mean to the stability of
the region. Would it eventually go into the arms of the neighboring Arab states,
given the large military and political support the Eritrean rebels, Christian and
Moslem alike, received from them? After all, the majority of the Eritrean population is Moslem. Although the Christian faction was consistently the more dominant of the two main factions, that could not still be a guarantee for the U.S. that
Eritrea would not eventually fall under the strong influence of the Arab states.
And, if that happened in the end, how would that affect the regional balance of
power, considering Eritrea's strategic location along the Red Sea?

On top of that, even low-level political support from the United States to
rebel factions seeking independence would have made the U.S. unpopular among
most African countries, as they feared it would set a bad precedence for the interference of outside powers in matters of their own territorial integrity. After considering all these factors, the U.S. chose to stay with its ambiguous position of
"peaceful settlement" throughout the Eritrean conflict.

Like the Eritrean rebel movement, the Sudanese People's Liberation Movement started its guerrilla warfare against the government in Khartoum in 1983
seeking independence from the Moslem North. The war started at a time when
the Sudanese regime of General Nimeri was a strong U.S. ally in direct contrast
to the hostile communist regime of Col. Mengistu Hailemariam of Ethiopia.
Despite its warm relations with the Nimeri regime, the United States chose to be
on the sidelines when it came to the Southern Sudan question. As on the Eritrean
question, here again it was filled with uncertainty over what position to take. The

State Department expressed empathy with the cause of the Southern Sudanese at heart, given the second-class citizenship those people had to endure under a strong Moslem government, but at the same time it would not want to offend a strong ally in a troubled Horn of Africa by supporting secessionists. Moreover, it would not want to offend all other African countries, most of which are preoccupied with fragile unity of their territories.

And, most important, the U.S. government was feeling uneasy over the fate of the Nile if Southern Sudan were to secede. The more the number of nations controlling the Nile, the more the potential for a wider regional conflict over its use, as each nation would have its own policy concerning it. And that could be detrimental to Egypt, a very crucial ally of the United States. Ever since the Sudanese fundamentalist Islamic government came to power in 1989, it has been hostile to the U.S. government. Even so, the State Department has chosen to remain on the sidelines with regard to the conflict in Southern Sudan.

Finally, it is important to note that while the U.S. had varying relationships with the different regimes of Ethiopia and Sudan, its policy toward the two rebel movements remained constantly ambiguous within the study periods, regardless of the changing administrations. The explanation of this constancy may lie in the fact that a clear policy would either way affect not only the antagonistic parties, but also other countries in the region. That's why a change in U.S. administrations did not have any effect on the ambiguity of the policy toward these conflicts. Also, change of administration does not often affect U.S. foreign policy as it does domestic policy. This shows that there is little change between Democrats and Republicans in their outlook of the rest of the world because what dictates here is American national interest.

Using the Eritrean and Southern Sudanese scenarios, the researcher in this study shall attempt to answer the following research questions:

(1) Are the media more likely to present balanced reporting on all sides of the conflict at a time of uncertainty on the part of the U.S. policymakers?

(2) Do the media tend to diversify their use of sources in reporting on foreign conflicts about which U.S. policy is uncertain?

C. THEORETICAL FRAMEWORK: THE POLICY UNCERTAINTY MODEL

As noted earlier, while the propaganda model may be a valuable tool to explain U.S. media's reporting of events within the context of the East-West conflict, it has shortcomings in dealing with situations which U.S. foreign policy is uncertain or ambiguous about. Therefore, an attempt shall be made here to develop a theoretical model which would explain media coverage of such international scenarios. The model will be known as *policy uncertainty model*, and will later be tested in the Eritrean and Sudan case studies.

1. Uncertainty—A Look at Different Perspectives

In the social sciences, the principle of uncertainty is primarily applied in economic and political theories. The economist Anthony Downs (1957, p. 77) defines uncertainty as "any lack of sure knowledge about the course of past, present, future, or hypothetical events." Uncertainty then assumes ambiguity of stand stemming from a limitation of knowledge on a given event.

In a study of organizational decision making, March and Simon (1958) define uncertainty in terms of the completeness and accuracy of the decision-maker's knowledge. Such a definition assumes lack of knowledge both in quantity and quality. They say that this lack of completeness and accuracy of knowledge about a situation hinders decision makers from assigning "definite probabilities to the occurrence of particular consequences" (p. 37). Thus, the question of probability is central to the uncertainty principle. Lack of probability leaves actors with ambiguity, hence resulting in indecision or inaction. To March and Simon, uncertainty has to do with the state of mind of the decision makers.

March in a later work (1981, pp. 226–227) distinguishes between two kinds of ambiguities associated with organizational decision making. The first type he calls "ambiguities of history," which stem from a problem of interpreting the past. He reasons that history is difficult to interpret, especially when the sample of observations is insufficient and there are no experimental controls. The second type he refers to as "ambiguities of preferences." These, according to him, are a result of imprecise, inconsistent, and unstable goals within an organization.

In an earlier work, March and Olsen (1976, p. 18) suggested another pair of categories from a different perspective: environmental uncertainty and outcome uncertainty. They said that environmental uncertainty stems from ambiguity that is inherent in the event itself. Environmental actions are often ambiguous because of observation difficulties and conflicting interpretations (Daft & Macintosh, 1981, p. 219). The North Korean submarine mission to the territorial waters of South Korea in September 1996 may be taken as an example of environmental uncertainty. Yet, in this type of uncertainty, it is only the environmental element that distinguishes it from the other type of uncertainty as we shall see in a moment, because, in the final analysis, uncertainty has to do with the state of mind of the decision-making body. In the above example, although the hostility between the two nations was obvious, the South Koreans could hardly get at the specific motive of this mission.

Outcome uncertainty refers to disagreement about the existence and nature of cause/effect relationships surrounding a given event. It is "the state arising from predicting outcomes from the actions taken to achieve them" (Leblebici & Salancik, 1981, p. 580). Again taking the Korean scenario, what will the continuing economic crisis in North Korea mean to the future of the peninsula as a whole? Will North Korea invade the South out of desperation, or will it bow to its economic crisis and propose to be united with the South, thus ending the 50-year-old hostility between the two nations? In this example of outcome uncertainty, then, the focus is on cause and effect.

2.   Uncertainty In Foreign Policymaking

Michael Smith (1988) observes that policymaking on a situation of uncertainty is more of an art than science as it requires the application of judgment, opinion, belief, selective estimates of the situation, plus whatever objective data is available. Smith identifies four stages in which foreign policymakers encounter uncertainty in the decision-making process: the policy arena, policy design, policy process, and policy implementation. Uncertainty in the policy arena stems from the fact that the international environment is diffuse, complex, and indeterminate. A variety of actors participate in a certain domain, and they often play by conflicting sets of rules. Information is unreliable and puzzling, often fragmentary. Besides, what is acceptable abroad may be contested domestically, or vice versa. Then in designing foreign policy (that is, defining principal objectives, strategies and values), decision makers must deal with a situation in which attempting to predict the future based on the present or the past is often self-defeating. Secondly, given the heterogeneity of global society, foreign policymakers may be unable to clearly communicate their strategies and intentions, however unequivocal they may try to be. Problems may also arise in the policymaking process stage in terms of setting priorities and preferences. These problems may actually be exacerbated by elaborate organizational and bureaucratic structures which, while reflecting the need to reduce uncertainties, have their own disadvantages. The routine application of standard operating procedures as a basis for predictable policymaking in these bureaucratic structures may be an obstacle to the recognition of genuine uncertainties and a hindrance to the kinds of flexibility these uncertainties demand.

Policy implementation is itself rife with uncertainty. Specific operational procedures and the technicalities they entail have unpredictable consequences. First, there may be a problem of communication and credibility. What is the relationship between the message sender and receiver in the process of implementing the policy? A second issue is one of co-ordination and control, particularly where the national policy machinery is complex and interlinked with international or multinational agencies. A final problem is evaluation of the implementation itself. How many policymakers say when a policy is completed? And, secondly, how can they know whether a policy has succeeded or failed, particularly when criteria for judging successes have not been established and/or are in doubt?

3.   Media Reporting in Times of Uncertainty

Araby (1989) studied the role of the elite press in the process of U.S. foreign policymaking by examining three Middle East cases: the sale of AWACS to Saudi Arabia (1981), the deployment of U.S. Marines in Lebanon (1984), and the raid on Libya (1986). He studied these cases by analyzing the commentaries of *The New York Times, Washington Post, Los Angeles Times*, and *Christian Science Monitor*. The study focused on one fundamental question: What are the conditions under which the press exercises more or less autonomy in reporting and commenting on foreign policy affairs? Araby found that when the two foreign policymaking institutions—the Presidency and Congress—agreed on defining U.S. national interest in a given case, as in the case of the raid on Libya, the press concentrated its discussion on this consensus view, to the virtual neglect of alternative views. He further found that in such conditions of bipartisan consensus, the press filtered out the ideas that threatened the policy consensus, hence defining the boundaries of acceptable public debate. This finding of Araby's is consistent with the long-standing view of the role of the press as a defender of consensus ideas and values (Mills, 1956; Gitlin, 1980; Altschull, 1984; Arno & Dissarayake, 1984; Hallin, 1987; Donohue, Tichenor & Olien, 1995).

In contrast, when the two foreign policymakers disagreed on what constitutes U.S. national interest, as in the case of the AWACS sale to Saudi Arabia and the Marines deployment in Lebanon, the press discussed the issues as two legitimate views. It also presented opinions and arguments along the lines of both positions. In short, the press treated the opposing views as legitimate controversies between two legitimate institutions. By taking such a stand in such circumstances, says Araby, the press is conferring status on the two important branches of the American government. Bennett (1990, p. 106) brings out even more clearly this role of status conferral of the press in times of disagreement over a policy with his press indexing theory. After examining the *New York Times'* coverage of U.S. funding for the Nicaraguan Contras between 1983 and 1986, he concludes: "Mass media news professionals tend to 'index' the range of voices and viewpoints in both news and editorials according to the range of views expressed in mainstream government debate about a given topic."

Zaller and Chiu's (2000, p. 61) classic study of the role of the press in foreign policy crises during the Post-World War II period supports Bennett's theory of press indexing. They find out that the media generally tend to support the government during foreign policy crises. They say that in their study of 42 foreign policy crises between 1946 and 1999, they find strong evidence that "reporters do, as Bennett suggests, appear to wax hawkish and wane dovish as official sources lead them to do." However, the two researchers add that despite a strong indexing effect over the entire post-World War II period, during the post-Cold War era the media have tended to be more independent of Congress and the president, though not necessarily more independent of government officials generally. Despite this slight change in the post-Cold War era, Zaller and Chiu's finding is still consistent with the general thrust that the media are supporters of the government and, indeed, U.S. foreign policy.

McCoy (1992), in his study of the *New York Times'* coverage of El Salvador in the 1980s and early 1990s, contends that the daily foreign affairs practices of the paper rarely disturb Washington's foreign-policy strategies and their communication to the American people. He explains that reporters who are brought along according to the usual socialization process display a definite pattern of compliance to the system of news gathering and an acceptable, limited range of perspectives from which to present news that often involves life, death and human dignity.

These findings run counter to Cohen's (1963) view of the press as a participant in the foreign policymaking process, "a political actor of tremendous consequence" (p. 268). Nor does it sit well with Reston's (1967) belief that the press generally influences foreign policy. On the other hand, these findings reinforce the view held by several scholars that the press is simply a supporter and follower of the foreign policymakers, even manipulated, as some say (Sigal, 1973; Halberstam, 1979; Gans, 1979; Paletz & Entman, 1981; Dorman & Farhang, 1987; Hertsgaard, 1988).

4. Conceptualizing Uncertainty in Foreign Policy

The policy uncertainty model departs from the premise that the media do their international affairs reporting based on U.S. foreign policy. It articulates that the media follow U.S. foreign policy whenever the policy is clear. But they find it difficult to decide which way to report when they cannot receive guidance from the foreign policymakers as a result of uncertainty on the part of the latter. Thus, uncertainty is conceptualized here as a state of indecision by foreign policymakers on a given international conflict, to the extent that it would leave the media unsure as to how they should report about it as they have no road map to follow. The policy uncertainty concept then does not end at the policymakers, but also extends to the uncertainty it leaves in media reporting. Nicholas Berry best sums up the media's level of discomfort at such times: "When foreign policy officials are divided or uncertain, the press will focus on the struggle to define the foreign policy assumptions that guide specific policies. It will ask questions on page one. It will focus on the players. It expects a single authority to define foreign policy. It wants some coherence from Washington in order to report foreign affairs" (Berry, 1990, p. xiv).

Uncertainty on the part of the foreign policymakers is marked by one of the following situations:

(1) impossibility of assigning a probability to the outcome of an event;
(2) ability to assign probabilities, but indecision to act because of disliking all the available consequence options;
(3) stalemate on decision due to division between policymakers over what position to take on a given issue or what strategy to follow in implementing an agreed policy.

a. Hypotheses

H-1

To the degree that U.S. policymakers are uncertain of what position to take on a given foreign conflict, the media tend to report on all sides of the conflict without applying dichotomized treatment.

The rationale behind this hypothesis is that uncertainty on the part of policymakers creates media uncertainty. Under such circumstances, the media do not have the policymakers (e.g., the State Department) to provide them with a road map of the unstable condition in the given country. Therefore, the media tend to gather news from and report on all sides of the conflict. The ultimate result will be neutral or balanced coverage on the warring parties. The policy uncertainty model assumes that in times of high predictability of outcomes in a given foreign conflict, the media tend to follow the lead of the dominant elite in their reporting. Up to this point then, this model goes hand in hand with the propaganda model. However, when authority is in a state of ambivalence or discord, the media tend to present balanced reporting.

H-2

To the extent that U.S. policy is ambiguous toward a given foreign conflict, the media are likely to gather news from all sources without giving any special priority to certain groups over others.

The impetus to get at all perspectives of the situation stirs the media to gather news from all sources involved in the conflict or those having proximity to it. Therefore, unlike the propaganda model where we have two differential standards for measuring the credibility of sources, in the policy uncertainty model any news source, until proven otherwise, will enjoy credibility and therefore is likely to be quoted in filing a story.

D. METHODOLOGY

The study takes *The New York Times* and *The Washington Post* as representatives of U.S. media in foreign news reporting. It examines their coverage of Eritrean and Southern Sudan conflicts between 1962 and 1991 and between 1983 and 1996, respectively. Coverage is examined in terms of portrayal of actors and usage of sources. The data from the two papers are collected using their respective indexes, Lexis/Nexis database, and microfilms.

1. Sampling

The two case studies were divided into regime-based political periods—the Sudan conflict into four periods, and the Eritrean War into two. Subsequently, selection of stories for the study was based on these political periods. Where the number of newspaper articles under a given period of study was found to be small (e.g., Period 1 in the Sudanese case study, which is the Nimeri regime during which *The New York Times* published only 23 stories), the universe was examined. On the other hand, where the data size was too large (e.g., 78 stories in Period 4, which is the Bashir regime, 1989–1996), sampling was called for. In such instances, the researcher applied the method of systematic sampling to arrive at a sample of 39, in this particular instance, by randomly selecting the starting number and taking every other story in the population from a chronologically ordered list.

The ratio applied in the systematic sampling of the study varied from period to period, depending on the size of the population (e.g., *The New York Times* had a population of 325 articles for Period 2 of Eritrean case study, whereas it had only 61 for Period 3 of Southern Sudan conflict). The rule of thumb followed here was that each period of study would be the unit of analysis is the news story in its entirety. Here, news story is broadly defined to include news stories, features, editorials, and commentaries. Photos, cartoons, maps and charts remain outside the scope of this study.

Our independent variable is uncertainty, and the dependent variables are neutral coverage (or balanced reporting) and source diversity (for a definition of uncertainty, see subdivision C.1.)

Our predictions are as follows:

(1) Press reports reflecting uncertainty among U.S. foreign policymakers will more likely be neutral toward key actors, compared with press reports reflecting certainty.
(2) Press reports reflecting uncertainty among U.S. foreign policymakers will contain greater diversity of sources than will press reports reflecting certainty.

2. Coding Scheme and Procedures

The following variables will be examined in the course of testing the two hypotheses: subject of coverage, direction of coverage, and quoted source within coverage. The variables are coded based on the following categories and definitions:

1. *Quoted source:* refers to an individual, group, institution or government used in the story by the staff reporter or wire service as a source of information. *Categories: U.S. government, Sudanese government, Ethiopian government, other government, rebel group, Sudanese nongovernment, Ethiopian nongovernment, nongovernment International, unspecified/anonymous, Dual source.*
2. *Subject:* Subject is defined here as an issue (or event) that is treated within a given story; it must be at least a paragraph long. There may

be more than one subject category within a story. Therefore, any number of them that the coder thinks have appeared in that story are coded. *Sub-categories: Cause of rebellion, military activity, external support for warring parties, human rights abuse/terrorism, famine/refugee/relief, peace effort, crisis/instability, foreign relations, anti-Western sentiment/measures, other, not applicable.*

3. *Direction of coverage:* favorable, unfavorable, neutral.
4. *Uncertainty of U.S. foreign policymakers:* This refers to the issue or issues of uncertainty of U.S. foreign policymakers during a given political period of the conflict.

An inter-coder reliability test conducted between two graduate students yielded a score of 91.8 percent.

E. DATA ANALYSIS

A total of 387 stories were examined from both case studies. Of these, 241 were from the Sudan case study, and the remaining 146 were from the Eritrean case study.

To the degree that U.S. policymakers are uncertain of what position to take on a given foreign conflict, the media tend to report on all sides of the conflict without applying dichotomized treatment.

Dichotomization assumes grouping into two mutually exclusive or contradictory categories. Therefore, in the course of this analysis, dichotomous coverage refers to cases where one of the contesting groups is treated favorably in more than half of the stories, and where the other group is treated unfavorably in more than half of the stories.

H-1 deals with the direction of media coverage toward the government and the rebels in both the Sudanese and Eritrean conflicts.

The data from all four periods of the Southern Sudan case study were combined for testing the hypothesis. Similarly, the data for the two periods of the Eritrean case study were combined for the same test. The tests were based on the treatment of each actor in each case study. The primary statistical test employed was the chi-square.

1. Sudan Case Study

Among the 126 stories focusing on the uncertainty of U.S. foreign policymakers, only 36.5 percent are coded as neutral in their treatment of the government of Sudan. This compares with 41.8 percent of the stories which do not dwell on the issues of uncertainty of the U.S. foreign policymakers. This nonsignificant difference (36.5 vs. 41.8 percent) is not in the predicted direction of the hypoth-

TABLE 1 Stories With and Without Uncertainty by Case Study and by Time Period

Sudan

Period	Stories With Uncertainty	Stories Without Uncertainty	Total
1 (1983–85)	25	13	38
2 (1985–86)	24	28	52
3 (1986–89)	57	21	78
4 (1989–96)	32	41	73
Total	138	103	241

Eritrea

Period	Stories With Uncertainty	Stories Without Uncertainty	Total
1 (1962–74)	37	25	62
2 (1974–91)	19	65	84
Total	56	90	146

esis. Similarly, 46.9 percent of the stories of uncertainty had neutral coverage toward the Sudanese rebels, as compared to 52.5 percent for the stories without uncertainty. Again this difference (46.9 vs. 52.5) is not in the predicted direction of the hypothesis.

In light of the above findings, it was important to examine the extent to which dichotomized treatment of the various actors actually occurred. Coverage of the Sudanese government in Period 1 was primarily neutral, while toward the rebels it was predominantly unfavorable. The rebels received unfavorable coverage in more than four times as many stories as did the Sudanese government. By contrast, the rebels received favorable coverage in only a third as many stories, compared with the government of Sudan. The government received neutral coverage in more stories than did the rebels. In this first period, then, the coverage was more directional in character, with the media favoring the pro-U.S. Nimeri regime over the rebels who were at the time being supported by anti-U.S. Libya and Soviet-backed Ethiopia. This pattern of findings is consistent with the propaganda model of Herman and Chomsky.

In Period 2, during which U.S.-Sudanese relations were ambiguous because of Sudan's closer ties with Libya, mention of both the government and the rebels tended to be neutral. However, among stories that did contain direction, there were more stories unfavorable toward the rebels than toward the Sudanese government. By contrast, the coverage was favorable toward the government in more than four times as many cases as for the rebels. Thus, in Period 2, there is some directional treatment still favoring the Sudanese government, though the difference is not as sharp as in Period 1.

In Period 3, both the government and the rebels received predominantly unfavorable coverage, since both parties were accused of using civilians as pawns in the war by blocking relief efforts from reaching the starving masses in each other's controlled territories. Within the U.S. government, Congress was highly vocal against this alleged form of human abuse, while the Reagan Administration chose to be silent on the matter. The result was that, in this period, the U.S. was in what might be termed a "love-hate" relationship with the Sudan government, which was swaying between Libya and the U.S. The U.S. appeared to adopt a wait-and-see attitude. There was little favorable coverage of either the Sudanese government or the rebels in the third period. In a sense, it might be termed coverage that conferred "a pox on both their houses." Slightly more than a tenth of the stories were favorable toward the Sudanese rebels, and under 6 percent were favorable toward the Sudanese government. More than half of the stories about either party were unfavorable. This leaves a little more than a third that were neutral, for the government as well as for the rebels. In general, then, in Period 3 the government and the rebels were treated more or less equally.

In Period 4, on the other hand, the Sudanese government received predominantly unfavorable coverage, while coverage of the rebels was predominantly neutral. Indeed, there were more than twice as many stories unfavorable toward the Sudanese government as were unfavorable toward the rebels. By contrast, the rebels received nearly 2.5 times as many neutral stories in this period as did the government. It should be pointed out again that Period 4 in the Sudanese conflict was a time when relations between Sudan and the U.S. were at their lowest point of the entire study period. This was especially true after 1993, when the Islamic Al-Bashir regime was implicated in the World Trade Center bombing. Also in Period 4, both the government and the rebels were widely accused of using food as a weapon against the civilians in each other's territory. Yet, the Sudanese rebels received primarily neutral coverage, while the Sudanese government received highly unfavorable coverage.

One might speculate that in terms of national values perceived by the two newspapers under study, the implication of terrorism by the Sudanese government in the World Trade Center bombing far outweighed the implication of interference in food distribution to starving populations on the part of the rebels. It is important to note here that there was a pattern of unfavorable coverage toward those regarded by the U.S. as pariah or enemy states, consistent with the propaganda model. The direction of coverage toward Libya in its role in the Sudanese conflict is a case in point. Libya, as a longstanding U.S. enemy, received far more unfavorable coverage than neutral or favorable. In all four periods combined, Libya was treated unfavorably in 72.2 percent of the stories in which it was mentioned, followed by neutral coverage in 25.9 percent of the stories, and favorable coverage in only 1.9 percent of the stories.

On the other hand, Iran, another adversary of the U.S., was mentioned only in stories that appeared within Period 4, in connection with its support to the Islamic government of Sudan in its war with the rebels. Iran was portrayed unfavorably in 55.6 percent of the stories in which it was mentioned, and in neutral terms in 44.4 percent of these stories. There was no favorable coverage about Iran.

2. The Eritrean Case Study

In this case study, among the stories of uncertainty, 68.1 percent have neutral coverage toward the Ethiopian government; this compares with 46.5 percent for the stories without uncertainty. Here, a positive relationship is observed between uncertainty of U.S. foreign policymakers and neutrality of media coverage. The relationship is statistically significant at the .017 level and is in the predicted direction. On the other hand, barely over 48 percent of the stories with uncertainty had neutral coverage toward the Eritrean rebels, as compared to just over 50 percent for the stories without uncertainty. This difference is neither in the predicted direction nor statistically significant. When it comes to dichotomous treatment, the Ethiopian government and the Eritrean rebels both received more coverage that was neutral than in any other category. Yet, the favorable/unfavorable coverage showed a certain amount of directional treatment, apparently based on the state of the U.S. government's relationship with the Ethiopian government across the two periods.

For example, in Period 1 during the pro-U.S. imperial regime, the Eritrean rebels were portrayed unfavorably in more than twice as many stories as was the Ethiopian government. In direct contrast, the Ethiopian government received favorable coverage in more than twice as many stories as did the rebels. At the same time, both the government and the rebels were treated unfavorably more frequently than favorably.

In Period 2, at the time of the communist regime, the Ethiopian government was mentioned unfavorably in about 2.5 times as many stories as were the Eritrean rebels, who were mentioned favorably in about four times as many stories as was the communist government of Ethiopia. Such a pattern of shifting to proportionately more unfavorable stories about a regime that turns communist, and at the same time to proportionately more favorable stories about the rebels fighting such a government, is again very consistent with the propaganda model of Herman and Chomsky.

On the other hand, the pattern of dichotomization toward the Soviet-block countries involved in the Eritrean conflict was not as marked as what the propaganda model would suggest. While the Soviet-block nations collectively received neutral coverage in 53.3 percent of the stories they appeared in, unfavorable coverage was found in only 26.7 percent of the stories. In fact, 20 percent of the stories gave favorable coverage. One reason for such a result could be the smoother relationship between the U.S. and the USSR with the policy shift introduced by Gorbachev as of 1985. Another reason could be the low-level and, in fact, indirect engagement of the Soviet-block countries in Period 1 of the Eritrean conflict which gave them more neutral coverage than unfavorable coverage.

To sum up, the findings from the Eritrean and Southern Sudan case studies show that in three of four instances there is no significant relationship between uncertainty of U.S. foreign policymakers and neutrality of media coverage. Thus, it may be concluded that the data show, at best, marginal support for the hypothesis. Also, regarding dichotomous treatment, the above findings indicate that in a given period, coverage may be predominantly neutral toward warring parties. At the same time, as long as the U.S. has close ties or clear antagonism against the host governments, there is likely to be a certain amount of dichotomized treatment between the parties in conflict. Yet, it must be emphasized that this dichotomous treatment is not at the level that Herman and Chomsky suggest. Coverage by the media in these cases is neutral in between one-fourth and two-thirds of the stories, depending upon the country and the period of time. This suggests that the ambiguities facing the U.S. government and the resulting uncertainty in its policy positions are reflected to a certain degree in media reporting about the issues.

To the extent that U.S. policy is ambiguous toward a given foreign conflict, the media are likely to gather news from all sources without giving any special priority to certain groups over others.

In their discussion of the propaganda model, Herman and Chomsky note that the media exercise dichotomized treatment through their selective use of sources. That is, they generally use sources from the "friendly" party involved in the conflict. This raises a question: how diverse would the use of sources by the media be in covering issues of U.S. uncertainty? Would there be any difference in the degree of diversity of sources between those stories dealing with the issues of uncertainty and the others?

In the Sudanese case study, there has been found no relationship between the two variables.

TABLE 2. Sudan Case Study: Diversity of Sources In Stories

	With Uncertainty	Without Uncertainty
Stories with Low Diversity	63.8%	62.1%
Stories with High Diversity	36.2%	37.9%
Total	100.0%	100.0%

d.f.1

chi-square.067

In the Eritrean case, too, there is no relationship between uncertainty of U.S. foreign policymakers and diversity of sources in media coverage. The difference is that while in the Sudan's case the majority of both stories with and without uncertainty showed a tendency to use a low diversity of sources, in the Eritrean case the reverse was true; the majority of both groups of stories tended to use a high diversity of sources.

In any event, the findings from the two case studies regarding diversity of sources do not support the hypothesis. Since the hypothesis received no support, it was deemed relevant to learn whether the media displayed any preference in their use of the warring parties as sources, as Herman and Chomsky suggest in their propaganda model.

In the southern Sudan case study, the government was quoted in nearly eight times as many stories as were the rebels. The amount of space devoted to the Sudanese government as a source compared to the rebels was 9.6 inches to one. Similarly in Period 2, the government was quoted in nearly five times as many stories as were the rebels. The ratio of column inches pertaining to the Sudanese government as a source compared to that of the rebels was four to one. In Period 3, the gap in frequency distribution narrows down to 1.6 to one, still in favor of the government. Interestingly enough, however, the rebels are quoted for an average length of 2.8 inches per story, as contrasted with 1.3 inches per story for the government. This may be due, in part, to the repeated exclusive interviews the reporters held with the rebels in this period. In Period 4, despite souring relations between the U.S. and the Sudanese government, the media used the latter as a source in three times as many stories as they did with the rebels. Similarly, the amount of space devoted to the Sudanese government as a source was nearly three times as much as for the rebels.

In the Eritrean case study, the same trend of using the government as a source more often and more widely than the rebels is observed, but to a lesser degree. In Period 1 the Ethiopian government was quoted in 1.5 as many stories as were the

TABLE 3. Eritrean Case Study: Diversity of Sources In Stories With and Without Uncertainty

	With Uncertainty (n 56)	Without Uncertainty (n 90)
Stories with Low Diversity	33.9%	40.0%
Stories with High Diversity	66.1%	60.0%
Total	100.0%	100.0%

d.f. 1

chi-square 0.542

Eritrean rebels. In terms of length, the ratio is 1.7 inches to one in favor of the Ethiopian government.

Such findings raise some questions about the propaganda model which would have expected the Ethiopian government to be much more frequently quoted and given more space in Period 1 than the rebels, because of the government's friendly relations with the U.S. The opposite would have been expected in Period 2, because of the hostility of the new government to the U.S.

3. Uncertainty and Length of Coverage

With the two uncertainty-related hypotheses receiving little support, it was considered useful to test for the existence of a relationship between uncertainty and length. While this relationship was not hypothesized, it is relevant to the more general question of whether uncertainty has any bearing on the nature of coverage. The relationships were studied for coverage of quoted sources as a whole, and for length of stories in their entirety. As with the two hypotheses tested earlier, the assumption behind this test is that in their coverage of issues of uncertainty, the media would devote a greater amount of space to their quoted sources than they would in a situation of relative certainty. This tendency, presumably, would reflect an attempt to gather as much information as possible about the given events or issues and thereby give them clarity and meaning. The same logic applies for the relationship between uncertainty and length of stories.

Indeed, while the case studies produce no support for the hypothesis of a relationship between uncertainty of U.S. foreign policymakers and source diversity in media coverage, they tend to show a relationship between uncertainty and length of coverage of quoted sources. In both case studies, stories with uncertainty tend to devote more space to their quoted sources than do the stories without uncertainty. However, this relationship is not statistically significant, as can be shown in Table 4.

Also, stories with uncertainty tend to be longer than stories without uncertainty. Again, however, the difference is not statistically significant.

TABLE 4. Average Length of Coverage of Quoted Sources Per Story In Sudan and Eritrean Case Studies

	With Uncertainty		Without Uncertainty		d.f.	t-value	P (1-tail)
	N	*Mean*	*N*	*Mean*			
Sudan	138	5.40	103	4.55	239	1.559	.060
Eritrea	56	4.98	90	4.53	144	0.637	.263

To sum up, it appears from the data that media coverage of events of uncertainty may not differ systematically in the direction of coverage between the warring parties, nor in the diversity of sources used. No significant difference has been found either in the amount of space devoted to coverage of quoted sources or length of stories as a whole. The only consistent pattern is in the differing use of the warring parties as sources of information.

F. CONCLUSIONS

The data revealed in just one of four test cases a relationship between uncertainty and neutrality of coverage, thus suggesting marginal support for the first hypothesis. On the other hand, the data indicate more neutral coverage in times of uncertainty on the part of U.S. foreign policymakers than the propaganda model would suggest in a dichotomized conflict scenario. Coverage by the media in the Sudan and Eritrean cases has been found neutral in between one-fourth and two-thirds of the stories, depending upon the country and the period of time. This suggests that the ambiguities facing the U.S. government, and the resulting uncertainty in their policy positions are reflected to a certain degree in media reporting about the issues. At the same time, the data indicate that as long as the U.S. has either close ties or clearly antagonistic relations with the governments, there is likely to be a certain amount of directional treatment of the parties in conflict, even when coverage as a whole is predominantly neutral. Yet, this directional coverage does not constitute the completely dichotomous treatment that Herman and Chomsky suggest.

It is also important to note that the differential treatment toward the warring parties shown in the data was not strictly based on the "friendly" versus "enemy" dichotomy. For example, while the Sudanese government was an ally of the U.S., particularly in the first three periods, the rebels were not labeled the "enemy" or pariah group by the U.S. policymakers, hence not by the media; they were simply what we might call, "the other" group. The same applies to the Ethiopian government and the Eritrean rebels in Period 1 in which the former was "friendly" to the U.S. and the latter the "other," neither friendly nor inimical. In Period 4 of the Sudan case study, although the U.S. included the Al-Bashir regime in its list of terrorist states (hence the "enemy"), it did not upgrade the rebels to the status of an ally (i.e., "friendly") group, either; the rebels were still considered and treated as "the other" and not inimical. The same pattern is seen in Period 2 of the Eritrean case study in which the communist regime of Ethiopia was treated as "the enemy" state, while the Eritrean rebels were still treated as the "other."

One might say it is this "other" attitude of the U.S., which is neither friendly nor hostile toward the rebels, that keeps U.S. policymakers uncertain of their position in these conflicts. This uncertainty reflects the complexity of foreign policymaking, which carries over directly to media reporting. This, in turn, means that only in situations where the two Cold War superpowers directly backed the warring parties, as in the case of El Salvador and Nicaragua, is the U.S. government seen adopting a clear policy of "friendly"/"enemy" dichotomy, then followed by the media, as can be deduced from the propaganda model (Herman & Chomsky, 1988, pp. 30–35).

Even clearer was the result of the test on source diversity. The data showed no relationship between uncertainty of U.S. foreign policymakers and source diversity, hence lending no support to the second hypothesis. Governments were quoted more frequently than were the rebels, regardless of the nature of the relations between these governments and the United States. This may seem contrary to the policy uncertainty model offered here, and it is not quite what the propaganda model would imply, either. Yet it is entirely consistent with the more general proposition from the literature that media coverage concentrates more on established power positions, i.e., governments, than on groups that may be challenging these governments.

The pattern that appears is not always a "friendly" versus "enemy" compartmentalization, although such categorizing may appear at times. Governments have the structural advantage to release information about the given conflict from time to time, and to be more accessible than rebel organizations. Rebel groups are often poorly equipped so far as information infrastructure is concerned and, typically, are not as organizationally resourceful as governments. In addition, their clandestine and fugitive character often works against their being accessible for media coverage. Of course, the Eritrean rebels had a much better information infrastructure than did the Southern Sudan rebels, yet they could by no means compete with the Ethiopian government.

Finally, although uncertainty tended to vary with length of coverage, both in terms of the average length of sources per story and average length of stories, this association was not statistically significant. Based on these findings, it appears that the impact of uncertainty of U.S. policymakers on media coverage of a foreign conflict was minimal. In these two case studies, uncertainty of U.S. foreign policymakers did not fundamentally affect the way the media cover events in foreign conflict.

The following are suggestions for further research:

1. Other hypotheses may be tested using the same model. One, for example, would be: "The greater the uncertainty, the less sharp the difference in directional coverage of confrontational actors." Such a hypothesis is still based on the assumption of the direct link between the situation of policymakers and media coverage. Where there is no definite position on the part of policymakers toward a given foreign scenario, the U.S. media are also without a clear direction.

Methodologically, such a hypothesis may be tested by coding each individual story according to where on an interval scale of favorability/unfavorability the warring parties are placed. This way, one would get a scalar difference in each story, so that degree of this scalar difference may indicate degree of dichotomization. This variable could then be related to the degree of uncertainty among policymakers.

2. The existence of a relationship between uncertainty and length of coverage, though not found significant, raises the question of issue intensity as a point for further study. Thus, the following hypothesis may be tested: "The greater the uncertainty on an issue, the more intense the coverage." There are numerous studies on issue intensity pertaining to coverage of elections as well as other prominent events and incidents. These studies have provided scales of measuring intensity. Such scales may be applied or refined in studying intensity of coverage with regard to issues of uncertainty in a foreign conflict situation.

3. The data in this study have led to the suggestion that level of development of information infrastructure may play a role in the degree of differential use of sources between contesting groups in a conflict. The assumption here is that where a given group's information is used by the media, that group will be quoted as a source.

Such a study might be patterned along the lines of an investigation by Corbett (1994, pp. 275–283) who studied media coverage of environmental groups in an attempt to learn whether there is a relationship between bureaucracy level, specialized information services, and success of publicity efforts. By using such studies as a springboard, it would be valuable if future research could examine the role that level of information infrastructure might play in the degree to which an actor is used as a source in a foreign conflict scenario. It might also be useful to determine whether directional coverage of actors is indeed affected by, for example, the degree of formal organization of information agencies.

4. The above three suggestions for further research are based on the assumption that the media follow or reflect U.S. foreign policy. A researcher taking the reverse approach may also study whether media coverage of foreign conflicts, about which policymakers are uncertain, play a role in shaping policies toward those given conflicts. Such a study would be based on the assumption that U.S. foreign policymakers rely, at least partly, on media information about the given conflict at a time of uncertainty in an effort to come up with a policy decision. One needs to be careful in undertaking such a study, since policy decision making is influenced by many factors, and therefore it requires a multi-dimensional study. In undertaking such a study, methods of discriminating the influence of one factor on policymakers as opposed to another must be worked out. That way, the researcher may be able to gauge the level of influence media information may have in policy decision making.

Besides, the media information on which policymakers depend would include not only American media, but those in the host country of the conflict as well as in other nations that might have keen interest in the conflict. Therefore, a researcher attempting such a study should include media organizations from these countries as well. Finally, the growing importance of the media in world affairs, along with increasing U.S. role in seeking to resolve regional disputes, makes the continued study of media role in coverage of these conflictual situations especially urgent.

REFERENCES

Altschull, H. J. (1984). *Agents of Power: The Press and Human Affairs*. New York: Longman.

Araby, O. (1989). *The Press and Foreign Policy: A Comparative Study of the Role of Elite Press In U.S. Foreign Policies In the Middle East*. (Unpublished doctoral dissertation: University of Minnesota).

Arno, A. & Dissarayake, W. (Eds.) (1984). *The News Media in National and International Conflict*. Boulder: Westview Press.

Bennett, W. L. (1990). Toward a Theory of Press-State Relations in the United States. *Journal of Communication, 40(2)*, 103–125.

Berry, N. O. (1990). *Foreign Policy and the Press: An Analysis of The New York Times' Coverage of U.S. Foreign Policy*. Westport, CT: Greenwood Press.

Chang, T. K. (1990). The News and U.S.-China Policy: Symbols In Newspapers and Documents. In L. J. Martin & R. E. Hiebert (Eds.), *Current Issues In International Communication*. New York: Longman.

Chang, T. K. (1993). *The Press and China Policy: The Illusion of Sino-American Relations, 1950–1984*. Norwood, N.J.: Ablex Publishing Corp.

Cohen, B. C. (1963). *The Press and Foreign Policy*. Princeton, N.J.: Princeton University Press.

Corbett, J. B. (1994). *Media, Bureaucracy, and the Success of Social Protest: Media Coverage of Environmental Movement Groups*. (Ph.D. Dissertation: University of Minnesota).

Daft, R. L. & Macintosh, N. B. (1981). A Tentative Exploration Into the Amount and Equivocality of Information Processing In Organizational Work Studies. *Administrative Science Quarterly, 26(2)*, 207–224.

Donohue, G., Tichenor, P. J. & Olien, C. (1995). A Guard Dog Perspective On the Role of Media. *Journal of Communication, 45(2)*, 115–128.

Dorman, W. A. & Farhang, M. (1987). *The U.S. Press and Iran*. Berkeley, CA: University of California Press.

Downs, A. (1957). *An Economic Theory of Democracy*. New York: Harper and Row.

The Freedom Forum Media Studies Center Research Group. (1993). *The Media and foreign Policy in the Post-Cold War World*. New York: the Freedom Forum Media Studies Center.

Gans, H. J. (1979). *Deciding What's News: A Study of CBS Evening News, NBC Nightly News, Newsweek and Time*. New York: Pantheon Books.

Gitlin, T. (1980). *The Whole World Is Watching: Mass Media in the Making and*

Unmaking of the New Left (1965–1970). Berkeley: University of California Press.

Halberstam, D. (1979). *The Powers That Be*. New York: Alfred A. Knopf.

Hallin, D. C. (1987). Hegemony: The American News Media from Vietnam to El Salvador. In D. L. Paletz (Ed.), *Political Communication Research*. Norwood, N.J.: Ablex Publishing Corp.

Herman, E. S. & Chomsky, N. (1988). *Manufacturing Consent*. New York: Pantheon.

Hertsgaard, M. (1988). *On Bended Knee: The Press and the Reagan Presidency*. New York: Farrar, Straus & Giroux.

Leblebici, H. & Salancik, G. R. (1981). Effects of Environmental Uncertainty On Information and Decision Processes In Banks. *Administrative Science Quarterly, 26(4)*, 578–596.

March, J. G. (1981). Decision-Making Perspective. In A. H. Van DeVen (Ed.), *Perspectives On Organization Design and Behavior*. NY: Wylie.

March, J. G. & Simon, H. A. (1958). *Organizations*. NY: Wylie.

March, J. G. & Olsen, J. P. (1976). *Ambiguity and Choice In Organizations*. Bergen: Universitets firkaget.

McCoy, T. (1992). The New York Times' Coverage of El Salvador. *Newspaper Research Journal, 13(3)*, 67–84.

Mills, C. W. (1956). *The Power Elite*. New York: Oxford University Press.

Paletz, D. L. & Entman, R. M. (1981). *Media Power Politics*. New York: The Free Press.

Reston, J. B. (1967). *The Artillery of the Press: Its Influence on American Foreign Policy*. New York: Harper & Row.

Sigal, L. V. (1973). *Reporters and Officials: The Organization and Politics of Newsmaking*. Lexington, MA: D.C. Heath.

Smith, M. (1988). The Reagan Administration's Foreign Policy 1981–1985: Learning To Live With Uncertainty. *Political Studies, 36*, 52–73.

Zaller, J. & Chiu, D. (2000). Government's Little Helper: U.S. Coverage of Foreign Policy Crises. In B. Nacos, R. Shapiro, & P. Iserna (Eds.), *Decisionmaking in a Glass House*. Lanham: Rowman and Littlefield.

PART III. MEDIA AND THE PUBLIC

CHAPTER 13

THE SOUTH AFRICAN PRESS:
NO STRANGERS TO CONFLICT [1]

Arnold S de Beer [2]

*What is important is not only to attain victory for democracy, it is to
retain democracy.*   —Nelson Mandela, 1997.

A. INTRODUCTION

South Africa and its press are no strangers to conflict. Since the early begin-
nings of white colonization in 1652, racial and cultural strife have marked the history of the country. For many present day observers, the first democratic elections
of 1994 heralded a new beginning to move away from conflict in what was then
the vogue to call "the Rainbow Nation," a term coined by Nobel laureate
Archbishop Desmond Tutu (Burton, 1996).

It was also assumed that the press would play a major role in President
Nelson Mandela's call for 'nation building,' moving away from conflict and strife,
and finding new peaceful ways to build a nation (see "On reconciliation," by
Mandela, in Crwys-Williams, 1997, p. 68). This seemed a viable role during the
sports euphoria of the mid-1990s (Strelitz & Steenveld, 1996). It was especially
true at the time of the world rugby cup finals during which Mandela appeared
before 80 000 cheering (mostly white) rugby supporters in the No. 6 jersey of the
Springbok rugby captain. For a while it seemed as if sports would unite a racially
torn, though sports mad nation, especially after the South African soccer team,
the Bafana-Bafana, won the African cup in 1996. But this was not to be.

Almost a decade down the line, the legacy of apartheid is not only still lin-
gering on the fringes of society, but is felt throughout all institutions and social
circles. For a large segment of the white population "they" (blacks in general and

---

[1] Though it is not customary, the author wishes to dedicate this chapter to his godchild,
Lize Jansen Van Rensburg-Coetzee, who died of cancer on the day the chapter was completed.
Throughout her young adulthood she fought, often against great odds, for a peaceful South
Africa. She was a resolute believer in the values of a liberal democracy and of peaceful nego-
tiations and actions to resolve societal conflict.

[2] The author wishes to thank Wadim Schreiner (see note 3) for his input in the formulation of sections D to F, and for the results of the Media Tenor analysis used in this chapter.

the ANC government in particular) are to be held accountable for the scourge of crime, the falling value of the rand and the lack of deliverance in many crucial areas of the public sphere. For blacks, the main stumbling block to a fuller democracy greater than that merely obtained at the polling booth, was for whites to embrace the idea of a multi-racial nationhood and to fully support the movement to an African renaissance (see Mandela in Crwys-Williams, 1997, p. 65–67; p. 6–87; for President Thabo Mbeki's point of view on the African renaissance, see Steyn, 2002a, p. 6).

In the 1960s and 1970s the South African press, even though functioning within the confines of the apartheid system, was regarded as one of the freest in Africa. However, the second half of the 1980s witnessed prohibitive emergency regulations muzzling both the local, national and international press covering the last years of apartheid, while the country was torn by conflict, civil unrest and violence (Hachten & Giffard, 1984). The April 27, 1994 democratic elections not only ushered in unprecedented hopes for peace, but press freedom was also guaranteed in the new constitution (Seleoane, 1996) and confirmed by President Nelson Mandela on numerous occasions (e.g. at a speech before the Foreign Correspondents' Association in Southern Africa; *The Star*, February 12, 1996, p. 14).

This chapter deals with some of the most pertinent issues on the South African press agenda as they relate to conflict and peace. The purpose is to analyze the role played by the South African press (more specifically a certain group of daily and weekly newspapers) as generators of conflict vis-à-vis their role as facilitators of the post-apartheid democratization process. This role will be discussed against the background of theoretical analysis by, among others, Galtung and Vincent (1992), Hachten (1987), Pinkney (1993), and Wilson and Gutiérrez (1995). The rest of the chapter deals with research findings by Media Tenor— Institute for Media Analysis in South Africa aimed at the issues discussed.[3]

We realize that one should constantly be aware of one's own perceptions and their impact on the research process. Therefore, this chapter does not attempt to be more than an exploratory and individualized effort from an eclectic functional point of view (Tichenor, 1981, p. 17) to come to grips with some of the more perplexing issues of conflict and peace confronting the press and the people of South Africa during their first decade of building a democracy.

---

[3] Media Tenor—Institute for Media Analysis is an international media research organization with institutes in Germany, the United Kingdom, America, and South Africa. Media Tenor South Africa analyses on a daily basis every news report in both the news and business sections of the South African dailies, *Beeld, Business Day, The Citizen, The Star* and *Sowetan*, as well as the weekend newspapers *City Press, The Sunday Times, The Independent on Sunday, Rapport, World on Sunday*. Over 26,000 news reports were coded from February 1, 2000 to January 31, 2002 to establish a profile of the differences and similarities in the way the newspapers presented the news. Details on the projects mentioned above is obtainable from: www.mediatenor.co.za and/or from the Managing Director, Wadim N. Schreiner, at wn.schreiner@mediatenor.co.za.

The concepts used in terms of the press being generators (vehicles; instruments) of conflict or facilitators (mediators) of peace are used within the context of the theoretical models mentioned earlier. Though it is not correct in the strict political sense of the word, state, government, and ANC are at times being used interchangeably.

B. THEORETICAL POINT OF DEPARTURE

The central point of departure for this chapter is a liberal democratic (Pinkney, 1993, pp. 5–7) or a Western (Hachten, 1987, pp. 19–23) one, namely that press freedom, i.e., the right to discuss politics openly and to report and criticize government and political parties without impunity, is central to the functioning of a democratic state. Within the South African context, this basic freedom has been denied to the majority of South African citizens during the apartheid years (Hachten & Giffard, 1984).

We will not be arguing that non-Western, "developing" or "Third World" societies, such as South Africa, are by necessity conflict-ridden. As Roelofse (1983, pp. 4–5, 12) shows, conflict in any discursive society is natural, due to the simple fact that people will always have different perceptions and attitudes. However, in a country such as South Africa, which virtually moved overnight from a white minority oligarchy to a parliamentary democracy, and where an inability and/or unwillingness to provide conditions for press and other freedoms to the majority prevailed for more than four decades, the possibility for conflict remains. One reason is that all former systems of autocracy, oligarchy and dictatorships (where freedom was possible, even in the supreme, but only for the elected few) will at least, for a certain period of time, be at the peril of those to whom freedom was denied. This could also happen in South Africa where the main task for the press and other institutions could be seen by the new order as that of manifestly cultivating the concept of democracy held by government.

In the South African situation, conflict between the liberal democratic tradition with its emphasis on the importance of the individual and individual rights vis-à-vis collective participatory or social democracy exacerbate the potential for conflict (Held, 1983). This is not only applicable to South Africa as such, but also to the continent of which it forms a part. It is within this context that distinctive elements of the modern democratic state, namely the role of the press in peace and conflict (and its variant violence), could be considered.

1. Historical Stages in News Reporting

Societies experiencing conflict, especially race conflict, and press reporting thereof, often face similar problems. For instance, Wilson and Gutiérrez (1995, p. 150) identify five stages experienced by the press in the U.S. Looking at these phases, the present press situation in South Africa seems to reflect all five stages collapsed into one. Exclusionary coverage, threatening issues, confrontation and stereotypical selection still hamper the development towards a fully multi-racial form of coverage. These phases have become the latent or manifest press policy norm for South Africa, as will be discussed.

a. Exclusionary Phase

The history of apartheid news reporting is to a large extent that of racial exclusion. In the apartheid era, even some liberal minded newspapers treated black people as part of the "native question" during the first half of the 20th century while the Afrikaans press promoted the idea of "separate development" (De Beer & Steyn, 1993; see the collection of articles on this topic in the special edition of *Ecquid Novi* "Focus on media and racism," Vol. 21(2), 2000). Spokespersons for the black majority still feel that in the new South Africa not enough news is being made available to and about the black community. On the other hand, many white (especially Afrikaans speaking whites) feel they are being excluded from the new societal structures and are considered as "bywoners in die land van hul geboorte" (share-croppers in the land of their birth; Dic Burger, January 7, 1997, p. 14).

b. Threatening-Issue Phase

While many arguments were offered for the implementation of apartheid, the perceived "threat posed by black people" was grounded to a large extent in the fear the white minority felt in being surrounded by a majority of black Africans on the southern tip of the continent.

This fear is now apparent in especially the conflict-ridden reports on crime. Racial polarization (Wilson & Gutiérrez, 1995, p. 154) is again the order of the day through news reporting that create the perception of blacks being the cause for the tide of crime engulfing the country, while at the same time fuelling white fears and new racial strife.

c. Confrontation Phase

While in the apartheid era black South Africans were considered to be "outside" the system, many whites, but also possibly the majority of unemployed (mostly illiterate) blacks, now feel the same way due to unfulfilled election promises (see *Sunday Times*, May 4, 1997, p. 22). Though the press might not have the manifest meaning to do so, much of the news is still perceived as "us versus them." What was found by the Turner Commission in the U.S. regarding the civil disorders, namely that there was a historical trend by a press that "has too long basked in a White world, looking out of it, if at all, with White men's eyes and a White perspective" (Wilson & Gutiérrez, 1995, p. 154), this was also taken to the extreme in South Africa, though the opposite seems to be taking place in post-1994 South Africa (Williams, 1996).

d. Stereotypical Selection Phase

After racial confrontation over decades, a peaceful negotiated revolution was obtained in South Africa in 1994. Social order (Wilson & Gutierrez, 1995, pp. 156–158) had to be restored, and a transition to a post-conflict period had to be made. While black society argued that the press is still not dealing with news topics that affect black people in a "natural" way, white people felt endangered when they perceived themselves to be on the receiving end of violent crime, and found employment doors shut in their faces, as is regularly reported in the press (*Rapport*, April 13, 1996, p. 14).

e. Multi-Racial Coverage Phase

"Multi-racial news coverage is the earlier antithesis of exclusion" (Wilson & Gutiérrez, 1995, pp. 158–161). If it is to become the goal and policy of the (South African) news press, the last vestiges of prejudice and racism must be removed from the (news) gatekeeper ranks. This does not mean that all news about non-whites will be good news, but that non-whites will be reflected in all types of news. News will be reported from the perspective that "us" represents all citizens (Wilson & Gutiérrez, 1995, pp. 158–161).

As in the U.S., the main thrust in obtaining such an ideal situation is apparently by affirmative action and black empowerment policies. However, the reality remains that the South African press is still very much divided, e.g., Afrikaans newspapers, such as *Beeld* and *Die Burger*, emphasizing news important to their reader base, and black English language newspapers, such as *Sowetan* and *New Nation*, almost exclusively covering news related to the black community. Where large broadcast institutions like the SABC were being changed to reflect the true demographic profile of the country (read black majority), many whites were turning their radio and television receivers off in response to what they perceived as "black" or "ANC" news and actuality programs (*Rapport*, April 13, 1996, p. 14).

This raised a question of critical proportions: how to deal with press freedom in a new democratic society, not only behest by a legacy of socioeconomic and political conflict, but which was also part of Africa, and which also showed many of this continent's conflictual characteristics, e.g., the rise of a "party-dominant system" (Friedman, 1996; Berger & Godsell, 1988) and its concomitant effect on the press.

C. THE AFRICAN CONTEXT

When writing about the press and South Africa, and more specifically on the role of the press in the process of conflict and peace, researchers and observers often fail to see the connection between South Africa and the rest of sub-Saharan Africa.

The worldwide trend is apparently to believe the South African democratic success story is an absolute example of the attainment of Western ideals and expectations in Africa. Western press observers often want to believe that the press in South Africa now functions within a First World or Western (Hachten, 1987, pp. 19–23) framework (Randall, 1996; *The Star*, January 11, 1996). Five years later, this issue was still not resolved, with the government chastising the press for not being patriotic enough, and not placing the "national interest" above the application of Western concepts of news values (Harvey, 2000, p. 37), while the rest of Africa suffered by and large under similar pressures from governments (see *So this is democracy?*, 2000; 2001).

What seemed clear was, that while on the one hand, South African and other sub-Saharan countries were building the basic structures of democracy (such as holding free and regular elections), keeping the press at bay (see *So this is democracy?, 2000; 2001*) was too often seen as a "solution" to a country's ills (e.g., in 2001/2002 the South African press was accused of being responsible for the falling value of the rand due to over zealous crime reporting, to the misfortunes of the country's sporting teams).

South Africa, though clearly one of the best examples of a democracy in Africa, was still struggling, like African countries elsewhere, to find a niche between the Western liberal-democratic concept of governance and a socialist democratic version of the developmental model where the press could be "used" whenever the government felt a need to alleviate tension and conflict, or to use it as a tool for conciliation projects, such as nation building (see Hachten, 1987, pp. 30–34 for a discussion of the different models).

While debates on relative merits of capitalism and communism hardly find a platform in Europe and America outside the university environment, in South Africa "such arguments will determine the future" of the country and its press (Mallaby, 1993, pp. 3–4). For the point often negated, is that the ANC government (as well as other governments in Africa), stem from strong Marxist socialist roots, while its senior partners in government and cabinet are trade unions (Cosatu) and the South African Communist Party (editorial in *The Star*, April 15, 1997, p. 10). In Africa the combination of democratic ideals and socialist reality did not always bode well for the press.

At the 1996 "The right to know: Access to information in African countries" conference, held in Harare and organized by the International Federation of Journalists (IFJ), the conference heard that when it came to access to information and vital communication between the government and the people, South Africa showed the most positive prognosis, while a dismal picture was painted about the situation in the rest of sub-Saharan Africa (Sboros, 1996). In most other African countries a climate of secrecy prevailed, and governments were under no legal obligation to supply information or reply to questions from the press. Five years later, the situation did not improve (see *So this is democracy*, 2000/2001).

While it is relatively easy to speak of the *de facto* functions of the press in the West, the main question for the African (and eventually South African) press is: What functions the press in South Africa ought to have in terms of conflict and peace reporting? Should the press (Miller, 1995) be seen as independent agents playing a watchdog role in an adversarial and eventual conflicting relationship with the government, or should it be part of a nation-building driven peace process? We will argue that the latter is becoming more and more applicable to South Africa.

However, the "role of the press" and "democracy" itself are very illusive terms to come to grips with (Pinkney, 1993, p. 136). The process by which the legacy of conflict between the defenders of authoritarianism (such as the National Party during the apartheid period) and the proponents of democracy (the black freedom struggle of the ANC and other groups) is resolved, would not be an easy one to either observe or analyze. Even so, when one probes the broad political structure and dynamics of present day South Africa, it seems that, like elsewhere and earlier in Africa, a socialist democracy (see Pinkney, 1993, pp. 6–7 for criteria) within the framework of the developmental model (see Hachten 1987, pp. 30–34 for criteria) is taking form with a concomitant effect on the press and its reporting on peace and conflict issues.

D. SOUTH AFRICA'S POLITICAL AND PRESS DISPENSATION

1. The Developmental Model

Given South Africa's apartheid legacy on the one hand, and the history of the political and press dispensation in post-colonial Africa on the other, we would aver in this section that one could analyze present-day South African government press policies and practices, as well as newspaper reporting on aspects such as peace and conflict, within the framework of what Hachten (1987, p. 30–34) and others (e.g., McQuail, 1987) call the developmental model. Or to put it differently, we will argue that South Africa is moving towards a socialist democracy within the framework of the developmental model, rather than towards a (often implied) libertarian democracy (even with a considerable body of new liberal laws in place and underway).

Western social scientists have posited a major role within the developmental model for mass communication in the process of nation-building in newly independent countries (McQuail, 1987). In this sense, liberal Western models might have unintentionally provided a rationale for autocratic press controls in developing countries (Hachten, 1987), of which South Africa might, to a greater or lesser degree, become another "African example" in the new century.

2. The Press as Vehicle for Nation-Building

In a developmental society, the government could use all the instruments of mass communication to aid in the great task of nation-building. This could mean that government must step in to provide adequate press services when the private sector is unable to do so.

In a "party-dominant democratic system," the dominant party as government relies primarily on the symbolism acquired and approved in the "struggle" against colonial or minority rule and is perceived by the electorate as an expression of a nation or group's desire for self-determination (Friedman, 1996, p. 4).

By 2002 it was still a problem for government that the ANC did not have a newspaper that was supporting it full-out in its nation-building program. A number of senior government officials have made strong statements in this regard. President, Thabo Mbeki, for instance, had a "serious problem" that "the major segment of political opinion was not well represented in the press." Mbeki has also made direct calls on print press ownership to change (Makhanya, 1996; Golding-Duffy, 1996b) in order to give expression to the needs of the majority of the country. This viewpoint was carried through to national discussions on the role of the press between government and the press in 2001 at the so-called Sun City deliberations.

Speaking at a joint gathering of the African Correspondents Association and the Freedom Forum in Washington, Mbeki made it clear that he believed the South African press based its reporting on the wrong assumption that the press' relationship with the government was necessarily adversarial. While in a front-page profile in *The New York Times* Mbeki deplored the lack of press support for the new government. Mbeki was quoted as saying (Fabricius, 1996):

> No one can tell me that the relationship of the London *Daily Telegraph* with the Conservative Party is adversarial. It supports the party whether it is in government or out. I'm not saying it crawls on its belly to support the Conservatives but it supports their policy.

Mbeki said that the South African press had correctly adopted an adversarial approach to the National Party government to destroy apartheid. Now that apartheid was gone, this "anti-system attitude was no longer appropriate." For instance, he had debated the issue with a senior South African editor who had told him: "It's not my duty to report you have built a dam but to report that you have failed to build a dam" (Fabricius, 1996). For Mbeki this was not satisfactory.

On a number of occasions, President Nelson Mandela also strongly called for a redistribution of access to and ownership of the press (e.g., "Era of white press dictators over," in: Reuter, 1996) in order to give the majority a voice in the process of nation-building.

3. The Press and the HIV/Aids Issue

Few issues in South Africa stirred so much controversy on conflict in the press, as that of Aids, and especially President Mbeki's stance that there is not necessarily a causal connection between the HIV-virus and Aids.

Media Tenor's research[4] shows that with the exception of the June 1999 international conference held in South Africa on Aids, the press gave relatively little coverage of this epidemic. It is calculated that by 2004, with the next general elections, South Africa is expected to have 35 percent of its population infected with Aids.

Presidential spokesperson Parks Mankahlana, responsible for taking the flak for President Thabo Mbeki's pronouncements on HIV not being the cause for Aids, died in October 2002 of what was widely rumored being an illness induced by HIV/Aids. This led to a critical debate between government spokespersons and the press on the right of the press to have covered the rumors. In more than one way, it highlighted the controversy between government and press on the issue of privacy (in the "national interest") and the "public's right to know" (Louw, 2000).

According to the *Sunday Times* (October 29, 2000, p. 14) Mankahlana said that providing HIV-positive women with anti-retroviral drugs would in the long run create a problem for the South African government, since it would be unable to deal with the growing numbers of Aids orphans. The government expressed "deep sadness" at Mankahlana's death, but did not confirm the cause of his death.

Even with the extent of Aids in South Africa, Media Tenor's data show that public health has a rather insignificant place on the press' agenda. Among all news stories reported in the five dailies and five weekend newspapers in the Gauteng province in the period from February to September 2000 (N = 28 398), the issue of public health (including Aids) was only the tenth most reported issue (with sports and crime being by far the issues most reported on).

The topic of Aids only start featuring on the press' agenda as a run-up to the international Aids convention in Durban in July 2000. A total of 478 stories on Aids were published in July, almost as much as in the period January till June (497 stories). Despite President Mbeki's position, that the link between HIV and Aids is not proven, the delegates at the Durban conference signed a petition that HIV did indeed cause Aids. The late Mankahlana had referred to this petition as "belonging into the presidential dustbin."

For Mbeki the conference offered the opportunity to give to the world his version of the cause of Aids: Poverty in the Third World, caused by debt to the Western World.

The effect of Mbeki's stance on Aids, was mirrored in a nationwide poll by the Institute for Democracy in South Africa (Idasa) which showed that Mbeki's popularity had plunged to previously unknown lows in 1999. In May, nearly 71 percent of South Africans thought he was performing well, people changed their opinion after July (when the international Aids conference was held) to a 66 per-

---

[4] In April 2002 the Government changed its position on this issue.

cent approval, and to 50 percent in September. A total of 46 percent of black women said Mbeki was doing a good job, while 11 percent of white females approved of him. The same survey also indicated that just 38 percent of South Africans were approving the way the ANC was handling the HIV/Aids issue.

HIV/Aids is very much a social issue that rippled out to matters pertaining to the society in which it is rampant, such as education and labor, but the representation of these groups are conspicuously low on the press agenda. Although an estimated 16–20 percent of all South African teachers are HIV positive, mention of the Minister of Education on this issue, surfaced in only 15 articles on Aids, and the affected group were voiced in a mere seven articles. Teacher absenteeism was attributed to their Aids-related illnesses—a labor-related issue and yet unions, representative of the majority of the South African workforce, featured in only 15 articles during this period with union representatives quoted in 26. However, this was mostly in support of the government's eventual introduction of generic drugs to hospitals and clinics.

This representation is again reflected in the relatively high number of white representation (26.1 percent) in Aids reports considering that this segment of community is far less affected by the pandemic than the black African group (65.8 percent)—where a far higher percentage of representation should be expected. This, almost disproportionate attention, was again illustrated in the proportionately low representation of the group probably the hardest hit with the disease and its results: females with 55.6 percent, compared to males with 44.4 percent. At the level of care givers there was no dispute that this group should by implication receive far greater attention in the media, as a result of their higher HIV/Aids infection: the babies born contracting the disease from their mothers, and the so-called aids orphans. Aids orphans were mentioned in only 13 articles during the period researched that contrasts with the extraordinarily high number of 570 reports on cholera in the first quarter of 2000.

In his 2002 State to the Nation speech in Parliament, Mbeki was still not giving clear signals whether he accepted that there was a causal link between HIV and Aids (*Saturday Star*, February 9, 2002, p. 01).

4. To Criticize or Support Government

South Africa is in a state of flux, desperately seeking to invent a new national culture, one that unites the rainbow nation, while allowing vibrant individual cultures to flourish. The media should be supportive of the good, teach tolerance of everyone's best attempts, kindly in criticism, but preaching intolerance of crime in communities or corruption in governance.

By stating *The Star*'s (August 30, 2001, p. 14) vision in the fashion mentioned above, the editor, Peter Sullivan, encapsulated much of what most of the traditional media in South Africa would underscore: being a supportive, but vigilant and critical watchdog. Sullivan also stated that his newspaper "share a passion for Africa." But herein lies the dilemma for the South African media. When one considers media coverage of government in the 12 months from February 2000 to January 2001, it is (according to Media Tenor's data) clear that the South African press was both critical and positive. However, when being too critical, government spokespersons, editorials and letters in newspapers aimed at black audiences, were almost unanimous in their contention that much of the criticism was fueled by racism.

Few stories encapsulated the tension between being a supportive press vis-à-vis a critical one more than the debacle over the South African government's controversial R3-billion arms acquisition program and the concurrent accusations of large-scale corruption.

Though the Minister of Defense, Mosiuoa Lekota, was the first within the ANC's party leadership to publicly voice the possibility of money changing hands in exchange for defense contracts, the continuing controversy surrounding the arms deal has been influenced (according to the African National Congress Youth League) by "the racist notion that a Black government could not rule." Judge William Heath, whose special investigating unit was barred from looking into the possibility of corruption, elicited more accusations of racism when he said that evidence he had of corruption could not be passed on to President Thabo Mbeki and Justice Minister Penuel Maduna for fear of jeopardizing his sources.

The Heath saga took many twists and turns in the media and was still not resolved by February 2002. For instance former President Nelson Mandela, as well as President Mbeki, was apparently implicated by Judge Heath in an organogram disclosed by Mbeki during a televised announcement. It later turned out that the organogram was not Heath's, but was compiled by the editor of a satirical magazine.

E. THABO MBEKI AND THE SOUTH AFRICAN PRESS

The relationship between the press and President Thabo Mbeki was one of the main ongoing themes in South African media coverage in 2001. The press received strong criticism from Mbeki and the Minister in the President's Office, Essop Pahad. In an interview Mbeki suggested that there exists a hostility in the minds of his media critics which is a product of unconscious racist impulses, while Pahad alleged there was a "systematic, vile and vicious campaign against the head of state."

What was clear from Media Tenor's analysis is that for almost a year Mbeki's image suffered across all newspapers included in the research project. About half of the reporting on Mbeki in *The Citizen* was negative (52 percent), while the most positive reporting came from *Sowetan* (29 percent) and *The Star* (30 percent). Similar to its dealing with news on government, almost half of the reporting in *Beeld* was classified as neutral towards the President (51 percent), with 13 percent of the reporting as explicitly positive.

In the first week of February 2001 there was an upswing in favorable media coverage on Mbeki following his second State of the Nation Address. Much of the improvement in media coverage apparently was due to Mbeki's departure from his earlier "two nation" speech in which he asserted that South Africa was a nation divided between black and poor—white and rich. After much criticism in the press, Mbeki said South Africa should become a land of hope. (*The Star*, March 11, 2001, p. 25):

> South Africans "are a people of many colors, races, cultures, languages and ancient origins. Yet we are tied to one another by a million visible and invisible threads. We share a common destiny from which none of us can escape because together we are human, we are South African, we are African."

Herein lies the crux of the matter. It seems that government and the media do not always have the same idea of how a human(e), South African press should report on the President and the government.

A major part of government's criticism of the press is based on the fact that the major newspapers in the country continue to emphasize in their reporting what seems to be the never-ending spiral of crime. The following four important dailies published more reports on crime than any other category of news. In the case of *Beeld* it was 21 percent; *Sowetan* was also 21 percent, while *The Citizen* (22 percent) and *The Star* (19 percent) were also in the same range. As one could expect, the overwhelming tone of the coverage in all four newspapers on crime was negative.

The high percentage of number of reports on crime should be seen against the context of how the newspapers dealt with all other topics on the news agenda. For instance, in its news columns *Sowetan* and *The Citizen* spent 11 percent each on business, and *The Star* 8 percent. Issues such as education, culture, the environment and energy issues, as well as gender received 2 percent and less in all four newspapers.

So pervasive is the impact of crime on the news agenda, that sports and party politics—two great South African past times—received a small slice of the coverage in the news sections. In the case of *Beeld*, it was 5 percent for sports and 4 percent for party politics; *Sowetan* 3 percent and 4 percent; *The Citizen* 4 percent and 5 percent; *The Star* 3 percent and 4 percent, respectively.

F.   PUBLIC INTEREST: THE DILEMMA OF THE PRESS

At a time when White House spokesperson, Ari Fleischer cautioned the American media to "watch what you say," the polemical debate between national and public interest within the media, was once again haunting the Southern African journalistic community in 2001. Resurfacing during a climactic meeting in June between the South African Editor's Forum and government, the latter once again voiced its concern about the media's reluctance to embrace the concept of national interest.

The government's position was that the press should make national interest its main objective, while the press emphasized its role to serve public interest. "In its emphasis on the national interest, the Government apparently revealed a lack of understanding of the public interest principle which drives the media. The Government might regard proposed new legislation as being in the national interest, while the media might regard rejection and vocal opposition to the legislation as being in the public interest" (Raymond Louw in *The Citizen*, April 22, 2001, p. 10). This showed the basic problem: the difference in opinion about the essence of democracy, the role of the press, the concepts of national and public interest, and the function of news reporting.

In a free press system, a relatively peaceful, homogenous society with a highly developed social, economic and technical infrastructure, can afford a pluralist adversarial press. Such a press can criticize at will the President and his government's policy in the public interest as defined by the press. In a developmental system, freedom of the press is restricted according to the cultural, political, socio-economic priorities and developmental needs of society, i.e., serving the national interest should be the media's paramount task (McQuail, 1987). This schism underlies the present rift between government and the press, especially as it relates the image of the President and South Africa. How do newspapers see their role fulfilling the mandate of national and/or public interest?

South African newspapers constitute a wide spectrum of opinion. *The Sowetan* with its sub-title *Building the Nation* is perhaps best know for its nation-building initiative. The paper endeavours to create a positive, committed national state of mind that will make South Africans the leaders of a redeveloping world. Media Tenor's research shows for *The Sowetan* a negative rating of government of 30 percent as well as an approval of 35 percent. In contrast, the weekly *Mail & Guardian* claims its role as a defender of the public interest, and recently stated its policy beneath a banner-headline reading: Remember the last time people said: "'We didn't know what was happening' Think. Again." *The Mail & Guardian* sees its task as being "independent, fearless, provocative, truthful, offering in-depth journalism and the watchdog of the people in power" (M&G Advertisement in *Rhodes Journalism Review*, 20, p. 2, 2001).

Media Tenor's analysis shows that government is rated between 50–75 percent negative and only 15 percent positive. The discrepancy between the positions indicates that for the South African press, the dilemma is how to perceive, and act upon its mandate. Does its prime alliance lay with government and the latter's perception of the national interest, or should it follow its own adversarial notion of the public interest? Or is the answer somewhere in-between?

G. INDIVIDUAL RIGHTS AND SOCIAL PROBLEMS

Individual rights of expression and other civil liberties are somewhat irrelevant in the face of the overwhelming problems of poverty, disease, illiteracy and ethnicity. Freedom of the press could be restricted, according to the development needs of society.

Again, this element of the developmental model is not, as far as we could ascertain, concretely based on any new existing governmental regulations or laws, but as was discussed previously, there are a number of indicators that opened the possibility of the ANC government taking more strident action in this regard.

It is in this context that attitudes towards freedom of expression and the right to information will have to be weighed up against the needs of society. As Van Zyl and Kantor (1995, p. 41) argue:

> Although freedom of expression and freedom of the press have often been proclaimed by the liberation movements of the past, the heritage of censorship and repression of the apartheid era, may be difficult to evade. (Actions by government have) sent alarm waves through the country's press, who are fearful of the repeat of past impositions . . . With the election of the first democratic government, a hegemonic shift has occurred towards national unity and nation-building and away from the ethnic and racial separatism of the apartheid era. With this, there could be a danger that outspoken criticism of the new order will quickly translate into an anti-South Africanism, where critics of government policy will be dismissed as unpatriotic and destructive.

This issue was also underscored by Williams (1996) who argued that the pressures on journalists in the new South Africa were "informal" but "extremely powerful":

> When a journalist was invited by Mandela "to brief him on the matter that the President felt had been overlooked in (an) editorial . . . can anyone of us begin to imagine the pressure to conform when singled out for personal attention in this way by a man widely regarded as the outstanding moral figure of the twentieth century?"

Unlike the *Saturday Star*, Williams (1996) took a different view in *The Citizen* regarding the way newspaper journalists are becoming "susceptible to pressure." According to Williams, the "insidious pressure" is to be "politically correct":

> It manifests in newspapers writing editorials telling people not to complain about the new South Africa; virtually apologizing when they do criticize the government; publicizing their internal affirmative action agreements; and

bending over backwards to fill their business and sports pages with Black-orientated material (but still not being able to attract Black readers, who can sniff window dressing).

It became quite plain that a number of newspapers in South Africa were adopting a form of self-censorship in deference to the new order, though the *Saturday Star* (November 25, 1996) took a different line:

> In any democracy, tension between the state and the press is healthy. In this context, the debate on South African journalism is to be encouraged rather than treated with alarm and misplaced concern that press freedom is under threat.

However, the consequence of the *Saturday Star*'s point of view could be that the press should show some restrain for the sake of nation-building when what they believe to perceive as signs of authoritarianism on the part of government came on to the news agenda. For instance, how would (or should) newspapers report on the following statements, namely that: a number of ANC measures "spell bad news for a free society," e.g., in the form of "state control of school curricula; powers to a gender commission to investigate law-abiding citizens; targeting unpopular speech with censorship measures (as is the case with hate speech) and the 'mooting of compulsory racial audits in the work place in the name of employment equity" (Douglas, 1997), and criticism of the government in general. On a structural level it was clear that the press had the right to report and comment freely as is the case in liberal democracies.

But in reality there were a number of tell-tale signs of a movement towards authoritarianism as were discussed and symbolized by ANC Woman's League leader Winnie Madikizela-Mandela's call on the eve of the 1997 International press Freedom Day that 'women' of the country would find ways to close down press that write 'absurdities' about her (*Sunday Times*, May 4, 1997, p. 22).

H. CONCLUSION

There is a growing feeling among South African whites that the country is moving more and more towards a radical democracy where the tyranny of the majority rules the way through its elite. The coercion that presently takes place in certain sectors of society to achieve socialist democratic objectives underscores this feeling. The specter of an "authoritarian free market state" (such as is underway in China) remains more than a possibility.

On the other hand the black majority feels that a participative democracy, as Siluma (1996, p. 3), editor of the *Sowetan*, names it, is not yet obtained. And, that unless South Africa is prepared to be bogged down with the legacy of apartheid, urgent and radical measures are needed to redress the situation. This might also include "press remedies," such as calls to give government its own voice on news in broadcast and newsprint, as elsewhere in Africa (Saidi, 2001).

The end-result is not clear. The fundamental question would be:. How much room will there be for "press individualism" in the Western sense? On paper, South Africans have created a near miracle by first going, after decades of apartheid, in a peaceful way through the process of negotiation and elections, and then writing and adopting a constitution that could be considered as a modern-day beacon of liberal democratic ideals. In terms of perception, the country's first President became, with the enthusiastic support of the press, the personification of hope and reconciliation.

In the final analysis it seems that South Africa might be able to offer to its own citizens and the world at large an innovative solution: the merging of Western individualistic democratic ideals with the participatory and collective humanism which are encapsulated in the Nguni word *ubuntu* (Sparks, 1993, p. 14). Westerners still have to come to an understanding of this particular form of humanism that finds expression in the African communal context (*People are people through other people*) rather than in the individualism of the West.

After all is said and done, ubuntu is perhaps more than anything else the underlying force that made it possible for freedom fighters like Nelson Mandela to forgive and to embark on a road of freedom and reconciliation.

REFERENCES

Berger, P. L. & Godsell, B. (Eds.) (1988). *A future South Africa—missions, strategies and realities*. Cape Town: Human & Rousseau.

Burton, S. (1996). Politics, communication and development in South Africa: methodology and mediations in a period of transformation. *Ecquid Novi, 17(2)*, 159–178.

Crwys-Williams, J. (Ed.) (1997). *In the words of Nelson Mandela*. London: Penguin Books.

De Beer, A. S. & Steyn, E. (1993). The National Party and the press: a special kind of symbiosis. In: P. E. Louw, (Ed.), *South African press policy. Debates of the 1990s* (pp. 204–226). Bellville: Anthropos.

Douglas, C. (1997). Complacency: threat to freedom. http://www2.inc.co.za/ archives. January 13, 1997.

Fabricius, P. (1996). SA journalists lack training, says Mbeki. *The Star*. http:// www.inc.co.za. July 25, 1996.

Friedman, S. (1996). No easy stroll to dominance: party dominance, opposition and civil society in South Africa. *Towards democracy—Journal of the Institute for Multi-party Democracy, 5(4)*, 4–15.

Hachten, W. A. & Giffard, C.A. (1984). *Total onslaught. The South African press under attack*. Johannesburg: Macmillan.

Hachten, W. A. (1987). *The world news prism. Changing press, changing ideologies*. Ames: Iowa State University Press.

Harvey, E. (2000). Who, what defines national interest? *Mail & Guardian*, August 11–17, 2000, 37.

Held, D. (1983). Introduction: Central perspectives on the modern state. In D. Held, J. Anderson, B. Gieben, S. Hall, L. Harris, P. Lewis, N. Parker & B. Turok (Eds.), *States and societies*. (pp. 1–55). Oxford: Basil Blackwell.

Louw, R. (2000). The death of Parks Mankahlana and the question of universal news values. *Ecquid Novi, 21(2)*, 243–249.

Makhanya, M. (1996). Mandela wants press to be free, not unfair. http://www2. inc.co.za/archives. November 28, 1996.

Mallaby, S. (1993). *After apartheid. The future of South Africa*. New York: Times Books.

McQuail, D. (1987). *Mass communication theory. An introduction*. London: Sage.

Miller, S. (1995). Freedom of the press. *Politikon, 22(1)*, 24–35.

Pinkney, R. (1993). *Democracy in the third world*. Buckingham: Open University Press.

Reuter. (1996). Era of white press dictators over. http://www2.inc.co.za/archives. December 3, 1996.

Roelofse, J. J. (1983). *Towards rational discourse*. Cape Town: Juta.

Saidi, B. (2001). Mugabe's media Bill is a desperate bid to hold on to power. It must be blocked. *Sunday Times*, December 9, 2001, p. 18.

Sboros, M. (1996). The right to know, a yardstick of any democracy, is more or less okay in South Africa, but often a travesty elsewhere. *The Star.* http://www.inc.co.za/archives. August 13, 1996.

Seleoane, M. (1996). Freedom of Expression: the challenges ahead. *Journal of the HRC Center for Constitutional Analysis, 7(4)*, 1–4.

Siluma, M. (1996). Journalists need an editorial charter; but more importantly, they need other groups to agree on it. *Rhodes Journalism Review, 3*, December.

So this is democracy? (2000 & 2001). Report on the state of the media in Southern Africa. Windhoek: Media Institute of Southern Africa.

Sparks, A. (1993). *The mind of South Africa. The story of the rise and fall of apartheid*. London: Mandarin.

Steyn, P. (2002a). Mbeki soek wêreld se steun vir die Afrika-herlewing. *Rapport*, March 2, 2002, p. 6.

Steyn, P. (2002b). SA gaan 'n magsmal Mugabe nie meer duld. *Rapport*, March 2, 2002. p. 6.

Strelitz, L & Steenveld, L. (1996). (Article translated by Elanie Steyn.) Sport en nasiebou in Suid-Afrika: die betekenis van die 1995 Rugby Wêreldbeker. *Ecquid Novi, 17(2)*, 137–158. ("Sport and nation-building in South Africa: the significance of the 1995 Rugby World Cup").

Tichenor, P. J. (1981). The logic of social and behavioral science. In G. H. Stempel, & B. H. Westley (Eds.), *Research methods in mass communication* (pp. 10–28). Englewood Cliffs: Prentice-Hall.

Van Zyl, J. & Kantor, L. (1995). Monitoring the press: a shift from vertical to horizontal monitoring. *Communicare, 13(2)*, 23–43.

Williams, M. (1996). Pressure on press. *The Citizen*, November 16, 1996, p. 6.

Wilson, C. C. & Gutiérrez, F. (1995). *Race, multiculturalism, and the press. From mass to class communication*. Thousand Oaks: Sage.

CHAPTER 14

CULTURAL CONFLICT IN THE MIDDLE EAST: THE MEDIA AS PEACEMAKERS

Dov Shinar

The premises of this chapter are that unlike other violent confrontations, the Middle Eastern conflict is fundamentally cultural, particularly in its Palestinian-Israeli version; that cultural conflicts are "intractable" (Lederach, 1998; Burgess & Burgess, 1996; Kraybill, 1995), in the sense that they are very difficult, perhaps impossible to resolve; that reconciliation is not the only possible nor desirable outcome of conflict: transformation (Vayrynen, 1991) is another viable option; that mistaken interpretations of conflict-resolution strategies can lead to "crises of expectations" in policymaking, in the media, and in public opinion; and that the media play important roles in these processes.

A. THE MIDDLE EAST: A CASE OF CULTURAL CONFLICT

The Middle Eastern conflict is deeply rooted in culture. Like some other instances, such as the Balkans or the former Soviet Union, the conflict is anchored in the most profound symbols of the search, formulation, and preservation of Israeli and Palestinian collective identities. This view stands in contrast with most diagnoses proposed to explain the conflict on uni-dimensional or bi-dimensional bases of nationality, religion, ethnicity, ideology or territory. It is true that like most wars in the recent centuries, such dimensions exist in the Middle Eastern conflict. But none of them, neither on its own nor in pairs or groups, has sufficed to fully explain the conflict's nature, characteristics and implications.

On the other hand, alternative concepts offered by anthropologists, political psychologists and others, have improved the exploration of conflict in general, and in the Middle East in particular. Clifford Geertz (1973), for example, sees "essentialism"—primordial affinities and inherited symbols, of blood, race, language, land, or religion—as crucial elements in conflicts involving symbols of collective consciousness and identity. And Herbert Kelman (1979, 1986, 1992a, 1998) focuses on the complex character of such conflicts, particularly in the Middle East, arguing that they are more than international or intergovernmental, as they affect the societies involved at the deepest levels of identity and existence.

B. CULTURAL CONFLICT: EXCLUSIVE, DEEP, LONG LASTING, TOTAL, GLOBAL

Wars rooted in culture differ from classic conflicts in exclusivity, depth, duration, totality and globality. The concept "Jihad" illustrates the exclusivity of cultural conflict. Barber (1992, 1995) has used this concept to describe the retribalization of human society, expressed since the end of the cold war in the dilution of nation-states, the establishment of new boundaries, and the strengthening of specific identities. Jihad's centrifugal movement has revived forgotten divisions, closed communities, and fundamentalist movements. Its essentialist nature, rejects the centripetal character of Barber's second major current: "McWorld," the transnational socioeconomic and cultural homogenization, inspired by globalizing markets, technology, and communications, and by a rapid diffusion of Western products. The tribal refusal to accept "the other," typical of cultural conflict, is a fundamental feature of Jihad.

Territory is another, at least in the Middle East, where it represents a raison d'etre as much as (perhaps more than) a strategic or economic resource.

Territory provides symbols essential to the formation, existence, and preservation of collective identity. Jerusalem, the Galilee, Hebron, Bethlehem, Judea, and Samaria, all and each of them, as well as the tracts of land between them, are exclusive symbols of being Jewish, Moslem, Christian, Palestinian or Israeli. The difficulty of compromise with respect to such sentiments is the core of the Middle Eastern conflict. Unlike conflicts in which violence and war are political, economic or ideological tools, the essentialist exclusiveness of Jihadist thinking and action fuels the view of war as a manifestation of acceptable primordial sentiments, in which mutual recognition is almost impossible, suspicion and animosity permeate all spheres of life at all times, and violence is legitimized by-and-large.

The strength of such feelings clarifies the depth of cultural conflict. Depth has to do with roots. The view of the conflicts in the Middle East, The Indian sub-continent or the Balkans as mere national confrontations is artificial, irrelevant, and inadequate. Nationalism, a 19th century European invention, is capable of explaining cases of war and reconciliation in the context of territorial or economic conflict, but fails to explain the persistence of cultural conflict. Thus, the failure of all ideologies developed in the 19th century, including nationalism, to deal with cultural conflict, triggered a search for alternative, "tighter" frames of collective identity.

The continuity of cultural conflicts differs from the dynamics of conventional belligerence, in which war is an eruption of violence between more or less organized armies, that interrupts periods of relative or absolute peace.

This does not happen in many cases of cultural conflict, where violence does not necessarily stop when peace agreements are signed. Israelis and Arabs have fought five conventional wars: in 1948, 1956, 1967, 1973, and 1982. In contrast, however, with the cyclical alternation of war and peace in conventional conflict, hostility has never stopped in the area since the early 20th century, conducted by official forces, secret services, armed militias, terrorist/guerrilla organizations, and civilians. The "low intensity" and "irregular" categories of war elsewhere, have found intense daily expressions in the Middle East: during the 1950s and 1960s they included the activities of Arab "infiltrators," Israeli retaliatory measures, and Israel-Syria or Israel-Egypt clashes; in the "war of attrition" that followed the 1967 war; in the PLO arrival in the area, and the attempts made by Israel, Jordan, and others to unsettle the organization since the 1970s; during the Israeli occupation of Lebanon in the 1980s and its pull-out more than a decade later; in the first and second Intifadas; and in the terrorist/guerrilla activities interspersed over the entire period. The pattern has not really changed in the peace process that resulted from the Oslo agreements. Israel and the PLO officially pledged mutual recognition and peaceful conduct, but violence has been going on.

Totality and globality are defined by span and space. Cultural conflict is not confined to official military battle zones, as in conventional war. In the Middle East, this has been demonstrated by Palestinian violence against airline passengers, Olympic athletes, and civilians in and outside Israel; by the violence of Israeli occupation forces and settlers against Palestinians; by battles between the Mosad and Palestinian organizations, in which no difference was made between guilty and innocent. For the Israelis, the totality of war has been expressed in acts of terrorism against military personnel and civilians; in the universal long military service for men and women; in the constant state of alert; and in the magnitude and frequency of deaths and injuries. For the Palestinians, the totality of war has been expressed in the infringement of human rights and the humiliating contacts with military occupation; in the daily physical danger of bodily harm and death; and in terrorist actions taken by Israeli settlers and others. No Palestinian family has been immune to this reality.

These characteristics clarify the extent to which conflicts rooted in culture are difficult, perhaps impossible to resolve.

C. "END-OF-CONFLICT" AND RECONCILIATION VERSUS TRANSFORMATION

Lessons from the Middle East—the Oslo agreements and the second Intifada, for example—allow for viewing at least two perceptions of peace processes: the first maintains that peace agreements mean "end-of-conflict" and reconciliation. The other maintains that negotiations and treaties represent no more than a transformation of the conflict's nature.

"End-of-conflict" and reconciliation are concepts applicable to one or more dimensions of conflict—territorial, political, economic, ideological, ethnic, religious. These concepts are adequate to conflicts that do not result from the search for identity symbols, and whose solution does not affect essentialist sentiments. But they do not seem to function in the contradictory coexistence of peace treaties and eruptions of violence, which are typical of cultural conflict. Thus, since the mid-1990s, a stance of doubt has been accompanying the hopes that had emerged from the Palestinian-Israeli peace process.

These doubts referred to the now irrelevant question of whether the Oslo peace process was irreversible. Indeed, doubts emerged with the assassination of Prime Minister Yitzhak Rabin; with the political downfall of his partners, his party and his peace camp; with the victory of the Israeli right and its anti-Oslo positions in the elections of 1996 and 2001; with the escalating violence employed by Palestinians and Israelis, not always well thought, not always proportional, and always condoned by right-wing, left-wing, and national unity governments. On the other hand, hopes about the success of the process have been nurtured by an unprecedented and paradoxical handing back of large and important tracts of land to the Palestinians, by Benjamin Netanyahu's right-wing government in 1996–1999; by public expressions supporting the process, including Ehud Barak's election in 1999; and by a more or less viable Israeli-Palestinian coexistence, at least until September 2000. The contradiction of these tendencies has been expressed, first, in the gulf between declarations made by both sides in favor of peace vis-a-vis their radically opposed essentialist positions on the questions of Jerusalem, the settlements, or the Palestinian right of return. A second expression of the contradiction, particularly since September 2000, has been the consistent breach of cease-fire agreements, mostly by Arafat, but also by Israel.

In order to understand this contradiction, concepts other than reconciliation and end-of-conflict are necessary. The exclusivity, depth, continuity, totality, and globality of cultural conflict do not allow for viewing peace processes as full or even partial and gradual reconciliation. This clarifies why the solution of the conflict is so difficult, why cultural wars do not end with the silence of the canons, and why peace does not start with the signing of agreements.

D. CONFLICT TRANSFORMATION

Another vision is that peace processes in cultural conflicts do not lead to reconciliation but to a transformation of the conflict (Burgess *et al.*, 1997; Lederach, 1995; Vayrinen, 1991). The terms "conflict resolution" and "conflict management" serve to clarify this vision. The former implies the possibility and need to end conflict. This implication assumes that conflict is a short-term phenomenon that can be "resolved" permanently. The assumption behind "conflict management" is that conflicts are long-term processes that often cannot be quickly resolved. But the notion of "management" suggests that people in conflict can be directed or controlled. In addition, "management" suggests that the goal is to reduce or control conflict volatility rather than dealing with the real source of the problem.

"Conflict transformation" does not suggest to simply eliminate or contain conflict, but recognizes the complex nature of some conflicts, in which relationships are changed, communication and patterns of social organization are altered, and images of the self and of the other are transformed. This is the case of cultural conflict. Conflict transformation is also a prescriptive concept. It suggests that while conflict is destructive, it can be transformed, and that self-images, relationships, and social structures can be improved. This involves transforming perceptions of issues, actions, and other people or groups.

Since conflict usually transforms perceptions by accentuating the differences between people and positions, effective conflict transformation can work to improve mutual understanding. Even when people's interests, values, and needs appear to be different or non-reconcilable, progress can be made if groups in conflict gain a relatively accurate understanding of the other.

Thus, the Presidents, government ministers, politicians, diplomats, and journalists, who took part in the celebrations of the Israeli-Palestinian peace agreements, undoubtedly participated in historic events. Together with billions of TV spectators around the globe, they witnessed the end of an era and the beginning of another. However, the optimism of the agreements, and the less euphoric reality of ongoing violence, did not signify usual post-war peacemaking. They represent, at best, a changing pattern in the relations of long-standing warring parties. Instead of a frontal confrontation, this new structure has featured an interaction of two coalitions, new in their transnational orientation, and rare in their intercultural composition. On one hand, a hitherto impossible "*peace coalition*," made up of the Israeli and Palestinian official positions, and supported by the governments of Jordan, Egypt, North Africa, the Gulf, the United States, Europe, and others, has been making efforts to provide the peace agreements with acceptable and durable contents. On the other hand, "*alliances of the extremes*," housing an unprecedented mix of radical right-wing Jewish Israelis, Islamic fundamentalists, PLO critics, and others, have been directly and indirectly supporting each other, through the use of verbal, diplomatic, and physical violence, to reject any agreement opposed to their essentialist-Jihadist convictions.

E. PEACEMAKING MODELS AND CRISES OF EXPECTATIONS

The confrontation of the coalitions explains the violence that accompanies the process, shows the resilience of cultural conflicts, even when political agreement is reached, and demonstrates the solid nature of cultural conflicts, even in the context of political treaties between powerful entities. Mistaken interpretations of the conflict might have serious consequences. Viewing the Oslo process as reconciliation ignores the importance of these factors. This and the belief that the process represents the end of the conflict produced the confusion, frustration and crisis of expectations that have been affecting all involved: right- and left-wing Israelis; settlers, and peaceniks; and Arafat's supporters and opponents, among the Palestinians and in the Arab world.

Those who interpreted the spirit of Oslo according to the transformation model, and considered the cultural environment and the realistic chances of reducing tension and violence, have developed a lower level of expectations, which enabled them to perceive the crisis less radically, and bear violence more rationally.

F. THE MEDIA IN WAR AND PEACE

How are the media involved in these processes? What is their share in creating crises of expectations and how can they contribute to easing them, and to promoting realistic peace processes? We now turn to these questions.

International communications in recent decades can be described along two major axes: the first is a modification of media functions; the second is media preference of war and violence rather than peace coverage.

1. Modification of Functions

The roles of the media in international relations have changed. The traditional chores of gathering and selecting facts, and of constructing, encoding, and representing realities (Tuchman, 1978; Hall, 1980) have been expanded. Journalists are not expected anymore just to present the news fairly and without bias in "language . . . unambiguous, undistorting." (Fowler, 1991, 1).

In recent decades, the media have assumed new roles. The 1970s' Kissinger media diplomacy, elaborated in academic detail two decades later (Kissinger, 1995), confirms Abba Eban's (1983) diagnosis of the impact open media diplomacy has had on the collapse of traditional diplomatic reticence. Media organizations and professionals participate at present in international relations, both at-large and as catalysts and "diplomatic brokers" (Larson, 1986; Gilboa, 1998).

As participants at-large, the media take part in exchanges between journalists, policymakers, and field-staff (Gitlin, 1980; Larson, 1988), as illustrated by the TV sets in decision-makers' offices and "situation rooms"; by briefings in official airplanes or in sealed compounds, such as in Grenada, Panama, and the Gulf War (Andersen, 1991; Servaes, 1991); and by media-monitored "secret negotiations" such as in Camp David (1979); Dayton, Ohio (1995); Stormont Castle (1997, 1998); and Wye River (1998). As catalysts, the media provide arenas and resources for international dialogue. They include shuttling diplomacy (Kissinger, 1995); "tomahawk diplomacy" used in the 1998 Kosovo and Iraq crises (Time, October 19, 1998); media exchanges (Clinton-Saddam, Rabin/ Netanyahu-Arafat/ Assad); and media events, such as summit meetings and the signing of peace agreements (Dayan & Katz, 1992; Gilboa, 1998).

As diplomatic brokers, the media conduct, and sometimes initiate international mediation, in ways that often blur the distinctions between the roles of reporters and diplomats. This is illustrated by the participation of the media in diplomatic processes, such as Walter Cronkite's paternity claim over Anwar

Sadat's 1977 voyage to Jerusalem (Cronkite, 1996; Gilboa, 1998); or ABC's Ted Koppel's live-on-air Jerusalem "town meeting," conducted during the Intifada in 1988, and featuring unprecedented face-to-face, Israeli-Palestinian negotiations (ABC News, 1988); and, by work behind enemy lines, such as CNN's Peter Arnett's in Baghdad, in the Gulf War (Arnett, 1991), Christian Ammanpour's in Iraq, during Operation "Desert Fox" in 1998, and Al Jazeera's coverage of the war in Afghanistan in 2001.

2. Media Preference of War and Violence

Professional and historical reasons explain the preference of war as media working material and symbolic inspiration. War is more compatible than peace with media professional standards, usual discourse and economic structures. War provides visuals and images of action. It is associated with heroism and conflict, focuses on the emotional rather than on the rational, and satisfies news-value demands: the present, the unusual, the dramatic, simplicity, action, personalization, and results (Galtung & Ruge, 1970; Bird & Dardenne, 1988; Goldstein, 1994).

This preference is magnified in the vivid colors, clear-cut polarities, unexpected features, and primordial sentiments typical of cultural conflict; and in its variety of images and voices exceeds that of plain conventional war conveying Aristotle's "pity and fear" at their "best." The typical peace coverage of press conferences, "talking heads" and airport scenes, has much lower news value.

The history of international journalism adds weight to this preference. Political constraints—mostly the Cold War's—caused the governmental rhetoric of power and violence to be adopted by the media as the "official discourse." "Peace talk" was tagged Communist in the 1950s and 1960s, and "challenger discourse" until the late 1980s, with low popularity and entry into the general audience media (Gamson, 1988; Meyer, 1995). This is also typical of communications research, where revisionist historians have been documenting the claim that the development of media research coincides with research done for official agencies since World War II. The work of some "founding fathers" was sponsored and funded by the Radio Bureau of the Office of War Information, the Information Division of the War Department, the U.S. Air Force, and the CIA (Robinson, 1988; Bruck, 1989; Simpson, 1994). Although there is no conclusive evidence of a direct and causal relation of war efforts with research directions, one cannot ignore that most of these researchers founded or joined leading communication departments and institutes (Rowland, 1983); that research on media coverage of Vietnam and the Middle East deals only briefly with the Paris and the Camp David talks; and that, compared with the multitude of media studies on Middle Eastern wars, there are only few studies on the media in the peace process.

G. A NEW MEDIA ENVIRONMENT

The new powers of the media as actors in international processes, have made a significant contribution to the crisis of expectations that has typified the peace process in the Middle East. The clarification of this argument calls for a discussion of the media climate since the end of the Cold War. The features of this new climate—concerted peacemaking and peacekeeping efforts, together with the revival of radical and sometimes violent separatist movements and demands (Barber, 1995)—have posed significant normative and practical challenges to the media.

One question is whether the media should use their new powers to promote peace. Conservative objections to a peace-oriented media on the grounds of loss of objectivity can be countered with the argument that the changing functions of the media in international relations are part of an ongoing erosion of mythical "objectivity" and of the acceptance of subjective reality construction concepts.

The question "whose version of peace should be promoted?" can be settled by demanding that free expression, professional integrity and ethics are secured, just as in the coverage of criminal activity. Even considering the differences in war and peace news-value, professional integrity and ethics demands that, together with legitimate considerations of sales and ratings, the media comply with basic values that match their critical stand to crime and drug traffic; and that, according to the code-of-conduct which calls for media responsiveness to social changes, they should join current peacemaking efforts.

Finally, if this position is accepted in general, it should be certainly adopted with regard to cultural conflict, because of both its frightening dimensions and the media aptitude to help in its transformation.

In this sense, the media should be required to produce persuasive symbols of security, alternative to those of war; to construct credible realities of change in the roles played by arch-enemies, once they become peacemaking partners; and to act as participants, catalysts, and brokers in the psychological adjustment—including in the reduction of dissonance, paranoiac feelings, etc.—to the unknown environment created in peace processes, that stands in traumatic contradiction with a long-term climate of war.

H.   THE MEDIA IN THE MIDDLE EASTERN CONFLICT

Another question is how can and how should the media be involved in the new international climate? The performance of local and foreign media in the Middle Eastern conflict can provide considerable insight into this topic. Since the Oslo process became public, the media have been dealing with the dilemma of how to function in a peacemaking era, and of choosing a model to guide coverage. Two phases are characteristic of this dilemma. In the first, between the mid-1990s and September 2000, coverage was inspired by the end-of-conflict and reconciliation model. However, like the leaders and politicians who adopted this model, the media had difficulty in explaining the violence that had been accompanying the process from as early as 1996, after which the peace camp began to lose momentum.

In the second phase, as from September 2000, the media have been forced, together with Israeli and other leaders, and with a changing public opinion, to abandon the reconciliation model, at least in order to settle the contradictions between the peace process and the ongoing violence.

1. Preference of the Reconciliation Model

Public opinion towards the peace process, led by the Oslo negotiators, and by the media—at least until September 2000—has shown a preference of reconciliation, negotiation and mutual concessions. This has been expressed, for example, in the wide coverage and in the tone of wondering admiration given by the media to the main actors in the process, to the signing of the agreements, and to events such as the awarding of the Nobel Prize for Peace to Arafat, Peres and Rabin. This is rather surprising, since it stands in contradiction with the traditional preference of the media to the action and the drama of war and violence. Background factors and professional reasons can provide at least some clarification.

Background factors include the emotional openness of the public towards peace; the symbiotic relations between the media and governments; and deductions from earlier peace processes.

- Emotional openness of the public: When the Oslo negotiations became public, a climate developed of emotional openness and psychological readiness to see the agreements in terms of reconciliation, particularly among the agreements' supporters. In this sense, it is interesting to note that the Israeli extreme right was more realistic than the left and than the media in its criticism against interpreting Oslo in terms of reconciliation. Right-wing activists and parties have supported and promoted the notion that the conflict has deep cultural roots. Even those who reject their radical conclusions, have to deal with the accuracy of this diagnosis.
- Media-government symbiotic relations: The tendency of the media to adopt official views in return for an open flow of information is well known. In the wake of the Cold War, particularly after Oslo, the Israeli and international media could not afford to ignore governmental and public opinion manifestations supporting the peace process.
- Deductions from earlier peace processes: the peace processes with Egypt and Jordan gave the media and the public an idea of what peace should look like. The deduction from these agreements to the Palestinian case seemed even more plausible with the recognition by the media that, even though the former agreements have not developed into full normal relations, they have included gestures of reconciliation on the part of Anwar Sadat, King Hussein, Menahem Begin, and Yitzhak Rabin; and a "tractable" amount of violence.

Professional reasons derive from the paradox that reconciliation has news value, particularly against a background of violence. A good example is the ample coverage given to King Hussein's visit to the Israeli town of Beth Shemesh in 1994, and the humble and friendly stance he used to apologize to the families of young women killed by a Jordanian soldier in a border incident. Thus, the media could not ignore the developing climate in favor of reconciliation. The professional factors related to this dynamics include some aspects of news value: polarization and contrast; and media events.

- Polarization and contrast increase the news value of an item. Within the reconciliation model the practices seem to convert the coverage of violence into the exception that proves the rule. Examples include the massacre perpetrated by Baruch Goldstein in Hebron's Cave of the Patriarchs in 1994; the violence which accompanied the opening of the Wailing Wall's tunnel in 1996, and even the first stages of the Intifada. They were covered by the media in an alternating style in which stories of violence were contrasted with coverage of the ongoing peace process, a factor that enhanced the news value of both types of stories.
- Media events: Dayan and Katz's media events theory (Katz & Dayan, 1985; Dayan & Katz, 1992) illustrates the emphasis on reconciliation in peace coverage. The perception of news-valuable reconciliation is evident in various types of media events coverage: The signing of peace agreements, in pre-planned highly performative, and widely covered rituals of new or renewed friendship, can be identified as "*coronation events*": "ceremonial parades . . . ritual transformation of the hero from one status to the next." (Katz & Dayan, 1985, p. 306).

Also a tone of reconciliation, accompanied by high news value, is present in "*conquest events*," where a "hero—facing insuperable odds—enters the enemy camp . . ." (Katz & Dayan, 1985, p. 306), as in Sadat's visit to Jerusalem. Examples of this type of matching between reconciliation and news value in the Middle East, include official and unofficial visits of Egyptian, Jordanian, Palestinian and Israeli officials in each others' cities and sites, during negotiations; the presence of Arab leaders in Yitzhak Rabin's funeral; Arafat's visit of condolences to Lea Rabin; the participation of Israeli leaders in King Hussein's funeral, etc.

The coverage of "*contest events*," "rule-governed battles of champions in sports and politics, such as the World Cup or presidential debates . . ." (Dayan & Katz, 1992, p. 26), in terms of reconciliation, also enjoys added news-value. This was demonstrated by Netanyahu's highly promoted negotiation discourse ("if they give [security] they get [land], if they don't give they don't get"); or in the already famous scene in which Ehud Barak and Arafat play the role of gentlemen pushing each other at the entrance of the White House, in the best tradition of slap-stick movies.

2. Abandoning the Reconciliation Model

There is little surprise in the fact that the escalation of violence in the fall of 2000 did not allow for theories of reconciliation to survive. Ehud Barak's spectacular downfall in the Israeli election of 2001 provides irrefutable evidence to that effect. The media, local, regional, and international alike, discontinued the promotion of such perceptions. They did not go all the way, however. Abandoning the reconciliation model did not mean adopting the conflict transformation model, a result of the conflict's cultural nature. Thus, since the end of 2000, most explanations given by the media about changes in Palestinian-Israeli relations have dealt with the failure to reconcile rather than with the deep roots of the conflict. Media coverage of Israeli and Palestinian violence has focused on the vanished dream of ending the conflict rather than on its complex cultural nature and context. Here too, the reasons are linked with the contradictory nature of professional requirements of news value and efficiency, in the adoption and abandoning of the reconciliation model on one hand, and in the conflict transformation model on the other.

- *Results:* The adoption of the reconciliation model by the media created "end-of-conflict expectations." Abandoning the model made the media emphasize the escalation of violence. These are clear and sharp results. In contrast, the open-endedness of the transformation model does not allow for a sharp presentation of results, a fact that imposes additional work on media professionals, reduces interest and produces lower news value.
- *Complexity:* The transformation model demands the media to present, and audiences to understand complex processes, whereas both the media adoption and abandoning of the reconciliation model focus on simple events, which increase production efficiency, and have higher news value.
- *Historical Duration:* The transformation model requires the media to describe, (and audiences to perceive) the long course of events. Also historical insight must be provided and understood. This requires more work, and reduces news value. In contrast, the adoption and abandoning of the reconciliation model emphasize the present, demand less effort on the part of the media and their audiences, and have higher news value.
- *Rationality:* As it emphasizes logic and rationality, the transformation model requires investment of more effort by the media and by the audiences. The adoption and abandoning of the reconciliation model involve emotional factors, which have higher news value, and are less labor consuming in media production and consumption alike.

- *Personalization and Concretization:* The transformation model focuses on collective values and abstract symbols, while the adoption and abandoning of the reconciliation model involves relations between people and concrete entities. The latter is clearly less work consuming and has higher news value.

The characteristics of the transformation model with regard to these news value criteria are considered less attractive by media producers and consumers, at least comparing with the reconciliation model.

I. CONCLUSIONS

At least until September 2000, the media did not show much interest in the cultural nature of the conflict. Inspired by professional norms of efficiency and news value, the media preferred to emphasize the openness of public opinion to reconciliation, positive governmental attitudes in this direction, and historical deductions from previous peace processes. Two major professional strategies were used in this context: the first was polarization and contrast, focusing on reconciliation against a background of the violence that has preceded and accompanied the peace process. The second was the coverage of media events related to reconciliation.

By recurring to these practices, the media have contributed to the rise and fall of expectations that followed the failure of the process. The Intifada forced the media to abandon the discourse of reconciliation. Frustrated by the collapse of the process, along with the majority of the public, the media returned to focusing on the escalating violence rather than on the deep cultural aspects of the conflict.

The conclusion is that the media are required to make the crucial and necessary step in full: to internalize the cultural meanings of the conflict; to transmit these meanings to the public, in order to raise consciousness of their significance and consequences; and to encourage public debate, first on peacemaking under constraining cultural factors, and secondly, on the choice between an eternal bloody feud and a manageable yet heavy burden by means of a transformation of the conflict.

Adopting this strategy can pose a dilemma, calling upon the media to make a choice between the ideology of contributing to peacemaking and professional demands on efficiency and news value. Confronting this dilemma might help the media deal with the idiosyncrasies of the transformation model, and with the professionally uncomfortable dimensions of cultural conflict coverage. The satisfaction of these demands is difficult, because it means departing from current norms and standards. But this is the real test of ethics and morality that goes beyond technical levels of media professionalism.

REFERENCES

ABC News (1988). Israelis and Palestinians. *ABC News Nightline.*

Andersen, R. (1991). The press, the public, and the New World Order. *Media Development*, Special Issue, October, 20–26.

Arnett, P. (1991). Why I Stayed in Iraq and How I Got That Interview with Saddam. *Washington Post*, March 17.

Barber, B. R. (1992). Jihad vs. McWorld. *Atlantic Monthly Review*, March, 53–65.

Barber, B. R. (1995). *Jihad vs. McWorld.* New York: Times Books.

Bird, S. E. & Dardenne, R. W. (1988). Myth, Chronicle and Story: Exploring the Narrative Qualities of News. In J. Carey (Ed.), *Media Myths and Narratives* (pp. 67–84). Newbury Park: Sage.

Bruck, P. A. (1989). Strategies for Peace, Strategies for News Research. *Journal of Communication, 39*, 108–129.

Burgess, H. & Burgess, G., with Glaser, T. & Yevsyukova, M. (1997). *Transformative Approaches to Conflict*, Conflict Research Consortium, University of Colorado. (http://www.colorado.edu/conflict/index.html).

Burgess, H. & Burgess, G. (1996). Constructive Confrontation: A Transformative Approach to Intractable Conflicts. *Mediation Quarterly, 13*, 305–322.

Cronkite, W. (1996). *A Reporter's Life.* New York: Random House.

Dayan, D. & Katz, E. (1992). *Media Events: The Live Broadcasting of History.* Cambridge, MA: Harvard University Press.

Eban, A. (1983). *The New Diplomacy: International Affairs in the Modern Age.* New York: Random House.

Galtung, J. & Ruge, H. M. (1965). The Structure of Foreign News. *Journal of International Peace Research*, I, 64–90.

Gamson, W. A. (1988). Political Discourse and Collective Action. *International Social Movement Journal, 1*, 219–244.

Geertz, C. (1973). *The Interpretation of Cultures.* New York: Basic Books.

Fowler, R. (1991). *Language in the News: Discourse and Ideology in the Press.* London: Routledge.

Gilboa, E. (1998). Media Diplomacy: Conceptual Divergence and Applications. *Harvard International Journal of Press/Politics, 3*, 56–75.

Goldstein, I. (1994). Broadcasting International Crises. *Journal of International Communication, 1*, 53–59.

Hall, S. (1980). *Culture, Media, Language.* London: Hutchinson.

Henry III, W. (1991). History As It Happens. *TIME*, January 6.

Katz, E. & Dayan, D. (1985). Media Events: On the Experience of "Not Being There." *Religion, 15*, 305–314.

Kelman, H. C. (1979). An Interactional Approach to Conflict Resolution and its Application to Israeli-Palestinian Relations. *International Relations, 6*, 99–122.

Kelman, H. C. (1986). Interactive Problems Solving: A Social-Psychological Approach to Conflict Resolution. In W. Klasse (Ed.), Dialogue Toward Interfaith Understanding. Tantur/Jerusalem: Ecumenical Institute for Theological Research.

Kelman, H. C. (1992). Informal Mediation by the Scholar/Practitioner. In J. Bercovitch & J. Z. Rubin (Eds.) *Mediation in International Relations: Multiple Approaches to Conflict Management.* New York. St. Martin's Press.

Kelman, H. C. (1998). Interactive Problem Solving: An Approach to Conflict Resolution and its Application in the Middle East. *PS: Political Science & Politics.* June (http:www.findarticles.com).

Kissinger, H. (1995). *Diplomacy*. New York: Touchstone.

Kraybill, R. (1995). The Cycle of Reconciliation. *Conciliation Quarterly, 14*, 7–8.

Larson, J. F. (1986). Television and US Foreign Policy: The Case of the Iran Hostage Crisis. *Journal of Communication*, 36, 108–130.

Larson, J. F. (1988). Television Reporting on Asian Affairs: The Case of South Korea. In P. Desbarats & R. Henderson (Eds.), *Encounter '87: Media, Democracy and Development* (pp. 47–50). London, Ontario: Graduate School of Journalism, University of Western Ontario.

Lederach, J. P. (1998). *Journey Towards Reconciliation*. Harald Press. Chapter 8: "The Meeting Place." (http://www.colorado.edu/conflict/transform/jp/chpt.html).

Lederach, J. P. (1995). *Preparing for Peace: Conflict Transformation Across Cultures.* Syracuse: Syracuse University Press.

Meyer, D. S. (1995). Framing National Security: Elite Public Discourse on Nuclear Weapons During the Cold War. *Political Communication*, 12, 173-192.

Robinson, G. J. (1988). Here be Dragons: Problems in Charting the U.S. History of Communication Studies. *Communication*, 10, 97–119.

Rowland, W. (1983). *The Politics of TV Violence: Policy Uses of Communication Research*. Beverly Hills: Sage.

Servaes, J. (1991). Was Grenada a testcase for the "disinformation war"? *Media Development*, Special Issue, October, 44–49.

Simpson, C. (1994). *Science of Coercion: Communication Research and Psychological Warfare*. New York: Oxford University Press.

Tuchman, B. (1978). *Making News*. New York: Free Press.

R. Vayrynen (Ed.) (1991). *New Directions in Conflict Theory: Conflict Resolution and Conflict Transformation*. London: Newbury Park, New Delhi: Sage.

CHAPTER 15

THE MEDIA AND RECONCILIATION
IN CENTRAL AMERICA

Sonia Gutiérrez-Villalobos

A. INTRODUCTION

This chapter analyzes the roles of the media in reconciliation processes in Central America. It critically examines these roles in the context of several reconciliation models and Central American peace accords including the regional peace accord, *Esquipulas II: Procedures to Establish a Firm and Lasting Peace in Central America*, that was signed by the governments of El Salvador, Nicaragua, Honduras, Guatemala, and Costa Rica, on August 7, 1987; and the national peace accords signed by countries involved in war: Nicaragua, El Salvador, and Guatemala.[1]

The study concludes that both reconciliation models and peace treaties ignored the media and media professionals as actors in post-conflict situations. It identifies two main reasons for this neglect: the reconciliation concept as adopted and practiced in Central America, and the concepts of objectivity and diplomacy. The results also show that the national peace accords assigned the media a political-electoral role. For instance, the Salvadorian peace accord stated the need for a national reconciliation campaign, thus acknowledging the media role in education. The Guatemalan accord assigns the media two more roles: a cultural outlet for the different ethnic communities and development catalysts. The analysis and conclusion that offers a plan to insert and increase the media role in reconciliation are based on relevant studies on this topic (Kempf, 1999; Kempf & Gutiérrez, 2001; Galtung, 1998; Luostarinen, 1999; Shinar, 1999).

The peace accords signed in Central America from 1987 to 1996 set a new era in the region's history of military dictatorships, repression, poverty, foreign intervention, and war. Dictatorships in El Salvador contained uprisings against human rights violations, violence, environmental destruction, poverty, inequality, and the high concentration of resources in national and foreign elite's hands. This situation escalated the conflict into a war between the Farabundo Marti guerrillas

---

[1] The national peace accords were the mechanisms to implement the regional accord. In order to meet this goal, each country at war created its own National reconciliation Comission. For detailed accounts on the negotiation process leading to internal peace accords in each country at war, *see* UPEACE, 1999.

and the army. In Nicaragua, after 40 years of the Somoza family dictatorship, the Sandinista Revolution took power in 1979. During the 1980s, a civil war erupted between the Contras, a guerrilla force trained and financed by the Reagan administration, and the Sandinista army. In Guatemala, with support from the national elite, a 1954 U.S. intervention ousted a social democratic government and placed a military dictatorship in power. The war between the guerrillas, the army, and the paramilitary began in 1960 and lasted for 36 years. These were 36 years of human rights violations and mass killings, mainly among indigenous populations (UPAZ, 1999).

Honduras and Costa Rica were not at war. Military dictatorships in Honduras were violating human rights, and its territory harbored military bases to launch attacks against neighboring countries, mainly against Nicaragua. Costa Rica abolished the army in 1948 but had to deal with two neutrality problems: the Contra rebels used its territory for training and launching attacks against Nicaragua; and powerful media transmitters were stationed in Costa Rica to broadcast propaganda against the Nicaraguan government. The military ruled Panama and became involved in confrontation with the U.S. This situation downplayed the internal conflict for a while. In 1989, the Bush administration invaded Panama and established a civilian government (Gutiérrez, 1990; Gutiérrez *et al.*, 1994; Gilboa, 1995–1996).

These wars generated thousands of refugees, destroyed towns and exterminated people. The signing of *Esquipulas II* was the beginning of the post-conflict stage at the regional level. At the national level, however, the post-conflict situation began only after the signing of national peace accords or ceasefire agreements. Nicaragua was the first country to enter the post-conflict stage after declaring a ceasefire. El Salvador was the second after signing its national peace accord in 1992. The war in Guatemala went on until 1996 when the national peace plan was signed. Yet, in the Central American post-conflict situation new conflicts have occurred, for instance, around border waterways or international river basins, and the challenge has been to manage them in a way that fosters cooperation rather than confrontation.

B. RECONCILIATION CONCEPTS

There are two basic concepts of reconciliation: national reconciliation and re-encounter reconciliation that is more social and personal. The peace accords at both the regional and the national levels deal with the concept of reconciliation in *regional and national* terms. This approach is useful to end hostilities and highly suitable for regional and national peace accords. However, it has been criticized (Lederach, 1997; Ortega, 1997), because of its limitations in dealing with specific issues such as demobilization and reintegration of ex-soldiers and ex-combatants, as well as with the reconciliation process that occurred among them. Lederach (1997) argues that excessive focus on the reconciliation's national dimension hinders other dimensions such as social and inner reconciliation. In his view, national reconciliation is a rhetorical reference that needs more grounding at the micro levels of society. Writings about the way the ex-combatants[2] and ex-soldiers in Central America articulate and interpret their own encounter and reconciliation with their former enemies, deserve more attention.

According to Ortega (1997) the ex-soldiers' and ex-contras' demobilization testimonies in Nicaragua yielded a new perspective within which reconciliation is seen in a non-linear way. From this perspective, reconciliation is not just a way to understand nor to accept the past in order to move on to a future in a new relationship with the former enemy. Reconciliation is rather a multifaceted simultaneous encounter in which both past experience and present needs intersect and generate hopes for the future. Rather than passing from past to future, these elements converge and become a source for new relationships. In Ortega's view, time, healing, and survival constitute the basic tools to interpret both the past and the future. The former enemies share these tools so that reencounter begins with a common denominator.

The nonlinear approach to reconciliation highlights both healing and the dynamics between encounter and reencounter. The healing component is a resource for reconstructing personal and social lives. The reencounter component stresses the idea of reconciliation as an approach with what has already been known only from a confrontational or polarized perspective. Therefore, reencounter among former enemies seeking reconciliation presents an innovation, to redirect life in a non-confrontational way. Reencounter often requires transformation from confrontation to cooperation.

C. NEW CULTURE AND TYPES OF COVERAGE

Redirecting life in a non-confrontational and depolarized way demands awareness of the new situations that come with reconciliation. Former enemies reencountering themselves are surrounded by newness: new institutions, new identities, new relationships, and new types of media and media coverage. In sum, they have to deal with a new culture.

New institutions: National elections have received high priority in Central America. The elections created and highlighted new institutions such as political parties, tribunals, and international observers. On the other hand, hegemonic institutions such as the army and the guerrillas, lost power and influence. The army was compelled to demobilize its soldiers, while the guerrillas entered the electoral arena after demobilizing its combatants.

New identities: A demobilized soldier might return to a poor community and become poor like his relatives and friends, or become just an ordinary member of

---

[2] Ex-combatants refer to the ex-guerrilla members. Ex-soldiers or demobilized refer to the former army members.

an ethnic community. This change of identity that goes along with demobilization is a learning process. Demobilized people have to learn how to live with a new identity and, therefore, reconciliation implies reconstruction at the social and the personal level.

New relationships: New identities serve to create new relationships. It is a very different experience to be a member of a vertical institution such as the army, than to be part of a community. During wars the focus on the enemy overshadows any other relationships. Reconciliation opens a multifaceted encounter not only with the past and the future, but also with different changes in many attributes including the environment, age, space, nationality, class, ethnic and racial alliances, gender, and religion.

A new culture: Reconciliation implies a change from war culture to peace culture. In Central America, after several years of peace treaties, the war culture has managed to survive in areas other than the battlefields, and the task to edu-cate individuals and society about negotiation and consensus building is far from complete (UPAZ, 1999).

New types of media and media coverage: During post-conflict situations there is always a danger of conflict resumption. The media can help to prevent this. Kempf & Gutiérrez (2001) suggest that the media might contribute to peace culture in several ways: "*De-escalation* oriented coverage," (DOC) strengthening of civil society, and demolition of stereotypes.

- DOC is designed to promote cooperation among parties by focus-ing on cooperative actions and values. It emphasizes common inter-ests and cooperation benefits. It highlights positive emotions and respect among former enemies—two basic ingredients needed to cultivate empathy. A Salvadorian journalist reveals that during the post-conflict situation, "Our role is to communicate happiness and life rather than fear and death" (CENITEC, 1991, p. 103, translated from Spanish).
- Strengthening the civil society is a key step during reconciliation. Civil society's plurality of interests, institutions, voices, and identi-ties, adds diversity to reporting. Civil society also needs access to new media and new technologies for networking and knowledge production.
- Overcoming stereotypes and prejudices. Stereotypes and prejudices about former enemies can be transformed into new images of toler-ance, respect and cooperation.

These activities transform the media into mediators. The new types of jour-nalism resulting from mediation and DOC are expected to replace war discourse's polarization, escalation, and one-sided journalism into a more diverse, all-sided

Journalism, and peace discourse. Peace discourse needs DOC to create a depolarized and a cooperative environment, which fosters cooperative initiatives between former enemies. Sometimes, new types of coverage require new media. Some media underwent institutional changes in order to support the peace process: In El Salvador the newspaper *Diario Latino* changed ownership when the workers bought it. Radio Venceremos, a former guerrilla radio station, emerged from underground transmission and became self-sufficient (CENITEC, 1991).

The concept of reconciliation as a reencounter shows that chances for confrontation at levels other than the national, might even increase after the signing of ceasefires and peace accords. The accords envisioned the transition from confrontation to reconciliation through national elections. However, at the community level the confrontation increased with the rise of new issues and problems. Thus, the need for commonalities becomes clear. Based on this idea, in Central America, reconciliation includes "*concertacion.*" It means to concert or to agree, to build a consensus that satisfies the different interest groups.

D. RECONCILIATION MODELS AND MEDIA ROLES

Three reconciliation models are examined to observe media roles: The Arias Foundation Reconciliation Model, the Post-Conflict Reconstruction Model, and the Actors and Approaches Model. All these models show that the media haven't been assigned significant roles in reconciliation processes.

1. The Arias Foundation Reconciliation Model

This model (Fundacion Arias, 1997) has been selected because it deals with issues related to the third group of mandates stated by *Esquipulas II:* Demobilization of soldiers and combatants, reintegration of ex-soldiers and ex-combatants into society, repatriation of exiles, and pacification. According to the model, the actors responsible for enforcement are governmental and non-governmental organizations at the international, national, civil society, and local community level. The media were not mentioned, partly because of the concept of reconciliation itself. Not only people reconcile, but also institutions. The media were polarized institutions during the war and continued to polarize during the post-conflict stage. They also had to reintegrate into the new society.

The Arias Foundation Reconciliation Model suffers from Media Neglect Syndrome (Fisas, 1998). It would have been very useful if this model had included a training program in peace culture for media professionals. The experience of the group implementing the model in training ex-soldiers and ex-combatants would have provided journalists with the skills to report on the new situation (Arias Foundation, 1997). This training could have enabled reporters to approach confrontation and violence differently. After all, they assign meaning to daily violence/confrontation, or peace/reconciliation actions. For example, in

Guatemala people killed delinquents in the streets without trial. These murders were reported in an isolated manner, even in yellow journalism fashion. The coverage lacked a connection to war culture still prevalent even after the signing of the peace accords.

2. The Post-Conflict Reconstruction Model

Fisas' (1998) model presents a ten-point agenda for the reconstruction and reconciliation stage: support for democratization, human rights watch, strengthening the peace process, peace culture campaign, downsizing the military, removing land mines, demobilization and reintegration, repatriation, handicapped rehabilitation, and material reconstruction.

The model assumes that "Peace building is more difficult than war ending, and even more difficult than waging it." He argued that the mainstream media neglected the societies undergoing reconciliation: "Another regrettable reality affects the nations that have begun a reconstruction and reconciliation stage: They are forgotten by the media which used to pay them considerable attention during the war. This phenomenon can be called 'peace neglect syndrome'" (Fisas, 1998, p. 126, translated from Spanish). The peace building process suffers from a "Peace Neglect Syndrome" (p. 57).

The syndrome is a routine pattern in mainstream media that paid more attention to conflict situations when they escalated into violence and war than to post-conflict situations. After the war foreign reporters lost interest and departed for another conflict. The peace neglect syndrome affected the local media professionals as well. On the one hand, they had a greater chance to get involved because of the departure of the foreign media, but on the other hand they didn't have enough interest in peace issues. Their activity decreases compared to their war coverage. Kempf and Gutiérrez (2001) argue that the peace neglect syndrome embodies pro-escalation coverage. The more the conflict escalates towards violence and war, the more coverage it gets (Gutiérrez, Hertog & Rush, 1994). The pro-escalation coverage strengthens the war culture. The syndrome may also undercut international cooperation during the post-conflict situation and redirect it to other areas of conflict.

3. The Actors and Approaches Model

Lederach (1994) developed this model mostly on the basis of his experience in Central America. This is a pyramidal model that distinguishes among three levels of actors:

- High level: politicians and military leaders.
- Middle level: academics, Church, business leaders, NGOs, press.
- Grass roots level: community leaders and project directors.

The model highlights the key roles the middle and grass roots levels' leaders are able to play in the transformation of conflict. The model offers a Peace Building Frame to understand and marshal peace-building resources for a sustainable reconciliation process. It contemplates two aspects: economic resources and new ways of thinking and action. The author calls for the use of new categories for thinking and acting about peace-building, including preparing human resources and budgets for conflict resolution and reconciliation, as well as taxing the weapons industry and those who benefit from arms trade. Lederach argues that a tax has been already established for the tobacco and alcohol industries, and it should also be applied to the weapons industry.

This section has identified two factors responsible for the Media Neglect Syndrome: the concepts of objectivity and reconciliation. The mainstream media view themselves as objective institutions performing objective and professional tasks. This perception undermines recognition of the media as a salient actor in the reconciliation process, and prevents a discussion about their possible supporting roles in reconciliation stages. Reconciliation, conceived as a national phenomenon, highlights the parties in conflict: the armies and the guerrillas, and reconciliation takes place mainly between them. This reconciliation concept reflects a governmental perspective where the rivals meet and join forces in the political arena. However, reconciliation as a reencounter means that reconciliation occurs at several levels, and that not only people reconcile, but also institutions. When media institutions reconcile with the new situation created after the signing of the peace accords, it narrows the room for both Peace Neglect Syndrome and Media Neglect Syndrome.

E. MEDIA ROLES AND PEACE ACCORDS

This section examines the media-prescribed and actual roles in the following regional and national peace accords signed in Central America:

(1) Esquipulas II, the regional peace accord for Central America.
(2) The cease fire in Nicaragua.
(3) The Chapultepec Peace Accord, El Salvador's national peace accord.
(4) The Guatemalan Peace Accord.

1. The *Esquipulas II* Peace Accord

The regional peace accord *Esquipulas II* mandated the Central American governments to initiate dialogue, reconciliation, and democratization processes internally. The accord proposed a model based on peace, democracy, and development. It includes four groups of mandates:

(1) National reconciliation oriented to end hostilities, initiate dialogue and amnesty, and create a National Reconciliation Commission.
(2) Presidential elections.

(3) Demobilization, demilitarization, and disarming of the guerrillas and the army.

(4) Democratization (political pluralism; radio, press, and television freedom; and lifting the emergency status).

The accord's fourth group of mandates deals specifically and directly with the media. The main concern is censorship and therefore the main proposal is to lift censorship in order to create a pluralistic political space. The media were expected to enlarge the space and the attention given to political parties participating in national elections. Consequently, the accord assigned the media a political/electoral role. Since the accord conceives of the elections as a step towards democracy in the post war situation, it is a pro-democracy role. The *Esquipulas II* media role was first applied in Nicaragua before the presidential elections. Two media outlets benefited from the accord: the newspaper *La Prensa*, owned by the Chamorro family, and Radio Catolica, owned by the Catholic Church (Saballos, 1991).

The *Esquipulas II* media roles in the post-conflict situation focused on political participation in national reconciliation elections. This perspective is still governmental. A civil society and non-governmental perspective requires a chapter dedicated to the role of the media on a more permanent basis such as building a new political culture. Yet, historically, the assignment of a political/electoral role to the media in Central America represented a major departure from earlier practice. Traditionally, the media took a partisan position for or against one of the rival political forces. This new role contributed to the peace process, albeit in a limited fashion.

2. The Nicaraguan Cease Fire

Nicaragua did not sign an internal peace accord, but on April 18, 1990, it was the first country to implement a ceasefire (Garcia, 1990). The agreement on presidential elections was accompanied by an agreement to modify the media legislation so that access will be available to all the political parties participating in the elections (Saballos, 1991). The Nicaraguan media legislation applied the *Esquipulas II* mandate to lift media censorship. But lifting censorship does not mean that the media would favor reconciliation. In fact, the media remained polarized. The second ONUVEN's (UN Commission to verify Nicaraguan Elections) report on the Nicaraguan media after the ceasefire expresses concern for the media's violent language and polarization during the reconciliation elections:

> The main concern is how the media are used [in political elections]. The ones which belong to the government are highly biased towards the party in power. The disqualification of opponents are beyond reasonable limits. Likewise, the violent language that is being used by the media, as well as the information manipulation carried out by the largest media on both sides [government and opposition], is quite alarming. . . . The media reinforce Manichean per-

ceptions . . . that are translated into incitement to violence and political intemperance, which are an attempt to invalidate the entire electoral process. A call for illegitimacy of the reconciliation elections is risky because the elections are the source for a democratic reconstruction process very much needed for the nation (ONUVEN, 1989, p. 24, translated from Spanish).

The ONUVEN's report recognized that the media are important actors in the reconciliation elections when it acknowledged that incitement to violence and intolerance put the elections at risk. Yet, this role is described as a political/electoral one, which coincides with *Esquipulas II*'s second set of mandates. The characteristics of the media's role in the elections, can be explained by what media researchers call Journalism of Attachment, or "one-sided Journalism" (Kempf & Gutiérrez, 2001). In the Nicaraguan reconciliation elections, this type of journalism meant attachment to one side only, the Frente Sandinista lead by Daniel Ortega, or the Opposition Unity, lead by Violeta de Chamorro. It also meant oppressing of any potential for serious political debate.

Despite the political polarization, the two rival and attached newspapers, *Barricada* and *La Prensa*, dealt with the same issues including, amnesty, cease fire, democratization, aid to the Contras, and abstention from the use of national territory to wage war on neighboring nations. Table 1 shows the percentage of attention given to each topic by each paper (Saballos, 1991). Each newspaper frames the common agenda differently. For example, *Barricada* opposed amnesty and dialogue with the Contras, while *La Prensa* pressured the Sandinista government to comply with the accord's demands to end the war.

TABLE 1. Attention to Topics

Topic	Barricada	La Prensa
Compliance with *Esquipulas II*	24%	26%
The war	16%	14%
Presidential elections	16%	12%

The Nicaraguan media could have done much more to support reconciliation. First, they could have adopted depolarized reporting based on non-confrontational language. This coverage would have supported the national dialogue oriented towards consensus-building in which Nicaragua had been engaged after the cease-fire. This consensus aimed at setting the agenda for the new government. Considering the agenda-setting function of the media, the Nicaraguan media could have set a consensus-supporting agenda.

3. The Salvadorian Peace Accord

The Salvadorian Peace Accord was signed in Mexico City, on January 16, 1992. It ended the civil war between the unified guerrillas command of the Farabundo Marti Liberation Front (FMLN) and the military dictatorship in El Salvador (Béjar, 1997). The accord includes seven chapters: The army, the police, the judiciary, the voting system, the social and economic systems, FMLN's political participation, and the ceasefire.

The first reference to the media in this accord appears in Chapter 6, p. 34 and later in Annex 7. It refers to the FMLN's political participation in the election system. It recommends granting the FMLN the right to mass media licenses so that they can have their own media. The purpose of these licenses was to assure FMLN's political integration in the electoral system.

The second reference to the media in Annex 7, *Using Mass Media to Foster Reconciliation* contributes to the reconciliation process in the following way:

(1) The Salvadorian Government cannot scramble FMLN's radio broadcasts.
(2) Both parties, the guerrilla and the army, agree to:
   • support a national campaign to foster national reunification and reconciliation, and to
   • fully comply with this agreement in order to back the reconciliation process.
(3) COPAZ (Peace Commission) will be responsible for supervising this agreement and for making recommendations about the media roles in the national reconciliation campaign.
(4) ONUSAL (UN Commission in El Salvador) will verify this specific agreement.

What this accord states about the media is very close to what the regional peace accord had mandated: to lift censorship, and provide media space for the presidential election. The accord also deals with media ownership as the former guerrilla front was allowed to own its own media. This was a major change in media ownership patterns.

4. The Guatemalan Peace Accord

The Guatemalan Peace Accord was signed on December 29, 1996, in Guatemala City. It ended the 36-year war. This accord is similar to *Esquipulas II* and the Nicaraguan agreement in two areas:

(1) The request for media access. However, here there is a difference from the Salvadorian Peace accords. The previous peace accords were concerned with national elections and political parties' access

to the media. The Guatemalan Accord requests access for the Mayan people and other indigenous peoples. Thus, a multicultural issue underlies this request.

(2) The media are not conceived as actors. Here there is also a difference between this accord and the previous ones. In this accord, the media constitute transmission channels whose role is to serve as outlets for cultural, educational, and informational purposes. But the media are cultural-laden institutions and cannot be neutral channels.

The cultural concern incorporated in this accord recognizes the importance of oral communication, which characterizes indigenous cultures, and is closely linked to indigenous women. The professionals in oral communication are the people themselves. This is a significant complex aspect to study from a reconciliation perspective. Unfortunately, the accord only mentions it without prescribing mandates to assure its implementation. This accord also creates a link between media and development. It is a very needed media role in a post-war situation, but, again, it is only briefly mentioned without mandates for implementation. In general, in comparison to the other agreements, this accord places demands for a variety of media roles and stresses the need for cultural affirmation and human rights for the indigenous peoples of Guatemala.

In sum, it is important to point out that the *Esquipulas II* provision to lift censorship stemmed from the limitations of the conflict stage when the military and the government elite censored the media. The post-conflict reconciliation situation, however, provided opportunities for media and information technologies' proactive roles. Thus, the regional accord could have been used to recommend additional roles to the media and the new communication technologies beyond elections. The political/electoral role assigned to the media is one of pro-reconciliation for the political parties and their constituencies. The media were expected to play this role in two ways: first, in the way that they depict the electoral process, and second, in creating space for all political parties to express themselves.

The political role assigned by the accords to the media could have contributed not only to the redistribution of power that was evident in the elections, but also to the conformation of a new political culture based on inclusion and cooperation. Therefore, this role is more than political but also cultural. It empowers civil society in knowledge production and decision making. The convergence between media, new communication technologies, and civil society, results from the cultural role assigned to the media and media professionals. The convergence implies that the media produce and disseminate knowledge about the issues facing the peace-building process. This knowledge can strengthen the ability of civil society to bring about democracy, development, and sustainable peace.

The media could have played roles that weren't mentioned in the accords including using national campaigns to explain the peace accords to the people, and conducting a wide debate in each country about the peace accords short- and long-term advantages to individuals and society and the necessary changes that must happen if they were to succeed. They could have also helped to build credibility about the peace accords against the attacks of the alternative media which often described the accords as "paper peace." Finally, they could have demanded accountability from those responsible for the implementation of the accords.

F. CONCLUSIONS

This study shows that reconciliation models used in Central America have neglected the media and only accorded them a political and electoral role. This neglect resulted from the reconciliation concept defined as a national process, and the notion of objectivity. Multi-Track Diplomacy (Fisas, 1998; McDonald, 1993) deconstructs objectivity. It is also known as "parallel civil diplomacy" because it includes new actors, some of them rooted in civil society. This approach assigns the media significant roles in reconciliation processes. Peace accords should include a chapter on media roles and it should be the result of a joint effort of officials, journalists, peace communication researchers, and research networks. This effort should apply to peace accords, reconciliation and reconstruction models, and security models. Here are the objectives and details of a plan designed to accomplish this goal:

1. Objectives

(1) Including a chapter for peace communications in peace accords, and in reconstruction and reconciliation models.
(2) Proposing media roles in reconciliation processes.
(3) Creating follow up mechanisms and incentives.

2. Contents

(1) *Depolarization:* There is not only a need to depolarize society but also the media, reporters, and perhaps even peace communication researchers and consultants. Censorship sustains polarization and therefore should be replaced by Peace Journalism or All-Sided Journalism that assigns potential credibility to all sides involved in a conflict.

(2) *Peace discourse:* The old war faring language used to portray enemies, confrontation, violence, war, and devastation should be replaced. It also requires a new sensitivity towards "newness" (new institutions, identities, relationships, etc.) that reconciliation brings about.

(3) *New roles:* Stemming from the idea that the media are actors in the conflict, mainly when they are highly polarized in favor or against one of the parties involved, there is a need to change or "demobilize" the media from previous roles. The new roles of mediators,

non-elite consensus-builders, and development catalysts demand detachment from a single reality in favor of different realities offered by the reconciliation process.

3. Institutions

(1) *Establishing a peace communication commission:* The tasks of this body would be to organize a reconciliation campaign, to monitor news, make recommendations to media institutions and journalists on how to improve reconciliation reporting and training.

(2) *Creating databases:* These will address key reconciliation issues such as demobilization, reintegration, repatriation, and democratization.

(3) *Forming reconciliation think tanks:* These will be designed to produce and distribute knowledge on issues such as development, cooperation, small businesses, education and training resources, loans, land distribution, etc. Currently, this issue becomes relevant with the proliferation of ICTs (information and communication technologies), believed to generate the fading of the divide between media and civil society.

(4) *Building networks:* These will include researchers and journalists whose aim would be to research, analyze, discuss and propose new agendas and roles of common interest. This is only a minimal and basic program and much more research and thinking is needed to substantially insert and expand media roles in post conflict situations and peacemaking processes.

REFERENCES

Aguilera, G. (1999). La arquitectura de una paz difícil: El caso de Guatemala. En: UPAZ (Ed.), *América Central: del Conflicto a la Negociación y el Consenso.* San José, Costa Rica: Editorama.

Arias Foundation for Peace and Human Progress. (1997). *Demobilization, Reintegration and Pacification in El Salvador.* San José, Costa Rica: Arias Foundation.

Béjar, R. G. (1997). Sociedad y Concertación en el Proceso de Pacificación en El Salvador. In PNUD, *La Sociedad Civil y los Procesos de Concertación en Centroamérica* (pp. 183–208). San José: PNUD.

Boutros-Ghali, B. (1992). *An Agenda for Peace.* New York: United Nations.

Bryant, J. & Zillmann, D. (Eds.). (1986). *Perpectives on Media Effects.* Hillsdale, New Jersey: Lawrence Earlbaum.

CENITEC-APES. (1991). *El Papel de los Medios de Comunicación el el Proceso de Reconciliación Post-bélica.* San Salvador, El Salvador: CENITEC.

Fernandez, G. (1989). *El Dasafío de la Paz en Centro America.* San Jose: Editorial Costa Rica.

Fisas, V. (1998). *Cultura de Paz y Gestión de Conflictos.* Barcelona: Icaria.

Galtung, J. (1998). *Peace Journalism: What, why, who, how, when, where.* Oslo: TRANSCEND.

García, V. (1990). El espejismo de la reconciliación. *Pensamiento Propio.* Anno VIII (70), Mayo, 20–23.

Gerbner, Gross, Morgan & Signorelli (1986). Living with television: The Dynamics of the Cultivation Process. In Bryant & Zillmann (Eds.). *Perpectives on Media Effects.* Hillsdale, New Jersey: Lawrence Earlbaum.

Gilboa, E. (1995–1996). The Panama Invasion Revisited: Lessons for American Policy in the Post-Cold War Era. *Political Science Quarterly, 110,* 539–562.

Gutiérrez, S. (1990). *Tactical and Strategic debate of the 1989 Panama Invasion.* University of Kentucky. Master's thesis.

Gutiérrez, S., Rush, R. & Hertog, J. (1994). Press Support for the U.S. Administration During the Panama Invasion. *Journalism Quarterly, 71(3),* 618–627.

Kempf, W. (1999). *De-escalation*-oriented conflict coverage? The Northern Ireland and Israeli-Palestinian peace processes in the German press. Paper presented at the IAMCR Scientific Conference at Leipzig, July 1999.

Kempf, W. & Gutiérrez, S. (2001). *Los Medios y la Cultura de Paz.* Berlin: Regener.

Lederach, J. P. (1997). Desmobilizados de Guerra en la Construcción de la paz en Nicaragua. En: *Cultura de Paz*, Año 3 (11), Marzo, 57–60.

Lederach, J. P. (1994). *Construyendo la Paz: Reconciliación Sostenible en Sociedades* Divididas. Tokio: Universidad de Naciones Unidas.

Luostarinen, H. (1999). Journalism and Cultural Preconditions of War. Paper presented at the IAMCR Scientific Conference at Leipzig, July 1999.

McDonald, J. (1993). *Guidelines for Newcomers to Track Two Diplomacy.* IMTD.

ONUVEN (UN Commission to verify Nicaraguan Elections). (1989). *La Situación en Centro América: Amenaza a la Paz y la Seguridad Internacionales e Iniciativas de Paz.* 1st. Report, October 17; 2nd, Report, December 1989; 3rd Report, January 1990.

Ortega, Z. (1997). *Desmobilizados de Guerra en la Construcción de la Paz en Centro América.* Managua: CEI.

Saballos, M. & Mena, M. (1991). Medios de Comunicación en el Conflicto Centroamericano. Managua: Unpublished manuscript.

Santamaría, O. (1999). El proceso de paz en El Salvador: Apreciaciones y experiencias. En: UPAZ (Ed.), *América Central: del Conflicto a la Negociación y el Consenso.* San José, Costa Rica: Editorama.

Shinar, D. (1999). "Media Diplomacy and 'Peace Talk': The Middle East and Northern Ireland." Paper presented at the IAMCR Scientific Conference at Leipzig, July 1999.

Solís, L. G. (1999). Esquipulas: Una experiencia centroamericana. En: UPAZ (Ed.), *América Central: del Conflicto a la Negociación y el Consenso.* San José, Costa Rica: Editorama.

Strobel, W. P. (1997). *Late-braking Foreign Policy.* Washington, D.C.: U.S. Institute for Peace.

Tehranian, M. (1982). International Communication: A Dialogue of the Deaf? *Political Communication and Persuasion, 2(1)*, 23–25.

Universidad R. Landivar–IDIES. (1997). *Acuerdos de Paz.* Ciudad de Guatemala: Guatemala.

UPAZ (2001). *Estado de la Paz y Evolución de las Violencias.* Montevideo: UPAZ.

UPAZ (1999). *América Central: del Conflicto a la Negociación y el Consenso.* San José, Costa Rica: Editorama.

CHAPTER 16

THE CRISIS IN KOSOVO: PHOTOGRAPHIC NEWS OF THE CONFLICT AND PUBLIC OPINION

Kimberly L. Bissell

A. INTRODUCTION

As in all wars, the atrocity stories published on the web and aired on CNN were aimed at molding public opinion . . . Among the most disturbing pictures the network's international correspondents brought home were sights and sounds of another reality depicting human suffering. The crippled grandmother pushed in a wooden wheelbarrow by her grandson, the wide-eyed girl clinging onto her mother's bosom, the wrinkled toothless man silently drying the oozing tears with the end of his ragged sleeve, all found shelter on the nation's comfortable couches as compassion-evoking crowds in a refugee camp.

(Dimitrova, 2001, p. 46)

Over the last century, the news media have capitalized on bringing the story of war home to viewers and readers via exclusive interviews, infographics, up-to-the-minute reports and visual imagery of hardship and suffering. With the technological improvements over the last decade, audiences have become inundated with still images, video, news stories and web sites devoted to covering international conflict. The Persian Gulf War was the first officially declared war with U.S. involvement since Vietnam, and thanks to the media's use of advanced technology, audiences were provided "24–7" coverage of the "Crisis in the Gulf." As Iyenger and Simon (1993) argue, the barrage of media coverage did not fall on deaf ears. They report that 70 percent of the Americans polled in January 1991 followed the news about the Gulf "very closely" (p. 366). Similarly, the Gallup Organization (1991) found that nearly 80 percent of the American

* An earlier version of this paper was presented to the Visual Communication Interest Group at the annual meeting of ICA in Washington, D.C. May 24–28, 2001. The data used in this study have been used in a similar paper to be published in *Political Communication.* I thank Martin Eicholtz, Hyo Lee, Gyong Ho Kim, Sang Hee Ryu, and Seung Kwan Ryu for their assistance in coding for this project.

public stayed up late to watch coverage of the Gulf Crisis. Along with increasing media coverage of the Gulf War, public concern for the war also increased (Iyengar & Simon, 1993).

Just like the Gulf War, the 1999 "strike against Yugoslavia" gave networks a boost in ratings as viewers around the world tuned in to see instantly transmitted images of "atrocities, massacres, genocide and ethnic cleansing" (Dimitrova, 2001, p. 3). During the initial stages of the "Crisis in Kosovo," (March 2, 1998 and March 23, 1999) 359 Kosovo-related stories were aired on network news programs (Media Monitor, May/June, 1999). However, from March 24, 1999—the start of the NATO airstrikes—to May 15, 1999, television networks aired 972 stories on the conflict (Media Monitor, May/June 1999). During a similar time period, between February 21, 1999, and June 10, 1999, national newspapers such as *The Washington Post, The Chicago Tribune*, and *The LA Times* ran approximately 100 news stories each in their respective front sections. Furthermore, according to reports from *The Media Monitor* and *Newsweek*, the bulk of media coverage emphasized only a few content categories: the air war, the plight of the refugees, UN/U.S. strategies, "ethnic cleansing," civilian damage, and diplomatic negotiations. The conflict in Kosovo undoubtedly gave media outlets a prime opportunity to provide readers and viewers with "live" reports from the region and instant video of refugees fleeing to the borders of Macedonia. Seaton (1999) argues the media take on a traditional role as messengers of information to the public during war times, but the media also play an important role in public opinion formation and foreign policy decision making because of their ability to instantly transmit words and pictures. News executives and journalism professors have even joked Saddam Hussein and the President relied on the news media during the Persian Gulf War to see what the other side was doing (Mueller, 1993). The "White House officials make decisions with one eye on the CNN report on the screens beside the telephones on their desks" (Seaton, 1999, p. 18).

Dimitrova (2001) says that as in all wars, the textual and visual display of atrocity is aimed at shaping public opinion. On April 26, 1999, 82 percent of those polled said they followed the news coverage of Kosovo either closely or very closely (The Gallup Organization, May 15, 1999). In addition, public support for the NATO mission in Kosovo increased on a weekly basis (The Gallup Organization, 1999). Thus, it seems that the media played an important role in keeping the public informed about the events in Kosovo. Furthermore, public interest in the conflict remained high because of the looming possibility of a full-scale war being waged against the Serbs and Milosevic.

This study examined the agenda-setting relationship between the media and the public during the Kosovo conflict. Newspaper articles and photos were used to measure media coverage of the Kosovo crisis, and "the most important issue" question from Gallup polls was used to measure public salience for the Kosovo crisis. Finally, public opinion was compared to content themes in textual and photographic news.

While the media certainly do not function as the only variable responsible for shaping public attitudes and beliefs, they may be responsible for contributing to the initial knowledge, beliefs, and perceptions about a conflict (Iyengar & Simon, 1993). In the case of the "Crisis in Kosovo," public salience for the Kosovo issue ranged from 0 to 15 percent. As previous agenda-setting studies indicate, such a shift in public salience for an issue can indeed be attributed to the increased media coverage of the issue (Johnson & Wanta, 1994).

B. THEORY

1. Trends in Wartime Public Opinion

The role of the mass media in public opinion formation has been hotly debated since Lazarsfeld, Berelson, and Gaudet's (1944) suggestion of the media's effect on voting behavior. Throughout much of the study of public opinion, scholars have examined multiple variables that shape or guide public attitudes. Mueller (1973) presented three assumptions regarding the relationship between war and public opinion. First is the suggestion that a war's duration has a direct effect on support for the war—the longer the war, the lower the approval ratings. Second, Mueller suggests that public support for a war increases over time as the public becomes "propagandized" through continuous media exposure. Mueller's third hypothesis asserts that there is no obvious trend in support for a war, and public attitudes swing in one direction or another, depending on the events of the war. However, empirical tests of the three hypotheses resulted in conflicting findings.

Everts (2000) suggests the much-disputed casualty hypothesis is an important factor in understanding the role between the media and public opinion. Everts says that when casualties occur on either side, support for the conflict drops off considerably.

2. War, News Values, and the Media

In addition to the above factors contributing to wartime shifts in public opinion, Mueller (1973) argues shifts in public opinion may also be attributable to national ideologies. He suggests the "rally-round-the-flag" phenomenon[1] influences public opinion when specific international events occur. As the "rally-round-the-flag" phenomenon pervades public sentiment, it is quite possible the sentiment extends to the media as well. World War II provides a good example of propaganda campaigns in full swing. "Pro-war" and "pro-U.S." literature littered newspapers, newsmagazines, advertisements, billboards, and the radio in the 1940s. While propaganda of this nature has not been evidenced since (Moeller, 1989), some experts argue media coverage of the Gulf War was similarly biased toward a pro-U.S. perspective (Cheney, 1993; Jowett, 1993; Kellner, 1993). In the

---

[1] This term is usually applied to describe presidential popularity ratings and a philosophical stance taken by a public when a country enters a war.

case of war, then, it is possible the "rally-round-the-flag" phenomenon intervenes with each issue's rank-ordered position in the most important issue poll. Mueller's suggestion is that because the war issue is so different from other issues, a national "rally-round-the-flag" ideology keeps the war issue high on the public and press agenda.

3. The Press and Public Opinion

This study's theoretical framework comes from two areas of literature—agenda setting and priming. Based on these theoretical frameworks, this study examined issue salience as well as how the public's evaluation of an issue changed due to media-based priming effects. The specific argument brought forward here is that the public's support for engagement in a conflict might depend on whether certain topics such as air strikes, diplomacy, or the condition of refugees are emphasized more than other topics.

The agenda-setting model (McCombs & Shaw, 1972) posits that the mass media have an influence on what the public recognizes as important issues, and the theory has been supported by a wealth of empirical studies. Since the news media are a dominant force in the dissemination of information about a conflict, they can increase the salience of particular conflict-related issues. "Through the day-by-day selection and display of the news, editors and news directors focus attention and influence the public's perceptions of what are the most important issues of the day. Our attention is further focused—and our pictures of the world shaped and refined—by the way journalists frame their news stories" (McCombs & Bell, 1996, p. 93).

Priming researchers contend that media presentations of particular issues will "prime" other semantically related concepts, thus heightening the likelihood that both are remembered in a similar fashion (Collins & Loftus, 1975). For example, if the media were to emphasize drugs as a major issue, their coverage would likely prime audiences to evaluate the President based on his handling of the drug issue. Johnson and Wanta (1999) found that the extensive media coverage of the drug issue during the 1990s had a stronger priming effect on public evaluations of Bush's drug policies than did general evaluations of the President. Thus, it appears that people rely on external cues—often supplied by the media—to "prime" a particular set of cognitive systems in order to make judgments and decisions (Johnson & Wanta, 1999; McNamara, 1992). As Iyengar and Kinder report (1987), the news media influence "the standards by which governments, presidents, policies, and candidates for office are judged . . . by calling attention to some matters while ignoring others" (p. 63).

Iyengar and Simon (1993) found that during the Gulf War, public evaluations of Bush—based on his foreign policy assessments—increased, meaning the public's overall assessment of the President was more positive based on being primed to think about foreign policy issues. Iyengar and Simon (1993) found in the same study that certain themes in the news led audiences to support a specific resolution to the crisis. They found that as broadcast coverage became more episodic, or event-oriented, the public was cued to think of the conflict in a particular way.

The argument presented here suggests priming can operate in a similar fashion with regard to photographs. Even though photographs may not be solely responsible for cueing audiences to think about issues in a particular way, the photographs still have the power to prime audiences to some degree. The photographs of the Kosovo crisis, published in traditional and online newspapers, gained widespread attention because of the often dramatic and emotional content. It's argued here these photographs acted in conjunction with newspaper stories, priming audiences to think about particular aspects of the conflict. Gibson and Zillmann (2000) found that when news stories were accompanied with photographs, the information contained in the photographs exerted "considerable influence on the readers' perception of the issue addressed in the story" (p. 364). They concluded that information provided via news photographs had a strong influence on viewer's perceptions of the same issue. Wanta (1986) found that with certain issues, the importance of that issue on the public's agenda increased when a dominant photograph of the issue was used. Dimitrova (2001) suggests the visuals provided during the Kosovo conflict served as confirmation and documentation of the atrocities by means of "literal and metaphoric proof of the perpetration of the crimes" (p. 50), and it is visuals such as these that may be priming audiences to think about the conflict in a particular way.

Previous studies (Johnson & Wanta, 1999) have examined how the public evaluates the U.S. President based on issues that were primed by the media. Johnson and Wanta (1999) suggest via media emphasis about some issues and not others, audiences are primed with certain aspects of the issues. The study here tests this premise. In addition, this study expands traditional agenda-setting and priming studies through the examination of news photographs. Regarding the priming hypotheses, it is argued that particular content themes guided public attitudes.

The following hypotheses are proposed:

H1: The more the news media cover the Kosovo story, measured by the total number of Kosovo stories and photographs on the front page, the more important the issue will be for the public.

H2: The more the news media cover the Kosovo story, measured by the total number of Kosovo stories and photographs on the front page, the more the public will favor U.S. engagement in the Kosovo conflict.

H3: The more the news media cover the Kosovo story, measured by the total number of Kosovo stories and photographs on the front page, the more the public will favor sending U.S. ground troops into the Kosovo region.

H4: The more particular content themes in newspaper front-page stories and photographs are emphasized, the more the public will favor U.S. engagement in the Kosovo conflict.

H5: The more particular content themes in newspaper front page stories and photographs are emphasized, the more the public will favor sending U.S. ground troops into the Kosovo region.

C. METHOD

To determine whether press coverage of the Kosovo conflict correlated with public salience for the Kosovo issue, a content analysis of the front pages of the following four U.S. newspapers was conducted: *The New York Times, The Washington Post, The Chicago Tribune*, and *The St. Louis Post-Dispatch*. The sampling strategy for newspaper content was designed based on the availability of public opinion data. Because the "most important issue" question was asked three times between January 1999 and May 1999, all newspaper front pages appearing in the four weeks prior to each poll were sampled. The use of only three dates of public opinion data could be contrived as a limitation to this study because any increase in public opinion could be attributable to the attention most issues receive when they are first covered by the media. That said, most studies using the "most important problem" question as a measure of the public agenda are similarly limited because the question is not a part of every poll taken.

To measure media coverage of the issue—the independent variable for hypotheses one through three—coders had to identify the total number of both Kosovo and non-Kosovo front page stories and record the count for each. Then, based on the total number of front-page stories, the percentage of stories dealing with the Kosovo conflict was calculated. The same procedure was used to measure photographic coverage.

Issue importance—the dependent variable for hypothesis one—was measured using the "most important issue" question in Gallup polls between January 1999 and May 1999. The percentage of respondents ranking the Kosovo issue as the most important issue was recorded for each poll date. This question was asked at three different times between January and May, and the data from the three points were used in this analysis.

Public support for U.S. involvement in the Kosovo region—the dependent variable for hypotheses two through five—was measured using two specific questions in Gallup polls between February 1999 and May 1999. Hypotheses two and four used the Gallup poll question, "Do you favor or oppose U.S. participation in the conflict in Kosovo?" and scores were based on the percentage of respondents who favored U.S. engagement. This question was asked 11 times between February 19, 1999, and May 24, 1999. Hypotheses three and five used the Gallup poll question, "Do you favor or oppose U.S. ground troops with other NATO countries to serve in combat in Yugoslavia?" and scores were based on the percentage of respondents who favored sending ground troops into the region. This question was asked ten times between March and June of 1999.

Hypotheses four and five used content themes present in front page newspaper stories and photographs as measures of the independent variable. Based on the content categories used by the *Media Monitor* in its analysis of news coverage of the Kosovo crisis, coders were trained to assign one of six content codes to each Kosovo story and photograph: Refugees, Serbs, diplomacy, deployment of troops into the region, NATO air strikes, and other.

Intercoder reliability for each of the variables ranged from .86 to .97, using Scott's pi.

D. RESULTS

Hypothesis one tested the original conceptualization of the agenda-setting model—the more the media emphasize a particular issue, the more important that issue will be for the public—and received strong support. Increasing coverage of the Kosovo crisis by the four newspapers under examination went along with increasing public attention to the issue ($r = .54$, $p < .01$). The hypothesis was also supported when each paper was analyzed separately, with individual correlation coefficients ranging from $r = .49$ ($p < .01$) for *The New York Times* to $r = .61$ ($p < .01$) for *The Chicago Tribune*.

When the agenda-setting relationship between the news media agenda and the public agenda was measured using Kosovo photographs instead of Kosovo articles, support was again found. As the four newspapers' visual coverage of the Kosovo crisis increased, the public increasingly became more concerned about the issue, ($r = .38$, $p < .01$). When the four papers were analyzed separately, similar results were found with correlation coefficients ranging from $r = .35$ ($p < .01$) for *The Washington Post* and *The St. Louis Post Dispatch* to $r = .46$ ($p < .01$) for *The Chicago Tribune*.

While hypothesis one tested the agenda-setting model in the traditional fashion—using the "most important issue" question to measure issue salience among the public—hypothesis two examined the relationship between the news media agenda and public attitudes toward the issue. In this case, the total number of Kosovo-related news stories and photographs on each day was correlated with public attitudes toward engaging in the conflict. As the number of news stories and news photographs of Kosovo increased, public attitudes toward engaging in the conflict also increased, ($r = .50$, $p < .01$), for news stories of the conflict, and ($r = .42$, $p < .01$), for visual coverage of the conflict. Again, the hypotheses were also supported for each individual paper.

TABLE 1: Correlations between the news media agenda (the number of newspaper front-page stories and photographs) and the public agenda.*

All newspapers	New York Times	Washington Post	Chicago Tribune	St. Louis Post Dispatch
Stories .54[a]	.49[a]	.57[a]	.61[a]	.59[a]
(n = 305)	(n = 83)	(n = 75)	(n = 67)	(n = 89)
Photos .38[a]	.41[a]	.35[a]	.46[a]	.35[a]
(n = 305)	(n = 83)	(n = 75)	(n = 67)	(n = 89)

* Public agenda measured using the "most important issue" question in Gallup polls.
[a] $p < .01$

TABLE 2: Correlations for news media agenda (the number of newspaper front-page stories and photos) and public support for engagement in the conflict in Kosovo.*

All newspapers	New York Times	Washington Post	Chicago Tribune	St. Louis Post Dispatch
Stories .50[a]	.60[a]	.54[a]	.50[a]	.43[a]
(n = 305)	(n = 83)	(n = 75)	(n = 67)	(n = 89)
Photos .42[a]	.56[a]	.44[a]	.40[a]	.26[a]
(n = 305)	(n = 83)	(n = 75)	(n = 67)	(n = 89)

* Public agenda measured using the following Gallup poll question: Do you favor or oppose engagement in the Kosovo crisis? Correlations were run with the percentage of respondents who favored engagement in the Kosovo crisis.
[a] $p < .01$

Hypotheses three was tested in a similar fashion—using the percentage of front page news stories and news photographs of Kosovo on any given day and comparing that percentage to percentage of the public who on that same day favored sending ground troops into the conflict. Hypothesis three was supported. Increases in the four newspapers' coverage of the Kosovo crisis correlated positively with the public in favor of sending U.S. ground troops into the Kosovo region for both textual coverage ($r = .70$, $p < .01$) and photographic coverage ($r = .57$, $p < .01$). The hypothesis was also supported for each individual paper. These results suggest the media can contribute to changing public salience for an issue and maybe even shape public attitudes toward an issue. While exposure to broadcast news can not be ignored or discredited, it is argued here that exposure to newspaper coverage of the conflict also contributed to shifts in public opinion.

Hypotheses four and five were based on priming theory and compared particular content themes in newspaper front page stories and photographs to public attitudes about the Kosovo issue. One-way ANOVA results support hypothesis four. Public support for U.S. engagement in Kosovo was significantly higher for particular content themes in newspaper articles. For example, during the earlier part of news coverage of the conflict, news stories and photographs focused on Serbian atrocities against Kosovar refugees. During the time when these stories were the greatest in number, February and early March, the public increasingly supported engaging in the conflict (F = 12.89, p < .001). Theories of news help explain these findings. Journalists learn very early on that human interest stories, which pit good versus evil with compelling photographs to boot, are the stories that get read the most because we, as a nation, are intrigued by international conflict and strife (Rich, 2000). Dimitrova (2001) says the story-telling devices used by the news media in textual and visual form helped provide "domestic audiences with the language to think about the participants in a faraway place and their agendas. In previous wars, atrocity stories have played an important preparedness and mobilization role because they illustrate the demonic nature of the enemy and thus provide the rationale for military involvement" (p. 48). The news media's emphasis of refugee stories during the Kosovo conflict is no different than the emphasis on Afghan refugees during the 2001/2002 conflict in the Middle East—we as a nation are intrigued by the stories of the displaced women and children. The refugee angle is a more straightforward story than a story about foreign policy issues. Subsequently, the

TABLE 3: Correlations for news media agenda (the number of newspaper front page stories and photographs) and public opinion regarding sending ground troops into the Kosovo conflict.

All newspapers	New York Times	Washington Post	Chicago Tribune	St. Louis Post Dispatch
Stories .70[a] (n = 305)	.75[a] (n = 83)	.83[a] (n = 75)	.72[a] (n = 67)	.58[a] (n = 89)
Photos .57[a] (n = 305)	.61[a] (n = 83)	.63[a] (n = 75)	.64[a] (n = 67)	.44[a] (n = 89)

* Public agenda measured using the following Gallup poll question: Do you favor or oppose U.S. ground troops with other NATO countries to serve in combat in Yugoslavia? Correlations were run with the percentage of respondents who favored sending U.S. ground troops to Yugoslavia.
[a] p < .01

TABLE 4: One-way analysis of variance for favoring U.S. engagement in the conflict and favoring sending U.S. ground troops into the Kosovo conflict by content themes in front page *newspaper stories and photographs*, means and standard deviations.

	Content themes					
Variables	Refugee	Serbs	Diplomacy	U.S. involvement	NATO airstrikes	Other
	Mean (SD)	Mean (SD)	Mean (SD)	Mean (SD)	Mean (SD)	Mean (SD)
% of respondents who favor U.S. engagement in the conflict	45.54 (20.37)	37.04 (24.88)	37.29 (21.81)	42.36 (18.63)	44.64 (20.86)	33.81 (20.86)
% of respondents who favor sending U.S. troops into the Kosovo conflict	32.73 (20.65)	19.39 (23.15)	16.80 (20.81)	20.45 (21.44)	31.34 (18.64)	18.62 (22.06)

* Post-hoc bonferroni tests found significant differences between the following groups:refugee and Serbs, refugee and diplomacy, refugee and other; Serbs and U.S. involvement, Serbs and NATO airstrikes, Serbs and other; diplomacy and U.S. involvement, diplomacy and NATO airstrikes, diplomacy and other; U.S. involvement and other; NATO airstrikes and other.

initial rise of refugee stories in the news media is not at all surprising, nor is the increase in public support for engagement in the conflict.

Hypothesis five was similar in that it measured the independent variable in the same way, but it used a slightly different question as a measure of the dependent variable. Public support for specific U.S. actions in Kosovo, such as sending in ground troops, was significantly higher for particular content themes found in front page stories and photographs. For example, shortly after the United States began the air strikes campaign against the Serbs, the public gradually began to support sending ground troops into the conflict ($F = 36.73$, $p < .001$). While an increase in refugee stories seemed to spur public attention to the conflict in general and seemed to bring about sympathetic attitudes in U.S. citizens, stories of the bombing campaign seemed to propel the public even more to think about engaging in the conflict and ending it quickly via sending in ground troops. During the Persian Gulf War, broadcast stories about the airstrikes were overwhelmingly positive (Iyengar & Simon, 1993) and emphasized the success of the "smart bombs," without mentioning the many "smart bombs" that missed their targets. In this case, the public attitudes toward the Kosovo conflict followed a pattern similar to that of Persian Gulf War public opinion. As the United States became more involved in the conflict via sending troops to Saudi Arabia, news stories emphasizing military strength appeared more frequently. On January 11, 1991, 29 percent of the respondents polled were against engaging in the war effort. On January 17, 1991, one day after the United States officially engaged in the war, that percentage dropped to 16 percent. It seems that once the United States officially became involved in the conflict, the public became more willing to send in ground troops in hopes of bringing the conflict to a quicker end.

In summary, all five hypotheses were strongly supported, suggesting that as the news media increased coverage of the Kosovo issue and emphasized particular content themes, public opinion followed suit.

E. DISCUSSION

This study examined the Kosovo crisis to test traditional agenda-setting hypotheses as well as hypotheses that link agenda-setting with priming theory. The agenda-setting model compares the media agenda with the public agenda and suggests that the news media influence the public's salience for particular issues while priming theory links the processing of news media information with public evaluations of political figures or issues. Combining agenda-setting with priming, Johnson and Wanta (1999) suggest that media coverage of an issue can also prime attitudes about the particular issue rather than just public officials. Therefore, this study tested the news media's ability to prime public attitudes toward specific issues in addition to the traditional agenda-setting measures.

The results indicate that public attitudes toward the Kosovo conflict correspond with the amount of related news media coverage as well as particular

TABLE 5: One-way analysis of variance for favoring U.S. engagement in the conflict and favoring sending U.S. ground troops into the Kosovo conflict by content themes in front page *newspaper stories and photographs*, means and standard deviations.

	Content themes					
Variables	Refugee	Serbs	Diplomacy	U.S. involvement	NATO airstrikes	Other
	Mean (SD)	Mean (SD)	Mean (SD)	Mean (SD)	Mean (SD)	Mean (SD)
% of respondents who favor U.S. engagement in the conflict	49.84 (5.93)	36.44 (25.94)	46.18 (16.71)	55.80 (2.77)	49.00 (15.61)	24.25 (28.74)
% of respondents who favor sending U.S. troops into the Kosovo conflict	34.45 (19.40)	23.81 (22.52)	28.45 (19.55)	44.00 (5.48)	34.29 (14.83)	13.81 (21.28)

* Post-hoc bonferroni tests found significant differences between the following groups: refugee and Serbs, refugee and U.S. involvement, refugee and other; Serbs and diplomacy, Serbs and U.S. involvement, Serbs and NATO airstrikes, Serbs and other; diplomacy and U.S. involvement, diplomacy and other; U.S. involvement and NATO airstrikes, U.S. involvement and other; NATO airstrikes and other.

themes found in the media coverage. These findings parallel results from other studies. For example, Neuman (1990) reported an "s-shaped" relationship between the media agenda and the public agenda for the Vietnam War issue. He found that as *The New York Times* initially increased its coverage of the Vietnam War, public concern for the issue also increased. However, this agenda-setting relationship reached a threshold after which increases in the press agenda were not followed by increases in the public agenda. Bissell's (1999) study of agenda-setting from WWII to the Persian Gulf War confirmed the existence of this threshold. The results from this study indicate a similar pattern (see Figure 1). Public concern for the Kosovo issue increased in a linear fashion then stabilized after a certain point. This certain point could have been reached during the air strike campaign, when it was conceivable the U.S. would have an upper hand in the conflict's outcome.

When discussing the examination of priming effects, it is important to note the comparisons to other content studies of the Kosovo crisis. *The Media Monitor* reported that stories of the Kosovar refugees and the air war dominated network news until the bombing of the Chinese Embassy in early May. In one week, March 24–March 30, 131 out of 182 broadcast stories focused on the air strikes. Between March 31 and April 6, the air war remained the main focus of network attention, 92 stories, but stories of the Kosovar refugees were covered almost as heavily, 85 stories (*Media Monitor*, p. 2). Print media coverage of the Kosovo issue followed a similar pattern. Stories about the plight of the refugees and the Serbian atrocities dominated early print coverage of the conflict. Starting in late March, stories about the air war and diplomatic negotiations seemed to come to the forefront in print news. Moreover, as the number of Kosovo stories began to decline in early May, so too did trends in public support for engagement in the conflict. From mid-February through the middle of April, public support for engagement in the conflict was on a gradual, but steady rise. These public opinion trends correspond to media coverage of the issue. Furthermore, public favorability toward sending in ground troops increased gradually from early March through April, but by early May, public support began to slightly decline and then increase later in the month. (see Figure 2).

While there seems to be a clear association between the news media agenda and the public agenda, there were differences found between the newspapers. Of the four newspapers, *The St. Louis Post-Dispatch* had the lowest correlation with the public agenda. Yet, the different findings between the newspapers simply suggest each newspaper may have devoted more or less time to the Kosovo issue than the others. Furthermore, some newspapers such as *The Washington Post* were more prone to running in-depth stories on the plight of the refugees than other newspapers, such as *The New York Times*. Despite variability in the correlation coefficients between the newspapers, the coefficients for all newspapers combined were fairly high, positive and significant. Despite the positive correlations found between the media and the public agenda, it could be assumed the initial

Figure 1: Public Opinion Trends of Favoring Engagement in the Military Action in Kosovo, 1999.

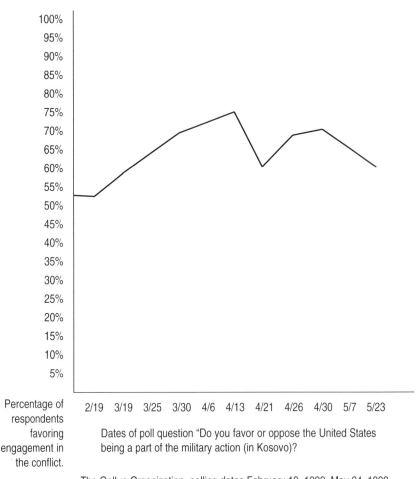

Percentage of respondents favoring engagement in the conflict.

Dates of poll question "Do you favor or oppose the United States being a part of the military action (in Kosovo)?

The Gallup Organization, polling dates February 19, 1999–May 24, 1999.

response to coverage of the crisis was propelled by the public's need for orientation or information about the conflict.

While the agenda-setting relationship has been modified to incorporate time lag, media credibility, and issue obtrusiveness into the equation, one of the most important findings in this area lies in an individual's need for orientation. Weaver (1977) suggests that a high need for orientation will lead individuals to seek out more information in the mass media, and in this method of alleviating uncertainty, greater agenda-setting effects are expected. Relying on the assumption that there

Figure 2: Public Opinion Trends of Favoring Sending Groups Troops into the Conflict in Kosovo, 1999.

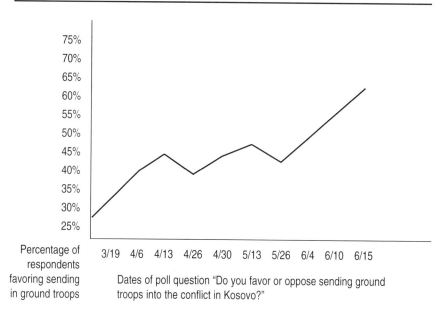

Percentage of respondents favoring sending in ground troops

Dates of poll question "Do you favor or oppose sending ground troops into the conflict in Kosovo?"

The Gallup Organization, polling dates March 19, 1999–June 15, 1999.

is a strong need for orientation for many individuals during times of war, the hypotheses predicted there would be positive correlations between the press agenda and the public agenda, and the need for orientation may explain why the correlation coefficients between the two agendas were so high.

Since the Kosovo issue never became *the* most important issue for the public, knowledge of what other issues the public favored is relevant. In January 1999 when the Kosovo issue recorded a 0, ethics, crime/violence, and education were of top concerns to the public. During May of 1999 when the Kosovo issue peaked at close to 15 percent, ethics, crime/violence, and education still remained on the top of the list. Yet, as the Kosovo issue became more important to the public, economic issues became less important to the public. As previously stated, the crisis in Kosovo started competing with the school shootings in Columbine High School after April 20, 1999.

The findings can also be interpreted in another way. During earlier coverage of the conflict, the heavy coverage of the Serbian atrocities led the public to think Milosevic would prevail in the war (*The Media Monitor*, p. 5). Coverage of the so-called "horse race" between Milosevic and NATO originally favored

Serbia, but once coverage of the air strikes increased, public attitudes shifted toward a more favorable assessment of NATO's prospects of winning the war. In this sense, media coverage of the conflict contributed to increases in knowledge about the war and increases in attitude formation about the conflict.

It is important to also address the issue of using photographs as one measure of the media agenda. While the photographs in newspapers are obviously not seen in isolation, the photograph still may play a role in (1) representing the media agenda as an accompaniment to stories and (2) helping with the transferal of salience of particular issues to the public. A single front page could have anywhere from five-to-ten stories on the front page. This same front page could also have anywhere from one-to-three images. If the still images represent issues also mentioned in the front-page stories, those particular issues are receiving even more prominent treatment by the newspaper. Thereby, the reinforcement of these issues in photographs may help shape viewers' impressions of the most important issue. Despite resounding support for each prediction, it would be erroneous to conclude this study was without its limitations. Researchers have had limited success arguing for the inclusion of photographs in the study of the media agenda. Yet, research in the area of newspaper readership trends suggests photographs are still often viewed before text. Furthermore, *The Media Monitor* reports the compelling nature of these specific photographs increased readership overall.

The application of priming in this study also went beyond the scope of what has been done previously. Even though few researchers (Johnson & Wanta, 1999) take priming in this same direction, no studies, to my knowledge, have tested the presumptions as in this study. That said, Scheufele (2000), Tulving and Watkins (1975) and Collins and Luftus (1975) all lay forth the groundwork for this study's premise. Each asserts that as individuals receive and process information, memory traces or activation tags are developed. "Activation tags or memory traces, therefore, influence subsequent information processing" (Scheufele, 2000, p. 299; Salancik, 1974). Furthermore, Iyengar and Kinder (1987) suggest the media's emphasis of particular issues influenced "the standards by which governments, presidents, policies, and candidates for public office are judged" (p. 63). This study chose to study policies rather than people or organizations as a whole.

This study also dealt with a few inevitable components of our culture—conflict, U.S. involvement in conflict, and media coverage of that conflict. This study merits attention because the findings explicate the study of two tried and true theories under new and different circumstances.

REFERENCES

Bissell, K. (1999). A century of war: An analysis of the president, the images and public opinion from the Spanish-American War to the Persian Gulf War. Unpublished doctoral dissertation, Syracuse University.

Brothers, C. (1997). *War and photography: A cultural history*. London, New York: Routledge.

Cheney G. (1993). We're talking war: Symbols, strategies and images. In B. S. Greenberg & W. Gantz, (Eds.), *Desert storm and the mass media*. Cresskill, N.J.: Hampton Press.

Cohen, B. C. (1963). *The press and foreign policy*. Princeton, NJ: Princeton University Press.

Collins, A. M. & Loftus, E. F. (1975). A spreading-activation theory of semantic processing. *Psychological Review, 82*, 407–428.

Dearing, J. W. & Rogers, E. M. (1996). *Communication concepts 6: Agenda-setting*. Thousand Oaks, CA: Sage Publications.

Dimitrova, A. K. (2001). Nightmares in the nightly news: CNN covers atrocities in Kosovo. *East European Quarterly, 35(1)*, 1–46.

Everts, P. (2000). When the going gets rough: Does the public support the use of military force? *World Affairs, 162(3)*, 91–108.

The Gallup Organization. (2001, 1999, 1991). Gallup Social and Economic Indicators.

Gibson, R. & Zillmann, D. (2000). Reading between the photographs: The influence of incidental pictorial information on issue perception. *Journalism and Mass Communication Quarterly, 77(2)*, 355–366.

Gutstadt, L. E. (1993). Taking the pulse of the CNN audience: A case study of the Gulf War. *Political Communication 10*, 399.

Iyengar, S. & Kinder, D. R. (1987). *News that matters: Agenda-setting and priming in a television age*. Chicago, IL.: University of Chicago Press.

Iyengar, S. & Simon, A. (1993). News coverage of the Gulf Crisis and public opinion: A study of agenda-setting, priming, and framing. *Communication Research, 20(3)*, 365–383.

Johnson, T. J. & Wanta, W. (1994). Influence dealers: A path-analysis model of agenda-building during Richard Nixon's war on drugs. Paper presented at AEJMC annual meeting in Atlanta, GA: August 1994.

Johnson, T. J. & Wanta, W. (1999). Nixon, the press, and the war on drugs: A comparison of agenda-setting and priming models. A paper presented at the ICA annual convention, San Francisco, CA: May 1999.

Jowett, G. S. (1993). Toward a propaganda analysis of the Gulf War. In B. S. Greenberg & W. Gantz, (Eds.), *desert storm and the mass media.* Cresskill, N.J.: Hampton Press.

Kellner, D. (1993). The crisis in the Gulf and the lack of critical media discourse. In B. S. Greenberg & W. Gantz, (Eds.), *Desert storm and the mass media.* Cresskill, N.J: Hampton Press.

Lazarsfeld, P. F., Berelson, B. & Gaudet, H. (1944). *The people's choice: How the voter makes up his mind in a presidential campaign.* New York: Duell, Sloan and Pearce.

McCombs, M. E. & Bell (1996). The agenda-setting role of mass communication. In M. B. Salwen & D. W. Stacks, (Eds.), *An integrated approach to communication theory and research.* Mahwah, New Jersey: Lawrence Erlbaum Associates, Publishers.

McCombs, M. E. & Shaw, D. (1972). The agenda-setting function of the mass media. *Public Opinion Quarterly, 36,* 176–185.

McNamara, T. P. (1992). Theories of priming. Associative distance and lag. *Journal of Experimental Psychology: Learning, Memory, and Cognition. 18,* 1173–1190.

The Media Monitor. (May/June, 1999). Crisis in Kosovo: TV news coverage of the NATO strikes on Yugoslavia. Center for Media and Public Affairs. 13(2).

Moeller, S. D. (1989). *Shooting war: Photography and the American experience of combat.* New York: Basic Books.

Mueller, J. E. (1973). *War, presidents, and public opinion.* New York: John Wiley and Sons.

Mueller, J. E. (1971). Trends in popular support for the wars in Korea and Vietnam. *The American Political Science Association, 35(2),* 358–375.

Mueller, J. (1993). American public opinion and the Gulf War. In S. A. Renshon (Ed.), *The political psychology of the gulf war* (pp. 199–226). Pittsburgh, PA.: University of Pittsburgh Press.

Neuman, W. R. (1990). The threshold of public attention. *Public Opinion Quarterly, 54,* 159–176.

Rich, C. (2000). *Writing and reporting news: A coaching method.* Belmont, CA: Wadsworth Publishing Co.

Salancik, J. R. (1974). Inference of one's attitude from behavior recalled under linguistically manipulated cognitive sets. *Journal of Experimental and Social Psychology, 10,* 415–427.

Scheufele, D. A. (2000). Agenda-setting, priming and framing revisited: Another look at cognitive effects of political communication. *Mass Communication & Society, 3(2 &3),* 297–316.

Seaton, J. (1999). Why do we think the Serbs do it? The new 'ethnic' wars and the media. *Political Quarterly, 70(3),* 254–271.

Tulving, E. & Watkins, M. J. (1975). Structure of memory traces. *Psychological Review, 82,* 261–275.

Wanta, W. (1997). *The public and the national agenda: How people learn about important issues.* Mahwah, NJ: Lawrence Erlbaum and Associates.

Wanta, W. (1986). The agenda-setting effects of dominant photographs. Paper presented at the AEJMC conference in Norman, OK.

Wanta, W. & Lee, T. (1997) Agenda-setting and priming. A comparison of two theoretical models. Paper presented at the annual convention of the ICA, Montreal, Canada.

Weaver, D. H. (1977). Political issues and voter need for orientation. In D. L. Shaw & M. E. McCombs (Eds.), *The emergence of American political issues: The agenda-setting function of the press*. (pp. 107–120). St. Paul, MN: West Publishing.

Weaver, R. L. III (1983). *Understanding public communication*. Westport, Conn: Praeger.

CHAPTER 17

INTERNET PUBLIC RELATIONS: A TOOL FOR CRISIS MANAGEMENT

Shannon B. Campbell

A. INTRODUCTION

Currently, public relations and (more recently) integrated marketing communications (IMC) are crucial organizational components for the sustenance of success in the today's marketplace. In order for public relations to remain an effective strategic tool for management, it must embrace communication integration and position itself as a tech-savvy organizational function. Today innovation is synonymous with success. The way(s) practitioners choose to utilize the Internet (or innovate) with regard to the primary functions of the profession—like crisis management—will determine whether the practitioners and the organizations they represent will continue to flourish throughout the 21st century. The most significant test for any organization comes when it is hit by a major accident or disaster. How it handles itself in the midst of a crisis may influence how it is perceived for years to come. This chapter investigates Internet trends and the ways in which public relations practitioners can use the Net in times of crises. Furthermore, it examines the inextricable relationship between the practitioner, the journalist and the Net and their interdependence. No change has affected communications practices as fast as new media or online services, especially the World Wide Web. The technology is ripe, economic barriers to entry are low and there are almost no regulatory hurdles. Cyber-IMC often provides an inexpensive alternative to traditional media, which can be time intensive (in terms of revisions, mistakes and so on). Moreover, it adds a new dimension—interactivity for the IMC planner and the campaign. The Internet serves as a new tool in the public relations arsenal, one that will become increasingly more useful and commonplace with technological improvements and the increase of "wired" journalists (Middleberg, 1997). For practitioners to dismiss the new generation of cyber journalists and the online communication they prefer is not only incompetent but borders on negligence.

With the explosive popularity of the Internet, many businesses and not-for-profit agencies are either already on the Internet or are flocking to it. Unfortunately, many websites are uninteresting, redundant, monotonous and quite frankly, dull—thus rendering them ineffective. Even traditional communications professionals view the Internet as a principle component of marketing strategy. However, before any business can establish a successful Internet marketing strategy, it must first establish Internet public relations. An effective website managed by a professional PR practitioner can greatly aid in maintaining mutually beneficial relationships between an organization and its target publics. A well-developed interactive site provides practitioners with pertinent information regarding users, thus allowing the practitioner to provide tailored messages to individual users. As the Internet continues to gain global popularity at astounding rates, cyber savvy users are able to wade through unprecedented amounts of information, pausing only to examine the information they deem pertinent or interesting. As such, simply targeting a public may no longer be sufficient when utilizing the Net as a strategic tool. Instead, tailoring messages for specific users, while addressing their precise concerns, represents the hallmark of Internet public relations. Practitioners with a sound technological background are highly valuable to organizations as they are able to retrieve pertinent information about users and provide them with tailored messages. But it takes more than a competent PR/IMC practitioner with a desire to establish an effective website for successful Internet public relations to occur. In fact, there are several strategic questions an Internet PR practitioner must ask before creating a web site. These questions include:

1. What is the goal of the site?
2. What content will be included?
3. How often will the site be edited?
4. How interactive will the site be?
5. How will practitioners track use?
6. Who will be responsible for managing the site?

Ogden (1998) offers additional several warnings when communicating in cyberspace:

1. Don't use the entire budget for site construction.
2. Don't create cyber campaigns that are too wide (in other words, narrowly define the target audience).
3. Don't treat online and offline campaigns the same way.
4. Don't provide information in which your target public isn't interested.
5. Don't try to save money by getting a cheap web host.
6. Don't exclude technical staff from planning.

B. INTERNET PUBLIC RELATIONS

While advertising involves buying television or radio airtime or space in a newspaper or magazine, marketers conduct research about a public's attitudes. Marketers determine what people are thinking and the strengths and weaknesses of a company or organization's image. Marketers use advertising or tools such as direct mail and brochures to address certain issues and concerns, thus creating demand for a product or service. Public relations is different than advertising and marketing. Advertising and marketing in conjunction create or define a need and encourage people to seek a certain solution, whereas public relations is generally considered a more long-term program or investment. Public relations is the art of persuasion in practice. It is making certain not only that a corporate/client's message is the right one for its goals, but also that the message gets to the public who needs it. Public relations simply defined, is the practice of doing the right thing— of performing—and communicating the substance of that performance. For the purpose of this chapter, pubic relations is the management of a company's image through communication. While digital marketing consulting involves understanding a client's Internet business and creating successful business solutions based on proven strategies, Internet public relations involves creating Internet-savvy communication programs that translates a client's positioning strategy and key messages from traditional media to the Internet. Internet PR may involve audience development, where the focus is on guiding high-quality visitors to corporate/ client web sites via search engines and targeted link networks; or brand building, where establishing new or virtual brands and migrating existing brands onto the Internet is paramount; or even Internet media management, where the notion of researching and managing Internet media buys enables one's organization/client to maximize the value of their expenditures. Traditional public relations, marketing and advertising materials are often expensive (brochures, product sheets, catalogs, etc.). Utilizing new media can reduce the cost of printing, storing and shipping large volumes of data to clients, journalists and other target publics. Practitioners can create CD-ROMS for approximately five cents per megabyte of information. "A CD-ROM disc is capable of holding 660 megabytes of data, the equivalent of approximately one-half million pages of text" (Ogden, 1998). In addition practitioners can add sound, animation, and still or moving video images. CD-ROMs can be: distributed at trade shows, mailed to prospective clientele, used to support sales or distributed as a promotional item (in lieu of "gifts" or business cards).

Internet public relations is about building reputations, developing relationships, creating a positive image, and informing and persuading people. Results are measured through image surveys examining the public's attitude toward an organization or industry; motivation research which looks at why the public's perception is favorable or not; effectiveness surveys that examine the impact of public relations on public opinion; and content analyses that measure how much media coverage an organization gets and how much of it is positive versus negative. While Internet advertisers and marketers are concerned with hits and pages, Internet public relations practitioners are more concerned with impressions and establishing long-term relationships with constituents.[1] The daunting task for the cyber PR practitioner is to demonstrate clearly to line management how these on-line activities (including media relations, community relations, investor relations,

---

[1] A page refers to any HTML page and all the graphics or other components included on that page. A hit, on the other hand, is a request for a single file, image or other unit of information.

etc.) contribute to the success of a company. To that end, Internet PR oftentimes requires more strategic planning and measurement of public perceptions, attitudes and awareness than traditional PR.

Publicity is the fundamental purpose of most organizational websites, making public relations one of the primary business functions served by the Internet and a company website—certainly, more so than sales or advertising. And since most journalists use the Internet for article research and reference, it can be a powerful media relations tool (Ross & Middleberg, 1997). Although there has been a steady growth in the number of Internet practitioners, compared to some other industries, public relations professionals have been relatively slow to use the Internet to advance their own messages and those of their clients (Ross, 1997). Nevertheless, Seitel (1998) feels use of the Net by practitioners will continue to grow exponentially in the future due to (1) the public's demand to be educated versus sold, (2) the need for real time performance and (3) the need for customization.

Internet public relations is a key building block to e-commerce or any successful online business venture and forms the framework upon which Internet marketing strategies can be built. In terms of e-commerce, an effective PR person can go a long way toward creating interesting content that will not only attract new customers, but also help retain current ones. The entire process from creating a positive image of an organization, to creating a need or desire for a product or service, to influencing potential buyers behavior can happen through a website (Avila & Sherwin, 1998). In short, Internet public relations lays the foundation for business activities by managing image and cultivating a climate of public trust. As more practitioners find themselves creating and maintaining websites to profile companies, promote products or position issues, it's imperative that they adhere to an Internet public relations perspective which dictates that websites should (1) shoot squarely—honesty really is the best policy—(2) give service— don't just use websites to publicize, provide newsworthy, interesting and timely information and pictures/images—(3) be succinct—sites should not be flooded with irrelevant or frivolous links and/or information. Federal Express applied this perspective when designing its web site. Federal Express, for example, set two goals for its web site: to do business and to provide up-to-date, unfiltered news (Jack O'Dwyers Newsletter, 1996). As such, Federal Express has reaped the fiscal benefits from having a "credible" web site.

Whether an organization chooses to manage it or not, if it has a website, it has an online image. This image can either help or hinder an organization's Internet marketing efforts. All organizations with websites on the Internet can benefit from sound public relations principles. Strategic planning is a significant function of PR. For the Internet practitioner then, having a solid plan outlining what an organization wants to accomplish with a website is marquise. Managing online organizational imagery requires a person with public relations savoir-faire who recognizes the link between image management and effective advertising and marketing. Internet PR practitioners employ a two-way asymmetrical approach to PR. The approach is asymmetrical in nature as Internet practitioners are expected to create and manage sites that promulgate their client's/organization's positive image. They are expected to produce a site that conceptualizes corporate/client values while simultaneously publicizing product superiority. The communication is two-way in that there exists a constant monitoring of dissenting Internet "conversation" and rogue sites by the practitioner. A rogue site is a website established to criticize, mobilize negative opinion and sometimes even slander businesses, products or people. Critics, detractors, customers or competitors frequently create rogue sites with relative ease. The existence of rogue sites oftentimes, creates a forum for practitioners to update their organization's website.

From an Internet public relations perspective, there are some topics practitioners should examine when updating their site which include:

- Evaluating the existing image in marketplace,
- Defining the desired image for the marketplace,
- Identifying the goals and objectives of the Internet effort,
- Defining the target public(s),
- Determining the strategies and tactics for achieving the online goals,
- Determining the specific messages for target public(s),
- Defining the criteria and methods for evaluating the site's effectiveness.

C. INTERNET DEMOGRAPHICS

The Internet has generally made the work of public relations professionals easier—that is, they can reach more people, more quickly. Net users represent an undeniably large population for an organization/client to tap into. How large of a population and who logs onto the Net? Since 1996 nearly 50 million people have used the Internet. Another 12 million annually take the Internet plunge (Seitel, 1998). The number of people accessing the Internet doubles every six months (Ogden, 1998). In 1996 Internet accessibility was available in 40.5 percent of all homes in the United States and that number has continued to grow exponentially (Ragans Interactive Public Relations, 1996). Approximately 30 percent of Internet users are in the 25 to 34 year old population. Although women comprise 45 percent of users, males are heavier Internet users by three-to-one (Snider, 1997). Internet users predictably are smart and affluent. Nearly 50 percent have completed college or have graduate degrees. The mean income of Internet users is $62,000 annually (Ragans Interactive Public Relations, 1996). Acura Division, the luxury arm of American Honda Motor Co. certainly recognizes Internet demographics. In August (1999) the company placed a customized version of its interactive dealership kiosks into consumers' homes through the @Home broadband service. The site included music, voice-overs, more than 200 screens, 30 videos and thousands of pages of information (Guilford, 1999). An Acura spokesperson said that it was not just necessarily high numbers that they were after; it was qualified high numbers (Guilford, 1999). In essence, Acura used *rich* media to bring qualified customers closer to a buying decision, rather than using the Net to attract casual shoppers.

While the Internet has made it easier to reach more people, it has also splintered publics. In fact, mass communication is weakening; in its place are very targeted communications strategies. The notion of public opinion is becoming more difficult to analyze. As demographic shifts become a mainstay in the new millennium, narrowing the audience demographic will become necessary for organizational success. Practitioners must keep this in mind while simultaneously recognizing that the trend will be for corporate websites to be more integrated with other communications activities.[2] Successful public relations practitioners in the 21st century will not only recognize but also acknowledge the explicit ties between public relations, marketing and advertising. Moreover, they must be technologically savvy enough to successfully navigate corporate/client campaigns through the information superhighway. The trend toward communication integration is undeniable. Practitioners must consider the campaign they're running offline and how they're going to follow through when a user logs onto their site. During a crisis pertinent information regarding organizational stances/views should take center stage on a site.

D. CRISIS MANAGEMENT AND THE INTERNET

For the PR practitioner, crisis management can be described as a kaleidoscope of ever-changing functions that do not so much proceed as crystallize anew each time. With each turn (as with each event or crisis) a new configuration forms (Pinsdorf, 1999). What worked previously helps in understanding the new cluster, but in truth, each public relations crisis is different. To be effective, a fusion must occur between strategic communications and the sobering realities of the times and the business it seeks to serve. Realities today mean understanding shrinking rather than expanding markets, the dismantling economy, and motivating employees that are increasingly less loyal and more demanding. Today's employees are seeking more individualism and are gathering more information from the Internet and each other than from traditional print sources. On one hand, the Internet has provided a new tool for business communicators who want to address internal and external publics. It allows the cyber practitioner to use his/her imagination in ways that never existed for the practitioners of previous decades. On the other hand, it has brought a new forum for critics to post complaints about organizational practices and procedures. Now *anyone* can embarrass a company worldwide with the push of a button. It is important to remember, as easily as a corporation can post information on its website, someone else can develop a site critical of a corporation. Whether the critic is a disgruntled employee, an activist/watchdog group, or a competitor, once rumors are spread on the Internet they are difficult to catch and stop. In a world of instantaneous communications,

---

[2] An example of which are television commercials we see that end with URLs.

the number and depth of crises affecting business, government, labor and non-profits have expanded exponentially.

Risk and magnitude, visibility and liability vary enormously from crisis to crisis and from industry to industry. While some wounds are self-inflicted, others burst violently on a company. Keeping this in mind, there are essentially two types of crises—acute and chronic. An acute crisis can be an explosion or labor dispute. A chronic crisis is ongoing. A chronic crisis is one without frame; there is usually no definite beginning and an unknowable end. While the goal in all crisis communications plans is to always communicate clearly to key audiences, one's tactics may change depending on whether the crisis is acute or chronic. Maintaining open communication throughout a chronic crisis can be a drain on resources and often leads to practitioner burn out. Websites provide a viable option for continuing communication throughout a crisis regardless of whether it is acute or chronic in nature.

Business crises are no longer the exception, but in most cases are to be expected, and are often inevitable. Crises fanned by the oxygen of publicity (whether in traditional or new media) are more visible and can be quite severe. Despite the horror stories in today's business news, many companies and its executives are abysmally unprepared.

There are three possible results of a crisis: (1) the organization is put out of business, ruined, possibly sued, and key executives possibly charged with crimes; (2) the organization continues to exist, but has lost respect and rapport with its target publics; (3) the organization wins the war of public opinion and is seen as favorably as before or perhaps more favorably. Effective crisis management includes crisis communications that not only can alleviate or eliminate the crisis, but can sometimes bring the organization a more positive reputation than before the crisis. Fern-Banks (1996) defines crisis management as a process of strategic planning for a crisis or negative turning point, a process that removes some of the risk and uncertainty from the negative occurrence and thereby allows the organization to be in greater control of its destiny. She defines crisis communications as the communication between the organization and its publics prior to, during and after the negative occurrence. The communications are designed to minimize damage to the image of the organization. A crisis has five stages:

1. Detection
2. Prevention/preparation
3. Containment
4. Recovery
5. Learning

The detection phase may begin with what Barton (1993) describes as prodromes or the prodromal stage, that is, noting the warning signs. Prodromes are crucial, since prevention is the best medicine for a crisis. When an organization in the same business suffers a crisis, practitioners should heed the warning. In other words, a pharmaceutical organization doesn't have to wait until a cyanide poisoning occurs (i.e., Tylenol) to provide tamper resistant products.

Crisis prevention occurs when organizations incorporate ongoing public relations programs and regular two-way communication, building relationships with key publics and thereby preventing crises, lessening the blows of crises or limiting the duration of crises. A manual (or intranet link) telling each key person on the crisis team what his/her role is, whom to notify, how to reach people, what to say and so on—or the crisis communications plan—is the primary tool of preparedness.

Containment refers to the effort to limit the duration of the crisis or keep it from spreading to other areas affecting the organization, while recovery refers to the efforts to return the company to business as usual. Organizations seek to leave the crisis behind and restore normalcy as soon as possible.

The learning phase is a process of examining the crisis and determining what was lost, what was gained and how the organization performed in the crisis. It is an evaluative procedure also designed to make the crisis a prodrome for the future.

One important lesson practitioners have learned from past crises, is that the less publics know about what is happening during a crisis, the more they fear the consequences. Hence, the Net is an invaluable instrument in the orchestration of crisis management. Many business failures and damaging public performances are the fault not simply of limited resources and unscrupulous competition. Rather, it is the poverty of imagination that restricts solutions to the manageable and thinkable. The Internet provides the practitioner with a tool that is as pliable and vast as his/her own imagination. As a result practitioners must use the Internet as a means for implementing proactive rather than reactive strategies when responding to markets and environments during times of crises. Ongoing proactive public relations programs of any kind are insurance policies against crises. Hence, the key to handling crises effectively is being proactive and employing issues management.

Issues management anticipates the issues that are potential crises and ranks them in order of possible damage to the organization. Then strategies and tactics are developed and implemented to lessen the likelihood of crises. In short, issues management is being prepared and it plays a vital role in crisis management. According to Seitel (1998), issues management is a five-step process that (1) identifies issues with which an organization must be concerned, (2) analyzes each issue with respect to its impact on constituent publics (3) displays the various strategic options available to an organization, (4) implements an action program to communicate the organizational view, and (5) evaluates the program in terms of reaching organizational goals. Although prevention remains the best insurance for any organization, crisis management has become one of the most coveted skills in the practice of PR. There is nothing complicated about the goals of crisis management. They are (1) to terminate the crisis quickly, (2) limit the damage, and (3) restore credibility (Wallace, 1991). The Internet provides an effective communication channel during times of crises. Official corporate websites allow organizations to be prepared, available and credible. When sites are managed effectively they support communication professionals' ability to provide prompt, frank and full information directly to target publics.

Undoubtedly, Internet communication can be an effective tool, especially in times of crises. Effectively managing one's own interactive website enhances the opportunity for two-way communication. Effective PR programs based on the mutual understanding model are said to be *excellent* programs (based on Grunig and Hunt's excellence theory). Managing one's own website gives an organization/client the flexibility and freedom of getting "news out" without having it filtered by an intermediary, which is the case in normal journalistic channels. Hence, during a crisis practitioners can use the website to disseminate information without fear that someone else might edit their message. The Internet also provides a medium where interviews with CEOs or key personnel can be conducted in real time online during a crisis. Journalists report an enormous growth in the use of e-mail over the past few years to work with sources and story providers (Ross & Middleberg, 1997). This is good news for the Internet practitioner during a crisis situation; e-mail interviews allow time for CEOs or key personnel to answer questions in a more thoughtful way than do traditional press conferences. E-mail is clearly becoming more important for day-to-day communications among journalists.

E. INTERDEPENDENCE OF JOURNALISTS, PRACTITIONERS AND THE NET

Anyone who has been online lately is aware that news organizations have been busy creating electronic products for the new medium. The print media are in the middle of a production revolution. The copy production process, even at small publications has become heavily computerized (Ross & Middleberg, 1997). Ross and Middleberg surveyed 3,800 magazine and newspaper editors and 2,000 magazine managing editors in late September 1996 and found that journalists are becoming more comfortable and familiar with the Internet and exhibit a distinct preference for digital/electronic imagery. Their survey also noted that the preference for online submission by journalists jumped from 17 percent in 1994 to 20 percent in 1995, and from 20 percent in 1995 to 29 percent in 1996. Respondents expect this growth trend to continue in the future. Fully 65 percent of respondents say they will likely prefer online submissions within five years. Journalists have clearly embraced online services; only 13 percent of responding journalists didn't have Internet access in 1996—down from 37 percent the previous year.[3]

---

[3] Yahoo is the most popular search engine for journalists—followed by Netscape's home page and Alta Vista.

As with all public relations, Internet practitioners' first priority should be to develop solid, mutually beneficial relationships based on trust, reliability and usefulness that journalists and the public will have confidence in. It's equally important for Internet practitioners to establish relationships with editors and/or reporters at online sources. Publics are turning to the Internet for their news. Hence, online magazines, TV affiliations and trade publications must be included in contact lists. Thus, the relationship practitioners have with online communication professionals should be well established before a crisis occurs. There are certain online practices and guidelines practitioners should adhere to during a crisis to ensure communication effectiveness. The following are adaptations from Cutlip, Center and Broom's (1994) "Guidelines for working with press."

- A website should present information from the viewpoint of the public's interest, not the organization.
- Practitioners must make the information easy to read and use.
- If practitioners don't want information quoted they must not publish it on the organization's website
- When addressing informational inconsistencies or rogue sites, don't argue or bicker with chat or Usenet groups.
- If a question from a constituent or media professional contains offensive language or simply words that make the practitioner uncomfortable, do not publish them electronically, even to deny them.
- On interactive sites, if asked a direct question give an equally direct answer.
- Do not add links to news releases unless the release contains "real" news.
- Always TELL THE TRUTH (even if it hurts).

It's no secret that users/journalists will expect to see an organization's side of the story at its site. However, any organization should, of course, tell the whole, honest story on its web site. If the organization has erred, it is usually better to reveal the mistake at once, apologize and make amends. During a crisis a website must address the following:[4]

What happened?
Were they any deaths or injuries?
What was the extent of the damage?
Why did it happen?
Who or what is responsible?
What is being done about it?
Has it happened before?
Were there any warning signs of the problem?

---

[4] This list is an adaptation from Fern-Banks (1996) "The media want to know . . . list."

Unlike any other media, it's undemanding for journalists using search engines to visit (corroborating or conflicting) sites along with the organizational site. As such, sins of omission will certainly be punished. Since journalistic tendency leads to suspicion and journalists describe business-oriented sites as less credible than their nonprofit/public counterparts, it's essential that practitioners be honest and forthright with cyber information.

A PR practitioner's concern is not only how a company will handle a crisis, but also how it communicates its handling and how it keeps a lid on inevitable rumors. With technological advances, these issues are now even more critical— no longer can a practitioner simply address a crisis with a press conference and leave it at that. Practitioners now must scan the newsgroups and mailing lists in an effort to catch rumors and dispel myths. E-mail boxes can possibly get jammed in a major crisis with the public and even the media asking questions and wanting immediate answers.

It's essential that a company directly address a crisis situation at the website either through a special link to an official statement or posting up-to-the-minute news releases regarding the crisis. Although there is a tendency to go overboard with fancy website video and audio feeds, especially where site operators want to attract a more general audience, note that the "razzle-dazzle" doesn't typically sway journalists. The media in cyberspace III national survey (1997) suggests that operating a site with a fast loading home page, then providing a "journalist's track," is a good strategy for practitioners to institute during a crisis. Journalist's tracks provide an effective and efficient means for the press to get company data during a crisis.

Many corporations (including not-for-profit agencies) have had to deal with Internet crises in recent years. The American Cancer Society incorporated an online crisis communications plan when an e-mail hoax circulated throughout the Internet. The e-mail told the sad story of a little girl who was dying of cancer. Her dying wish was to raise awareness of cancer so the e-mail encouraged people to make many copies of the message and distribute it to friends, colleagues, Usenet groups, and so on. The e-mail went on to say the American Cancer Society was sponsoring the project and would donate a certain amount of money toward cancer research for every message that was duplicated. As far as the American Cancer Society could tell, there was no such little girl and no such case. The American Cancer Society instituted a relatively quick and inexpensive solution. They immediately posted a warning on their website explaining the hoax.

Public relations and marketing professionals are "control freaks." They try to control the message, control the use of logos and now control rogue websites— or at least contain the potential damage they can cause. Perhaps it is the very lack of control (over illegitimate sites) that contributes to the low number of Internet practitioners. Let's face it; the Internet is equivalent to communication anarchy for the PR practitioner. The Internet provides an extension to the organizational grapevine with a speed and proliferation never before seen. Mark Twain once said that a lie travels half way around the world while the truth is putting on its shoes. The Internet provides a vehicle for false statemehts to travel around the world instantly. Culturally, public relations practitioners and marketers are going to have to give in on this [need for control] if they expect to feed the constant desire for content and serve their target audience. Nonetheless, dealing with rogue sites over which a practitioner has no control will become increasingly important as Internet use continues to infiltrate mainstream practice.

Recently, Ford Motor Company had to deal with a "rogue" site. A group called the "Association for Flaming Ford Owners" sponsored the site. The group demanded that Ford recall millions of vehicles they claimed were not safe.

Fast-food chain McDonald's faced a situation similar to that of Ford Motor Company, when "McSpotlight" went online with anti-McDonald's messages. The group posted information on a libel case McDonald's was lodging against two people who published a "fact sheet" on the Internet entitled "What's wrong with McDonalds?" In a 12-week period, their site logged more than 1.7 million hits.[5] There are numerous rogue sites on the Internet including: K-Mart, Intel, Snapple, Prudential Life Insurance, Nike, Wells Fargo Bank, and Walt Disney—to name a few. The question is not whether or not communications professionals should monitor these sites, since it is an essential component in maintaining favorable corporate image. For many organizations then, the question quickly becomes how much/many resources to allocate to resolve the "misinformation" perpetuated by these sites. Shell International, London ran banners on potentially hostile web sites to spur dialogue with activists who criticized its human rights and environmental practices (Guilford, 1999). Banners also run on sites operated by CNN, Environmental News Network and Environmental Data Exchange to name a few.

F. CONCLUSIONS

The Internet is proving to be an effective and affordable way to advertise business services, sell products and promulgate corporate identity. There is no question that the Internet will become an increasingly powerful communications vehicle and a progressively important vehicle for public relations practitioners in the new millennium. The World Wide Web is at the center of profound changes that will forever alter the way practitioners do business as well as the way they communicate. The agencies/companies that will fare best in the coming years are those riding the cutting edge of technology. Tech-savvy companies that recognize this trend as the future of public relations and go online now are in a position to grow with the web and enhance organizational sites as the technology continues

---

[5] Rogue sites are of particular importance for Internet practitioners as search engines often lead publics to rogue sites when an organizational "key word" is input.

to mature. Those who fail to embrace this new technology will cease to be effective players in the marketplace of the future.

While the Internet provides practitioners with a high impact, graphically rich medium, the traditional skills of writing and media and communications knowledge will continue to be essential for practitioners in the future. Added to the traditional skills however, will be the necessity of understanding technology and of being proficient in negotiating the Net. It is crucial as we continue to forge into the 21st century that practitioners master the interactive workplace: cyberspace, the Internet, the World Wide Web. Practitioners must possess the specific knowledge necessary to use the web to enhance communication with target publics, and increase their organization's competitive advantage in conducting research and learning more about their competition. While most companies and organizations now recognize the value of an Internet presence for corporate communications, many need guidance with regard to effectively managing their sites and readily identifying the important role of the Internet public relations practitioner. The Internet PR practitioner assists organizations in determining Internet demographics, statistics, features, and (perhaps most importantly) what the competition is doing. An Internet PR practitioner is still a practitioner and despite all of the high-tech advancements, traditional public relations skills remain paramount for success in the field.

REFERENCES

Avila, E. & Sherwin, G. (1998). *Connecting online: Creating successful image on the Internet*. Oasis: New York.

Barton, L. (1993). *Crisis in organizations*. Cincinnati: South-Western Publishing Co.

Cutlip, S., Center, A. & Broom, G. (1994). *Effective public relations*. Englewood Cliffs, NJ: Prentice Hall.

Cyberspace's value as a PR tool touted. (1996, June 6). *Jack O'Dwyer's Newsletter*, 7.

Fern-Banks, K. (1996). *Crisis communications: A casebook approach*. Mahwah, NJ: Lawrence Erlbaum Associates.

Guilford, D. (1999, August). Acura sees rich value on @Home's network. *Advertising Age*. [Internet] Crane Communications Inc.

Guilford, D. (1999, August). Shell takes banner ads to its critics. *Advertising Age*. [Internet] Crane Communications Inc.

Middleberg, D. (1997). *Media in cyberspace III: A national study*. http://www.mediasource.com/study/cont.htm.

Ogden, J. (1998). *Developing a creative and innovative integrated marketing communication plan: A working model*. Prentice Hall: Upper Saddle River, NJ.

Pinsdorf, M. (1999). *Communicating when your company is under siege*. New York: Fordham Press.

Ross, S. (1997). *Media in cyberspace III: A national study*. http://www.mediasource.com/study/cont.htm.

Ross, S. & Middleberg, D. (1997). *Media in cyberspace III: A national study*. http://www.mediasource.com/study/cont.htm.

Ross, S. & Middleberg, D. (1995, February). *The media in cyberspace (a national survey of journalists*. New York.

Seitel, F. (1998). *The practice of public relations*. Simon & Schuster: Upper Saddle River, NJ.

Snider, M. (1997, February 19). Growing on-line population making Internet "mass media." *USA Today*, A1.

Wallace, T. (1991, November). Crisis management: Practical tips on restoring trust. *The Journal of Private Sector Policy*, 14.

Who is using the Internet? (1996, July 21). *Ragan's Interactive Public Relations*, 8.

INDEX

ABC (American Broadcasting Company), 34, 195, 201, 205, 287
  See also Nightline
Actors and Approaches Model, 299, 300–01
Advertising, 120, 332–33, 336
Affiliation, 72–78
Afghanistan, 141, 213–14, 231, 245, 287, 319
Africa, 3, 30, 47, 51, 53–55, 57
  See also specific countries
African Correspondents Association, 270
African National Congress, 264–65, 269, 273, 277
Afrikaans press, 267, 274
Agenda*setting, 97, 119–20, 155, 218, 312–14, 317, 321, 324–25*
AIDS coverage, 270–72
Al*Hayat* (London), 202
Al-Jazeera, 287
Al-Qaeda, 20, 233
Alta Vista, 339
Alternative media, 32, 34–35, 331
Al-Wasat (London), 202
American Society of Newspapers Editors, 11
Amin, Hafizullah, 213
Ammanpour, Christian, 287
Anglo-Irish Agreement, 144
Anti-globalization, 4, 6, 8–10, 19–20, 25–26, 30–31
Apartheid, 148, 263, 269–70
Arab-Israeli conflict, 194, 281–284, 288
  See also Israel
Arab states, 198, 240
  See also specific countries
Arafat, Yasser, 68, 71, 82, 194, 206–07, 284–86, 289–90
Arias Foundation Reconciliation Model, 299–300
Arnett, Peter, 287
Asahi Shinmun (Japan), 96, 98, 100–02, 104, 106–08, 110–111
Ashrawi, Hanan, 203–04
Asia, 15, 30, 46–47, 53, 55, 57
  See also specific countries

Assad, Hafez el-, 197, 201–02, 286
Audience perceptions, 45, 50, 58–59, 96, 121, 265, 313–14, 334
Austin-American Statesman, 123

Baghdad, 197, 199
Baker, James, 206
Balkans, 3, 163, 281–82
  See also specific countries
Barak, Ehud, 284, 290–91
Bargaining, 79, 84
Barnett, Michael, 177, 185–86.
Barricada (Nicaragua), 303
BBC (British Broadcasting Corporation), 138–39, 148
Beeld (South Africa), 264, 267, 274
Begin, Menachem, 199–201, 289
Belfast, 142–43, 145
Beijing, 46
Bennett, W. Lance, 4, 140, 147, 149, 244
  See also "indexing hypothesis"
Berlin Wall, 217
Binary frame, 120
bin–Laden, Osama, 233
Blair, Tony, 141–44, 146–47
Bosnia, 45, 159, 161–67, 176–180, 183–85
  See also Dayton Peace Agreement
Bosnian Serbs, 176–78, 183–85
Boutros-Ghali, Boutros, 179
Breaking news, 51–53, 55–56
Bretton Woods Agreement, 25
Bridging, 193, 195, 202–04
Britain, 137, 141, 177–78, 200
Broadcast media, 11, 13–14, 19, 71, 139, 148, 178, 199, 312–13, 315, 321
  See also specific networks
Bruton, John, 141
Buchanan, Patrick, 5
Budennovsk Hostage Crisis, 223–24
Burns, Nicholas, 197
Bush, George, 17, 19, 197, 206, 296, 314
Bush, George W., 7, 19–20
Business communication, 336, 338, 343
Business Day, (South Africa), 264
Business Week, 284, 290–91

Camp David,
  Conference and accords 1978, 65,
    205–06, 286
  Conference 2000, 85, 286–87
Canada, 29, 30, 53
Capitalism, 4, 6, 8, 92
Carter administration, 200
Casualty hypothesis, 313
CBS (Columbia Broadcasting System),
  10, 13–15, 180, 195, 199–201
Censorship, 137–39, 219, 233, 277, 302,
  304–05
Center for Strategic and International
  Studies, 16
Central America, 3, 239, 295–96, 300
  See also specific countries
Central Intelligence Agency (CIA), 287
Chamorro, Violeta de, 303
Characterization frames, 117–18, 125–26.
Chechnia, 214–15, 221, 224, 227–232
Chernomyrdin, Victor, 223, 225
Chicago Tribune, 312, 316–19
China, 7, 20, 48, 59, 94, 214, 239, 277
Chirac, Jacques, 178
Chomsky, Noam, 237–38, 253
  See also propaganda model
Chosun Ilbo (South Korea), 96–102,
  104–08, 110
Christian Science Monitor, 244
Christopher, Warren, 179, 181
Cisneros, Henry, 122–23
Citizen (South Africa), 264, 273–74, 276
Civil society, 298, 305
Clinton, William, 17, 147–48, 286
  and Arab–Israeli negotiations, 68, 194,
    198, 206
  and Bosnia, 163, 178, 181–82, 187
  and NAFTA, 5, 7
  and WTO, 13–14, 18–19, 31, 33, 37
  Impeachment, 148
Closed–Door Diplomacy, 193
CNN (Cable News Network), 45, 148,
  175–76, 186–89, 287, 311–12, 342
CNN Effect, 175–76, 186–87
Cognitive systems, 118, 314
Cold War, 3, 4, 6–8, 9, 10, 19, 59, 95, 138,
  205, 215–16, 237, 239, 282, 288–89
Collective identity, 281–82
Columbia Journalism Review, 11

Commentaries, 55–56, 99–100, 105–09, 160
  See also op-ed articles
Communication, 119, 336–37, 341, 343
Communication technologies, 3, 25, 282,
  305, 307
Computer mediated communication, 26
  See also Internet, World Wide Web
Conflict management, 65–66, 70, 94–96,
  108, 284, 298
Conflict resolution, 45–47, 51–56, 58, 65,
  110, 148–49, 176, 186–89, 197–98,
  218, 281, 284, 301
Conflict transformation, 281, 284–85, 291
Confidence building, 67, 157, 193, 195,
  199, 202–04, 207–08
Congo, 165
Consensus building, 9, 93, 103, 109, 111,
  118–19, 127, 141, 307
Conservatives, 6
Consumers International, 34
Content analysis, 28, 48–49, 52–53, 57,
  72, 96–97, 159–161, 333
Contact Group Plan, 185
Contras, 244, 296, 303
  See also Sandinista
Corporate media, 35, 38
Costa Rica, 295–96
Council of Canadians, 29
Countervailing power, 20
Criminal justice, 135, 137, 288
Crisis, 48, 54, 331, 337–38, 341
  See also international crisis
Crisis management, 153, 331, 336–39, 341
Croatia, 177, 179, 183, 184–85
Cronkite, Walter, 194, 199–201, 207–08,
  286–87
Cultural conflict, 47, 281–83
Cultural diversity, 6, 164
Cyber journalists, 331
Cyberspace III National Survey, 341

Dagestan, 214, 225, 229, 231–32,
Dallas Morning News, 123
Daily Mail, 143–44
Damascus, 195, 202
Dayan, Daniel, 148, 204–07, 286, 290
  See also media events
Dayton Peace Agreement, 161, 167, 177,
  183, 286

Decision-making, 9–10, 26, 84, 117, 286
  See also policymaking
De-escalation, 70, 157–59, 161–62, 166, 298
Demobilization, 297–98, 300
Democratic Leadership Committee, 5
Democrats, 7, 16, 19
Demonization, 4, 8, 50
Deutsche Bank, 4, 18
Developing countries, 47–49, 51, 54–55, 57, 59, 265
Development model, 268–69, 276
Dialogue, 37, 203–04, 286
Diario Latino (El Salvador), 299
Die Burger (South Africa), 267
Digital Imagery, 339
Direct Action Coalition, 7–8, 9, 39
Discourse, 3, 6, 65, 81, 92, 124, 135, 137, 148, 287
Disney, Walt, 342
Dissent, 3, 4
Documentaries, 146–47
Domestic politics, 158–59, 162–63
Donga Ilbo (South Korea), 96, 98, 100–02, 104–08, 110
Double hermeneutic, 16
Dudaev, Johar, 224–25, 230
Durban, 199, 271

Eban, Abba, 286
E-commerce, 334
Ecquid Novi (South Africa), 266
Editorials, 3, 11, 52, 49, 56, 66–67, 96, 100, 109–112, 114, 124, 140–44, 148, 164
Edwards Aquifer Dispute, 119, 121–123
Edwards Underground Water District, 117, 121–22, 124
Egypt, 68, 194–95, 199–202, 205, 241, 289
  See also Sadat
Electronic imagery, 339
Elites, 3, 4, 6, 9, 11, 14, 19–20, 120, 138
Elite hegemonic control, 4
Elite press, 11, 15, 56, 142, 160, 164–65, 167–68, 239, 243
El Salvador, 239, 245, 255, 295–96, 299, 301, 304
E-mail, 29, 36, 339, 341
Emancipatory communication, 28

"End of conflict" approach, 283–84, 288, 291
Entman, Robert, M. 4
Environmental Data Exchange, 342
Environmental issues, 13, 26–27, 29, 120–21, 128, 135
Environmental News Network, 342
Eritrea, 165
Eritrean conflict, 240, 251–254, 256
Escalation, 46, 119, 124, 126, 128, 157–58, 160–61, 165, 292, 298, 300
Esquipulas II, 295–96, 299, 301–05
Ethnic cleansing, 312
Ethnocentrism, 92
Euikihiko, Ikeda, 90
Europe, 29, 47, 53, 55, 57, 163, 268, 285
European Union, 5, 7, 165
Event oriented coverage, 315
Exclusionary coverage, 265
Exclusive Economic Zone (EEZ), 90
Exit polls, 7
Express (Britain), 143
External cues, 314
External hyperlinks, 29

Falklands, 138–39, 141
Farabundo Marti Liberation Front (FMLN), 295, 304
Federal Express, 334
Fleischer, Ari, 274
Florida, 7
Financial Times, 142
Foreign correspondents, 99, 103, 196, 222, 288, 291, 300
Framing, 4, 11, 14, 26, 46, 48, 50, 52, 57, 63–64, 69, 84–85, 91, 103, 105, 117–18, 121–
124, 154, 159, 167–68, 180–82, 189, 220, 223–24, 303, 314
France, 7, 178, 221
Freedom Forum, 270
Freedom of the press, 264–65, 276
  See also censorship
Free press theory, 156
Free trade, 18, 33
Friedman, Thomas, 17–18, 198
Front page articles, 13, 66, 142, 180, 316–19, 322
Front page photographs, 17, 316–19, 322

Galbraith, Kenneth, 20
Gallup organization, 311–12, 316,
 318–19, 324–25
Galtung, Johan, 47, 148
Gates, Bill, 18
Geneva, 25
Georgia, 214–15
Germany, 221
Giddens, Anthony, 4, 16
Gittlin, Todd, 10, 16, 92
Glasnost, 213, 216–17
Global Arcade, 37
Global communications, 25, 48, 197, 207,
 286
Global economy, 5, 7, 16
Global Exchange, 6
Global institutions, 8
Global Trade Watch, 5, 12
Global village, 16
Global warming, 120
Globalization, 4, 6, 9, 11–12, 17, 25–26,
 39, 282–83
 See also anti–globalization
Golan Heights, 197–98
Good Friday Agreement, 147–48
Gorazde safe area, 178, 181–82
Gorbachev, Mikhail, 206, 213, 216–17, 224
Gore, Albert, 6–7, 31, 167
Grachev, Pavel, 220
Greenpeace, 27
Grenada, 141, 286
Grozny, 215, 220, 229
Guardian, 138, 141–43
Guatemala, 239, 295–96, 300–01, 304–5
Gulf War, 49–50, 141, 194, 197, 199, 205,
 286–87, 311–14, 321, 323

Haass, Richard, 203
Hailemarian, Mengistu, 240
Hallin, Daniel, 3, 138, 147
Hangyoreh Shinmun (South Korea), 96,
 98, 100–8, 110
Headlines, 48, 52–55, 141–42, 180
Hegemony theory, 238
Herman, Edward, 93, 237–38, 253
 See also propaganda model
Hewlett-Packard, 12
High modernism, 3
Holbroke, Richard, 181, 183–84

Home broadband service, 335
Honduras, 295–96
Horn of Africa, 241
Houston Chronicle, 123
Human interest stories, 48, 319
Human rights, 13, 16, 27, 82, 220, 233,
 296, 300
Humanitarian intervention, 158–59,
 162–63, 168, 175–76, 183–89
Hume, John, 142
Hume-Adams Initiative, 144
Hurd, Douglas, 139
Hussein King of Jordan, 289–90
Hussein, Saddam, 50, 187, 197, 199, 205,
 286, 312
Hyperlinks, 29, 35–36

Identity frames, 117–18, 124–26, 283
Image management, 96, 114, 137, 141,
 177, 185–86, 333–35
 See also public relations
Independent (Britain), 142–43, 206
Independent Television Channel (NTV
 Russia), 222–23, 233
"Indexing hypothesis," 4, 19, 49,140–41,
 146–47, 244
India, 7
Indigenous Environment Network, 33
Infographics, 311
Information technologies, 3–4, 6, 137, 307
 See also communication technologies
Institute for Agricultural Trade and Policy,
 29, 36
Institute for Democracy in South Africa,
 271
Integrated marketing communication, 331
Intellectual property rights, 25
Interactive problem solving, 67, 281
Interest groups, 3, 9
International conflict, 45, 47, 56, 58, 69,
 89–90, 93–94, 138, 193, 215, 319
International communications, 25, 48, 286
 See also global communications
International community, 65, 187, 189
International crisis, 54, 153, 157–58, 197
International Federation of Journalists, 268
International journalism, 287, 222
 See also foreign correspondents
International Labor Organization (ILO), 31

International law, 5, 91, 113
International Monetary Fund (IMF), 5, 25, 40
International negotiation, 56, 67
    See also negotiation
International news, 45–49, 51, 54, 56, 59
International trade, 25, 48
Internet, 9, 15, 17–18, 20, 25, 26–27, 38–40, 331, 333, 335, 339, 341–43
Internet demographics, 335–36
Internet public relations, 332–34, 343
Interpersonal communication, 45, 67, 69, 83
Inter Press Service (IPS), 34
Intervention, 3, 34, 140, 165, 175–176, 185
    See also humanitarian intervention
Intifada, 203, 283, 287, 290, 292
Intractable disputes, 118–19, 122, 124, 126–27, 281
Investigative reporting, 9, 136, 140
Iraq, 46, 175, 187, 197, 286–87
    See also Hussein Saddam
Iran, 197, 251
Iranian hostage crisis, 197
Iran-Iraq war, 45, 164
Irish peace process, 141–45
Irish Republican Army (IRA), 139, 142–44
Islamic fundamentalism, 285
Isolationism, 164–65
Israel, 194, 197–199, 283–84
Israeli media, 48, 65, 198–99, 202, 291
Israel and Palestinians, 48, 54, 194, 203–07, 281, 283–04, 285, 291
    See also Oslo negotiations
Issue importance, 314, 316
Issues management, 338
Izvestia, 216–18, 227–32

Japan, 15, 89–96, 111–14
Japanese press, 89–92, 94, 96–97, 99, 103, 105, 112
    See also specific newspapers
Jerusalem, 81–82, 194, 200–3, 284
Jihad, 282, 285
Johannesburg, 46
Jordan, 194, 205, 285, 289
"Journalism of Attachment," 303
Judea and Samaria, 282

Kabul, 231
Kalb, Bernard, 196
Kalb, Marvin, 195–96
Karmal, Babrak, 213, 219, 228, 231
Katz, Elihu, 148, 204–07, 286, 290
    See also media events
Kazakhstan, 215
Kelman, Herbert, 67, 281
Kissinger, Henry, 17, 193, 195–96, 201–02, 208
Knowledge creation, 29, 32–36, 38
Kohl, Helmut, 178
Koppel, Ted, 194–96, 202–04, 207–08, 287
Kosovo, 141, 175, 286, 312, 317–19, 322–23
Kosovar refugees, 319, 323
Kovalev, Sergei, 220–21, 229
Kurds, 187
Kyoto Protocol, 19

Labour (Britain), 142, 144, 147
Labor unions, 8
Lake, Anthony, 178
Laissez-faire, 5–6, 12
Language analysis, 117, 124
La Prensa (Nicaragua), 302–03
Latin America, 30, 46–47, 53, 57
    See also specific countries
Leadership, 16, 50, 82, 141, 176, 179–80, 193, 197, 204–05, 229–30, 273
Leaks, 103, 136, 195–97
Lebanon, 194, 243, 283
Lebed, Alexander, 220, 225, 230
Le Mond, 34
Lexis–Nexis Academic Universe, 71
Liberation, 10
Libya, 197, 244, 249
London, 46, 142, 147, 199
London Conference on Bosnia, 178
Los Angeles, 46, 214
Los Angeles Times, 11, 15–18, 34, 45, 244
    and WTO's meeting in Seattle, 11, 15, 17–18
    foreign news coverage in, 46, 48–49, 51–56, 58–59
    Kosovo crisis coverage in, 312, 316–19
Low intensity conflict, 283

Macedonia, 312

Madrid Peace Conference, 194, 198, 205–07
Mail and Guardian (South Africa), 275
Mainichi (Japan), 96, 98, 100–02, 104–8, 110–12
Mainstream media, 15, 29, 32, 34–35, 38, 140, 301
Major, John, 142–43, 146, 178
Malaysia, 35–36
Mandela, Nelson, 263–64, 270, 273, 276, 278
"Manufacturing consent," 238
    See also propaganda model
Marketing, 332–33, 336
Maskhadov, Aslan, 225, 230, 232
Mass media, 3, 4, 9, 20, 45–46, 50–51, 59, 69, 71, 89, 91, 304, 314, 336
Mayan people, 239, 305
Mbeki, Thabo, 264, 270–73
McDonalds, 342
McWorld, 282
Media–Broker Diplomacy, 194, 199–202, 286
Media Diplomacy, 193–197, 286
Media events, 148, 204–08, 286, 290, 292
Media independence, 154, 219
Media Monitor, 312, 317, 323, 326
Media Neglect Syndrome, 299, 301
Media production, 92, 94, 119, 135–37, 154
    See also news value
Media Tenor (South Africa), 271, 273, 275
Mediation, 118, 124, 127, 193, 199–202, 208
Mermin, Jonathan, 4, 49, 140–41, 146–47
Meta communication, 52–53, 206
Mexico, 53
Mexico City, 46, 304
Middle East, 3, 47, 51, 53–57, 66–67, 148, 281–82, 319
    See also specific countries
Milosevich, Slobodan, 184, 312, 325
Mirror (Britain), 138, 143–44
Mirror image, 46, 95
Mobilization, 6, 9, 28, 38, 156, 159, 193, 205, 207
    See also self–mobilization
Moscow, 46, 214
Motive image, 71, 73
Mowlem, Mo, 143

Mueller, John, 313
Multilateral Agreement on Investment, 17
Multi-racial coverage, 266–67
Multi-track diplomacy, 306
Mutually Enhancing Opportunity, 65–66, 70, 79, 81–82
Mutually Hurting Stalemate, 65, 70, 81–83

Nader, Ralph, 5, 7, 12, 14
Nation, 16
National Broadcasting Company (NBC), 195
National integration, 95, 157, 165–66
National Party (South Africa), 269–70
National Press Club, 198
National reconciliation, 296, 298
    See also reconciliation
National Wildlife Federation, 35
Nationalism, 5, 282
Nation-building, 269–70
Nation-State, 4, 16, 50, 52, 54, 89, 269, 282
    See also sovereignty
Negotiation, 65–70, 78–79, 81, 83, 84, 89, 113, 136, 148, 193–94, 201–03, 289
    See also secret diplomacy
Netanyahu, Benjamin, 284, 286, 290
Netscape, 339
Networking, 38, 307
New Left, 10
New media, 137, 331
New Nation (South Africa), 267
New York Post, 200
New York Times, 198, 200, 202, 204–05, coverage of
    Bosnia crisis, 160–63, 180
    China, 34–35, 48
    conflicts in Africa, 246–255
    conflicts in Central America, 244–45
    Kosovo crisis, 316–19, 320, 323
    WTO, 11, 17–18, 35
NEWSBANK Database, 123
News blackout, 31, 65
News channels, 103–05
Newsday, 16
Newsmaking,
    See media production
News photographs, 315
News value, 49–50, 287–88, 290, 292

Newsweek, 312
Nicaragua, 140, 255, 295–97, 301–03
  See also Contras
Nightline, 202–04, 208, 287
Nike, 9, 342
Nixon, Richard, 195
Non-Governmental Organizations, 25, 27,
  29–40, 103
North Africa, 285
  See also specific countries
North American Free Trade Area
  (NAFTA), 7
North Atlantic Council, 179
North Atlantic Treaty Organization
  (NATO), 179
  operations in Bosnia, 176–79, 184–86
  operations in Kosovo, 175, 312, 316–17,
  325–26
Northern Iraq intervention, 175, 187
Northern Ireland conflict, 139, 141–148
Northern Ireland Information Service, 145
Northern Ireland Office, 143, 145
North Korea, 45, 93, 197, 242
Norway, 68, 83
  See also Oslo negotiation
Nuclear arms, 9–10, 53–54

Objectivity, 92, 135, 138, 208, 288, 298, 301
Olmert, Ehud, 203–04
Olympic Games 1980, 1984, 214
On-line media, 315, 331, 339–40
Op-ed articles, 11, 15–19
  See also editorials
Operation Allied Force, 175, 187, 189
Operation Deliberate Force, 183–85
Operation Desert Fox, 287
Oral communications, 305
Organization for Security and Cooperation
  in Europe, 221
Ortega, Daniel, 303
Oslo negotiations, 65–69, 71–85, 135,
  148, 194, 203, 206, 283, 285, 288–89
Other, 46, 49, 58, 282, 285, 297–98
  See also Self

Pakistan, 213–14, 231
Palestine Liberation Organization (PLO),
  68, 82, 194, 198, 283, 285
  See also Israel

Palestinian autonomy, 68, 194, 206
Palestinian terrorism, 81–82, 194
  See also Intifada
Pan-African News Agency, 34
Panama, 49, 141, 286, 296
Participatory dialogue, 29, 36–38
Passive media, 136, 155, 299, 301
Patriarch paper, 184
Peace building, 176–77, 300–01, 305
Peace culture, 298–300, 306
Peacekeeping, 45, 53–54, 57
Peres, Shimon, 289
Perestroica, 213, 216
Perot, Ross, 7
Policymaking, 2, 4, 86, 136–37, 140–41,
  144, 147, 149, 159–60, 163, 167, 175,
  178–183, 188–89, 193, 195, 197, 207,
  232, 237, 243, 245, 248, 251, 255,
  281, 312
Policy-media interaction model, 179
Policy uncertainty, 180–82, 241–43
Political contest model, 135, 218–19,
  226
Political economy, 3
Political opportunity structure, 6
Political participation, 302
Political psychology, 72
Polls, 6, 15, 147, 222, 271–72, 275,
  311–12, 316–320, 322, 324–25
Popular press, 11, 96, 168
Positive nationalism, 16
Post-Cold War era, 3, 8, 57, 159, 288
Post-conflict periods, 267, 285, 295–96,
  298, 300
Post-Conflict Reconstruction Model,
  299–300
Power, 71–78, 136, 166
Prague, 40
Pre-negotiation, 67, 193–94, 203
  See also negotiation
Presidential documents, 160–63
Pravda, 217
Press releases, 32–33, 38
Primary definition, 136
Priming, 165, 314–15, 321, 326
Problem solving, 73
Prodromes, 337–38
Progressive reform, 6, 8–10, 18
Propaganda, 91, 137, 145, 193, 222, 313

Propaganda model, 93, 95, 114, 138, 237–39, 241, 249, 251–256

Public opinion, 3, 4, 8–9, 20, 45–46, 59, 90, 94–96, 99, 103, 105–06, 121, 146–47, 155, 165–67, 194, 204, 218, 271–72, 281, 284, 289, 312–13, 320–22, 324–25, 333–34, 336

Public relations, 12, 92, 96, 121, 137, 331–34, 336

Public sphere, 26, 146, 148–49, 264
    See also sphere of consensus

Putin, Vladmir, 232–33

Quebec city, 40

Rabin, Yitzhak, 65, 68, 71, 196, 198, 206–07, 284, 289–90

Radio Catolica, (Nicaragua), 302

Radio Venceremos, (El Salvador), 299

"Rallying–around–the flag," 4, 7–8, 15, 165–66, 313–14

Reagan administration, 18–19, 93, 140, 296

Reconciliation, 67, 111, 193, 207, 268, 278, 281, 283–84, 289–92, 307

Red Sea, 240

Reform Party (United States), 5

Relational Order Theory, 67, 69–71, 81, 83

Republicans, 7, 16, 20

Resource Mobilization Theory, 6, 9

Reuters, 34

Rhetoric, 73, 81–82, 84, 287

Ripeness Theory, 65–66, 70–71, 81, 83

Rogue site, 335, 340, 342

Ross, Denis, 198

Ruckus Society, 12

Rumors, 341

Russia, 214, 217, 220
    conflict with Chechnya, 214–15, 221, 225–27, 230, 232
    media in, 213, 216–17, 222, 226, 232–33
    public opinion in, 221–23, 232

Rwanda, 45, 165, 187

Sadat, Anwar, 194, 199–201, 205, 286, 289–90

Safire, William, 200

Salvadorian Peace Accord, 295, 304

Sam Kim Young, 91, 112

San Antonio, 121–23, 125–27

San Antonio Express News, 124

Sandinista, 296, 303 See also Contras

Sankei (Japan), 91, 96–98, 100–8, 110–11

Sarajevo, 179, 184, 186–87

Saudi Arabia, 243–44, 321

Saunders, Harold, 203

Seal, Patrick, 201–02, 207

Search engines, 333, 341

Seattle, 3, 6, 8, 14, 16–17, 25–26, 31, 39

Seattle Post-Intelligencer, 34

Seattle Times, 34

Secret diplomacy, 65, 68, 79, 82, 145, 193–94, 197–98, 206, 230, 286
    See also Oslo negotiations

Self, 46, 49, 58, 282, 285, 297–98

Self censorship, 277
    See also censorship

Self empowerment, 29, 30–32

Self mobilization, 156–58, 166–67
    See also mobilization

Seoul, 99, 111, 114

Seoul Shinmun (South Korea), 96, 98, 100–08, 110–111, 114

Shales, Tom, 197

Shara, Farouk al, 198–99

"Shuttle Diplomacy," 195–96, 201, 286

Sierra Club, 30, 121, 126

Signaling, 89, 193, 195, 197–99, 207–8

Singapore, 15

Sinn Fein, 139, 142–45

Six Day War, 197, 282

Sky News, 148

Social conflict, 119–20, 127

Social reality, 70, 92

Somalia, 165, 175, 187

Somoza family, 296

Sources, 4, 35, 48, 99–103, 135, 140, 196, 219, 226, 237, 241, 246–47, 256

Source media analysis, 135

South Africa, 45, 148, 263–64, 269–70

South African Broadcasting Corporation (SABC), 267

South African Editor's Forum, 275

South African press, 264, 269
    See also specific newspapers

South Korea, 45, 89–96, 111–14

South Korean press, 89–92, 94, 96–97, 99, 103, 105, 112
    See also specific newspapers

Sovereignty, 3–5, 8, 13, 89–91, 103, 105
Soviet Union, 3, 7, 93, 95, 159, 215
  invasion of Afghanistan, 213–14, 281
  media in, 213, 216, 231
  military of, 219–20, 232
  opposition in, 220
Sowetan (South Africa), 264, 267, 273–75,
  277
Sphere of consensus, 138–39, 146
Spin, 137, 145, 148
  See also image management
Srebrenica safe area, 178–79, 181, 186
Sri Lanka, 17, 240
Stalin, Joseph, 215
St. Louis Post-Dispatch, 316–19
Star (South Africa), 264, 272–74, 277–76
Starbucks, 14
Stereotypes, 50, 94, 266, 298
Stewardship framing, 120
Strategic planning, 334, 337
Sub-Sharan Africa, 267–68
Sudan, 165, 240, 248–51
Sun (Britain), 143
Sun City Deliberations, 270
Syria, 194–95, 197–199, 201–02, 206,
  283

Tabloid press, 143
Takeshima
  See Tokdo
Taliban, 20
Tel Aviv, 81–82
Telegraph (Britain), 142–43, 270
Terrorism, 48, 53, 81–82, 143–44
  See also al Qaida, Palestinian terrorism
Texas, 121–25
Texas Natural Resource Conservation
  Commission (TNRCC), 122–24
Thames Television, 139
Thatcher administration, 137, 144
Third party intervention, 66, 69, 83, 119,
  127, 175, 193–94, 197, 201–02, 208,
  219
Third Way, 5
Third World Network, 35, 39
Tikkun, 16
Time magazine, 200
Times (Britain), 142–43
Times (South Africa), 264, 272

Times of India, 50
Tokdo crisis, 89–91, 96–97, 105–13
Top down communication, 28
Toronto, 137
Total war, 283
Track–Two Diplomacy, 67–68, 193–94,
  202–04
Transnational corporations, 33
"Trial balloon," 197
Turner Commission, 266
TWA hostage crisis, 197
Two way asymmetrical approach, 335

United Nations (UN),
  Commission in El Salvador, 304
  Commission to Verify Nicaraguan
    Elections, 302–03
  Conference on Racism, 199
  Maritime Treaty, 90
  Protection Force (UNPROFOR),
    176–77
  safe areas in Bosnia, 178, 181–83
  Security Council, 165
United Press International (UPI), 128
United States (US), 8–9, 49, 58, 93 94,
  159, 163, 168, 177–80, 221, 241,
  246–254, 285, 296, 315, 319
U.S. Air Force, 287
U.S. Chamber of Commerce, 13
U.S. Congress, 35, 148, 250
U.S. Department of Justice, 17
U.S. Department of State, 35, 160–63,
  197, 203, 241, 246
U.S. Fish and Wildlife Service, 122, 126
U.S. Office of War Information, 287
U.S. Trade Representative, 26, 35
USA Today, 10, 12–13, 19
Utilitarian frame, 120

Valeriani, Richard, 195–96
Vietnam War, 3, 10, 138, 140, 168, 196,
  216, 287, 311, 323
Village Voice, 34
Visual imagery, 311

Walters, Barbara, 201
War of Attrition, 283
War culture, 298–300
Washington, D.C., 140, 197–98, 203, 206

Washington Post, 197, coverage of
  Bosnia crisis, 160–63, 180
  China, 98
  conflicts in Africa, 246–255
  conflicts in Central America, 244–45
  Kosovo crisis, 312, 316–19, 323
  WTO, 11, 17
"Watch dog" role, 149, 157–58, 165–67
Watergate, 140
Websites, 25, 28, 31–32, 332, 337, 339, 341
  See also Internet
West Bank, 68
Wire services, 48, 128
World Bank, 25, 40
World Cup Games 2002, 111, 114
World public opinion, 94, 96, 203
World Trade Organization (WTO), 4–5, 7
  mission of, 4
  opposition to, 8, 12, 25–26, 28
  Seattle meeting, 3, 26, 30, 33

  structure of, 12, 25
  transparency of, 5, 33
  Website of, 36
World War I, 139, 163
World War II, 157, 313
World Wide Web, 25, 28, 31–32, 337,
  339, 341
  See also Internet
Wye River Conference, 286

Yahoo, 339
Yeltzin, Boris, 215, 218, 221–22, 225, 229
Yomiuri (Japan), 96, 98, 100–02, 104,
  106–08, 110–12
Yonhap (South Korean News Agency), 91
Yugoslavia, 185

Zartman, I. William, 65–66, 83, 193
  See also Ripeness Theory